T0207428

Lecture Notes in Computer Science 14665

The series Lecture Notes in Computer Science (LNCS), including its subseries Lecture Notes in Artificial Intelligence (LNAI) and Lecture Notes in Bioinformatics (LNBI), has established itself as a medium for the publication of new developments in computer science and information technology research, teaching, and education.

LNCS enjoys close cooperation with the computer science R & D community, the series counts many renowned academics among its volume editors and paper authors, and collaborates with prestigious societies. Its mission is to serve this international community by providing an invaluable service, mainly focused on the publication of conference and workshop proceedings and postproceedings. LNCS commenced publication in 1973.

Albert Meroño Peñuela · Anastasia Dimou ·
Raphaël Troncy · Olaf Hartig · Maribel Acosta ·
Mehwish Alam · Heiko Paulheim ·
Pasquale Lisena
Editors

The Semantic Web

21st International Conference, ESWC 2024
Hersonissos, Crete, Greece, May 26–30, 2024
Proceedings, Part II

 Springer

Editors
Albert Meroño Peñuela (ID)
King's College London
London, UK

Anastasia Dimou (ID)
KU Leuven
Sint-Katelijne-Waver, Belgium

Raphaël Troncy (ID)
EURECOM
Biot, France

Olaf Hartig (ID)
Linköping University
Linköping, Sweden

Maribel Acosta (ID)
Technical University of Munich
Heilbronn, Germany

Mehwish Alam (ID)
Polytechnic Institute of Paris
Palaiseau, France

Heiko Paulheim (ID)
University of Mannheim
Mannheim, Germany

Pasquale Lisena (ID)
EURECOM
Biot, France

ISSN 0302-9743   ISSN 1611-3349 (electronic)
Lecture Notes in Computer Science
ISBN 978-3-031-60634-2   ISBN 978-3-031-60635-9 (eBook)
https://doi.org/10.1007/978-3-031-60635-9

This Springer imprint is published by the registered company Springer Nature Switzerland AG
The registered company address is: Gewerbestrasse 11, 6330 Cham, Switzerland

If disposing of this product, please recycle the paper.

Preface

This volume contains the main proceedings of the 21st edition of the European Semantic Web Conference (ESWC 2024). ESWC is a major venue for discussing the latest in scientific results and innovations related to the semantic web, knowledge graphs, and web data. This year we aimed at acknowledging recent developments in AI with a special tagline, "Fabrics of Knowledge: Knowledge Graphs and Generative AI". By doing so, and adapting the program as described below, we intended to open up the conference to fundamental questions about how we acquire, represent, use, and interact with knowledge in the advent of Generative AI and large language models.

This year ESWC's Research track addressed the theoretical, analytical, and empirical aspects of the Semantic Web, semantic technologies, knowledge graphs and semantics on the Web in general. The In-use track focused on contributions that reuse and apply state-of-the-art semantic technologies or resources to real-world settings. The Resource track welcomed resource contributions that are on the one hand innovative or novel and on the other hand sharable and reusable (e.g. datasets, knowledge graphs, ontologies, workflows, benchmarks, frameworks), and provide the necessary scaffolding to support the generation of scientific work and advance the state of the art.

The main scientific program of ESWC 2024 contained 32 papers selected out of 138 submissions (62 research, 19 in-use, 57 resource): 13 papers in the Research track, 5 in the In-Use track, and 14 in the Resource track. The overall acceptance rate was 23% (20% research, 26% in-use, 24% resource). Due to last year's success in innovating with the ESWC review process, this year we kept the approach of not including a final overall score before the rebuttal phase in the Research and Resource tracks. This enabled reviewers to focus on their reviews rather than scores, and on asking specific questions and to use the answers provided by authors in the rebuttal in their final assessment. The program chairs are grateful to the 40 senior PC members, the 240 PC members, and the 25 external reviewers for providing their feedback on the scientific program, and to all other community members who contributed in reviewing. Each paper received an average of 3.6 reviews, with both the Research and Resources being dual anonymous, and In-Use being single anonymous. We adopted ACM's terminology in all calls to improve ESWC's Diversity, Equity, and Inclusion principles in how we communicated review guidelines.[1]

We welcomed invited keynotes from three world renowned speakers, spanning industry and academia and in keeping with our theme of building understanding between the knowledge graph and generative AI communities: Elena Simperl (King's College London & Open Data Institute), Peter Clark (Allen Institute for Artificial Intelligence, AI2), and Katariina Kari (IKEA Systems B.V.).

As part of the conference's special topic, ESWC 2024 featured a Special Track on Large Language Models for Knowledge Engineering, providing a venue for scientific discussion and community building for early work on this exciting new area of research.

---

[1] See "Words Matter" https://www.acm.org/diversity-inclusion/words-matter.

The track had 52 submissions, demonstrating the importance of research in this direction. The number of selected papers for presentation and publication for this track is reported in the Satellite Volume.

ESWC 2024 also had a record-breaking number of workshop and tutorial proposals, of which 16 workshops and 2 tutorials were accepted. Their large variety of topics included data management, natural language processing, sustainability, and generative neuro-symbolic AI, aligning with this year's conference topic.

The conference also offered other opportunities to discuss the latest research and innovation work, including a poster and demo session, workshops and tutorials, a PhD symposium, an EU project networking session, and an industry track. We thank Joe Raad and Bruno Sartini for organising the Workshop and Tutorials track, which hosted 16 workshops and 2 tutorials covering topics ranging from knowledge graph construction to deep learning with knowledge graphs. We are also thankful to María Poveda-Villalón and Andrea Nuzzolese for successfully running the Posters and Demos track. We are grateful to Marta Sabou and Valentina Presutti for coordinating a very special PhD Symposium aiming at bridging the ESWC PhD and the International Semantic Web Summer School (ISWS) alumni, which welcomed 14 PhD students who had the opportunity to present their work and receive feedback in a constructive environment. Thanks go to Irene Celino and Artem Revenko for their management of the Industry Track which welcomed submissions from several large industry players. We also thank Cassia Trojahn and Sabrina Kirrane for increasing the networking potential of ESWC by running the Project Networking Session. A special thanks to Tabea Tietz and Stefano De Giorgis for their amazing job as Web and Publicity chairs, and to Pasquale Lisena for preparing this volume with Springer and the conference metadata. We thank STI International for supporting the conference organization, and in particular Umut Serles and Juliette Opdenplatz for their invaluable support. We thank our sponsors for supporting ESWC 2024 and also our sponsorship chairs Nitisha Jain and Jan-Christoph Kalo for securing them. Finally, we are also grateful to Dieter Fensel, John Domingue, Elena Simperl, Paul Groth, Catia Pesquita and the ESWC 2023 organising committee for their invaluable support and advice.

As we reflect on both the past and the future, and our role as researchers and technologists, our thoughts go out to all those impacted by war around the world.

April 2024

Albert Meroño Peñuela
Anastasia Dimou
Raphaël Troncy
Olaf Hartig
Maribel Acosta
Mehwish Alam
Heiko Paulheim
Pasquale Lisena

Organization

General Chair

Albert Meroño Peñuela   King's College London, UK

Research Track Program Chairs

Anastasia Dimou   KU Leuven, Belgium
Raphaël Troncy   EURECOM, France

Resource Track Program Chairs

Mehwish Alam   Télécom Paris, Institut Polytechnique de Paris, France
Heiko Paulheim   University of Mannheim, Germany

In-Use Track Program Chairs

Olaf Hartig   Linköpings Universitet, Sweden
Maribel Acosta   Ruhr University Bochum, Germany

Special Track on Large Language Models for Knowledge Engineering

Oscar Corcho   Universidad Politécnica de Madrid, Spain
Paul Groth   University of Amsterdam, Netherlands
Elena Simperl   King's College London, UK
Valentina Tamma   University of Liverpool, UK

Workshops and Tutorials Chairs

Joe Raad   University of Paris-Saclay, France
Bruno Sartini   Ludwig-Maximilians University of Munich, Germany

Poster and Demo Chairs

Andrea Nuzzolese   ISTC-CNR, Italy
María Poveda-Villalón   Universidad Politécnica de Madrid, Spain

PhD Symposium Chairs

Marta Sabou   Vienna University of Economics and Business,
                                      Austria
Valentina Presutti   University of Bologna, Italy

Industry Track Program Chairs

Irene Celino   Cefriel, Italy
Artem Revenko   Semantic Web Company GmbH, Austria

Sponsorship

Nitisha Jain   King's College London, UK
Jan-Christoph Kalo   University of Amsterdam, Netherlands

Project Networking

Cassia Trojahn   IRIT, France
Sabrina Kirrane   WU Vienna, Austria

Web and Publicity

Stefano De Giorgis   University of Bologna, Italy
Tabea Tietz   FIZ Karlsruhe, Germany

Proceedings and Conference Metadata

Pasquale Lisena   EURECOM, France

Program Committee

Nora Abdelmageed	Friedrich-Schiller-Universität Jena, Germany
Ghadeer Abuoda	Aalborg University, Denmark
Maribel Acosta	TU Munich, Germany
Shqiponja Ahmetaj	TU Wien, Austria
Aljbin Ahmeti	Semantic Web Company GmbH and TU Wien, Austria
Mehwish Alam	Télécom Paris, France
Céline Alec	Université de Caen-Normandie, France
Vladimir Alexiev	Ontotext Corp., Bulgaria
Panos Alexopoulos	Textkernel B.V., Netherlands
Alsayed Algergawy	University of Jena, Germany
Reham Alharbi	University of Liverpool, UK
Bradley Allen	University of Amsterdam, Netherlands
Doerthe Arndt	TU Dresden, Germany
Natanael Arndt	eccenca GmbH, Germany
Luigi Asprino	University of Bologna, Italy
Ghislain Auguste Atemezing	ERA, France
Maurizio Atzori	University of Cagliari, Italy
Sören Auer	TIB Leibniz Information Center Science, Germany & Technology and University of Hannover, Germany
Carlos Badenes-Olmedo	Universidad Politécnica de Madrid, Spain
Booma Sowkarthiga Balasubramani	University of Illinois at Chicago, USA
Konstantina Bereta	National and Kapodistrian University of Athens, Greece
Abraham Bernstein	University of Zurich, Switzerland
Russa Biswas	Hasso Plattner Institute, Germany
Christian Bizer	University of Mannheim, Germany
Peter Bloem	Vrije Universiteit Amsterdam, Netherlands
Martin Blum	University of Trier, Germany
Carlos Bobed	University of Zaragoza, Spain
Fernando Bobillo	University of Zaragoza, Spain
Pieter Bonte	Ghent University, Belgium
Andreas Both	DATEV eG, Germany
Alexandros Bousdekis	Institute of Communication and Computer Systems-National Technical University of Athens, Greece
Loris Bozzato	Fondazione Bruno Kessler, Italy
Janez Brank	Jozef Stefan Institute, Slovenia

Adrian M. P. Brasoveanu	MODUL Technology GmbH, Austria
Olivier Bruneau	University of Lorraine, France
Carlos Buil Aranda	Universidad Técnica Federico Santa María, Chile
Maxime Buron	Inria, France
Davide Buscaldi	Université Sorbonne-Paris-Nord, France
Jean-Paul Calbimonte	University of Applied Sciences and Arts Western Switzerland, Switzerland
Pablo Calleja	Universidad Politécnica de Madrid, Spain
Antonella Carbonaro	University of Bologna, Italy
Valentina Anita Carriero	Cefriel, Italy
Sylvie Cazalens	LIRIS - INSA de Lyon, France
Irene Celino	Cefriel, Italy
Renato Cerqueira	IBM Research - Brazil, Brazil
Yoan Chabot	Orange Labs, France
Javad Chamanara	Technische Informationsbibliothek, Germany
Pierre-Antoine Champin	LIRIS, Université Claude Bernard Lyon 1, France
David Chaves-Fraga	Universidade de Santiago de Compostela, Spain
Lihu Chen	Inria Saclay, France
Gong Cheng	Nanjing University, China
Philipp Cimiano	Bielefeld University, Germany
Andrea Cimmino Arriaga	Universidad Politécnica de Madrid, Spain
Michael Cochez	Vrije Universiteit Amsterdam, Netherlands
Diego Collarana	Fraunhofer IAIS, Germany
Pieter Colpaert	Ghent University, Belgium
Oscar Corcho	Universidad Politécnica de Madrid, Spain
Francesco Corcoglioniti	Free University of Bozen-Bolzano, Italy
Julien Corman	Free University of Bozen-Bolzano, Italy
Marco Cremaschi	University of Milano-Bicocca, Italy
Claudia d'Amato	University of Bari, Italy
Mathieu D'Aquin	LORIA, University of Lorraine, France
Jennifer D'Souza	TIB Leibniz Information Centre for Science and Technology University Library, Germany
Enrico Daga	The Open University, UK
Jérôme David	Inria, France
Jacopo de Berardinis	King's College London, UK
Victor de Boer	Vrije Universiteit Amsterdam, Netherlands
Stefano de Giorgis	University of Bologna, Italy
Ben De Meester	Ghent University, Belgium
Daniele Dell'Aglio	Aalborg University, Denmark
Gianluca Demartini	The University of Queensland, Australia
Elena Demidova	University of Bonn, Germany
Kathrin Dentler	Triply, Netherlands

Danilo Dessì	GESIS – Leibniz Institute for the Social Sciences, Germany
Gayo Diallo	University of Bordeaux, France
Stefan Dietze	GESIS – Leibniz Institute for the Social Sciences, Germany
Dimitar Dimitrov	GESIS – Leibniz Institute for the Social Sciences, Germany
Anastasia Dimou	KU Leuven, Belgium
Christian Dirschl	Wolters Kluwer Germany, Germany
Daniil Dobriy	Vienna University of Economics and Business, Austria
Milan Dojchinovski	Czech Technical University in Prague, Czech Republic
Ivan Donadello	Free University of Bozen-Bolzano, Italy
Mauro Dragoni	Fondazione Bruno Kessler, Italy
Kai Eckert	Mannheim University of Applied Sciences, Germany
Vasilis Efthymiou	Harokopio University of Athens, Greece
Shusaku Egami	National Institute of Advanced Industrial Science and Technology, Japan
Fajar J. Ekaputra	Vienna University of Economics and Business (WU), Austria
Vadim Ermolayev	Ukrainian Catholic University, Ukraine
Paola Espinoza Arias	Universidad Politécnica de Madrid, Spain
Lorena Etcheverry	Universidad de la República, Uruguay
Pavlos Fafalios	Technical University of Crete and FORTH-ICS, Greece
Alessandro Faraotti	IBM, Italy
Catherine Faron	Université Côte d'Azur, France
Anna Fensel	Wageningen University and Research, Netherlands
Javier D. Fernández	F. Hoffmann-La Roche AG, Switzerland
Mariano Fernández López	Universidad San Pablo CEU, Spain
Jesualdo Tomás Fernández-Breis	Universidad de Murcia, Spain
Sebastián Ferrada	Universidad de Chile, Chile
Agata Filipowska	Poznan University of Economics, Poland
Erwin Filtz	Siemens AG Österreich, Austria
Giorgos Flouris	FORTH-ICS, Greece
Flavius Frasincar	Erasmus University Rotterdam, Netherlands
Naoki Fukuta	Shizuoka University, Japan
Michael Färber	Karlsruhe Institute of Technology, Germany
Mohamed H. Gad-Elrab	Bosch Center for Artificial Intelligence, Germany
Alban Gaignard	CNRS, France

Luis Galárraga	Inria, France
Fabien Gandon	Inria, France
Aldo Gangemi	Università di Bologna and ISTC-CNR, Italy
Raúl García-Castro	Universidad Politécnica de Madrid, Spain
Andrés García-Silva	Expert.ai, Spain
Daniel Garijo	Universidad Politécnica de Madrid, Spain
Manas Gaur	Wright State University, USA
Yuxia Geng	Zhejiang University, China
Genet Asefa Gesese	FIZ Karlsruhe – Leibniz-Institut für Informationsinfrastruktur, Germany
Pouya Ghiasnezhad Omran	Australian National University, Australia
Martin Giese	University of Oslo, Norway
Jose M. Gimenez-Garcia	Universidad de Valladolid, Spain
Francois Goasdoue	Université de Rennes 1, France
Jose Manuel Gomez-Perez	Expert.ai, Spain
Simon Gottschalk	Leibniz Universität Hannover, Germany
Floriana Grasso	University of Liverpool, UK
Damien Graux	Huawei Research Ltd., UK
Paul Groth	University of Amsterdam, Netherlands
Claudio Gutierrez	Universidad de Chile, Chile
Peter Haase	metaphacts GmbH, Germany
Mohad-Saïd Hacid	Université Lyon 1, France
Torsten Hahmann	University of Maine, USA
George Hannah	University of Liverpool, UK
Andreas Harth	Friedrich-Alexander-Universität Erlangen-Nürnberg and Fraunhofer IIS, Germany
Olaf Hartig	Linköping University, Sweden
Oktie Hassanzadeh	IBM, USA
Ivan Heibi	University of Bologna, Italy
Veronika Heimsbakk	Capgemini, Norway
Nicolas Heist	University of Mannheim, Germany
Lars Heling	Stardog Union, Germany
Nathalie Hernandez	IRIT, France
Daniel Herzig	metaphacts GmbH, Germany
Ryohei Hisano	ETH Zurich, Switzerland
Pascal Hitzler	Kansas State University, USA
Rinke Hoekstra	Elsevier, Netherlands
Aidan Hogan	Universidad de Chile, Chile
Andreas Hotho	University of Wuerzburg, Germany
Wei Hu	Nanjing University, China
Thomas Hubauer	Siemens AG Corporate Technology, Germany

Andreea Iana	University of Mannheim, Germany
Luis Ibanez-Gonzalez	University of Southampton, UK
Ana Iglesias-Molina	Universidad Politécnica de Madrid, Spain
Filip Ilievski	Vrije Universiteit Amsterdam, Netherlands
Antoine Isaac	Europeana & Vrije Universiteit Amsterdam, Netherlands
Hajira Jabeen	GESIS – Leibniz Institute for the Social Sciences, Germany
Nitisha Jain	King's College London, London, UK
Mustafa Jarrar	Birzeit University, Palestine
Ernesto Jimenez-Ruiz	City, University of London, UK
Milos Jovanovik	Ss. Cyril and Methodius University in Skopje, North Macedonia
Simon Jupp	Elsevier, Netherlands
Jan-Christoph Kalo	University of Amsterdam, Netherlands
Eduard Kamburjan	University of Oslo, Norway
Maulik R. Kamdar	Optum Health, USA
Katariina Kari	Inter IKEA Systems B.V., Finland
Tomi Kauppinen	Aalto University, Finland
Mayank Kejriwal	University of Southern California, USA
Natthawut Kertkeidkachorn	Japan Advanced Institute of Science and Technology, Japan
Ali Khalili	Deloitte, Netherlands
Sabrina Kirrane	Vienna University of Economics and Business, Austria
Tomas Kliegr	Prague University of Economics and Business, Czech Republic
Matthias Klusch	DFKI, Germany
Haridimos Kondylakis	Institute of Computer Science, FORTH, Greece
George Konstantinidis	University of Southampton, UK
Stasinos Konstantopoulos	NCSR Demokritos, Greece
Roman Kontchakov	Birkbeck, University of London, UK
Manolis Koubarakis	National and Kapodistrian University of Athens, Greece
Kozaki Kouji	Osaka Electro-Communication University, Japan
Maria Koutraki	Leibniz Universität Hannover, Germany
Anelia Kurteva	TU Delft, Netherlands
Tobias Käfer	Karlsruhe Institute of Technology, Germany
Birgitta König-Ries	Friedrich Schiller University of Jena, German
Jose Emilio Labra Gayo	Universidad de Oviedo, Spain
Frederique Laforest	INSA Lyon, France
Sarasi Lalithsena	IBM Watson, USA

Andre Lamurias	NOVA School of Science and Technology, Portugal
Davide Lanti	Free University of Bozen-Bolzano, Italy
Danh Le Phuoc	TU Berlin, Germany
Maxime Lefrançois	École des Mines de Saint-Étienne, France
Huanyu Li	Linköping University, Sweden
Sven Lieber	Royal Library of Belgium (KBR), Belgium
Stephan Linzbach	GESIS – Leibniz Institute for the Social Sciences, Germany
Anna-Sofia Lippolis	University of Bologna and ISTC-CNR, Italy
Pasquale Lisena	EURECOM, France
Wenqiang Liu	Xi'an Jiaotong University, China
Giorgia Lodi	Istituto di Scienze e Tecnologie della Cognizione (CNR), Italy
Vanessa Lopez	IBM, Ireland
Pierre Maillot	Inria, France
Maria Maleshkova	Helmut-Schmidt-Universität/Universität der Bundeswehr Hamburg, Germany
Maria Vanina Martinez	IIIA-CSIC, Spain
Miguel A. Martinez-Prieto	University of Valladolid, Spain
Jose L. Martinez-Rodriguez	Autonomous University of Tamaulipas, Mexico
Patricia Martín-Chozas	Universidad Politécnica de Madrid, Spain
Edgard Marx	Leipzig University of Applied Sciences (HTWK), Germany
Philipp Mayr	GESIS – Leibniz Institute for the Social Sciences, Germany
Jamie McCusker	Rensselaer Polytechnic Institute, USA
Lionel Medini	CNRS, France
Albert Meroño-Peñuela	King's College London, UK
Franck Michel	Université Côte d'Azur, CNRS, I3S, France
Nandana Mihindukulasooriya	IBM Research AI, USA
Nada Mimouni	CEDRIC lab - CNAM Conservatoire National des Arts et Métiers Pari, France
Daniel Miranker	The University of Texas at Austin, USA
Victor Mireles	Semantic Web Company, Austria
Pascal Molli	University of Nantes, France
Pierre Monnin	Université Côte d'Azur, Inria, CNRS, I3S, Sophia Antipolis, France
Boris Motik	University of Oxford, UK
Enrico Motta	The Open University, UK
Diego Moussallem	Paderborn University, German
Paul Mulholland	The Open University, UK
Varish Mulwad	GE Research, India

Raghava Mutharaju   IIIT-Delhi, India
María Navas-Loro   Universidad Politécnica de Madrid, Spain
Fabian Neuhaus   University of Magdeburg, Germany
Vinh Nguyen   National Library of Medicine, NIH, USA
Andriy Nikolov   AstraZeneca, UK
Nikolay Nikolov   SINTEF, Norway
Andrea Nuzzolese   ISTC-CNR, Italy
Cliff O'Reilly   City London University, UK
Femke Ongenae   Ghent University, Belgium
Francesco Osborne   The Open University, UK
Ankur Padia   UBMC, USA
George Papadakis   National Technical University of Athens, Greece
Pierre-Henri Paris   Telecom Paris, France
Heiko Paulheim   University of Mannheim, German
Terry Payne   University of Liverpool, UK
Tassilo Pellegrini   University of Applied Sciences St. Pölten, Austria
Maria Angela Pellegrino   Università degli Studi di Salerno, Italy
Bernardo Pereira Nunes   Australian National University, Australia
Romana Pernisch   Vrije Universiteit Amsterdam, Netherlands
Catia Pesquita   Universidade de Lisboa, Portugal
Rafael Peñaloza   University of Milano-Bicocca, Italy
Guangyuan Piao   National University of Ireland, Ireland
Francesco Piccialli   University of Naples Federico II, Italy
Lydia Pintscher   Wikimedia Deutschland, Germany
Dimitris Plexousakis   Institute of Computer Science, FORTH, Greece
Axel Polleres   Vienna University of Economics and Business,
                                 Austria
Livio Pompianu   University of Cagliari, Italy
María Poveda-Villalón   Universidad Politécnica de Madrid, Spain
Nicoleta Preda   University of Versailles
                                 Saint-Quentin-en-Yvelines, France
Valentina Presutti   University of Bologna, Italy
Joe Raad   University of Paris-Saclay, France
Alexandre Rademaker   IBM Research and EMAp/FGV, Brazil
Helen Mair Rawsthorne   École des Mines de Saint-Étienne, France
Simon Razniewski   Bosch Center for Artificial Intelligence, Germany
Diego Reforgiato   Università degli studi di Cagliari, Italy
Artem Revenko   Semantic Web Company GmbH, Austria
Mariano Rico   Universidad Politécnica de Madrid, Spain
Célian Ringwald   Université Côte d'Azur, Inria, CNRS, I3S, France
Giuseppe Rizzo   LINKS Foundation, Italy
Mariano Rodríguez Muro   Google, USA

Sergio José Rodríguez Méndez	Australian National University, Australia
Edelweis Rohrer	Universidad de la República, Uruguay
Julian Rojas	Ghent University, Belgium
Maria Del Mar Roldan-Garcia	Universidad de Malaga, Spain
Oscar Romero	Universitat Politècnica de Catalunya, Spain
Miguel Romero Orth	Universidad Adolfo Ibáñez, Chile
Henry Rosales-Méndez	University of Chile, Chile
Catherine Roussey	INRAE, France
Sebastian Rudolph	TU Dresden, Germany
Anisa Rula	University of Brescia, Italy
Alessandro Russo	STLab, ISTC-CNR, Italy
Marta Sabou	Vienna University of Economics and Business, Austria
Harald Sack	FIZ Karlsruhe, Leibniz Institute for Information Infrastructure & KIT Karlsruhe, Germany
Afshin Sadeghi	Fraunhoder IAIS, Germany
Angelo Antonio Salatino	The Open University, UK
Muhammad Saleem	AKSW, University Of Leizpig, Germany
Bruno Sartini	Ludwig-Maximilians University of Munich, Germany
Felix Sasaki	Cornelsen Verlag GmbH & TH Brandenburg, Germany
Fatiha Saïs	University of Paris-Saclay, France
Ralf Schenkel	Trier University, Germany
Stefan Schlobach	Vrije Universiteit Amsterdam, Netherlands
Daniel Schwabe	PUC-Rio, Brazil
Mario Scrocca	Cefriel, Italy
Juan F. Sequeda	data.world, USA
Umutcan Serles	STI, University of Innsbruck, Austria
Bariş Sertkaya	Frankfurt University of Applied Sciences, Germany
Cogan Shimizu	Wright State University, USA
Pavel Shvaiko	Informatica Trentina, Italy
Lucia Siciliani	University of Bari, Italy
Leslie Sikos	Edith Cowan University, Australia
Gerardo Simari	Universidad Nacional del Sur (UNS) and CONICET, Argentina
Elena Simperl	King's College London, UK
Hala Skaf-Molli	University of Nantes, France
Blerina Spahiu	University of Milano-Bicocca, Italy
Marc Spaniol	Université de Caen Normandie, France
Kavitha Srinivas	IBM, USA

Steffen Staab   UNI Stuttgart, Germany
Bram Steenwinckel   Ghent University, Belgium
Kostas Stefanidis   Tampere University, Finland
Nadine Steinmetz   University of Applied Sciences Erfurt, Germany
Armando Stellato   University of Rome Tor Vergata, Italy
Simon Steyskal   Siemens AG Österreich, Austria
Lise Stork   Vrije Universiteit Amsterdam, Netherlands
Umberto Straccia   ISTI-CNR, Italy
Chang Sun   Institute of Data Science at Maastricht University,
                                       Netherlands
Zequn Sun   Nanjing University, China
Vojtěch Svátek   Prague University of Economics and Business,
                                       Czech Republic
Ruben Taelman   Ghent University, Belgium
Yousouf Taghzouti   École des Mines de Saint-Étienne, France
Valentina Tamma   University of Liverpool, UK
Olivier Teste   IRIT, France
Krishnaprasad Thirunarayan   Wright State University, USA
Elodie Thiéblin   Logilab, France
Ilaria Tiddi   Vrije Universiteit Amsterdam, Netherlands
Tabea Tietz   FIZ Karlsruhe, Germany
Konstantin Todorov   University of Montpellier, France
Ioan Toma   STI Innsbruck, Austria
Riccardo Tommasini   INSA Lyon, France
Sebastian Tramp   eccenca GmbH, Germany
Trung-Kien Tran   Bosch Center for Artificial Intelligence, Germany
Cassia Trojahn   IRIT, France
Raphaël Troncy   EURECOM, France
Yannis Tzitzikas   University of Crete and FORTH-ICS, Greece
Jürgen Umbrich   Vienna University of Economy and Business
                                       (WU), Austria
Ricardo Usbeck   Leuphana University Lüneburg, Germany
Marieke van Erp   KNAW Humanities Cluster, Netherlands
Frank Van Harmelen   Vrije Universiteit Amsterdam, Netherlands
Miel Vander Sande   Meemoo, Belgium
Guillermo Vega-Gorgojo   Universidad de Valladolid, Spain
Ruben Verborgh   Ghent University, Belgium
Maria-Esther Vidal   TIB, Germany
Serena Villata   CNRS, France
Fabio Vitali   University of Bologna, Italy
Domagoj Vrgoc   Pontificia Universidad Católica de Chile, Chile
Kewen Wang   Griffith University, Australia

Ruijie Wang   University of Zurich, Switzerland
Xander Wilcke   Vrije Universiteit Amsterdam, Netherlands
Honghan Wu   King's College London, UK
Zhe Wu   eBay, USA
Josiane Xavier Parreira   Siemens AG Österreich, Austria
Guohui Xiao   University of Bergen, Norway
Nadia Yacoubi Ayadi   Université Claude Bernard Lyon 1, France
Fouad Zablith   American University of Beirut, Lebanon
Hamada Zahera   Paderborn University, Germany
Ondřej Zamazal   Prague University of Economics and Business,
                                   Czech Republic
Xiaowang Zhang   Tianjin University, China
Ziqi Zhang   Accessible Intelligence, UK
Yihang Zhao   King's College London, UK
Antoine Zimmermann   École des Mines de Saint-Étienne, France
Sara Zuppiroli   ISTC-CNR, Italy
Hanna Ćwiek-Kupczyńska   University of Luxembourg, Luxembourg
Kārlis Čerāns   University of Latvia, Latvia

Additional Reviewers

Akaichi, Ines   Ondraszek, Sarah Rebecca
Antakli, Andre   Patkos, Theodore
Bruns, Oleksandra   Peng, Yiwen
Cardellino, Cristian   Pons, Gerard
Cintra, Paul   Qu, Yuanwei
Djeddi, Warith Eddine   Ragazzi, Luca
Fanourakis, Nikolaos   Raoufi, Ensiyeh
Fischer, Elisabeth   Ratta, Marco
Gaur, Manas   Ringwald, Célian
Gautam, Nikita   Schlör, Daniel
Gui, Zhou   Schraudner, Daniel
Martín Chozas, Patricia   Shao, Chen
Montiel-Ponsoda, Elena   van der Weijden, Daniel
Morales Tirado, Alba Catalina   Viviurka Do Carmo, Paulo Ricardo
Nayyeri, Mojtaba   Xiong, Bo
Olivier, Inizan   Yumusak, Semih
Omeliyanenko, Janna

Sponsors

Platinum Sponsors

VideoLectures.NET is an award-winning free and open access educational video lectures repository. The lectures are given by distinguished scholars and scientists at the most important and prominent events like conferences, summer schools, workshops and science promotional events from many fields of science. The portal is aimed at promoting science, exchanging ideas and fostering knowledge sharing by providing high quality didactic contents not only to the scientific community but also to the general public. All lectures, accompanying documents, information and links are systematically selected and classified through the editorial process taking into account also users' comments.

Gold Sponsors

Ontotext is a global leader in enterprise knowledge graph technology and semantic database engines. Ontotext employs big knowledge graphs to enable unified data access and cognitive analytics via text mining and integration of data across multiple sources. Ontotext™ engine and Ontotext Platform power business critical systems in the biggest banks, media, market intelligence agencies, car and aerospace manufacturers. Ontotext technology and solutions are spread wide across the value chain of the most knowledge intensive enterprises in financial services, publishing, healthcare, pharma, manufacturing and public sectors. Leveraging AI and cognitive technologies, Ontotext helps enterprises get competitive advantage, by connecting the dots of their proprietary knowledge and putting in the context of global intelligence.

Silver Sponsors

Springer is part of Springer Nature, a leading global research, educational and professional publisher, home to an array of respected and trusted brands providing quality content through a range of innovative products and services. Springer Nature is the world's largest academic book publisher, publisher of the world's most influential journals and a pioneer in the field of open research. The company numbers almost 13,000 staff in over 50 countries and has a turnover of approximately €1.5 billion. Springer Nature was formed in 2015 through the merger of Nature Publishing Group, Palgrave Macmillan, Macmillan Education and Springer Science+Business Media.

Founded over 350 years ago, the **University of Innsbruck** today is the most important research and educational institution in western Austria, offering a wide range of programmes across all disciplines. Located in the heart of the Alps, it offers 28,000 students and 5,500 employees the best conditions.

Bronze Sponsors

metaphacts is a German software company that empowers customers to drive knowledge democratization and decision intelligence using knowledge graphs. Built entirely on open standards and technologies, our product metaphactory delivers a low-code, FAIR Data platform that supports collaborative knowledge modeling and knowledge generation and enables on-demand citizen access to consumable, contextual and actionable knowledge. metaphacts serves customers in areas such as life sciences and pharma, engineering and manufacturing, finance and insurance, retail, cultural heritage, and more. For more information about metaphacts and its products and solutions please visit www.metaphacts.com.

eccenca Corporate Memory is cutting-edge Knowledge Graph technology. It digitally captures the expertise of knowledge workers so that it can be accessed and processed by machines. The fusion of human knowledge with large amounts of data, coupled with the computing power of machines, results in powerful artificial intelligence that enables companies to execute existing processes as well as innovation projects of all kinds at high speed and low cost. And it creates an impressive competitive advantage.

Through eccenca.my you can register and create an eccenca Corporate Memory Community Edition Sandbox for evaluation. Join pioneers like Bosch, Siemens, AstraZeneca and many other global market leaders – our world-class team of Linked Data Experts is ready when you are.

Contents – Part II

Contents – Part I

In-Use

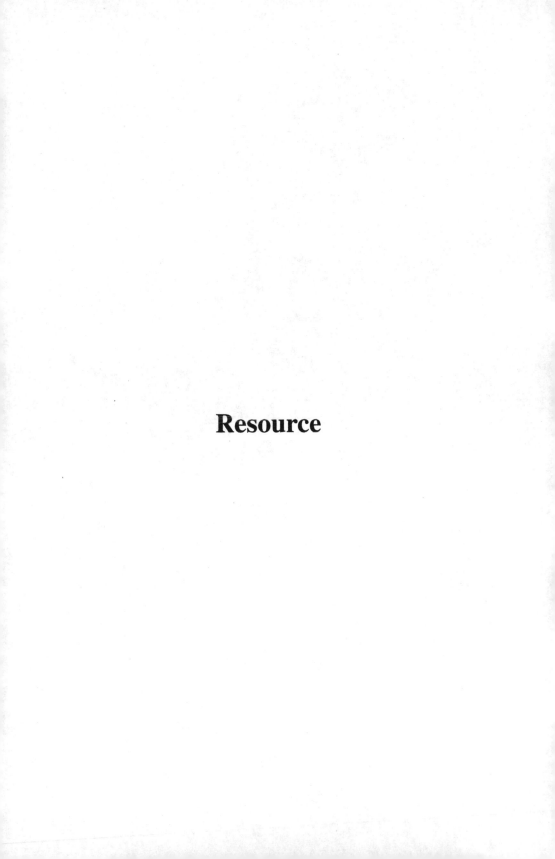

Resource

PyGraft: Configurable Generation of Synthetic Schemas and Knowledge Graphs at Your Fingertips

Nicolas Hubert[1,2]([✉])[iD], Pierre Monnin[3][iD], Mathieu d'Aquin[2][iD],
Davy Monticolo[1][iD], and Armelle Brun[2][iD]

[1] Université de Lorraine, ERPI, Nancy, France
{nicolas.hubert,davy.monticolo}@univ-lorraine.fr
[2] Université de Lorraine, CNRS, LORIA, Nancy, France
{mathieu.daquin,armelle.brun}@univ-lorraine.fr
[3] Université Côte d'Azur, Inria, CNRS, I3S, Sophia-Antipolis, France
pierre.monnin@inria.fr

Abstract. Knowledge graphs (KGs) have emerged as a prominent data representation and management paradigm. Being usually underpinned by a schema (*e.g.*, an ontology), KGs capture not only factual information but also contextual knowledge. In some tasks, a few KGs established themselves as standard benchmarks. However, recent works outline that relying on a limited collection of datasets is not sufficient to assess the generalization capability of an approach. In some data-sensitive fields such as education or medicine, access to public datasets is even more limited. To remedy the aforementioned issues, we release PyGraft, a Python-based tool that generates highly customized, domain-agnostic schemas and KGs. The synthesized schemas encompass various RDFS and OWL constructs, while the synthesized KGs emulate the characteristics and scale of real-world KGs. Logical consistency of the generated resources is ultimately ensured by running a description logic (DL) reasoner. By providing a way of generating both a schema and KG in a single pipeline, PyGraft's aim is to empower the generation of a more diverse array of KGs for benchmarking novel approaches in areas such as graph-based machine learning (ML), or more generally KG processing. In graph-based ML in particular, this should foster a more holistic evaluation of model performance and generalization capability, thereby going beyond the limited collection of available benchmarks. PyGraft is available at: https://github.com/nicolas-hbt/pygraft.

Keywords: Knowledge Graph · Schema · Semantic Web · Synthetic Data Generator

Resource type: Software
License: MIT License
DOI: https://doi.org/10.5281/zenodo.10243209
URL: https://github.com/nicolas-hbt/pygraft

1   Introduction

Knowledge graphs (KGs) have been increasingly used as a graph-structure representation of data. More specifically, a KG is a collection of triples (s, p, o) where s (subject) and o (object) are two entities of the graph, and p is a predicate that qualifies the nature of the relation holding between them [16]. KGs are usually underpinned by a schema (*e.g.*, an ontology) which defines the main concepts and relations of a domain of interest, as well as the rules under which these concepts and relations are allowed to interact [14].

KGs are being used in a wide array of tasks, in many of which a limited collection of KGs established themselves as standard benchmarks for evaluating model performance. However, there are some concerns around the sole usage of these specific mainstream KGs for assessing the generalization capability of newly introduced models. For example, for the particular task of node classification, it has been demonstrated that mainstream datasets such as CiteSeer, Cora, and PubMed feature similar statistical characteristics, especially homophily [24]. Consequently, new models are assessed with respect to a collection of statistically similar datasets. Therefore, their performance improvement does not always hold beyond the standard benchmark datasets [24]. Similarly, it has been shown that many link prediction train sets suffer from extremely skewed distributions in both the degrees of entities and the occurrence of a subset of predicates [28]. In addition, some of the established link prediction datasets are plagued with data biases [27] and include many occurrences of inference patterns [8, 21, 22] that predictive models are able to incorporate, which may cause overly optimistic evaluation performance [8]. For example, the mainstream FB15k and WN18 datasets are substantially affected by these biases. Therefore, more diverse datasets are needed [27]. In this situation, it is of utmost importance to provide a way for researchers to generate synthetic yet realistic datasets of different shapes and characteristics, so that new models can be evaluated in a wide range of data settings.

Worse than relying on a limited number of KGs is the lack of publicly available KGs in some application fields. Conducting research in domains such as education, law enforcement, or medicine, is particularly difficult. On the grounds of data privacy, collecting and sharing real-world knowledge may not be possible. As such, domain-oriented KGs are barely accessible in these areas. However, engineers, practitioners, and researchers usually have precise ideas of the characteristics of their problem of interest. In this context, it would be beneficial to generate a synthetic KG that emulates the characteristics of a real KG [11].

The aforementioned issues led to several attempts at building synthetic generators of schemas and KGs, even though in most cases these two aspects have been considered separately. Stochastic-based generators have been proposed to output domain-agnostic KGs [1, 10, 25]. However good these methods are at generating large graphs quickly, their data generation process does not allow to take an underlying schema into account [11]. Therefore, the resulting KGs are not guaranteed to accurately mimic the characteristics of real-world KGs in a desired application field. In contrast, schema-driven generators are able to synthesize KGs that resemble real-world data. However, most works focused on generating synthetic KGs on the basis of an already existing schema [23]. Synthesizing both a schema and a KG underpinned by it is a more challenging task that has been considered but with only limited success so far [23].

In this work, we aim at addressing this issue. In particular, we present PyGraft, a Python-based tool to generate highly customized, domain-agnostic schemas and KGs. The contributions of our work are the following:

- To the best of our knowledge, PyGraft is the first generator dedicated to the generation of both schemas and KGs in a unique pipeline, while being highly tunable based on a broad array of user-specified parameters. Notably, the generated resources are domain-agnostic, which makes them usable for benchmarking purposes regardless of the application field.
- The generated schemas and KGs are built with an extended set of RDFS and OWL constructs and their logical consistency is ensured by the use of a DL reasoner, which allows for both fine-grained description of resources and strict compliance with common Semantic Web standards.
- We publicly release our code with a documentation and accompanying examples for ease of use.

The remainder of the paper is structured as follows. Related work is presented in Sect. 2. In Sect. 3, PyGraft is detailed and accompanied with necessary background knowledge and comparisons with other available generators. In Sect. 4, a thorough performance analysis of PyGraft is presented. A discussion on current potential use cases, limitations, and future work can be found in Sect. 5. Lastly, Sect. 6 sums up the key insights presented in this paper.

2   Related Work

The generation principle governing synthetic graph generators leads to differentiate between *stochastic-based*, *deep generative*, and *semantic-driven* generators. Along the description of these families of generators, Table 1 provides details on current and open-source implementations. These tools are also compared with PyGraft regarding several criteria.

Stochastic-based generators are usually characterized by their ability to output large graphs in a short amount of time. Early works are represented by the famous Erdős-Rényi model [10]. The Erdős-Rényi model generates graphs by independently assigning edges between pairs of nodes with a fixed probability. The Barabási-Albert model [1] exhibits scale-free degree distributions and is based on the principle of preferential attachment, where new nodes are more likely to attach to nodes with higher degrees. The R-MAT model [5] generates large-scale power-law graphs with properties like power-law degree distributions and community structures. More recently, TrillionG [25] – presented as an extension of R-MAT – represents nodes and edges as vectors in a high-dimensional space. TrillionG allows users to generate large graphs up to trillions of edges while exhibiting lower space and time complexities than previously proposed generators. In Table 1, stochastic-based generators are represented by igraph[1],

---

[1] https://github.com/igraph/python-igraph/.

NetworkX^2, and Snap^3. Although they are not specifically designed for graph generation, they provide off-the-shelf implementations for generating random graphs, such as the Erdős-Rényi and Barabási-Albert models. They are domain-agnostic and scalable, but do not take into account any semantics.

Deep generative graph generators are trained on existing graph datasets and learn to capture the underlying patterns of the input graphs. Deep generative graph models are typically based on generative adversarial networks (GANs) and graph neural networks (GNNs), recurrent neural networks (RNNs), or variational autoencoders (VAEs). GraphGAN [31] leverages the GAN structure, in which the generative model receives a vertex and aims at fitting its true connectivity distribution over all other vertices – thereby producing fake samples for the discriminative model to differentiate from ground-truth samples. GraphRNN [32] is a deep autoregressive model that trains on a collection of graphs. It can be viewed as a hierarchical model adding nodes and edges in a sequential manner. A representant of the VAE family of generators is NeVAE [29], which is specifically designed for molecular graphs. NeVAE features a decoder which is able to guarantee a set of valid properties in the generated molecules. In particular, MolGAN [7] and NeVAE [29] are bound to molecular graph generation. Therefore, they are not domain-agnostic (Table 1). The other generators of this family are, but they do not take a schema as input when generating random graphs, *i.e.*, they are not schema-driven (Table 1).

Semantic-driven generators, in contrast, incorporate schema-based constraints or external knowledge to generate graphs that exhibit specific characteristics or follow certain patterns relevant to the given field of application. In [15], the Lehigh University Benchmark (LUBM) and the Univ-Bench Artificial data generator (UBA) are presented. The former is an ontology modelling the university domain while the latter aims at generating synthetic graphs based on the LUBM schema as well as user-defined queries and restrictions. Similarly, the Linked Data Benchmark Council (LDBC) [2] released the Social Network Benchmark (SNB), which includes a graph generator for synthesizing social network data based on realistic distributions. gMark [3] has subsequently been presented as the first generator that satisfies the criteria of being domain-independent, scalable, schema-driven, and highly configurable, all at the same time. However, it still requires already existing schemas as input. In [23], Melo and Paulheim focus on the synthesis of KGs for the purpose of benchmarking link prediction and type prediction tasks. The authors claim that there is a need for more diverse benchmark datasets for link prediction, with the possibility of having control over their characteristics (*e.g.*, the number of entities, relation assertions, number of types, etc.). Therefore, Melo and Paulheim propose a synthesizing approach which replicates input real-world graphs while allowing for controlled variations in graph characteristics. Notably, they highlight the fact that most works, including theirs, focus on synthesizing KGs based on an existing schema, which leads them to formulate the desiderata of generating both a schema and a KG from scratch as a promising venue for future work – which PyGraft actually does.

---

^{2} https://github.com/networkx/networkx/.
^{3} https://github.com/snap-stanford/snap-python/.

Subsequently, Feng *et al.* [11] proposed a schema-driven graph generator based on the concept of Extended Graph Differential Dependencies (GDD^x). However, their approach cannot generate domain-agnostic schemas and thus requires an existing schema as input. The DLCC benchmark proposed in [26] features a synthetic KG generator based on user-specified graph and schema properties. Beyond asking for a given number of nodes, relations and degree distribution in the resulting KG, it allows for specifying a few RDFS constructs for the generation of the underpinning schema.

None of the aforementioned semantic-driven generators perform a logical consistency check of the generated graphs (see Table 1). Additionally, they can only produce final KGs based on an input schema. Some of them are also domain-specific. DLCC [26] is the closest work to ours, and, to the best of our knowledge, this is the first and only work that allows to generate both a schema and a KG while being domain-agnostic. However, it only features 3 schema constructs, namely rdfs:domain, rdfs:range, and rdfs:subClassOf. These sole three constructs do not pose any constraints on triple generation (hence the consistency checking is not needed) and do not fully feature all Semantic Web possibilities that could exist in KGs. This is also why the resources generated with the DLCC generator do not undergo any logical consistency checks (see Table 1).

In the present work, we aim at going a step further and taking numerous RDFS *and* OWL constructs into account, as PyGraft features a broad range of schema constructs (see Tables 2 and 3). Considered together, these constructs lead to many potential sources of inconsistencies that need to be carefully avoided with specific procedures and a final consistency check using a DL reasoner. However, this more challenging setting allows PyGraft to generate KGs that feature a broader range of Semantic Web possibilities.

3 PyGraft Description

This section starts by formally introducing the notions of schema and knowledge graph. The schematic overview of PyGraft is presented in Sect. 3.2. PyGraft schema and KG generation pipelines are presented in Sects. 3.3 and 3.4, respectively.

3.1 Preliminaries

On the one hand, a schema – *e.g.*, an ontology – refers to a explicit specification of a conceptualization that includes concepts, properties, and restrictions within a particular domain of knowledge [14]. It helps ensure consistency, clarity, and interoperability when representing and sharing knowledge. In our work, we consider schemas to be represented as a collection of concepts $\mathcal{C}$, properties $\mathcal{P}$, and axioms $\mathcal{A}$, *i.e.*, $\mathcal{S} = \{\mathcal{C}, \mathcal{P}, \mathcal{A}\}$. Schemas are typically represented using formal languages such as RDFS[4] (Resource Description Framework) and OWL[5] (Web Ontology Language).

---

[4] https://www.w3.org/RDFS/.
[5] https://www.w3.org/OWL/.

Table 1. Feature comparison of graph generation tools. Dashed line is used when a feature is not applicable due to the characteristics of the described generation tool. Domain-agnostic denotes whether a given tool is able to potentially operate with schemas of different application fields.

Tool	Domain-agnostic	Schema-driven	Schema generation	Schema properties	Graph properties	Scalable	Consistency check
igraph[a]	✓	✗	✗	–	✓	✓	–
NetworkX[b]	✓	✗	✗	–	✓	✓	–
Snap[c]	✓	✗	✗	–	✓	✓	–
GraphGen [13]	✓	✗	✗	–	✓	✓	–
GraphRNN [32]	✓	✗	✗	–	✓	✓	–
GraphVAE [30]	✓	✗	✗	–	✓	✗	–
GraphWorld [24]	✓	✗	✗	–	✓	✓	–
MolGAN [7]	✗	✗	✗	–	✓	✗	–
NeVAE [29]	✗	✗	✗	–	✓	✓	–
UBA-LUBM [15]	✗	✓	✗	–	✓	✓	✗
SNB [2]	✗	✓	✗	–	✓	✓	✗
gMark [3]	✓	✓	✗	–	✓	✓	✗
Melo *et al.* [23]	✓	✓	✗	–	✓	✓	✗
GDD^x [11]	✓	✓	✗	–	✓	✓	✗
DLCC [26]	✓	✓	✓	3	✓	✓	✗
PyGraph (ours)	✓	✓	✓	13	✓	✓	✓

[a] https://github.com/igraph/python-igraph/
[b] https://github.com/networkx/networkx/
[c] https://github.com/snap-stanford/snap-python/

Regarding KGs, distinct definitions co-exist [4, 9]. In this work, we stick to the inclusive definition of Hogan *et al.* [16], *i.e.,* we consider a KG to be a graph where nodes represent entities and edges represent relations between these entities. The link between schemas and KGs lies in the fact that schemas are often used to define the structure and semantics of a KG. In other words, a schema defines the vocabulary and rules that govern entities and relationships in a KG. In this view, a KG is a data graph that can be potentially enhanced with a schema [16].

3.2 Overview

From a high-level perspective, the entire PyGraft generation pipeline is depicted in Fig. 1. In particular, Class and Relation Generators are firstly initialized with user-specified parameters, and are then used for building the schema incrementally. The logical consistency of the schema is subsequently checked using HermiT reasoner [12] through the `owlready2`[6] Python library. If the user is also interested in generating a KG based on this schema, the KG Generator is initialized with KG-related parameters, and takes the previously generated schema as input in order to sequentially build the KG. Ultimately, the logical consistency of the resulting KG is assessed with HermiT. More details on the schema-level generation are provided in Sect. 3.3, while Sect. 3.4 describes the KG generation procedure.

---

[6] https://github.com/pwin/owlready2/.

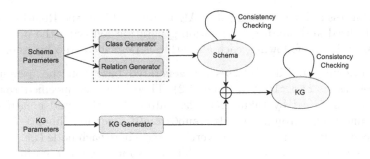

Fig. 1. PyGraft general overview.

3.3   Schema Generation

Table 2. User-defined parameters for schema and KG generations.

	Parameter	Description
Classes	num_classes	Number of classes
	max_depth	Depth of the class hierarchy
	avg_depth	Average class depth
	inheritance_ratio	Proportion of rdfs:subClassOf
	avg_disjointness	Proportion of owl:DisjointWith
Relations	num_relations	Number of relations
	prop_profiled_relations	Proportion of rdfs:domain and rdfs:range
	relation_specificity	Average depth of rdfs:domain and rdfs:range
	prop_asymmetric	Proportion of owl:AsymmetricProperty
	prop_symmetric	Proportion of owl:SymmetricProperty
	prop_irreflexive	Proportion of owl:IrreflexiveProperty
	prop_reflexive	Proportion of owl:ReflexiveProperty
	prop_transitive	Proportion of owl:TransitiveProperty
	prop_functional	Proportion of owl:FunctionalProperty
	prop_inversefunctional	Proportion of owl:InverseFunctionalProperty
	prop_inverseof	Proportion of owl:inverseOf
	prop_subproperties	Proportion of rdfs:subPropertyOf
Individuals	num_entities	Number of entities
	num_triples	Number of triples
	relation_balance	Relation distribution across triples
	prop_untyped	Proportion of untyped entities
	avg_depth_specific	Average depth of most specific class
	multityping	Whether entities are multi-typed
	avg_multityping	Average number of most-specific classes per entity

The schema generation follows a well-defined series of steps. In particular, the Class Generator in Fig. 1 is initialized first, and generates the class hierarchy and disjointness axioms as detailed in Algorithm 1. Then, the Relation Generator is initialized and handles the relation generation following the procedure of Algorithm 2. In the following, each algorithm is described step by step.

Class Generation. First, classes are generated based on the user-specified number of classes `num_classes` (lines 1–2). Then, the user-specified `max_depth` parameter is satisfied by taking one class after the other and creating child-parent connections through the `rdfs:subClassOf` assertion (lines 3–7). At this point, the class hierarchy is a purely vertical tree where each node (*i.e.,* class) has exactly one child, except the leaf node. The class hierarchy is then further filled by taking each remaining class sequentially, and connecting it with other classes so that `avg_depth` and `inheritance_ratio` are satisfied (lines 8–13). It is worth mentioning that with some probability α chosen to be moderately low, a freshly picked class can be placed randomly (lines 10–11). This does not necessarily go in the direction of `avg_depth` and `inheritance_ratio` target parameters, but it allows adding stochasticity and realism in the characteristics of the generated class hierarchy. Besides, when a low number of classes are still to be connected, this randomness is deactivated so that each subsequent class connection is in line with `avg_depth` and `inheritance_ratio` fulfilment. Finally, class disjointnesses are added to the schema by picking two classes A and B, ensuring that none of them is a transitive parent or child of the other, and extending class disjointness to their respective children, if any (lines 14–16).

When generating classes, anomalies may occur. For instance, choosing values such that `avg_depth` > `max_depth` triggers an error. In a few other situations, the schema is generated but the user requirements might not be completely fulfilled. This can happen because of competing parameter values. For example, the constraints `num_classes` = 6 (`root` excluded), `max_depth` = 3, `avg_depth` = 1.5, and `inheritance_ratio` = 2.5 cannot be simultaneously satisfied (Fig. 2). In this situation, the schema is generated with a best-effort strategy, seeking to build a schema with statistics as close as possible to the user requirements.

Relation Generation. Before presenting the procedure for generating relations and their properties, it is worth mentioning that PyGraft allows relations to be described by multiple `OWL` and `RDFS` constructs. This leads to more realistic schemas and KGs, at the expense of higher risk of inconsistency: some property combinations are not logically consistent, *e.g.,* a relation cannot be simultaneously qualified by `owl:ReflexiveProperty` and `owl:IrreflexiveProperty`. Based on the relation properties available in PyGraft (Table 3), all combinations were extracted and for each combination, a new graph was serialized using `rdflib`[7]. This graph contains a unique relation which is qualified by the given property combinations[8]. Based on the simplified schema, the HermiT reasoner

---

[7] https://github.com/RDFLib/rdflib/.

[8] An instance triple should also be added. This is because some property combinations such as `owl:SymmetricProperty` and `owl:AsymmetricProperty` are not flagged as logically inconsistent *per se* in `OWL`. However, a relation qualified by these two properties is not allowed to connect any instances.

performs consistency checking. Finally, a dictionary stores all possible property combinations. Knowing valid and invalid property combinations is necessary for guiding relation property assignment and minimize logical inconsistency likelihood before actually running the reasoner.

In Algorithm 2, this dictionary of valid property combinations is loaded (line 3) just after initializing the number of relations specified by the user (lines 1–2). Then, each relation in the schema is qualified with properties based on a pre-defined order (lines 4–6). For example, `owl:ReflexiveProperty` and `owl:IrreflexiveProperty` are assigned first, then `owl:SymmetricProperty`, etc. These properties are named *attributes* as they characterize a relation *per se*. Next, the *relationship property* `owl:InverseOf` is assigned to relations (line 7), which poses constraints on relation domain and range assignments (line 8), which themselves pose constraints on relation pairings through the `rdfs:subPropertyOf` assertion (line 9), *e.g.,* domain and range of subproperties should not be disjoint with domain and range of superproperties.

In Table 3 are reported the relation properties that the current PyGraft version handles, along with their logical definition and accompanying examples.

Table 3. Relation properties covered by PyGraft.

Property	Definition	Example
`owl:AsymmetricProperty`	$\forall x \forall y : p(x, y) \Rightarrow \neg p(y, x)$	`isParentOf`
`owl:SymmetricProperty`	$\forall x \forall y : p(x, y) \Rightarrow p(y, x)$	`hasSibling`
`owl:ReflexiveProperty`	$\forall x : p(x, x)$	`hasSameColorAs`
`owl:IrreflexiveProperty`	$\forall x : \neg p(x, x)$	`isYoungerThan`
`owl:TransitiveProperty`	$\forall x \forall y \forall z : p(x, y) \wedge p(y, z) \Rightarrow p(x, z)$	`isCheaperThan`
`owl:FunctionalProperty`	$\forall x \forall y \forall z : (p(x, y) \wedge p(x, z)) \Rightarrow y = z$	`hasISBN`
`owl:InverseFunctionalProperty`	$\forall x \forall y \forall z : (p(x, y) \wedge p(z, y)) \Rightarrow x = z$	`isEmailAddressOf`
`owl:InverseOf`	$\forall x \forall y : p(x, y) \Longleftrightarrow q(y, x)$	`owns` $\Longleftrightarrow$ `isOwnedBy`
`rdfs:subPropertyOf`	$\forall x \forall y : p(x, y) \Rightarrow q(x, y)$	`hasMother` $\Rightarrow$ `hasParent`

3.4 Knowledge Graph Generation

In light of PyGraft overview (Fig. 1), this section explores how the KG generator is initialized with user parameters and used in conjunction with any generated schema to build the final KG. As for schema, we provide a step-by-step insight into Algorithm 3. Entities and the KG are generated (lines 1–3) and a schema dedicated to the KG generation is loaded (line 4). Based on **prop_untyped**, entities are assigned a class whose depth in the class hierarchy should be in a close range around **avg_depth_specific** (line 5). Based on **avg_multityping**, several of them are assigned other classes of the same depth, provided that they are not disjoint with any of the specific classes characterizing a given entity (lines 6–7). Then, triples are generated (lines 8–9) in a sequential manner. Namely, unobserved entities in U have sampling priority, to ensure that the required number of entities in the resulting KG is met as fully as possible. Ultimately, checking procedures are performed (line 10) before the KG undergoes logical

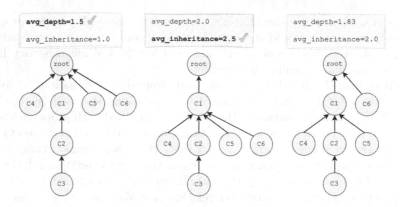

Fig. 2. Potential class hierarchies for the constraints: `num_classes` = 6, `max_depth` = 3, `avg_depth` = 1.5, and `inheritance_ratio` = 2.5. Left and middle class hierarchies are built with parameter priority. The right class hierarchy is built with a best-effort strategy, without specific parameter privilege.

consistency checking using a semantic reasoner (line 11). If the generated KG is inconsistent, a message warns the user but the KG is stored nevertheless. The user can then choose to restart the generation procedure. It is worth mentioning that the checking procedures (line 10) follow the relevant `OWL 2 RL/RDF` rules[9]. These rules – in the form of first-order implications – are implemented in PyGraft to ensure consistency pre-checking before the HermiT reasoner is deployed. In addition, the OntOlogy Pitfall Scanner![10] was also used for identifying several checking procedures and for ensuring compliance with common Semantic Web standards.

4   PyGraft in Action

4.1   Efficiency and Scalability Details

In this section, the efficiency and scalability of PyGraft are benchmarked across several schema and graph configurations. Each schema specification reported in Table 4 is paired with each graph specification from Table 5. This leads to 27 distinct combinations.

In particular, schemas from $S1$ to $S3$ are small-sized, schemas from $S4$ to $S6$ are medium-sized, and schemas from $S7$ to $S9$ are of larger sizes (Table 4). For each schema of a given size, the degree of constraints vary as they contain different levels of `OWL` and `RDFS` logical constructs. For example, $S1$ has less constraints than $S2$, which itself has less constraints than $S3$. Graph specifications G_1, G_2, and G_3 correspond to small-sized, medium-sized and large-sized graphs, respectively (Table 5).

---

[9] https://www.w3.org/TR/owl2-profiles/#ref-owl-2-rdf-semantics/.
[10] https://oops.linkeddata.es/.

Algorithm 1. Class Generation

1: Initialize the set of unconnected classes: $U = \{C_1, C_2, ..., C_m\}$
2: Initialize the set of linked classes: $L = \emptyset$
3: $C_1 \leftarrow$ U.POP(), L.ADD(C_1)
4: C_1 rdfs:subClassOf root
5: **while** max_depth is not satisfied **do**   ▷ Fulfilling class hierarchy depth
6:     $C_i \leftarrow$ U.POP(), L.ADD(C_i)
7:     C_i rdfs:subClassOf C_{i-1}
8: **while** $U \neq \emptyset$ **do**   ▷ Building class hierarchy
9:     $C_i \leftarrow$ U.POP(), L.ADD(C_i)
10:    **if** random$(0, 1) \leq \alpha$ **then**   ▷ Adding stochasticity
11:        Place it randomly
12:    **else**
13:        Place it s.t. avg_depth and inheritance_ratio are satisfied
14: **while** current_disj < disj_ratio **do**   ▷ Adds owl:disjointWith
15:    Pick classes A and B s.t. B is neither a parent nor a child of A
16:    Make A and B disjoint and extend disjointness to their respective children

---

Algorithm 2. Relation Generation

1: Initialize the set of unqualified relations: $U = \{R_1, R_2, ..., R_n\}$
2: Initialize the set of qualified relations: $Q = \emptyset$
3: Load compatible patterns
4: **while** $U \neq \emptyset$ and attribute proportions not satisfied **do**   ▷ Adding attributes
5:     $R_i \leftarrow$ U.POP(), Q.ADD(R_i)
6:     QUALIFY(R_i) based on priority order

7: INVERSE_PAIRING(Q)   ▷ Adding owl:inverseOf
8: RELATION_PROFILING(Q)   ▷ Adding rdfs:domain/range
9: SUBPROPERTY_PAIRING(Q)   ▷ Adding rdfs:subPropertyOf

Algorithm 3. Knowledge Graph Generation

1: Initialize the set of unobserved entities: $U = \{E_1, E_2, ..., E_p\}$
2: Initialize the set of observed entities: $O = \emptyset$
3: Initialize the knowledge graph: $\mathcal{KG} = \emptyset$
4: Load the underpinning schema $\mathcal{S}$
5: ASSIGN_CLASS(U)   ▷ Specific class attribution based on prop_untyped
6: **if** multityping **then**
7:     COMPLETE_TYPING(U)   ▷ Adding specific classes based on avg_multityping
8: **while** $U \neq \emptyset$ and num_triples not satisfied **do**
9:     $\mathcal{KG} \leftarrow$ GENERATE_TRIPLES($U, O, \mathcal{S}$)
10: CHECKING_PROCEDURES($\mathcal{KG}$)   ▷ Removing foreseeable inconsistencies
11: REASONING($\mathcal{KG}$)   ▷ HermiT reasoner

For these 27 unique configurations, execution times w.r.t. several dimensions are computed and shown in Fig. 3. Execution times related to the schema generation are omitted as they are negligible. Experiments were conducted on a machine with 2 CPUs Intel Xeon E5-2650 v4, 12 cores/CPU, and 128GB RAM.

It is worth mentioning that the 27 generated KGs were flagged as consistent at the first attempt. The breakdown of time executions differs according to the schema and graph sizes (see Fig. 3). For small graphs, the final consistency checking is the most time-consuming part. For large graphs, triple generation time dominates the rest. As graph sizes increase, all execution times grow but we observe that PyGraft is able to generate consistent KGs quickly, even for large KGs: with our experimental configuration, the total execution time for KGs with 10K entities and 100K triples is roughly 1.5 min. In addition, PyGraft scalability was assessed by asking a KG of 100K entities and 1M triples. On the same machine, it took 47 min to generate such a KG, which was again consistent at the first attempt.

Table 4. Generated schemas. Column headers from left to right: number of classes, class hierarchy depth, average class depth, proportion of class disjointness (cd), number of relations, average depth of relation domains and ranges (rs), and proportions of reflexive (rf), irreflexive (irr), asymmetric (asy), symmetric (sy), transitive (tra), and inverse (inv) relations.

	$|\mathcal{C}|$	MAX($\mathcal{D}$)	AVG($\mathcal{D}$)	cd	$|\mathcal{R}|$	rs	ref	irr	asy	sym	tra	inv
$\mathcal{S}1$	25	3	1.5	0.1	25	1.5	0.1	0.1	0.1	0.1	0.1	0.1
$\mathcal{S}2$	25	3	1.5	0.2	25	1.5	0.2	0.2	0.2	0.2	0.2	0.2
$\mathcal{S}3$	25	3	1.5	0.3	25	1.5	0.3	0.3	0.3	0.3	0.3	0.3
$\mathcal{S}4$	100	4	2.5	0.1	100	2.5	0.1	0.1	0.1	0.1	0.1	0.1
$\mathcal{S}5$	100	4	2.5	0.2	100	2.5	0.2	0.2	0.2	0.2	0.2	0.2
$\mathcal{S}6$	100	4	2.5	0.3	100	2.5	0.3	0.3	0.3	0.3	0.3	0.3
$\mathcal{S}7$	250	5	3.0	0.1	250	3.0	0.1	0.1	0.1	0.1	0.1	0.1
$\mathcal{S}8$	250	5	3.0	0.2	250	3.0	0.2	0.2	0.2	0.2	0.2	0.2
$\mathcal{S}9$	250	5	3.0	0.3	250	3.0	0.3	0.3	0.3	0.3	0.3	0.3

Table 5. Different graph specifications. Column headers from left to right: number of entities, number of triples, proportion of untyped entities, average depth of the most specific class, average number of most-specific classes per multi-typed entity.

	$|\mathcal{E}|$	$|\mathcal{T}|$	unt	asc	mul
$\mathcal{G}_1$	100	1,000	0.3	2.0	2.0
$\mathcal{G}_2$	1,000	10,000	0.3	2.0	2.0
$\mathcal{G}_3$	10,000	100,000	0.3	2.0	2.0

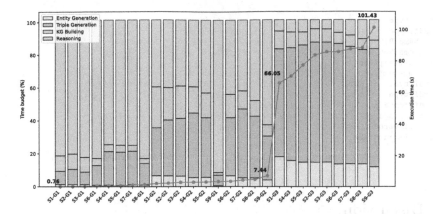

Fig. 3. Execution time breakdown for each configuration.

4.2 Usage Illustration

In this section, we briefly provide some usage examples to demonstrate how easy it is to use PyGraft. Desired characteristics of the output schema and/or KG can be specified with the path to a `yaml` or `json` configuration file. In the example presented in Listing 1.1, after importing PyGraft, we first generate a `yaml` configuration file in the current working directory. For the sake of simplicity, the generated template is left untouched, i.e., we keep the default parameter values. More advanced usage is provided in the official documentation: https:// pygraft.readthedocs.io/en/latest/. Then, we generate both a schema and KG in a single pipeline. The generated resources are subsequently stored in the current working directory.

```
import pygraft

pygraft.create_yaml_template()
pygraft.generate("template.yml")
```

Listing 1.1. Schema and KG generation with PyGraft.

By default, the generated graph is stored as an `rdf/xml` file. A snippet of a KG generated with PyGraft is provided in Listing 1.2.

```xml
<?xml version="1.0" encoding="utf-8"?>
<rdf:RDF
    xmlns:ns1="http://purl.org/dc/terms/"
    xmlns:owl="http://www.w3.org/2002/07/owl#"
    xmlns:rdf="http://www.w3.org/1999/02/22-rdf-syntax-ns#"
    xmlns:rdfs="http://www.w3.org/2000/01/rdf-schema#"
    xmlns:sc="http://pygraf.t/"
>

  <rdf:Description rdf:about="http://pygraf.t/C30">
    <rdf:type rdf:resource="http://www.w3.org/2002/07/owl#Class"/>
    <rdfs:subClassOf rdf:resource="http://www.w3.org/2002/07/owl#Thing"/>
    <owl:disjointWith rdf:resource="http://pygraf.t/C16"/>
  </rdf:Description>
  <rdf:Description rdf:about="http://pygraf.t/E324">
```

```
<rdf:type rdf:resource="http://pygraf.t/C4"/>
<rdf:type rdf:resource="http://pygraf.t/C17"/>
<schema:R15 rdf:resource="http://pygraf.t/E356"/>
<schema:R34 rdf:resource="http://pygraf.t/E44"/>
</rdf:Description>
<rdf:Description rdf:about="http://pygraf.t/R34">
<rdf:type rdf:resource="http://www.w3.org/2002/07/owl#ObjectProperty"/>
<rdf:type rdf:resource="http://www.w3.org/2002/07/owl#TransitiveProperty"/>
<rdfs:domain rdf:resource="http://pygraf.t/C17"/>
<rdfs:range rdf:resource="http://pygraf.t/C17"/>
<owl:inverseOf rdf:resource="http://pygraf.t/R15"/>
</rdf:Description>
```

Listing 1.2. Excerpt from a generated graph.

5   Discussion

5.1   Potential Uses

As mentioned, PyGraft can be used for generating several schemas and KGs on the fly, thereby facilitating novel approaches and model benchmarking on a wider range of datasets with diversified characteristics. In practice, this can be easily done with inspecting the configuration file we provide as template, and tweaking parameters as one sees fit.

Additionally, PyGraft can be used for generating anonymous data. Let us assume one is working in a data-sensitive field such as medicine or education, characterized by the paucity of readily available data. Thanks to PyGraft, it becomes much more accessible to experiment with sensitiveless testbeds, provided that the user has a rough idea of the scale and characteristics of the resources they want to mimic.

It is worth noting that a vibrant research community aims at incorporating schema-based information into the learning process with KGs [6,19,20]. Using information derived from the schema in addition to the facts contained in the KG aims at building more semantic-aware approaches [17], that are expected to result in more coherent predictions [18] and better predictive accuracy [6,17]. However, it is frequently reported that most KGs do not come with publicly available schemas that would facilitate the development of such schema-aware approaches. For this reason, PyGraft may also be helpful to generate both synthetic schemas with dependent KGs to foster the development of schema-driven, neuro-symbolic approaches, and to run ablation studies on specific schema constructs in isolation.

5.2   Limitations, Sustainability, Maintenance and Future Work

In this section, we discuss the current limitations of PyGraft and elaborate on our sustainability and maintenance plan, as well as future work opportunities.

First, it should be noted that PyGraft relies on `rdflib` for serializing triples. As part of supplementary experiments, we tried to push PyGraft capabilities to its limit by generating very large KGs with >10M entities and triples. In such cases, the serialization failed. In future work, we will develop independent serialization procedures so that bigger graphs can be generated.

Secondly, recall that our implemented checking procedures limit the likelihood of any inconsistency *before* the DL reasoner is ultimately applied on the generated KG. In case of inconsistencies that would remain undetected by the checking procedures, our actual use of the HermiT reasoner is able to detect such inconsistencies, but not to provide any information on the triples that should be removed so that the KG becomes consistent. In future work, we will implement such a functionality, so that the consistency of the generated KGs can be ensured in a single loop without requiring any input from the user's side.

More generally, we aim at maintaining the PyGraft library, a cornerstone in our commitment to robust software engineering practices and open-source community engagement. Our approach is to release new versions in response to emerging user requirements, ensuring that PyGraft not only meets but anticipates the needs of its users. For instance, a common request is the ability to generate literals – which we seek to achieve in the near future. Furthermore, we recently welcomed the suggestion of offering a hub that would gather different KG profiles generated by the community. To this aim, we welcome all contributions on Github (*e.g.,*, issues, forks, or pull requests) to make PyGraft useful to researchers of a large array of communities. We are dedicated to incorporating methodologies for continuous integration and deployment, fostering a test-driven development environment that guarantees reliability and efficiency. We also want PyGraft to fit within the Semantic Web community and be recognized as a useful tool for researchers and engineers working on KG-based applications.

In future work, we will showcase the impact of PyGraft in real-world use cases. Some relevant scenarios include recommender systems and ontology repairment. In particular, for the latter use-case, we envision the creation of voluntarily imperfect schemas, containing (known) contradictions to resolve. Link prediction also appears as an appropriate task to evaluate PyGraft's usefulness.

6   Conclusion

In this work, we presented PyGraft, a Python tool for generating synthetic schemas and KGs from user requirements. Several OWL and RDFS constructs are integrated to output realistic KGs that comply with Semantic Web standards. PyGraft allows researchers and practitioners to generate schemas and KGs on the fly, provided minimal knowledge about the desired specifications. Hence, PyGraft can prove useful for various applications. As it allows for generating schemas and KGs of controlled characteristics, it can serve as a well-suited tool for benchmarking novel approaches or models. Being domain-agnostic, PyGraft can be used to generate synthetic schemas and KGs resembling real ones in data-sensitive fields where access or publication of public data is scarce. Due to the richly described generated KGs in terms of OWL and RDFS constructs, PyGraft may also facilitate the development of schema-driven, neuro-symbolic models.

References

1. Albert, R., Barabási, A.L.: Statistical mechanics of complex networks. Rev. Mod. Phys. **74**, 47–97 (2002). https://doi.org/10.1103/RevModPhys.74.47
2. Angles, R., et al.: The linked data benchmark council: a graph and RDF industry benchmarking effort. SIGMOD Rec. **43**(1), 27–31 (2014). https://doi.org/10.1145/2627692.2627697
3. Bagan, G., Bonifati, A., Ciucanu, R., Fletcher, G.H.L., Lemay, A., Advokaat, N.: gMark: schema-driven generation of graphs and queries. IEEE Trans. Knowl. Data Eng. **29**(4), 856–869 (2017). https://doi.org/10.1109/TKDE.2016.2633993
4. Bonatti, P.A., Decker, S., Polleres, A., Presutti, V.: Knowledge graphs: new directions for knowledge representation on the semantic web (Dagstuhl seminar 18371). Dagstuhl Rep. **8**(9), 29–111 (2018). https://doi.org/10.4230/DagRep.8.9.29
5. Chakrabarti, D., Zhan, Y., Faloutsos, C.: R-MAT: a recursive model for graph mining. In: Proceedings of the Fourth SIAM International Conference on Data Mining, Lake Buena Vista, Florida, USA, 22–24 April 2004, pp. 442–446. SIAM (2004). https://doi.org/10.1137/1.9781611972740.43
6. d'Amato, C., Quatraro, N.F., Fanizzi, N.: Injecting background knowledge into embedding models for predictive tasks on knowledge graphs. In: Verborgh, R., et al. (eds.) ESWC 2021. LNCS, vol. 12731, pp. 441–457. Springer, Cham (2021). https://doi.org/10.1007/978-3-030-77385-4_26
7. De Cao, N., Kipf, T.: MolGAN: an implicit generative model for small molecular graphs. In: ICML 2018 Workshop on Theoretical Foundations and Applications of Deep Generative Models (2018)
8. Dettmers, T., Minervini, P., Stenetorp, P., Riedel, S.: Convolutional 2D knowledge graph embeddings. In: Proceedings of the Thirty-Second AAAI Conference on Artificial Intelligence, (AAAI-18), the 30th Innovative Applications of Artificial Intelligence (IAAI-18), and the 8th AAAI Symposium on Educational Advances in Artificial Intelligence (EAAI-18), New Orleans, Louisiana, USA, 2–7 February 2018, pp. 1811–1818. AAAI Press (2018)
9. Ehrlinger, L., Wöß, W.: Towards a definition of knowledge graphs. In: Joint Proceedings of the Posters and Demos Track of the 12th International Conference on Semantic Systems - SEMANTiCS2016 and the 1st International Workshop on Semantic Change & Evolving Semantics (SuCCESS'16) co-located with the 12th International Conference on Semantic Systems (SEMANTiCS 2016), Leipzig, Germany, 12–15 September 2016. CEUR Workshop Proceedings, vol. 1695. CEUR-WS.org (2016)
10. ERDdS, P., R&wi, A.: On random graphs I. Publ. math. debrecen **6**(290-297), 18 (1959)
11. Feng, Z., et al.: A schema-driven synthetic knowledge graph generation approach with extended graph differential dependencies (gdd^{x}s). IEEE Access **9**, 5609–5639 (2021). https://doi.org/10.1109/ACCESS.2020.3048186
12. Glimm, B., Horrocks, I., Motik, B., Stoilos, G., Wang, Z.: Hermit: an OWL 2 reasoner. J. Autom. Reason. **53**(3), 245–269 (2014). https://doi.org/10.1007/s10817-014-9305-1
13. Goyal, N., Jain, H.V., Ranu, S.: GraphGen: a scalable approach to domain-agnostic labeled graph generation. In: WWW 2020: The Web Conference 2020, Taipei, Taiwan, 20–24 April 2020, pp. 1253–1263. ACM/IW3C2 (2020). https://doi.org/10.1145/3366423.3380201

14. Gruber, T.R.: Toward principles for the design of ontologies used for knowledge sharing? Int. J. Hum Comput Stud. **43**(5–6), 907–928 (1995). https://doi.org/10.1006/ijhc.1995.1081
15. Guo, Y., Pan, Z., Heflin, J.: LUBM: a benchmark for OWL knowledge base systems. J. Web Semant. **3**(2–3), 158–182 (2005). https://doi.org/10.1016/j.websem.2005.06.005
16. Hogan, A., et al.: Knowledge Graphs. Synthesis Lectures on Data, Semantics, and Knowledge, Morgan & Claypool Publishers (2021). https://doi.org/10.2200/S01125ED1V01Y202109DSK022
17. Hubert, N., Monnin, P., Brun, A., Monticolo, D.: Enhancing knowledge graph embedding models with semantic-driven loss functions. CoRR abs/2303.00286 (2023). https://doi.org/10.48550/arXiv.2303.00286
18. Hubert, N., Monnin, P., Brun, A., Monticolo, D.: Sem@k: is my knowledge graph embedding model semantic-aware? CoRR abs/2301.05601 (2023). https://doi.org/10.48550/arXiv.2301.05601
19. Hubert, N., Paulheim, H., Monnin, P., Brun, A., Monticolo, D.: Schema first! learn versatile knowledge graph embeddings by capturing semantics with machine. CoRR abs/2306.03659 (2023). https://doi.org/10.48550/arXiv.2306.03659
20. Jain, N., Tran, T.K., Gad-Elrab, M.H., Stepanova, D.: Improving knowledge graph embeddings with ontological reasoning. In: Hotho, A., et al. (eds.) ISWC 2021. LNCS, vol. 12922, pp. 410–426. Springer, Cham (2021). https://doi.org/10.1007/978-3-030-88361-4_24
21. Jin, L., Yao, Z., Chen, M., Chen, H., Zhang, W.: A comprehensive study on knowledge graph embedding over relational patterns based on rule learning (2023)
22. Liu, S., Grau, B.C., Horrocks, I., Kostylev, E.V.: Revisiting inferential benchmarks for knowledge graph completion. CoRR abs/2306.04814 (2023). https://doi.org/10.48550/arXiv.2306.04814
23. Melo, A., Paulheim, H.: Synthesizing knowledge graphs for link and type prediction benchmarking. In: Blomqvist, E., Maynard, D., Gangemi, A., Hoekstra, R., Hitzler, P., Hartig, O. (eds.) ESWC 2017. LNCS, vol. 10249, pp. 136–151. Springer, Cham (2017). https://doi.org/10.1007/978-3-319-58068-5_9
24. Palowitch, J., Tsitsulin, A., Mayer, B., Perozzi, B.: GraphWorld: fake graphs bring real insights for GNNs. In: KDD 2022: The 28th ACM SIGKDD Conference on Knowledge Discovery and Data Mining, Washington, DC, USA, 14–18 August 2022, pp. 3691–3701. ACM (2022). https://doi.org/10.1145/3534678.3539203
25. Park, H., Kim, M.: Trilliong: a trillion-scale synthetic graph generator using a recursive vector model. In: Proceedings of the 2017 ACM International Conference on Management of Data, SIGMOD Conference 2017, Chicago, IL, USA, 14–19 May 2017, pp. 913–928. ACM (2017). https://doi.org/10.1145/3035918.3064014
26. Portisch, J., Paulheim, H.: The DLCC node classification benchmark for analyzing knowledge graph embeddings. In: Sattler, U., et al. (eds.) ISWC 2022. LNCS, vol. 13489, pp. 592–609. Springer, Cham (2022). https://doi.org/10.1007/978-3-031-19433-7_34
27. Rossi, A., Firmani, D., Merialdo, P., et al.: Knowledge graph embeddings or bias graph embeddings? A study of bias in link prediction models. In: CEUR Workshop Proceedings, vol. 3034. CEUR-WS (2021)
28. Rossi, A., Matinata, A.: Knowledge graph embeddings: are relation-learning models learning relations? In: Proceedings of the Workshops of the EDBT/ICDT 2020 Joint Conference, Copenhagen, Denmark, 30 March 2020. CEUR Workshop Proceedings, vol. 2578. CEUR-WS.org (2020)

29. Samanta, B., et al.: NEVAE: a deep generative model for molecular graphs. J. Mach. Learn. Res. **21**, 114:1–114:33 (2020)
30. Simonovsky, M., Komodakis, N.: GraphVAE: towards generation of small graphs using variational autoencoders. In: Kurkova, V., Manolopoulos, Y., Hammer, B., Iliadis, L., Maglogiannis, I. (eds.) ICANN 2018. LNCS, vol. 11139, pp. 412–422. Springer, Cham (2018). https://doi.org/10.1007/978-3-030-01418-6_41
31. Wang, H., et al.: GraphGAN: graph representation learning with generative adversarial nets. In: Proceedings of the Thirty-Second AAAI Conference on Artificial Intelligence, (AAAI-18), the 30th innovative Applications of Artificial Intelligence (IAAI-18), and the 8th AAAI Symposium on Educational Advances in Artificial Intelligence (EAAI-18), New Orleans, Louisiana, USA, 2–7 February 2018, pp. 2508–2515. AAAI Press (2018)
32. You, J., Ying, R., Ren, X., Hamilton, W.L., Leskovec, J.: GraphRNN: generating realistic graphs with deep auto-regressive models. In: Proceedings of the 35th International Conference on Machine Learning, ICML 2018, Stockholmsmässan, Stockholm, Sweden, 10–15 July 2018. Proceedings of Machine Learning Research, vol. 80, pp. 5694–5703. PMLR (2018)

NORIA-O: An Ontology for Anomaly Detection and Incident Management in ICT Systems

Lionel Tailhardat[1,2]([✉]) [iD], Yoan Chabot[3] [iD], and Raphael Troncy[2] [iD]

[1] Orange, Paris, France
lionel.tailhardat@orange.com
[2] EURECOM, Sophia Antipolis, Biot, France
[3] Orange, Belfort, France

Abstract. Large-scale Information and Communications Technology (ICT) systems give rise to difficult situations such as handling cascading failures and detecting complex malicious activities occurring on multiple services and network layers. For network supervision, managing these situations while ensuring the high-standard quality of service and security requires a comprehensive view on how communication devices are interconnected and are performing. However, the information is spread across heterogeneous data sources which triggers information integration challenges. Existing data models enable to represent computing resources and how they are allocated. However, to date, there is no model to describe the inter-dependencies between the structural, dynamic, and functional aspects of a network infrastructure. In this paper, we propose the NORIA ontology that has been developed together with network and cybersecurity experts in order to describe an infrastructure, its events, diagnosis and repair actions performed during incident management. A use case describing a fictitious failure shows how this ontology can model complex situations and serve as a basis for anomaly detection and root cause analysis. The ontology is available at https://w3id.org/noria and empowers the largest telco operator in France.

Keywords: Ontology · Network Supervision · Incident Management · Network Infrastructure · NORIA

1 Introduction

When managing large-scale IT & telco networks (broadband international backbones, corporate networks, Internet access networks), one is sooner or later involved into handling complex incident situations, such as general IT service disruption because of cascading failures or cyber-attacks. Incident management teams rely on decision support tools like Network Monitoring Systems (NMSs) [25,43] or Security Information and Event Management systems (SIEMs) [26]. These tools often use an elementary representation of the network

© The Author(s), under exclusive license to Springer Nature Switzerland AG 2024
A. Meroño Peñuela et al. (Eds.): ESWC 2024, LNCS 14665, pp. 21–39, 2024.
https://doi.org/10.1007/978-3-031-60635-9_2

infrastructures and services. Basically, an IT network is a set of computers, routers, and other devices connected and configured to allow data processing and sharing. Similarly, an IT service is the usage of this processing and sharing capability for specific purposes, from the most trivial ones (entertainment, ticket booking, home automation) to more challenging ones (stock exchange, road lights, or nuclear plant management). Although obvious at first glance, this level of description is not sufficient to scale up for maintaining high-standard quality of service on large-scale networks. This is due to the heterogeneity of the Information and Communications Technology (ICT) systems that compose them and the interdependencies between services and infrastructure: incident diagnosis and remediation is a challenging task as supervision teams must deal with multiple technologies, technical characteristics, monitoring systems, and stakeholders in siloed organizations. For example, one can consider a service architecture that combines virtual machines (VMs) distributed across data centers, which are interconnected through an IPoDWDM[1] network. To achieve efficiency, it is necessary to integrate and correlate data from various sources. This includes data from VM management tools, Optical Transport Network (OTN) layer management tools (which may be managed by a third-party operator), information about scheduled operations, and contact details for local servicing teams.

To tackle these cross-domain data interpretation and incident management challenges, we argue that a graph-based explicit knowledge representation would help capturing complex network situations (e.g. discrepancy of routing metrics with respect to an engineering rule, lack of redundancy in a distributed service) and reasoning on them (e.g. inventory list to scrutinize further, cause and remediation procedure search). Our main contribution in this regard is the NORIA Ontology (NORIA-O) for representing network infrastructures, incidents and operations on networks. This ontology re-uses and extends well-known ontologies such as SEAS [38,39], FOLIO [9], UCO [62], ORG [14], BOT [31] and BBO [2]. It also includes controlled vocabularies for handling data from various ICT systems and incident situations through a small set of shareable definitions. NORIA-O has been developed within the Orange[2] company, a leading international network infrastructure and service provider. Its long-standing experience on complex network management allows us to back NORIA-O with insightful details from domain experts and to evaluate the model with real-world data. In addition, NORIA-O has also been successfully used in a knowledge graph construction pipeline in an industrial setting [30] and for capturing and classifying incident contexts using graph embeddings [28]. The ontology, controlled vocabularies and their associated documentation are available at https://w3id.org/noria.

The remainder of this paper is organized as follows. In Sect. 2, we review RDF-based and non-RDF based data models enabling to represent network infrastructures and incidents. In Sect. 3, we describe the methodology we follow to design NORIA-O, starting from competency questions that capture the knowledge of experts. In Sect. 4, we deep dive into the different concepts as well as into the associated vocabularies. We evaluate the ontology with respect to our

---

[1] Internet Protocol over Dense Wave Division Multiplexing [19].

[2] https://www.orange.com/.

requirements and competency questions in Sect. 5. We exemplify how NORIA-O is used for the supervision of a network infrastructure in Sect. 6. Finally, we conclude and outline some future work in Sect. 7.

2   Related Work

Previous works have demonstrated that the use of semantic modeling is of interest for network infrastructure monitoring (e.g. INDL [37], CRATELO [1], UCO [62], ToCo [48], ACCTP [10], DevOpsInfra [42]). Several tools have also been proposed to facilitate the construction and utilization of knowledge graphs in different areas. These include RMLMapper [3] for data integration, SLOGERT [4] for log parsing and semantization, String2Vocabulary [44] for vocabulary reconciliation, and KG Explorer [55] and Gephi [36] for visualization purposes. We posit that these works partly cover the knowledge domains required for describing ICT systems and related activities (e.g. incident management, cybersecurity risk evaluation). For example, the combination of the SEAS and PEP [38,39] models is useful for describing technological systems, commands and observed values from probing devices. However, SEAS mostly targets the IoT domain and end-user devices, and the semantics of PEP relates to computer process. The DevOpsInfra [42] ontology describes sets of computing resources and how they are allocated for hosting services. However, concepts are missing for a finer grain description of the network topology. Moreover, the ontology mostly focuses on the provisioning activity and is not aligned with other well-known models such as SOSA [27] and the TMForum Open API[3] for interoperable definitions of states and operations. The CRATELO [1] model enables describing and reasoning on cyber-operations. Used in combination with the PACO [41] model, reasoning on network traffic from the defenders' and attackers' perspective is possible. However, concepts for network topology and operations are missing for contextualizing network traffic sessions within the network topology itself and the day-to-day operations.

In this paper, we aim to fill this gap in developing a comprehensive semantic model for describing and reasoning on the combination of network infrastructure characteristics (e.g. device type, links), network activity (e.g. user login, interface status change, processor overload alert) and operations (e.g. software upgrade, server reboot, link decommissioning). Based on various selection criteria, such as the coverage of our target knowledge domain and the enrichment of existing ontologies, we design NORIA-O so that it builds upon some of these existing semantic models as described in Sect. 3.

3   Methodology

In this section, we describe the knowledge engineering methodology we used to develop NORIA-O. First, we capture Competency Questions (CQs) from a panel of experts familiar with network operation issues and derive archetypes from these CQs for further analysis (Sect. 3.1). Second, we show how we designed the conceptual model (Sect. 3.2).

---

[3] https://github.com/tmforum-apis.

3.1 Competency Questions and Conceptualization

We gathered experts from several entities in the fields of engineering, operations, supervision, and incident management on networks and data centers, including teams from Network Operation Centers (NOCs) and Security Operation Centers (SOCs). This panel consists of 16 experts who collectively represent 150 operations team members. To effectively capture the knowledge of the experts, we followed a user-centered design methodology combined with ontology engineering methods. From our review of the literature, the Competency Question approach [61] turns out to be the most intuitive and straightforward with respect to how NOC and SOC teams use and talk about their tools. Indeed, this approach involves extracting the conceptual model of the knowledge domain by analyzing user queries expressed in natural language through a set of semantic patterns. During several iterations of knowledge capture meetings on a shared notebook, the experts could validate, invalidate, add and modify Competency Questions (CQs). At the end of this stage, the teams validated 26 CQs presented in Table 1. This includes questions on events, resources (e.g. server, router), applications (e.g. Domain Name System, Video-on-Demand platform), log and alarms (e.g. login, CPU overload) and operation plan (e.g. SSL/TLS certificate renew, IS-IS interface re-prioritization).

From the set of CQs, we derived a conceptual model of the domain of discourse by applying the "*Competency Question archetype mapping*" approach [61, §4.3]. For example, CQ#1 can be mapped to the "*Which [CE1] [OPE] [CE2]?*" archetype (ID: 1), yielding to breaking down the competency question into the following components: $CE1$ = Asset (resource/application/site), OPE = are-ContainedIn, and $CE2$ = Incident. We also adhered to the guidelines of the Linked Open Terms (LOT) methodology [33], which notably include reusing or aligning with existing vocabularies.

Upon scrutinizing the conceptual model and candidate vocabularies, two characteristics are observed. Firstly, concepts derived from the Table 1 can be referred to as "atomic concepts" (e.g. application, alarm, resource), representing concepts that are not defined by composition but are considered indivisible in nature. Thus, we can expect to use simple relationships (potentially hierarchical) between concepts during the modeling and implementation phases. Secondly, research domains related to ICT systems management (such as event spreading [32], software engineering [16], knowledge management, and automated reasoning [7]), exhibit abstract concepts common to these domains and the NORIA-O field, such as *physical vs functional* and *cause vs consequence*. Therefore, we suggest structuring the NORIA-O domain concepts using similar facets to leverage the approaches and tools applicable in these research domains, such as finite state automatons and Markov decision processes. For instance, combining the facets allows for a comprehensive analysis of the complexity and observability levels of networks, which we refer to as a hybrid "concrete-conceptual" model [29]. In this model, assets' states dynamically vary based on behavioral rules and are interpreted through higher-level composite concepts. Consequently, predicting the next set of states/concepts becomes a sequential decision under uncertainty problem. We further define these facets in the next section.

Table 1. NORIA-O Competency Questions (CQs). In this table, we list the NORIA-O CQs collected during knowledge capture meetings (Sect. 3.1), along with their corresponding archetype (Arch. ID, as defined in [61, §4.3]) and authoring tests results (Sect. 5, with the number of implemented queries for the evaluation stage). Facets (Sect. 3.2): S = structural, F = functional, D = dynamic, and P = procedural.

#	CQs	Facets	Arch. ID	AT Eval.
1	Which resource/application/site is concerned by a given incident?	S, F, D	1	OK (4)
2	What assets are shared by a given asset chain?	S, F	6	OK (1)
3	What logs and alarms are coming from a specified resource?	S, D	1	OK (1)
4	Which metrics are coming from a specified resource?	S	1	OK (1)
5	To which event family does this log belong and is this event normal or abnormal?	D, P	3	OK (1)
6	What events are associated with a given event?	D	1	OK (1)
7	Which agent/event/resource caused the event under analysis?	S, F, D, P	1	OK (3)
8	What do the various fields in the log refer to?	D	1, 3	OK (1)
9	Is there any pattern in a given set of logs/alarms?	D, P	1, 6	AI (1)
10	What interventions were carried out on this resource that could have caused the incident?	S, D, P	1, 6	OK (2)
11	What was the root cause of the incident?	D, P	6	AI (1)
12	Which sequence of events led to the incident?	D, P	6	OK (1)
13	On which resource did this sequence of events take place and in which order?	S, D	1	OK (1)
14	What past incidents are similar to a given incident?	D, P	6	AI (1)
15	What operation plan (automation, operating procedures, etc.) could help us solve the incident?	D, P	1, 3	AI (1)
16	What corrective actions have been carried out so far for a given incident?	D, P	1	OK (1)
17	What is the list of actions taken that led to the resolution of the incident?	D, P	1	OK (1)
18	Given all the corrective actions carried out so far for the incident, what assumptions covered the actions taken?	D, P	1, 4	AI (1)
19	What has been the effect of the corrective actions taken so far for the incident?	D, P	1	OK (1)
20	Given all the corrective actions carried out so far for the incident, what possible actions could we still take?	D, P	6	AI (1)
21	What is the summary of this incident and its resolution?	D	1	OK (1)
22	Which agents were involved in the resolution of the incident?	D	1	OK (1)
23	What is the financial cost of this incident if it occurs?	D	2	Ext.
24	How long before this incident is resolved?	D	1	AI (1)
25	What are the vulnerabilities and the associated risk levels of this infrastructure?	S, F, D	1, 2	AI (1)
26	What is the most likely sequence of actions that would cause this infrastructure to fail?	S, F, P	6	AI (1)

3.2 Domain of Discourse and Modeling Strategy

Facets. Considering dynamic ICT systems with constrained and multi-level functional behavior, we define the four following facets for structuring the knowledge domain. An illustration of these facets is provided in Fig. 1.

- **The structural facet** describes the physical and logical elements of the network. It allows modeling the equipment classes, connections and compositions. This facet aims to support calculations on network objects and

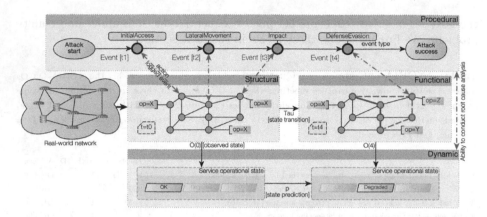

Fig. 1. ICT system state transition model and relations to the NORIA-O facets. The representation of a network can be divided into four facets: *structural, functional* (the blue path indicates an operational data flow, the red path a faulty flow), *dynamic,* and *procedural* (logged events are related to cyber-security attack tactics from the MITRE ATT&CK matrix [45]). *Tau* stands for state transition, $O(t)$ for observed state at time t, and p for state prediction. (Color figure online)

properties (direct or deduced) and calculations on the physical and logical structures (real or patterns).

– **The functional facet** describes services provided and diffusion areas. This facet makes it possible to meet the need for functional isomorphism (e.g. replacing one equipment with another performing the same function). It allows modeling the service types, interactions between them, and compositions. This facet allows calculations on network domains and their properties (direct or inferred) and calculations on services and streams (e.g. "end-to-end" notion).

– **The dynamic facet** describes the sequence of events. It allows modeling the occurrence of an event on a given equipment or service as well as precedence relationships. This facet aims to support time calculations (absolute, relative, membership) and causality calculations (first order or probabilistic).

– **The procedural facet** describes how things work and should be interpreted. Automation principles (e.g. fail-over mechanisms of redundant systems) or operation principles (e.g. doubt removal procedures) are expected parts of this facet. Associated application goals are deductive/abductive reasoning over facts and reflection over knowledge for automated learning (discovery/recommendation) of procedures (e.g. evolutionary search over targeted goals, composition calculus over sequences of events).

Modeling strategy. Considering the domains of anomaly detection and incident management, we consider incidents as a central concept for i) computing and reasoning about anomaly signatures, and ii) linking trouble tickets to anomaly signatures for root cause analysis tasks. We introduce the `noria` namespace, which encompasses the entire set of NORIA-O concepts and relations in a unified manner. To align with risk management and business modeling practices (such as the incident logging and categorization steps in the ITIL's Incident Management Process model – IMP [53]), we adopt a top-to-bottom modeling strategy, starting from the process and extending to objects. Due to the "atomic concepts" characteristic of the knowledge domain (Sect. 3.1) and our top-to-bottom approach, we primarily focus on an axiomatization based on subsumption with RDFS [13], and with OWL [50] for cases that require additional logical structuring (e.g. class disjointness, property qualification)[4].

Model re-use. Following the best practices in ontology development, we aim to re-use existing data models and vocabularies as a base and extend them to represent domain-specific classes and properties. From RDF-based ontologies, we interconnect and/or extend the following models: **BBO** [2] for describing activities from the business process modeling perspective in conformance to the Business Process Model Notation (BPMN); **BOT** [31] for describing resource locations and enabling geographical neighboring analysis for root cause analysis tasks; **DCTERMS** for standard management of NORIA-O instances as parts of a catalog; **DevOpsInfra** [42] for enabling potential interactions of NORIA-O with the DevOps perspective; **FOAF** [12] for describing social organizations; **FOLIO** [9] for enabling Root Cause Analysis (RCA) tasks based on the Failure Mode and Effect Analysis (FMEA) approach; **ORG** [14] for describing stakeholders and related organizations; **SEAS & PEP** [38,39] for describing technological systems, measures, commands, and results; **UCO** [62] for enabling cyber-security risk assessment on instances of NORIA-O; **SLOGERT** [4] for describing system logs and enabling potential usage of the SLOGERT log interpretation framework.

From non RDF-based data models, we take advantage of the concept hierarchy and vocabulary definitions from the **TMForum Data Model**[5] for enabling an interoperable definition of trouble tickets and change requests with third-party Operations Support Systems (OSSs) and Decision Support Systems (DSSs), **ITU-T** [20,21] for standard definitions of notifications and ways to handle them within the telecommunication industry, **IETF** for precise use of terminology in the context of a Request for Comments (RFC)[6].

We propose implementing alignment with third-party data models and vocabularies on a class or property basis when relevant, using the dedicated OWL and RDF constructs such as `owl:equivalentClass`, `rdfs:subClassOf`, or `rdfs:isDefinedBy`. Similarly, we aim to provide guidelines for directly instantiating these vocabularies in cases where aligning a class or property would be redundant.

Modeling observations. Considering observables and their state change (e.g. the operational state of a network interface, the temperature measurements from

---

[4] During implementation, cardinality restrictions were not prioritized as they were not considered crucial. Instead, we see cardinality restrictions as more beneficial for post-implementation data quality tasks using SHACL [17].

[5] https://github.com/tmforum-apis.

[6] https://datatracker.ietf.org/.

a sensor), we observe that modeling and logging observations can be done: (a) as a string, (b) as a concept from a controlled vocabulary, (c) as an instance, (d) as an instance with time property or time instance (e.g. using reification, or following the `sosa:Observation` model[7]). These four options are relevant for the NORIA-O application domain. The concern is not about choosing one option for all situations, but how we can mix them. Hence, we adopt the following selection criterion: 1) use (a) and (b) for invariant properties, 2) use (c) and (d) for time-dependent and/or specific use-case extensions to NORIA-O (i.e. additional observables are defined in a side vocabulary so the main ontology remains stable).

Controlled vocabularies. Because of potentially heterogeneous data incoming from varied ICT systems and incident situations to handle, we take notes of terms from datasets and other ontologies for building up a controlled vocabulary. This aims at efficient management of anomaly detection patterns, rules and methods by reducing the lexical range of possible situations to interpret. For this, we propose a set of domain-specific vocabularies (e.g. Incident Management Process, Application, Notification vocabularies) modeled as SKOS concepts within concept schemes (e.g. the milestones of the Incident Management Process). We add, whenever available, alternate definitions of the concepts for reconciliation of similar object attribute values through a single concept reference (e.g. communication devices may report the same status of network interfaces with varied terms such as *"active"*, *"up"* or *"enabled"*). We also use the concept scheme approach for enabling multiple interpretation of a similar concept. For example, an event may be categorized as an `integrityViolation` based on the analysis of the event text, which allows us to reason on the event type and infer a `SecurityAlarm` thanks to a dual membership of the `integrityViolation` concept definition. The implementation of the vocabulary reconciliation task (e.g. relating the observed network interface administrative status to the adequate concept reference with help of natural language processing) is out of the scope of this paper and is left to the NORIA-O user's choice.

4   NORIA-O: Formalization and Implementation

We have implemented the NORIA-O conceptual model in RDFS/OWL-2. NORIA-O consists of 59 classes, 107 object properties, and 71 datatype properties. It is organized with the four facets presented in Sect. 3.2 and illustrated in Fig. 2. Its expressivity is $ALCHOI(D)$ as per Protégé 5.1. In this section, we introduce some of the main concepts and properties.

4.1   Resources, Network Interfaces, Network Links and Applications

Within computer science, a resource is some *"part contributing to the functioning of an ICT system."* Similarly, as per the TMForum Data Model[8], a resource is

---

[7] https://www.w3.org/TR/vocab-ssn/#SOSAObservation.
[8] https://github.com/tmforum-apis/Open_Api_And_Data_Model.

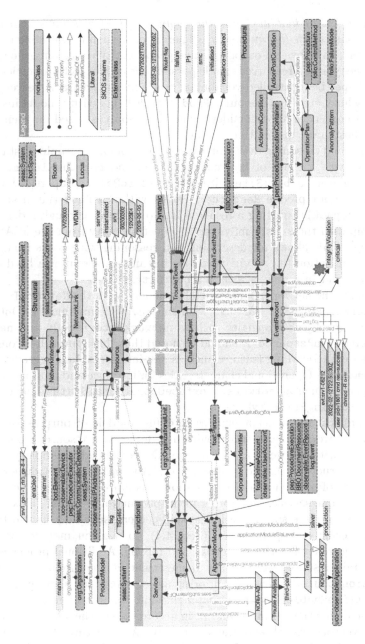

Fig. 2. Overview of the NORIA-O model. We depict the most important classes and properties, including related domain of discourse facets and relationships to third-parties models. noria is the default namespace. The red star indicates where events are characterized within the data model as incidents or anomalies. Examples are provided for the "literal" and "SKOS scheme" blocks. For the sake of clarity, some object properties are grouped (see "simplified object property") for a light representation of similar properties (i.e. same rdfs:domain or same rdfs:range). The diagram partly follows the Graffoo specification [52]. (Color figure online)

"an abstract entity that describes the common set of attributes shared by all concrete resources in the inventory". Therefore, we define the `Resource` class for describing any physical or logical manageable entity composing the network. Defining the type of a resource is made possible through object properties such as `resourceType` (i.e. controlled-vocabulary concepts such as rack, server, router, virtual machine, etc.) and `resourceProductModel` (i.e. entity model instances). Additional properties allow for identifying the resources based on their logistic identifier, hostname, installation date, etc.

Locating and reasoning over a physical entity from a geographical standpoint is available with a chain of `bot:containsZone` and `bot:hasElement` properties, starting from a `bot:Site` with `bot:hasZeroPoint` property, down to a `Locus` concept for precise `Resource` location within a `Room` (i.e. a specialization of `bot:Space`). Locating a resource is also available through a dependency relationship with the `seas:subSystemOf` object property from the SEAS SystemOntology[9]. This allows for describing and reasoning with parts from various levels of organization (e.g. a virtual router instance in a router, a hard drive in a server, a server in a rack, a rack in a `bot:Site`, etc.).

Describing the network topology itself is defined with the `NetworkInterface` and `NetworkLink` classes. We align with the SEAS CommunicationOntology[10] model through object properties such as `networkInterfaceOf` and `networkLinkTerminationResource`. It should be noted that this approach is compatible with advanced networking features such as sub-interfaces, link aggregation, virtual channels, etc. Operational characteristics for interface and links are available with properties such as `networkInterfaceOperationalStatus` and `networkInterfaceRoutingPriorityMetric`.

The `Application` concept enables to define models of purpose (e.g. internet access, network time, alarm monitoring) for sets of resources, and to categorize these with respect to their nature (i.e. controlled-vocabulary concepts such as infrastructure, service platform, etc.). An `ApplicationModule` is a concrete instance of a given model (e.g. national federated Internet access, corporate network time service, monitoring for in-production devices). This grouping level enables to relate specific technical skill centers, such as a named IP backbone engineering or support team (Sect. 4.4), to a given module for specific expertise (e.g. re-engineering, diagnosis and repair). Additional properties allow for finer grain resources and events management at the module level such as `applicationModuleSlaLevel` for prioritizing servicing teams, or `applicationModuleHotlineEnabled` for triggering night shift support teams.

We also define the `Service` concept in accordance to the TMForum TMF638 Service Inventory API[11] and the IETF SFC Architecture [22] for grouping instances of `ApplicationModule`, and thus enabling the data path and application composition perspectives of the functional facet (Sect. 3.2). The network topology related to a given service is inferred from the set of resources, net-

---

[9] https://w3id.org/seas/SystemOntology.
[10] https://w3id.org/seas/CommunicationOntology.
[11] https://github.com/tmforum-apis.

work interfaces and network links included in each application that is part of the service. We observe that, although deterministic, the data path granularity calculus for some communication session (e.g. a time-bounded IP/http query with its response) depends on the specificity of the resources included in `ApplicationModule` instances. For example, the resulting granularity for a "*national IP backbone infrastructure*" application instance will correspond to the routing domain.

4.2 Logs and Alarms

As per the International Telecommunication Union (ITU), "*the log is a repository for records*" (ITU-T Rec. X.735) [21] and an event log record "*represents the information stored in the log as a result of receiving notifications or incoming event reports*" (ITU-T Rec. X.721) [20]. Based on this definition, we define the `EventRecord` class for storing any event coming from managed objects (e.g. `Resource`, `Application`) such as system logs [49], SNMP Traps [34] and application specific messages (e.g. user applications, operational support systems, processing platforms). Fundamental properties such as `loggingTime`, `logText`, `logOriginatingManagedObject` and `logOriginatingManagementSystem` allow for keeping track of the event origin and content. Details about the message meaning are managed with the `dcterms:type` property that refers to a controlled-vocabulary for event type tagging[12] (e.g. state change, processing error alarm, integrity violation). The `alarmSeverity` property provides an indication of how it is perceived that the capability of the managed object has been affected, or how serious are the service affecting conditions (including for security alarms). Additional properties related to alarm management and interpretation are available with alignment to the DCTERMS and PEP models, such as: `alarmMitigatedBy` and `dcterms:relation` for aggregating events and building event signatures; `dcterms:conformsTo` for root cause analysis and repair planning; `dcterms:mediator` for responsibility follow up.

4.3 Trouble Tickets and Change Requests

We define the `TroubleTicket` concept accordingly to the TMForum DataModel where a trouble ticket is "*a record of an issue that is created, tracked, and managed by a trouble ticket management system*"[13]. It is not an event per se, but a mean to efficiently manage targeted resource/service (e.g. `troubleTicketRelatedResource` property) restoration operations through collaboration. Hence, we also consider trouble tickets as a product of the ITIL's Incident Management process [53], and relate them to ITIL's Problem Management process [54] and the BPMN by alignment to the `bbo:DataResource` class.

---

[12] Event type tagging can be carried-out at the data integration stage, or through a posteriori language processing of the "logText" property.

[13] http://datamodel.tmforum.org/en/master/Common/TroubleTicket/.

Corrective maintenance action details are logged as `TroubleTicketNote` and related to the parent `TroubleTicket` with the `dcterms:isPartOf` property. Actions' accountability is implemented with the `dcterms:creator` in relation to the `foaf:Agent` class (Sect. 4.4). Correlating actions to the digital traces (i.e. `EventRecord`) they produce at the structural and functional level (e.g. login, configuration change, upgrade) is available with the `dcterms:relation` property towards a `pep:ProcedureExecutionContainer` entity.

We provide additional properties for improving the incident diagnosis stage efficiency (e.g. `dcterms:hasPart` for hierarchical grouping of tickets), and moving towards root cause analysis based on the notion of Known Error Database (KEDB) (e.g. `troubleTicketCategory` and `problemCategory` for a priori and a posteriori categorization, respectively) and primary/secondary anomaly (cause-/effect) with alignment to the FOLIO model. With greater details, a trouble ticket is a document transitively referencing a set of corrective maintenance actions that can be abstracted into an issue remediation `OperationPlan` for solving the `AnomalyPattern` at hand. Reaching such abstraction from actions' digital traces is enabled by considering the PEP model with `TroubleTicket` as a specialization of a `pep:ProcedureExecutionContainer`, actions as `pep:ProcedureExecution` and `OperationPlan` as `pep:Procedure`.

Similarly to trouble tickets, we define the `ChangeRequest` concept according to the TMForum DataModel[14] for tracking scheduled change operations (as sets of `pep:ProcedureExecution` carried-out in correspondence to a given `OperationPlan`) with structural or functional impact, and computing (potential) causality for trouble tickets based on the set of correlated resources/applications and operations start/end time.

4.4 Agents, Teams and Organizations

From the incident management perspective, finding experts in short time is key for operational efficiency. One common approach is to form teams based on technical expertise (e.g. routing and international backbone, servers and virtual machines, forensics and malware retro-engineering) and assign them to manage specific equipment or services. External support and engineering services are also relied upon for specialized cases. To facilitate interoperability with complementary knowledge bases, we utilize the FOAF and ORG data models for representing entities such as agents and users (`foaf:Person`), organizational units (`org:OrganizationalUnit`), and organizations (`org:Organization`). Relationships with IT entities, such as `Resource` and `Application`, are modeled using properties like `elementManagedBy` and `applicationModuleRelatedParty`. We introduce the `CorporateUserIdentifier` class as a specialization of `foaf:OnlineAccount` and provide a controlled vocabulary for detailed role descriptions of agents, teams (e.g. Technical Support Group), and organizations (e.g. Manufacturer). This notably enables applying the cyber security

---

[14] http://datamodel.tmforum.org/en/master/Common/ChangeRequest/.

out-of-policy principle (i.e. what is not defined is not allowed) for tracking non-legitimate operations (unless facing an insider) by asserting access control groups as `org:OrganizationalUnit` and scrutinizing observed or declared user actions (e.g. `eventLogOriginatingAgent`, `dcterms:creator`).[15]

5 Evaluation

We have evaluated the NORIA-O implementation according to the ability of the model to answer the CQs that were collected in Sect. 3.1. The CQs have emerged from an iterative and collaborative process of capturing knowledge from domain experts. Therefore, we consider that translating these CQs into Authoring Tests (ATs) [23,61] and obtaining a satisfactory answer to these SPARQL [57] queries from the knowledge graph constitute a sound evaluation of NORIA-O. This evaluation aims to check that all the concepts and relations that are important for the experts' needs are included in NORIA-O. The set of authoring tests, available at https://w3id.org/noria/evaluation, has been defined and tested on two knowledge graph instances structured by NORIA-O. The first one describes a fictitious case of supervision and is publicly available (Sect. 6). The second one has been generated from Orange internal data (10 data sources encompassing 128 features over 15 tables) using an in-house data pipeline [30]; the size of the resulting RDF dataset is approximately 4 million triples for 400K entities, including streamed events spanning over 111 days.[16]

After this evaluation, we distinguish three situations depicted in column "AT Validation" of Table 1. First, a large number of CQs (16/26) can be answered using a single or several simple SPARQL queries and the ontology ("OK" in Table 1). 9/26 CQs ("AI" in Table 1) are partially satisfied using SPARQL queries, to which complementary AI techniques should be added to fully answer the CQs. For example, to answer CQ#11 *"What was the root cause of the incident?"*, the representation of alarms and logs associated with a given incident needs to be enhanced with root cause analysis algorithms (e.g. using semantic reasoners with failure mode descriptions [8], or similar incident context search [28]). Another example is CQ#25 *"What are the vulnerabilities and the associated risk levels of this infrastructure?"* that can be answered only by looking for non-desirable network topology shapes or relations to cybersecurity knowledge derived from network structure and security scanners (e.g. using the SHACL [17] toolset, or graph-based risk assessment [60] with UCO-labelled data [62]). Third, 1/26 CQs requires the introduction of new concepts or relations via an extension of NORIA-O ("Extension" in Table 1). The CQ #23 *"What is the financial cost of this incident if it occurs?"* involves information about the cost of an incident (e.g. leveraging the SEAS Failable System ontology [39] and calculating the number of users affected by a service impairment).

---

[15] We assume that companies' human-resource databases are reliable and accurate sources of truth.

[16] Due to confidentiality, this large dataset is not made public but the fictitious one has been created with the purpose of being a shareable resource.

6   Use Case: Modeling a Complex IT Infrastructure

We illustrate the usage and expressiveness of NORIA-O through a fictitious case of network infrastructure supervision. The Fig. 3 summarizes this use case by showing both the network topology and the corresponding entities. The dataset for this scenario is available at https://w3id.org/noria/dataset. 660 triples are needed for representing the full scenario with additional resources, organization and root cause analysis details.

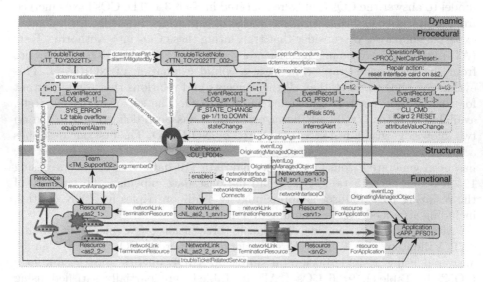

Fig. 3. NORIA-O instantiation example. A fault on an access switch (red star) impacts redundancy for critical application resources. The technician identifies the issue through an inferred alert $(t = t2)$, traces it back to the faulty equipment, and takes corrective action $(t = t3)$. The process is documented in a trouble ticket, including the cause and repair action. noria is the default namespace for classes and properties. "SKOS scheme" block values (e.g. *"equipmentAlarm"*, *"inferredAlert"*, etc.) are coming from the NORIA-O controlled vocabulary. (Color figure online)

Based on this scenario, we observe that NORIA-O enhances anomaly detection and analysis tasks with the following capabilities. **Data integration:** it consolidates data from various sources and provides a standardized interpretation using the `rdf:type` and `skos:Concept` constructs. For example, this allows entities in the structural and functional facets to combine data from network discovery tools, VM hypervisors, and the company directory. Events can also be looked up by their type, regardless of their originating signaling system. **Data querying:** it enables facet-wise checking of the network state and configuration in a rule-based approach using data retrieval. For example, a SPARQL query [57] can derive the scenario's inferred alert (a resilience problem) using a k out-of n graph pattern on `Resource` and `Application` entities. This would not have been possible with a single data source or without standardized interpretation of the data using controlled vocabularies. **Situation understanding & classification:** it enables gaining facet-wise insights about a situation and its ecosystem using graph traversal. For instance, a SPARQL query can calculate the network neighborhood for a specific incident or identify the teams involved in its resolution. Categorizing event patterns and root cause analysis is addressed using reasoning through complementary ontologies [8, 40] or rule engines [35, 47]. Additionally, the context of an incident, represented by the graph structure related to a `TroubleTicket` entity, can be captured and categorized using graph embeddings [28].

7   Conclusion and Future Work

In this paper, we presented NORIA-O, an ontology for representing network infrastructures, incidents and maintenance operations, that relies on and extends well-known semantic models such as BBO, BOT, FOAF, FOLIO, SEAS and UCO. NORIA-O is available at https://w3id.org/noria under a BSD-4 License, along with its documentation and a sample dataset. We conducted an evaluation of NORIA-O using the Competency Questions & Authoring Tests methodology [61], demonstrating its suitability according to the expert needs. We also illustrated the usage and expressiveness of the data model using a fictitious case of network infrastructure supervision. We showcased the complementary use of graph traversal techniques, reasoning, and incident context capture through graph embeddings.

Future work will focus on experimenting with NORIA-O for cross-domain alarm correlation and aggregation. First, event logs from heterogeneous data sources depicting an identical phenomenon need to be parsed and categorized in the same way. This can be achieved by incorporating specific technological domains, such as OTN or 5G mobile network specifications, into the NORIA-O controlled vocabulary. Techniques such as log parsing [24,51] and semantization [4] can be applied, either before or after the data integration stage. NLP-related techniques, including named entity recognition [5], topic modeling [18], and vocabulary reconciliation [44], are crucial in this process. Second, relating events to anomaly models [28] or attack scenarios [6], requires to filter-out event logs and alarms on both trouble tickets' timespan and impacted resources characteristics. Recent research on dynamic graphs with event streams has shown promising results in estimating the useful spreading of observables [11,15,56,59].

Finally, we note that network resilience and cybersecurity application domains will benefit from extensions of a NORIA-O knowledge graph with third-party data collection tools. For example, network topology anti-patterns and semantic interpretation of the ICT resources configuration [58] could be related to the network performance and issues. Similarly, integrating data from vulnerability scanners and cyber threat intelligence tools could enable cybersecurity risk evaluation and minimization (e.g. combining CVSS [46] data from OpenCTI[17] with optimized countermeasure placement techniques [60]).

---

[17] https://www.opencti.io.

References

1. Oltramari, A., Cranor, L., Walls, R., McDaniel, P.: Building an ontology of cyber security. In: 9th Conference on Semantic Technologies for Intelligence, Defense, and Security (STIDS) (2014)
2. Annane, A., Aussenac-Gilles, N., Kamel, M.: BBO: BPMN 2.0 based ontology for business process representation. In: 20th European Conference on Knowledge Management (ECKM) (2019)
3. Dimou, A.: High quality linked data generation from heterogeneous data. Ph.D. thesis, University of Antwerp (2017)
4. Ekelhart, A., Ekaputra, F.J., Kiesling, E.: The SLOGERT framework for automated log knowledge graph construction. In: Verborgh, R., et al. (eds.) ESWC 2021. LNCS, vol. 12731, pp. 631–646. Springer, Cham (2021). https://doi.org/10.1007/978-3-030-77385-4_38
5. Piplai, A., Mittal, S., Joshi, A., Finin, T., Holt, J., Zak, R.: Creating cybersecurity knowledge graphs from malware after action reports. IEEE Access (2020). https://doi.org/10.1109/ACCESS.2020.3039234
6. Elitzur, A., Puzis, R., Zilberman, P.: Attack hypothesis generation. In: European Intelligence and Security Informatics Conference (EISIC) (2019). https://doi.org/10.1109/EISIC49498.2019.9108886
7. Goertzel, B., Pennachin, C., Geisweiller, N.: Engineering General Intelligence, Part 1: A Path to Advanced AGI via Embodied Learning and Cognitive Synergy. Atlantis Press (2014)
8. Steenwinckel, B.: IBCNServices/Folio-Ontology (2019). https://github.com/IBCNServices/Folio-Ontology
9. Steenwinckel, B., et al.: Towards adaptive anomaly detection and root cause analysis by automated extraction of knowledge from risk analyses. In: 9th International Semantic Sensor Networks Workshop (SSN) (2018)
10. Brazhuk, A.: Threat modeling of cloud systems with ontological security pattern catalog. Int. J. Open Inf. Technol. (2021)
11. Xu, C., Nayyeri, M., Alkhoury, F., Yazdi, H.S., Lehmann, J.: Temporal knowledge graph embedding model based on additive time series decomposition. In: 19th International Semantic Web Conference (ISWC) (2020)
12. Brickley, D., Miller, L.: Friend of a Friend (FOAF) Vocabulary Specification (2004). http://xmlns.com/foaf/spec/
13. Brickley, D., Guha, R.V.: RDF Schema. W3C Recommendation, W3C (2014)
14. Reynolds, D.: The Organization Ontology. W3C Recommendation, W3C (2014)
15. Maillot-Tchofo, D., Triki, A., Laye, M., Puentes, J.: Clustering of live network alarms using unsupervised statistical models. In: 49th European Conference on Optical Communications (ECOC) (2023)
16. Kaur, H., Maini, R.: Identification of recurring patterns of code to detect structural clones. In: 6th International Conference on Advanced Computing (IACC) (2016). https://doi.org/10.1109/IACC.2016.80
17. Knublauch, H., Kontokostas, D.: Shapes Constraint Language (SHACL). W3C Recommendation, W3C (2017)
18. Harrando, I., Lisena, P., Troncy, R.: Apples to apples: a systematic evaluation of topic models. In: Recent Advances in Natural Language Processing (RANLP) (2021). https://doi.org/10.26615/978-954-452-072-4_055
19. ITU: ITU-T Rec. G.709/Y.1331 (06/20) – Interfaces for the optical transport network. Recommendation, International Telecommunication Union (ITU) (2020)

20. ITU/CCITT: ITU-T Rec. X.721 (02/92) Information Technology – Open Systems Interconnection – Structure of Management Information: Definition of Management Information. Recommendation, International Telecommunication Union (ITU) (1992)
21. ITU/CCITT: ITU-T Rec. X.735 (09/92) Information Technology – Open Systems Interconnection – Systems Management: Log Control Function. Recommendation, International Telecommunication Union (ITU) (1992)
22. Halpern, J., Pignataro, C.: Service function chaining (SFC) architecture. RFC 7665 (2015)
23. Potoniec, J., Wiśniewski, D., Ławrynowicz, A., Keet, C.M.: Dataset of ontology competency questions to SPARQL-OWL queries translations. Data in Brief (2020)
24. Zhu, J., et al.: Tools and benchmarks for automated log parsing. In: 41st International Conference on Software Engineering: Software Engineering in Practice (ICSE-SEIP) (2019). https://doi.org/10.1109/ICSE-SEIP.2019.00021
25. Chessman, J.: Magic quadrant for network performance monitoring and diagnostics. Technical report. G00463582, Gartner (2020)
26. Kavanagh, K., Bussa, T., Sadowski, G.: Magic quadrant for security information and event management. Technical report. G00348811, Gartner (2018)
27. Janowicz, K., Haller, A., Cox, S., Phuoc, D., Lefrançois, M.: SOSA: a lightweight ontology for sensors, observations, samples, and actuators. SSRN Electron. J. (2018). https://doi.org/10.1016/j.websem.2018.06.003
28. Tailhardat, L., Troncy, R., Chabot, Y.: Leveraging knowledge graphs for classifying incident situations in ICT systems. In: 18th International Conference on Availability, Reliability and Security (ARES) (2023). https://doi.org/10.1145/3600160.3604991
29. Tailhardat, L., Chabot, Y., Troncy, R.: NORIA: machine learning, ontology and reasoning for the identification of anomalies (2021). https://genears.github.io/pubs/IA2-2021-NORIA-POSTER.pdf, position poster, Institut d'Automne en Intelligence Artificielle (IA²), Sorbonne Center for Artificial Intelligence (SCAI), Paris, France
30. Tailhardat, L., Chabot, Y., Troncy, R.: Designing NORIA: a knowledge graph-based platform for anomaly detection and incident management in ICT systems. In: 4th International Workshop on Knowledge Graph Construction (KGCW) (2023)
31. Rasmussen, M.H., Lefrançois, M., Schneider, G.F., Pauwels, P.: BOT: the building topology ontology of the W3C linked building data group. Semant. Web J. (2020). https://doi.org/10.3233/SW-200385
32. Thapa, M., Espejo-Uribe, J., Pournaras, E.: Measuring network reliability and repairability against cascading failures. J. Intell. Inf. Syst. (2019)
33. Poveda-Villalón, M., Fernández-Izquierdo, A., Fernández-López, M., García-Castro, R.: LOT: an industrial oriented ontology engineering framework. In: Engineering Applications of Artificial Intelligence (2022)
34. Fedor, M., Schoffstall, M.L., Davin, J.R., Case, J.D.: Simple Network Management Protocol (SNMP). RFC 1157 (1990)
35. Proctor, M.: Drools: a rule engine for complex event processing. In: Schürr, A., Varró, D., Varró, G. (eds.) AGTIVE 2011. LNCS, vol. 7233, pp. 2–2. Springer, Heidelberg (2012). https://doi.org/10.1007/978-3-642-34176-2_2
36. Bastian, M., Heymann, S., Jacomy, M.: Gephi: an open source software for exploring and manipulating networks. In: 3rd International AAAI Conference on Weblogs and Social Media (ICWSM) (2009). https://doi.org/10.1609/icwsm.v3i1.13937

37. Ghijsen, M., et al.: A semantic-web approach for modeling computing infrastructures. Comput. Electr. Eng. (2013). https://doi.org/10.1016/j.compeleceng.2013.08.011
38. Lefrançois, M.: Planned ETSI SAREF extensions based on the W3C&OGC SOSA/SSN-compatible SEAS ontology patterns. In: Workshop on Semantic Interoperability and Standardization in the IoT (SIS-IoT) (2017)
39. Lefrançois, M., Kalaoja, J., Ghariani, T., Zimmermann, A.: SEAS Knowledge Model. Deliverable 2.2, ITEA2 12004 Smart Energy Aware Systems (2016)
40. Lazzari, N., Poltronieri, A., Presutti, V.: Classifying sequences by combining context-free grammars and OWL ontologies. In: Pesquita, C., et al. (eds.) ESWC 2023. LNCS, vol. 13870, pp. 156–173. Springer, Cham (2023). https://doi.org/10.1007/978-3-031-33455-9_10
41. Ben-Asher, N., Oltramari, A., Erbacher, R.F., Gonzalez, C.: Ontology-based adaptive systems of cyber defense. In: 10th Conference on Semantic Technology for Intelligence, Defense, and Security (STIDS) (2015)
42. Corcho, O., et al.: A high-level ontology network for ICT infrastructures. In: Hotho, A., et al. (eds.) ISWC 2021. LNCS, vol. 12922, pp. 446–462. Springer, Cham (2021). https://doi.org/10.1007/978-3-030-88361-4_26
43. Prasad, P., Chessman, J.: Market guide for IT infrastructure monitoring tools. Technical report. G00450400, Gartner (2019)
44. Lisena, P., et al.: Controlled vocabularies for music metadata. In: 19th International Society for Music Information Retrieval Conference (ISMIR) (2018)
45. Kaloroumakis, P.E., Smith, M.J.: Toward a knowledge graph of cybersecurity countermeasures. Technical report, The MITRE Corporation (2021)
46. Mell, P., Scarfone, K., Romanosky, S.: Common vulnerability scoring system. IEEE Security Privacy (2006)
47. Bonte, P., Tommasini, R., Valle, E.D., De Turck, F., Ongenae, F.: Streaming MASSIF: cascading reasoning for efficient processing of IoT data streams. Sensors (2018). https://doi.org/10.3390/s18113832
48. Zhou, Q., Gray, A.J.G., McLaughlin, S.: ToCo: an ontology for representing hybrid telecommunication networks. In: Hitzler, P., et al. (eds.) ESWC 2019. LNCS, vol. 11503, pp. 507–522. Springer, Cham (2019). https://doi.org/10.1007/978-3-030-21348-0_33
49. Gerhards, R.: The syslog protocol. RFC 5424 (2009)
50. Bechhofer, S., et al.: Web Ontology Language (OWL). W3C Recommendation, W3C (2004)
51. He, S., He, P., Chen, Z., Yang, T., Yuxin, S., Lyu, M.R.: A survey on automated log analysis for reliability engineering. ACM Comput. Surv. (2021). https://doi.org/10.1145/3460345
52. Peroni, S.: Graffoo: Graphical Framework for OWL Ontologies (2013). https://essepuntato.it/graffoo/
53. Kempter, S.: It process maps – incident management (2007). https://wiki.en.it-processmaps.com/index.php/Incident_Management
54. Kempter, S.: It process maps – problem management (2007). https://wiki.en.it-processmaps.com/index.php/Problem_Management
55. Ehrhart, T., Lisena, P., Troncy, R.: KG explorer: a customisable exploration tool for knowledge graphs. In: 6th International Workshop on the Visualization and Interaction for Ontologies and Linked Data, co-Located with the 20th International Semantic Web Conference (ISWC) (2021)
56. Wu, T., Khan, A., Gao, H., Li, C.: Efficiently embedding dynamic knowledge graphs. Knowl.-Based Syst. (2019)

57. W3C SPARQL Working Group: SPARQL Protocol and RDF Query Language 1.1 (SPARQL). W3C Recommendation, W3C (2013)
58. Atoui, W.S.: Toward auto-configuration in software networks. Ph.D. thesis, Institut Polytechnique de Paris (2020)
59. Li, Y., Ge, T., Chen, C.: Data stream event prediction based on timing knowledge and state transitions. VDLB Endow. (2020)
60. Naghmouchi, Y., Perrot, N., Kheir, N., Mahjoub, A.R., Wary, J.-P.: A new risk assessment framework using graph theory for complex ICT systems. In: 8th ACM CCS International Workshop on Managing Insider Security Threats (2016). https://doi.org/10.1145/2995959.2995969
61. Ren, Y., Parvizi, A., Mellish, C., Pan, J.Z., van Deemter, K., Stevens, R.: Towards competency question-driven ontology authoring. In: Presutti, V., d'Amato, C., Gandon, F., d'Aquin, M., Staab, S., Tordai, A. (eds.) ESWC 2014. LNCS, vol. 8465, pp. 752–767. Springer, Cham (2014). https://doi.org/10.1007/978-3-319-07443-6_50
62. Syed, Z., Padia, A., Lisa Mathews, M., Finin, T., Joshi, A.: UCO: a unified cyber-security ontology. In: AAAI Workshop on Artificial Intelligence for Cyber Security (2016)

FlexRML: A Flexible and Memory Efficient Knowledge Graph Materializer

Michael Freund[1]([✉]) [iD], Sebastian Schmid[2] [iD], Rene Dorsch[1] [iD],
and Andreas Harth[1,2] [iD]

[1] Fraunhofer Institute for Integrated Circuits IIS, Nürnberg, Germany
{michael.freund,rene.dorsch,andreas.harth}@iis.fraunhofer.de
[2] Friedrich-Alexander-Universität Erlangen-Nürnberg, Nürnberg, Germany

Abstract. We present FlexRML, a flexible and memory efficient software resource for interpreting and executing RML mappings. As a knowledge graph materializer, FlexRML can operate on a wide range of systems, from cloud-based environments to edge devices, as well as resource-constrained IoT devices and real-time microcontrollers. The primary goal of FlexRML is to balance memory efficiency with fast mapping execution. This is achieved by using C++ for the implementation and a result size estimation algorithm that approximates the number of N-Quads generated and, based on the estimate, optimizes bit sizes and data structures used to save memory in preparation for mapping execution. Our evaluation shows that FlexRML's adaptive bit size and data structure selection results in higher memory efficiency compared to conventional methods. When benchmarked against state-of-the-art RML processors, FlexRML consistently shows lower peak memory consumption across different datasets while delivering faster or comparable execution times.

Resource type: RML Processor
License: GNU AGPLv3
DOI: https://doi.org/10.5281/zenodo.10256148
URL: https://github.com/wintechis/flex-rml

Keywords: Knowledge Graph Construction · RML · Internet of Things

1 Introduction

Knowledge graphs (KGs) [13] have become increasingly popular in both industry and academia. For instance, KGs are used to enhance Large Language Models (LLMs) by supplementing them with additional factual information, thereby countering issues like hallucination [20]. In the context of Industry 4.0, KGs play an important role in enabling semantic interoperability between devices and services [2]. Additionally, as Internet of Things (IoT) devices generate large volumes of raw data, the application of Semantic Web technologies, such as RDF and ontologies, can add context and meaning to the data, which significantly increases its value [29].

A. Meroño Peñuela et al. (Eds.): ESWC 2024, LNCS 14665, pp. 40–56, 2024.
https://doi.org/10.1007/978-3-031-60635-9_3

One approach to constructing KGs, i.e., mapping non-RDF data such as CSV, JSON, or XML to RDF, is to use a generic mapping language such as the RDF Mapping Language (RML) [9]. RML mappings are represented as RDF graphs and outline the tasks for transforming a non-RDF data source, called *logicalSource*, into RDF format. The transformation process is organized by a construct called *triplesMap*. Within a triplesMap, the generation of RDF data is described by two main mappings: the *subjectMap* and the *predicateObjectMap*. The subjectMap is responsible for mapping elements from the logical source to RDF subjects. In turn, the predicateObjectMap handles the creation of predicates and objects for the RDF data by integrating a *predicateMap* that maps to RDF predicates and an *objectMap* that maps to RDF objects. If objects are generated using a join, the objectMap also specifies a *joinCondition*. The RML mappings are used in conjunction with RML processors, which are engines that interpret the mappings and transform non-RDF input data to output RDF data in serializations such as N-Quads. Well known RML processors are the RMLMapper[1], Morph-KGC [3], or the SDM-RDFizer [15].

The current generation of RML processors is implemented using high-level languages such as Java, JavaScript, and Python. The design choice to use high-level languages makes them well-suited for operation in unconstrained environments, such as cloud platforms. However, it also restricts their ability to function effectively in environments with limited memory, such as single-board computers or highly constrained microcontrollers. Additionally, these RML processors may not be optimal for real-time applications that are crucial in Industry 4.0 contexts, where processing needs to be reliably completed within strict time limits [14].

With the emergence of new and evolving domains such as LLMs and Industry 4.0, there is a growing demand for access to both semantic and factual data. To meet this demand, there is a need for an RML processor that is not only fast and memory efficient, but also versatile enough to operate in a variety of environments, whether constrained, unconstrained, or requiring real-time guarantees. The main challenge in developing such a framework is to ensure efficient management of available processing power and memory.

Our resource, FlexRML, is a flexible and memory efficient RML processor developed in C++ to ensure adaptability to various environments with different resource constraints. FlexRML uses an algorithm based on Bernoulli sampling to estimate the result size, specifically the number of unique RDF N-Quads to be generated. This feature allows FlexRML to select the most optimal hash functions for different data structures, balancing improved memory efficiency and increased processing time for KG materialization. From an implementation perspective, FlexRML optimizes at the mapping level using techniques such as self-join elimination, RML mapping normalization, and, where possible, replaces join operations with reference conditions. In cases where joins cannot be replaced, FlexRML uses a hash join algorithm to perform them. To increase memory efficiency, duplicate removal is handled by storing the hash of already generated RDF data, which carries the risk of hash collisions that can result in missing

---

[1] https://github.com/RMLio/rmlmapper-java.

output N-Quads. But the risk can be mitigated by choosing an appropriate bit size when computing hashes.

The key contributions of our work are as follows:

- Introduction of FlexRML, a memory-efficient RML processor capable of mapping data in cloud, edge, and IoT environments.
- Usage of a sampling-based algorithm to estimate N-Quads, enabling optimal hash function selection for improved memory efficiency.
- Comprehensive evaluation of FlexRML's performance against existing RML processors across cloud, edge, and IoT platforms, accompanied by the introduction of a dataset specifically tailored for evaluating IoT devices.

2   Related Work

There are several languages and techniques for building KGs from non-RDF data, notably SPARQL-Generate [19], SPARQL Anything [6], and D-REPR [28]. However, the dominant method relies on R2RML [7], a W3C recommendation, and its extension RML, which supports non-relational data sources such as CSV, JSON, and XML. The adoption of RML is underscored by the number of RML processors available [3,15,23,25], each with different conformance[2] and features, such as mapping partitions. These implementations in high-level languages are suitable for cloud environments, but are less optimal for resource-constrained devices. In contrast, we propose an RML processor designed for a wide range of devices, from cloud and consumer hardware to single-board computers and resource-constrained microcontrollers and IoT devices.

Semantic Web technologies such as RDF, RDFS, and OWL are considered key to semantic interoperability in IoT, as proposed by various authors [12,17]. Many proposed IoT architectures [1,18,22] share a common need to map IoT data to RDF for cloud storage and application use, typically using an edge device such as a gateway for mapping. However, FlexRML offers a simpler alternative by enabling direct data mapping on Internet-connected, constrained devices, enabling direct cloud uploads and bypassing the need for edge RML processors. Nevertheless, in scenarios where edge-based RML processors are required, FlexRML's memory efficiency makes it a viable option for edge deployment as well. The availability of RDF data directly on IoT devices is a prerequisite for device-level semantic interoperability, which can be used to enable data exchange in distributed IoT systems.

3   FlexRML: Architecture and Implementation

The FlexRML architecture integrates both high-level design and specific implementation details, providing a complete picture of how each component works within the system.

FlexRML performs two main steps: the *Preprocessing Step* and the *Mapping Step*, as shown in Fig. 1.

---

[2] https://rml.io/implementation-report/.

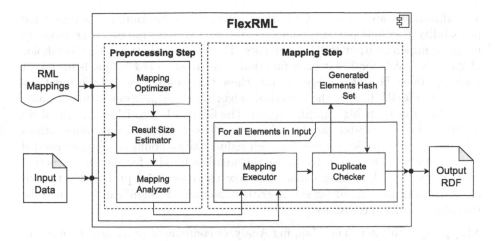

Fig. 1. The Architecture of FlexRML.

3.1 Preprocessing Step

The *Preprocessing Step* is designed to optimize input RML mappings for efficient processing. This involves preparing the correct physical data structures and hash functions, and extracting necessary processing steps from the RML mappings.

Mapping Optimizer. The Mapping Optimizer is designed to increase the efficiency of input RML mappings. This is achieved through a multi-step process: First, the component analyzes the input RML mapping and applies strategies such as self-join elimination [3] or mapping normalization [24]. In addition, the component evaluates the potential to replace join operations with reference conditions [27]. From a technical point of view, the optimizer uses the Serd[3] C library for RDF parsing. The component's functionality includes replacing self-joins with corresponding objectMaps, expanding constant shortcuts or classes, and decomposing complex predicateObjectMaps that may consist of multiple predicateMaps or objectMaps. Where appropriate, the optimizer also replaces standard joins with reference conditions in the RML mapping to improve materialization speed.

Result Size Estimator. The Result Size Estimator uses sampling methods described in Sect. 4 to estimate the number of N-Quads generated by the RML mapping. Based on the estimated total $\hat{T}$, the component determines the appropriate bit size for hash functions. The bit size corresponds to the number of possible unique hash values N and must be chosen according to $\hat{T}$. The decision which hash size to use is based on pre-calculated thresholds derived from the birthday problem in probability theory (see Eq. 1).

$$P = 1 - \frac{N!}{(N - \hat{T})! \cdot N^{\hat{T}}} \approx 1 - e^{-\frac{\hat{T}^2}{2N}} \tag{1}$$

---

[3] https://github.com/drobilla/serd.

The thresholds are computed to allow a worst-case maximum hash collision probability P of 0.05 percent, which has proven sufficient in our experiments to mitigate missing output RDF statements. Therefore, we have set the thresholds at 2,073 N-Quads for 32-bit hash functions, and 135,835,773 N-Quads for 64-bit hash functions. For estimates exceeding these thresholds, 128-bit hash functions are used. FlexRML uses the CityHash algorithm[4] to perform string hashing operations due to its high hashing speed. The CityHash algorithm is available in 32-bit, 64-bit and 128-bit variants. Using smaller bit sizes for hash computations not only speeds up the process, but also reduces the amount of memory needed to store hashes. The goal is to choose the smallest bit size for the hash function that keeps the risk of hash collisions below the predefined probability threshold. Choosing an optimal bit size is critical, as this will significantly reduce the probability of hash collisions.

Mapping Analyzer. The Mapping Analyzer component processes the normalized input RML mappings and extracts key information. The extracted information includes the number of predicateObjectMaps in each triplesMap, the classes corresponding to the subjectMap, and the details of objectMaps including the joinCondition. The data extracted by the Mapping Analyzer is organized into several arrays. These arrays form the basis of the mapping process and serve as directives to the Mapping Executor.

3.2 Mapping Step

The *Mapping Step* performs the actual mapping of the logical sources to RDF using the Mapping Executor, which interprets the extracted information generated by the Mapping Analyzer, creates N-Quads, and removes duplicates using a Duplicate Checker and a hash set to track hashes of already generated N-Quads.

The Mapping Step is parallelized in FlexRML using the Producer-Consumer design pattern. In this setup, each triplesMap is processed in a separate thread by a Mapping Executor acting as a producer, while the Duplicate Checker operates as a consumer in a separate thread. This design ensures that all generated N-Quads are checked before they are written to the output file, while allowing FlexRML to use multiple threads to speed up the materialization process.

Mapping Executor. The Mapping Executor component maps input data sources into N-Quads. The component processes each data element from the specified inputs, e.g., from a file on the local drive or from in-memory data structures such as the std::string class [8], converts the read element into the internal vector-based data representation, and generates a set of N-Quads for each element. Note that FlexRML currently supports only CSV data as input, due to limited support for the C++ standard library in some microcontroller environments, which restricts the use of existing parsing libraries. The N-Quad generation uses the extracted information from the RML mapping gathered by the Mapping Analyzer. If join operations cannot be substituted with a reference condition at the mapping level, the Mapping Executor performs a join using a hash join algorithm, and therefore must create an index on the data beforehand.

---

[4] https://opensource.googleblog.com/2011/04/introducing-cityhash.html.

Duplicate Checker. Each generated set of N-Quads is passed to the Duplicate Checker. This component uses a hash function with a bit size of either 32, 64, or 128, as specified by the Result Size Estimator. Each N-Quad is hashed, and the hash value is then evaluated for uniqueness. The evaluation is done by attempting to insert the hash into a hash set. If the hash already exists in the set, indicating a potential duplicate, the corresponding N-Quad is discarded. Otherwise the N-Quad is considered unique and written to the output file. Through this mechanism, the output RDF data is continuously and incrementally built. As new N-Quads are generated, they undergo the same duplication check. However, a risk of this method is the possibility of hash collisions where an N-Quad is mistakenly marked as a duplicate, resulting in its absence in the output. The risk can be mitigated by choosing an appropriate bit size.

4 Estimation of Generated RDF Elements

Estimating the number of RDF elements, such as N-Quads, that will be generated before executing an RML mapping is beneficial. For instance, in FlexRML, the estimate is used to select the appropriate bit size for hash functions. Generally, the estimation can serve other purposes similar to those in classical relational database systems, such as query optimization or the selection of efficient algorithms and access methods [16].

Independent Bernoulli sampling is an established technique for estimating result sizes [11, p. 348], especially for join operations [26]. In general the algorithm consits of following steps:

1. Generate a sample from the original dataset through simple random sampling, where each record is independently and randomly chosen.
2. Count the elements in the sample that exhibit the desired characteristic. The proportion of these elements in the sample is an estimate of their proportion in the entire dataset.
3. Use the identified proportion to estimate the number of elements with the desired characteristic in the entire dataset.

The method allows quick estimations by analyzing the distribution and properties of the data without processing the entire dataset, assuming sample sizes are large [21]. In KG construction, we sample the logical source data, perform the RML mapping on the sample, and enumerate the unique results, before estimating the unique results in the entire dataset.

When performing the estimation, we differentiate between two categories of triplesMaps and their corresponding objectMaps: those that require a join operation and those that do not.

4.1 Estimation of triplesMaps Without Join

To estimate the output size produced by triplesMaps consisting of objectMaps without join we assess the number of unique N-Quads U that will be generated when mapping each element of the logical data source A. Elements in the logical source can be, for example, rows in CSV files or JSON objects in JSON arrays.

To estimate U, we generate a Bernoulli sample S_A drawn from the original dataset A. The sampling process is performed with a given probability p. Using S_A, we perform the mapping and enumerate the generated unique N-Quads U'. Given that each element's inclusion in our sample is defined by p, the expected count of U' is U multiplied by p, or $E[U'] = U \cdot p$. From this, we derive our estimator $\hat{U}$, which represents the estimated total number of unique N-Quads that will be generated when mapping the entire logical source. To obtain $\hat{U}$, we scale U' by the inverse of the sampling probability, resulting in $\hat{U} = \frac{U'}{p}$. To calculate the expected value of $\hat{U}$, we consider the scaling of U', resulting in $E[\hat{U}] = E[\frac{U'}{p}]$. Substituting the expression for U', we further show that

$$E[\hat{U}] = E[\frac{U'}{p}] = E[\frac{U \cdot p}{p}] = E[U] \qquad (2)$$

which demonstrates that $\hat{U}$ serves as an estimator for U.

To estimate the total number of N-Quads, $\hat{U}_{total}$, generated by all triplesMaps with non-join objectMaps, we sum the individual estimates $\hat{U}$:

$$\hat{U}_{total} = \sum \hat{U} \qquad (3)$$

4.2 Estimation of triplesMaps with Join

When estimating the number of unique N-Quads J when mapping triplesMaps consisting of objectMaps with joins, it must be taken into account that there are two logical sources, A and B, instead of just one. Therefore, the estimation operation requires the creation of two samples using independent Bernoulli sampling: sample S_A from logical source A sampled with probability p_A, and sample S_B from logical source B sampled with probability p_B. The RML mapping is performed on the two samples, and the unique N-Quads J' generated are enumerated. To obtain the estimated number of unique N-Quads $\hat{J}$ when mapping the two entire logical sources, we again scale up J' by using the inverse of the two sampling probabilities p_A and p_B [26]. The inverse is used because the sampling probability represents the fraction of the logical source that is included in the sample. Thus, to estimate the number of unique RDF elements when mapping the entire content of the logical sources, we use $\hat{J} = \frac{J'}{p_A \cdot p_B}$.

To estimate the total number of unique N-Quads generated by triplesMaps with joins $\hat{J}_{total}$, we sum the scaled estimates of generated unique N-Quads:

$$\hat{J}_{total} = \sum \hat{J} \qquad (4)$$

4.3 Estimation of All triplesMaps

The estimate of the total number of unique N-Quads generated from all triplesMaps, $\hat{T}$, is therefore given by

$$\hat{T} = \hat{U}_{total} + \hat{J}_{total} \qquad (5)$$

By adding the unique estimates from predicateObjectMaps without joins to the unique estimates of predicateObjectMaps with joins, we arrive at an estimation of the total unique RDF elements generated through an RML mapping.

5 Empirical Evaluation

In the evaluation we aim to answer following three research questions:

- **R1:** How accurate is the estimation using the Result Size Estimator?
- **R2:** How does adaptive selection of the appropriate bit size for hash algorithms impact execution time and memory consumption?
- **R3:** How does FlexRML compare to state-of-the-art KG materializers in terms of execution time and memory consumption?

All results and scripts to run the benchmark can be found on GitHub[5].

Datasets. We evaluated FlexRML using three benchmarks. In a cloud and edge environment we used the GTFS Madrid benchmark [5] with scale factors of 10, 100, and 500, and the SDM Genomic Testbed[6] with dataset sizes of 10K, 100K, and 1M entries and a duplicate rate of 75 percent, with each element repeated 20 times. To the best of our knowledge, there are no datasets containing sensor data that are small enough to be mapped on IoT devices, so for this purpose we introduce a new RML-SENSOR benchmark[7] (SENS). The RML-SENSOR benchmark simulates data produced by two sensors and includes one metadata file. The data can be generated using small scale factors, which allows for the evaluation of the performance of RML processors on memory-constrained devices. All datasets used in the evaluation are in CSV format.

The SDM Genomic Testbed provides RML mappings[8] with different types of objectMaps: simple objectMaps without joins (POM), objectMaps with a self-join (REF), and objectMaps with a join (JOIN), the abbreviations are reused form [3]. The number of mappings of each type used is indicated by a number followed by the type, e.g. 1POM means that the mapping consists of one simple objectMap without join.

Metrics. For R1, we evaluate the Result Size Estimator by comparing the estimated number of generated N-Quads, obtained using various sampling probabilities, against the true value of generated N-Quads and the required execution time using the built-in chrono module. To address R2 and R3, we assess the KG materialization performance using two parameters: elapsed wall time and maximum memory usage. The latter was measured by the maximum resident set size. These parameters were evaluated on three systems with different levels of constraint. Both parameters, elapsed wall time and maximum resident set size, were obtained using the time command from the GNU time package[9]. Each

---

[5] https://github.com/wintechis/flex-rml-evaluation/.

[6] https://figshare.com/articles/dataset/SDM-Genomic-Datasets/14838342/1.

[7] https://github.com/wintechis/rml-sensor-benchmark/.

[8] https://github.com/SDM-TIB/SDM-RDFizer-Experiments/tree/master/cikm2020/experiments.

[9] https://www.gnu.org/software/time/.

experiment was conducted three times, and the average values for elapsed wall time and peak memory usage are reported. The exact hardware and software configurations of each tested device are detailed in Table 1. Better results are indicated by lower values in the diagram in both metrics.

Table 1. Evaluated Hardware and Systems.

Name	Type	Processor	Memory	Operating System
ESP32	IoT Device	2 × 240 MHz	512 KB	ESP-IDF FreeRTOS
Pi 4	Edge Node	4 × 1.5 GHz	4 GB	Raspberry Pi OS
VM	Cloud	8 × 2.0 GHz	64 GB	Ubuntu 22.04.3 LTS

5.1   Accuracy of Result Size Estimator

To evaluate R1, we performed experiments on the 100k SDM Genomic dataset using the combination of 4POM and 5JOIN mapping rules (Fig. 2), allowing us to evaluate the accuracy in a complex scenario combining objectMaps with and without joins. The evaluation is performed on the cloud based virtual machine.

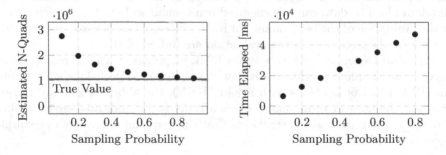

Fig. 2. Accuracy of estimated N-Quads compared to the true value, indicated by a red line, at 1,058,181 N-Quads (left) and elapsed time (right) of the Result Size Estimator on the 100k Genomic dataset using mapping rule 4POM combined with 5JOIN. (Color figure online)

Our results show that the estimated N-Quads follow an exponential decay as a function of the sampling probability and converge to the true value. The exponential decay is a result of diminishing returns in accuracy gains as the probability of sampling, and therefore the representativeness of the sample, increases; initially, small increases in probability yield significant improvements in estimation accuracy. However, as the probability and representativeness continue to increase, the incremental accuracy gains slow down. On the other hand, the execution time increases linearly with the sampling probability, which is to be expected since a doubling of the sampling probability results in twice as much data in the sample and thus requires roughly twice as much processing time.

In general, a higher sampling probability increases the accuracy of the estimated N-Quads, but at the cost of increased computational time. Conversely, lower sampling probabilities provide the benefit of faster estimation, but at the cost of reduced accuracy. Balancing these tradeoffs, FlexRML chooses a default sampling probability of 0.2.

5.2 Performance of Adaptive Hash Function Selection

To address R2, we evaluated FlexRML using an adaptive bit size selection for the hash algorithm and compared it to FlexRML$_{128}$, which represents a naive approach where a 128-bit hash function is used uniformly for all hash algorithms. The evaluation is performed on the cloud platform described in Table 1. For the SDM Genomic dataset, the RML mapping for 1POM is used. All mapped datasets produce the same output using both implementations, i.e. there are no hash collisions.

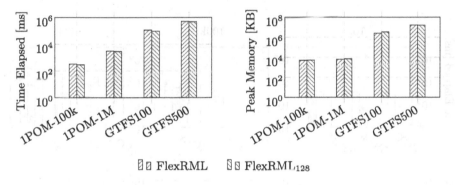

Fig. 3. Elapsed time (left) and peak memory usage (right) for FlexRML with Adaptive Hash Size (Blue) vs. FlexRML with Fixed 128-bit Hash Size (Red). (Color figure online)

The results show that the execution time of FlexRML$_{128}$ is consistently shorter compared to that of FlexRML (see Fig. 3, left diagram). This outcome is expected, as the algorithms used in the Result Size Estimator require additional processing time. However, as depicted in the right diagram of Fig. 3, FlexRML shows lower memory consumption when performing the mapping on all datasets, except in the case of the GTFS500 dataset, where both approaches require a 128-bit hash function. For instance, when mapping the GTFS100 dataset FlexRML requires about 1 GB less memory.

The evaluation shows that when a 128-bit hash function is unnecessary, the use of the Result Size Estimator can reduce the peak memory usage. However, this benefit is accompanied by an increase in processing time.

5.3 Comparison with Existing RML Processors

We perform a comparative analysis of FlexRML on three different platforms, as shown in Table 1: a virtual machine representing a cloud environment, a Raspberry Pi 4 representing an edge node, and an ESP32 microcontroller representing an embedded real-time IoT device. Note that the ESP32 has 512 KB of RAM, of which 300 KB are accessible to the heap. The comparison is made against other state-of-the-art RML processors, specifically Morph-KGC [4] and SDM-RDFizer [10]. Both RML processors are primarily implemented in Python, but use libraries written in C/C++ or Rust for performance-critical parts. When comparing FlexRML to the two RML processors, we took an outcome-based approach, focusing on comparing results using two metrics: materialization speed and memory usage, to evaluate KG materializers regardless of their implementation language. In the following, all figures have a logarithmic scale.

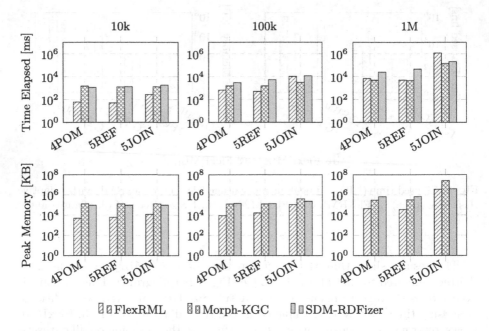

Fig. 4. Cloud: Elapsed time (top) and peak memory usage (bottom) for the SDM genomic dataset over data sizes of 10k, 100k, and 1M.

Cloud Environment. The data on elapsed time and peak memory usage for the SDM Genomic dataset (Fig. 4), shows FlexRML's better performance than Morph-KGC and SDM-RDFizer in processing predicateObjectMaps without join (POMs) or with self-join (REFs), and smaller datasets. However, for larger datasets, FlexRML is slower than Morph-KGC, and it is slower than both Morph-KGC and SDM-RDFizer when processing large datasets with JOIN mapping rules. Despite this, FlexRML's overall lower memory consumption across all datasets is a considerable compensating factor.

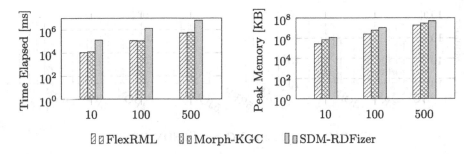

Fig. 5. Cloud: Elapsed time (left) and peak memory usage (right) for the GTFS Madrid benchmark using scale sizes of 10, 100, and 500.

In the GTFS Madrid benchmark (Fig. 5), FlexRML shows comparable performance to Morph-KGC in terms of processing time, while outperforming SDM-RDFizer. In addition, FlexRML demonstrates higher memory efficiency than the two other RML processors. The benchmarks show that FlexRML consistently outperforms other leading RML processors in memory efficiency across all datasets on cloud platforms. In situations where mappings consist entirely of POMs, REFs, or joins that are substitutable by reference conditions, FlexRML using the Result Size Estimator demonstrates processing speeds that are either superior to or on par with competing processors.

Edge Environment. The results from the SDM genomic dataset (Fig. 6) evaluation at the edge are consistent with those observed in the cloud. FlexRML shows greater memory efficiency and faster performance in mapping POMs or REFs. But for JOIN mappings, FlexRML's execution time exceeds that of the other two RML processors. Notably, Morph-KGC was not able to process the 5JOIN operation on the 1M dataset, due to insufficient memory of the edge.

In the case of the GTFS benchmark (Fig. 7), FlexRML again stands out, showcasing the shortest execution time and the least peak memory usage. This memory efficiency is significant in the context of the GTFS100 dataset, where FlexRML is the only RML processor evaluated that successfully maps the dataset within the 4 GB RAM limitation of the Pi.

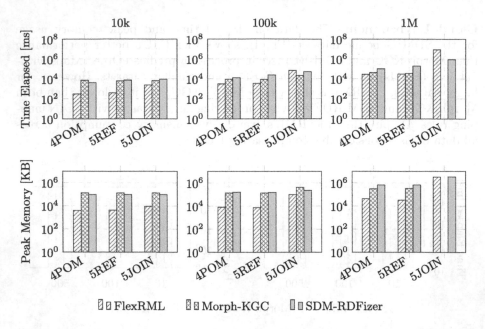

Fig. 6. Edge Node: Elapsed time (top) and peak memory usage (bottom) for the SDM genomic dataset. No bars indicate memory exhaustion and a process crash.

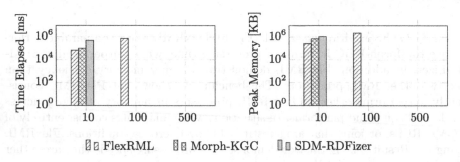

Fig. 7. Edge Node: Elapsed time (left) and peak memory usage (right) for the GTFS Madrid benchmark. No bars indicate memory exhaustion and a process crash.

Device Environment. FlexRML is the only RML processor capable of running on real-time microcontrollers due to its implementation in C++, so only FlexRML can be evaluated. In the device environment, the RML processor can only use in-memory data structures because the ESP32 microcontroller has no local storage, therefore both the RML mappings and the data to be mapped were stored in memory. Peak memory was measured by evaluating the heap memory used.

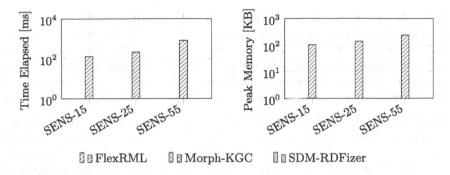

Fig. 8. IoT Device: Elapsed time (left) and peak memory usage (right) for the RML-SENSOR benchmark. Higher scales could not be mapped due to memory limitations.

The results in Fig. 8 show that FlexRML is capable of processing complex RML mappings, including joins, in a simple microcontroller environment. FlexRML can map up to 550 N-Quads, using the RML-SENSOR benchmark and a scale factor of 55, with only about 250 KB of memory. Such performance is considered sufficient and has the potential to enable semantic interoperability at the device level.

6   The Resource FlexRML

FlexRML is designed with several key aspects in mind to maximize usability, community adoption, and extensibility. These aspects include:

Availability. The FlexRML source code is actively maintained and publicly available in a GitHub[10] repository. FlexRML is released under the open source GNU AGPLv3 license. To ensure long-term accessibility and to support reproducibility, all releases of FlexRML are archived on Zenodo. Our future plans for FlexRML can also be found on the GitHub page. The roadmap outlines our upcoming features and reflects our commitment to continuous improvement and community engagement.

Novelty. FlexRML introduces a result size estimation technique for constructing KGs. The result size estimation feature is particularly important for devices with limited memory. Through this optimization and the implementation in C++, FlexRML expands the range of devices capable of mapping non-RDF data to RDF by focusing not only on unconstrained cloud environments, but also on resource-constrained devices and microcontrollers, a domain not previously explored by existing RML processors.

Reusability. FlexRML is designed with accessibility and ease of use in mind. Documentation, usage examples, and configuration files for various use cases are available in the GitHub repository, making it easy to use the resource. To further

---

[10] https://github.com/wintechis/flex-rml.

enhance user experience, prebuilt executables for multiple platforms are available. These executables align with the familiar process of installing or running programs for many users. By offering prebuilt versions, we eliminate the need to set up a build environment or install a specific language interpreter, tasks that require technical expertise. Each release of FlexRML is validated against the latest RML test cases to ensure full compliance with the RML specification.

Versatility. FlexRML uses a modular design that allows future enhancements, including the ability to handle additional data types such as JSON and XML. To handle each data encoding, a dedicated reader must be implemented. The reader is responsible for converting the read data to FlexRML's internal vector-based data representation. The FlexRML core can also be adapted to specific needs, as we have done with the CLI and ESP32 versions. The CLI version has an additional C++ file that handles command line arguments and calls the correct FlexRML functions based on the parameters, while the ESP32 version does not need CLI argument processing, but rather uses microcontroller specific libraries enabling, for example, serial communication.

7   Conclusion and Future Work

We introduced FlexRML, a flexible and memory-efficient resource for executing RML mappings to materialize KGs on a variety of devices, spanning different levels of constraints. FlexRML expands the range of devices capable of producing RDF, including those previously unable to run an RML processor. Our empirical evaluation shows that using the result size estimation algorithm reduces memory consumption compared to a naive fixed bit size approach, by allowing the use of smaller bit sizes in the hash function for duplicate removal without losing output quads. Additionally we found that FlexRML, using the adaptive bit size selection and memory advantages of C++, consistently shows lower peak memory consumption across different datasets when benchmarked against leading RML processors, and offers faster or comparable execution times. Looking ahead, our future development efforts will focus on implementing support for additional data formats, with a particular focus on JSON, incorporating compliance with the new RML specification, and reducing the execution time of non-substitutable joins by implementing join optimizations. In addition, an interesting future research direction we want to explore is the combination of mapping partitions and result size estimation to further improve memory efficiency.

Acknowledgements. This work was funded by the German Federal Ministry for Economic Affairs and Climate Action (BMWK) through the Antrieb 4.0 project (Grant No. 13IK015B).

References

1. Ahamed, J., Mir, R.N., Chishti, M.A.: RML based ontology development approach in internet of things for healthcare domain. Int. J. Pervasive Comput. Commun. **17**(4), 377–389 (2021)
2. Al-Osta, M., Ahmed, B., Abdelouahed, G.: A lightweight semantic web-based approach for data annotation on IoT gateways. Procedia Comput. Sci. **113**, 186–193 (2017)
3. Arenas-Guerrero, J., Chaves-Fraga, D., Toledo, J., Pérez, M.S., Corcho, O.: Morph-KGC: scalable knowledge graph materialization with mapping partitions. Semant. Web (Preprint) 1–20 (2022)
4. Arenas-Guerrero, J.: morph-kgc/morph-kgc: 2.6.4 (2023). https://doi.org/10.5281/zenodo.10171377
5. Chaves-Fraga, D., Priyatna, F., Cimmino, A., Toledo, J., Ruckhaus, E., Corcho, O.: GTFS-Madrid-Bench: a benchmark for virtual knowledge graph access in the transport domain. J. Web Semant. **65**, 100596 (2020). https://doi.org/10.1016/j.websem.2020.100596
6. Daga, E., Asprino, L., Mulholland, P., Gangemi, A., et al.: Facade-X: an opinionated approach to SPARQL anything. Stud. Semant. Web **53**, 58–73 (2021)
7. Das, S., Sundara, S., Cyganiak, R.: R2RML: RDB to RDF Mapping Language (2012). https://www.w3.org/TR/r2rml/
8. Dasoulas, I., Chaves-Fraga, D., Garijo, D., Dimou, A.: Declarative RDF construction from in-memory data structures with RML (2023)
9. Dimou, A., Vander Sande, M., Colpaert, P., Verborgh, R., Mannens, E., Van de Walle, R.: RML: a generic language for integrated RDF mappings of heterogeneous data. In: 7th Workshop on Linked Data on the Web, vol. 1184 (2014)
10. eiglesias34, Chaves, D., et al.: SDM-TIB/SDM-RDFizer: v4.7.2.7 (2023). https://doi.org/10.5281/zenodo.10101405
11. Freedman, D., Pisani, R., Purves, R.: Statistics. 4th edn. W. W. Norton & Co (2007)
12. Ganzha, M., Paprzycki, M., Pawłowski, W., Szmeja, P., Wasielewska, K.: Towards semantic interoperability between Internet of Things platforms. In: Integration, Interconnection, and Interoperability of IoT Systems, pp. 103–127 (2018)
13. Hogan, A., et al.: Knowledge graphs. ACM Comput. Surv. **54**(4) (2021). https://doi.org/10.1145/3447772
14. Hozdić, E.: Smart factory for industry 4.0: a review. Int. J. Mod. Manuf. Technol. **7**(1), 28–35 (2015)
15. Iglesias, E., Jozashoori, S., Chaves-Fraga, D., Collarana, D., Vidal, M.E.: SDM-RDFizer: an RML interpreter for the efficient creation of RDF knowledge graphs. In: Proceedings of the 29th ACM International Conference on Information & Knowledge Management, pp. 3039–3046 (2020)
16. Ioannidis, Y.E.: Query optimization. ACM Comput. Surv. (CSUR) **28**(1), 121–123 (1996)
17. Jabbar, S., Ullah, F., Khalid, S., Khan, M., Han, K., et al.: Semantic interoperability in heterogeneous IoT infrastructure for healthcare. Wirel. Commun. Mob. Comput. **2017** (2017)
18. Lakka, E., et al.: End-to-end semantic interoperability mechanisms for IoT. In: 2019 IEEE 24th International Workshop on Computer Aided Modeling and Design of Communication Links and Networks (CAMAD), pp. 1–6. IEEE (2019)

19. Lefrançois, M., Zimmermann, A., Bakerally, N.: A SPARQL extension for generating RDF from heterogeneous formats. In: Blomqvist, E., Maynard, D., Gangemi, A., Hoekstra, R., Hitzler, P., Hartig, O. (eds.) ESWC 2017. LNCS, pp. 35–50. Springer, Cham (2017). https://doi.org/10.1007/978-3-319-58068-5_3

20. Martino, A., Iannelli, M., Truong, C.: Knowledge injection to counter large language model (LLM) hallucination. In: Pesquita, C., et al. (eds.) ESWC 2023. LNCS, vol. 13998, pp. 182–185. Springer, Cham (2023). https://doi.org/10.1007/978-3-031-43458-7_34

21. Megill, N.D., Pavicic, M.: Estimating Bernoulli trial probability from a small sample. arXiv preprint arXiv:1105.1486 (2011)

22. Moons, B., Sanders, F., Paelman, T., Hoebeke, J.: Decentralized linked open data in constrained wireless sensor networks. In: 2020 7th International Conference on Internet of Things: Systems, Management and Security (IOTSMS), pp. 1–6. IEEE (2020)

23. Oo, S.M., Haesendonck, G., De Meester, B., Dimou, A.: RMLStreamer-SISO: an RDF stream generator from streaming heterogeneous data. In: Sattler, U., et al. (eds.) ISWC 2022. LNCS, vol. 13489, pp. 697–713. Springer, Cham (2022). https://doi.org/10.1007/978-3-031-19433-7_40

24. Rodriguez-Muro, M., Rezk, M.: Efficient SPARQL-to-SQL with R2RML mappings. J. Web Semant. **33**, 141–169 (2015)

25. Şimşek, U., Kärle, E., Fensel, D.: RocketRML - a NodeJS implementation of a use-case specific RML mapper. arXiv preprint arXiv:1903.04969 (2019)

26. Vengerov, D., Menck, A.C., Zait, M., Chakkappen, S.P.: Join size estimation subject to filter conditions. Proc. VLDB Endow. **8**(12), 1530–1541 (2015)

27. de Vleeschauwer, E., Min Oo, S., De Meester, B., Colpaert, P.: Reference conditions: relating mapping rules without joining. In: KGCW 2023, the 4th International Workshop on Knowledge Graph Construction (2023)

28. Vu, B., Pujara, J., Knoblock, C.A.: D-REPR: a language for describing and mapping diversely-structured data sources to RDF. In: Proceedings of the 10th International Conference on Knowledge Capture, pp. 189–196 (2019)

29. Wang, L.: Heterogeneous data and big data analytics. Autom. Control Inf. Sci. **3**(1), 8–15 (2017)

IICONGRAPH: Improved Iconographic and Iconological Statements in Knowledge Graphs

Bruno Sartini[✉][iD]

Ludwig-Maximilians-Universität München, Munich, Germany
`b.sartini@lmu.de`

Abstract. Iconography and iconology are fundamental domains when it comes to understanding artifacts of cultural heritage (CH). Iconography deals with the study and interpretation of visual elements depicted in artifacts and their symbolism, while iconology delves deeper, exploring the underlying cultural and historical meanings. Despite the advances in representing CH with Linked Open Data (LOD), recent studies show persistent gaps in the representation of iconographic and iconological statements in current knowledge graphs (KGs). To address them, this paper presents IICONGRAPH, a KG that was created by refining and extending the iconographic and iconological statements of ArCo (the Italian KG of CH) and Wikidata. The development of IICONGRAPH was also driven by a series of requirements emerging from research case studies expressed in competency questions (CQs) that were unattainable in the non-reengineered versions of the KGs. The evaluation results demonstrate that IICONGRAPH not only outperforms ArCo and Wikidata through domain-specific assessments from the literature but also serves as a robust platform for answering the formulated CQs. IICONGRAPH is released and documented in accordance with the FAIR principles to guarantee the resource's reusability. The algorithms used to create it and assess the CQs have also been made available to ensure transparency and reproducibility. While future work focuses on ingesting more data into the KG, and on implementing it as a backbone of LLM-based question answering systems, the current version of IICONGRAPH still emerges as a valuable asset, contributing to the evolving landscape of CH representation within KGs, the Semantic Web, and beyond.

Keywords: Knowledge Graph · Iconography · Iconology · Symbolism · Cultural Heritage · Digital Humanities · Knowledge Graph Generation

Resource type: Knowledge Graph
License: Creative Commons Attribution 4.0 International
DOI: https://doi.org/10.5281/zenodo.10294589
URL: https://w3id.org/iicongraph/
Documentation: https://w3id.org/iicongraph/docs/

1 Introduction

Using Linked Open Data (LOD) in the context of cultural heritage (CH) simplifies the organization, publication, connection, and reuse of knowledge within this domain, and also provides a structure capable of expressing the complex relationships that can emerge between CH artifacts [13]. Over the years, numerous Knowledge Graphs (KGs) have emerged that contain triples on CH, including those referenced in [1,5–7,12,28]. While some serve a general purpose and deal with various domains, others have been specifically crafted to incorporate and represent information about CH. However, recent studies [4] demonstrate that, in the artistic domains of iconography and iconology,[1] current KGs show two main issues: (i) iconographic and iconological statements lack granularity or are dumped[2] in free text descriptions [25], and (ii) cultural symbolism[3] is severely underrepresented.

This paper addresses these gaps by presenting *IICONGRAPH*, a KG developed from the iconographic and iconological statements of Wikidata [28] and ArCo [6], first re-engineered following the ICON ontology [23] structure, and then enriched with LOD on cultural symbolism taken from HyperReal [24]. These two KGs were chosen because they showed the greatest potential in the evaluation work by Baroncini et al. [4], obtaining the highest scores for the correctness of their iconographic and iconological statements, while showing limits when it comes to the level of granularity of these statements.[4] First, the same evaluation is conducted on IICONGRAPH to demonstrate its superior performance compared to the original sources, highlighting its impact through quantitative assessments. Second, the research potential of IICONGRAPH is tested by attempting to address domain-specific competency questions (CQs) that remained unanswered with the original data from Wikidata and ArCo. The rest of the paper is divided as follows. Section 2 gives a background of the work by presenting the resources included in IICONGRAPH, the ontology behind it, and the limitations of the KGs that were chosen as the initial data sources. Section 3 follows by describing the development and release of IICONGRAPH. In Sect. 4, IICONGRAPH is evaluated using the methodology proposed in [4]. The following Sect. 5 describes how the re-engineered KG can now be used to

---

[1] Iconography is the study and interpretation of visual symbols and images, often within the context of art or visual representation. It involves the identification and analysis of symbols, motifs, and elements within images in an artwork. Iconology instead involves the interpretation of images in a broader cultural and historical context, exploring the deeper layers of meaning, cultural ideologies, and socio-political influences associated with visual representations [17].

[2] Considering dumping as the phenomenon in which "important information for which no appropriate field was found, was forced as plain text inside a descriptive field, easy for humans to read but forever lost to any automatic tool" [2].

[3] Intended as the set of symbolic meanings that some CH objects (or the elements depicted in them) convey from specific cultural perspectives.

[4] In the mentioned study, both KGs performed poorly on the "structure" evaluation, which dealt with the possibility to differentiate between iconographic, iconological, and symbolic subjects, among other criteria explained in Sect. 4.

answer domain specific CQs. Section 6 contains a discussion reflecting on the results of the quantitative and research-based evaluations. Then, Sect. 7 mentions related work about the generation of artistic KGs. Finally, Sect. 8 contains final reflections on this work and mentions possible future work.

2 Background, Problem Statement, and Research Requirements

In this section, the resources used to develop and enrich IICONGRAPH are described. In the subsections about ArCo and Wikidata, their current issues in the representation of artistic interpretation domain are highlighted.

2.1 ICON Ontology 2.0

ICON [23] is an ontology that conceptualizes artistic interpretations by formalizing the methodology of E. Panofsky [17]. According to Panofsky, when performing an artistic interpretation, the interpreter can consider three levels. At a pre-iconographic level, artistic motifs and their factual or expressional meanings are recognized both as single entities and as groups (or compositions). The recognition of a tree, of the action of running or the emotion of crying would be considered pre-iconographical. At an iconographical level, the same motifs are now recognized as what Panofsky calls images, and these images represent characters, symbols, personifications, specific places, events or objects (such as Rome, World War II, and Thor's Hammer). At the same level, the artwork can be seen as depicting a story or an allegory (Panofsky uses "Invenzione" as a general term conveying both stories and allegories). At an iconological level, the artworks are then analyzed in comparison with the cultural context in which they were created, and they become a vessel to convey more in-depth cultural meanings or representing cultural values or cultural phenomena. ICON was updated (in version 2.0) to include three shortcuts that directly link an artwork to the element of pre-iconographic, iconographic or iconologic levels that it depicts or represents [22]. For a more comprehensive overview of ICON, refer to the documentation of IICONGRAPH[5] or to previous publications on the ontology [22,23]. The classes and properties of ICON used in this work are displayed in Fig. 1.

2.2 HyperReal

HyperReal is a KG that contains more than 40,000 instances of symbolism, also called simulations. A simulation is a connection between a symbol (like a cat) and its symbolic meaning (such as divinity) in a particular cultural context (e.g. Egyptian). HyperReal information comes from various sources such as symbols dictionaries [15], and encyclopedias [16] and is structured according to the Simulation Ontology framework. Figure 2 shows the graphical rendering of the *cat-divinity* simulation. The KG is available through its data dump at

---

[5] https://w3id.org/iicongraph/docs/.

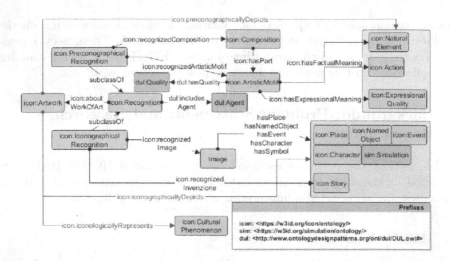

Fig. 1. Graphical Rendering of the ICON ontology classes and properties used in IICONGRAPH. The shortcuts of ICON 2.0 are red, imported classes are violet. (Color figure online)

https://w3id.org/simulation/data. HyperReal data are aligned with the corresponding Wordnet [9] and Babelnet [14] synsets to facilitate the process of aligning external data with its symbols and symbolic meanings [21]. HyperReal has been used in the back end of CH-related applications [26], and as a data source for quantitative comparative cultural studies [27]. In the context of IICONGRAPH, it is used to enrich the potential symbolism of artworks. For instance, a painting depicting a cat could be interpreted from an Egyptian point of view as symbolizing divinity. This kind of inference is agnostic from the intention of the creator of the work of art, but contributes to its understanding from a polyvocal and multicultural perspective.

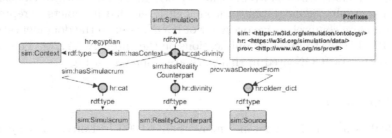

Fig. 2. Graphical Rendering of the *cat-divinity* simulation following the Simulation Ontology schema. The Simulacrum is the specific term used to represent symbols, while Reality Counterpart is the term used to represent symbolic meanings.

2.3   Wikidata

Wikidata [28] is a user-generated, open, comprehensive knowledge base, launched in 2012 by the Wikimedia Foundation, with a wide selection of content, available in various levels of detail and formats. It provides a platform for collaboration, sharing, integration, and a technology system for creating linked data. In the Digital Humanities domain, it is often used to annotate and improve project components, curating metadata to refine the interoperability of authority and local data sets about CH [30]. In the context of this work, the main focus was on the subset of Wikidata's statements regarding artworks and their depictions (the extraction methodology is explained in Sect. 3).

Wikidata Analysis and Problem Statement. When analysing the limitations of Wikidata's iconographic and iconological statements, the main focus is on the property *depicts* (wdt:P180) and its qualifiers. This property links an artwork with an element depicted in it. Its qualifiers, such as *wears* (wdt:P3828), and *expression, gesture, or body pose* (wdt: P6022), give more context to the depicted element. On the one hand, Wikidata contains more than 372,000 *depicts* statements[6] when the subject is a painting (wd:Q3305213), which is a great starting point for digital art history studies. On the other hand, this property is used for all three levels of interpretations, flattening the expressivity of those statements. When it comes to expressing symbolism, there are some exceptions. For, instance *symbolizes* (wdt:P4878) is a qualifier of *depicts* that links a depicted element to what it symbolizes. However, the property is rarely used (only 63 statements related to paintings).[7] **Therefore, the main issue with Wikidata is that when the data are present, the schema is lacking, and when the schema is present, the data are lacking.**

Formulation of Competency Questions for Wikidata. Following the previous statements, in Wikidata it is not possible to retrieve what the most symbolic paintings are and how many serendipitous symbolic connections exist between paintings. Serendipitous connections are defined here as

> "all the new connections that emerged between artworks in Wikidata, caused by the shared symbolic meaning **only**. [...]For example, if Painting A and Painting B both depict a heart, they will share the potential symbolism of love because they share the same symbol, this would not be a serendipitous connections. Contrarily, if Painting A contains a heart and painting C contains a red rose, they share the symbolic meaning of love without sharing the same symbol, which leads to a serendipitous discovery" [21].

---

[6] Query last run in December 2023: https://qlever.cs.uni-freiburg.de/wikidata/yKhv77.

[7] Query last run in December 2023: https://w.wiki/8QyF.

By using the current data in Wikidata, zero serendipitous connections emerge.[8] At the same time, it is also currently challenging to distinguish between the pre-iconographical and the iconographical elements depicted in Wikidata's paintings, a task that becomes even more difficult if the objective is distinguishing between the specific types of iconographical subjects (characters, places, attributes, etc.)

Given these premises, the following CQs have been formulated and will be answered in IICONGRAPH.

CQ1. How many serendipitous connections exist among artworks in Wikidata?
CQ2. Which artworks are associated with the most symbolic meanings?
CQ3. How are pre-iconographic and iconographic depictions distributed across Wikidata's *depicts.* statements in paintings?
CQ4. Among iconographical elements, which are the main classes (characters, places, attributes) that emerge as the most frequent?

Regarding CQ1 and CQ2, I hypothesize that after enriching Wikidata with HyperReal, the number of serendipitous connections will substantially increase, and after that it will be possible to rank Wikidata's painting according to their *symbolic temperature*. Addressing CQ3 and CQ4, the hypothesis is that by re-engineering the statements in Wikidata according to the ICON ontology, it will be possible to distinguish and measure the distribution of pre-iconographic and iconographic elements.

2.4   ArCo

ArCo [6] is a KG that describes a wide spectrum of artifacts from the Italian CH, containing items belonging to the architectural, ethnographic, and artistic domains. It follows the structure of the ArCo ontology, spread into different modules to address different levels of description of CH. In the context of this work, only a subset of statements related to artworks (which belong to the class *HistoricalOrArtisticProperty*) will be considered, with more limitations that will be explained in the following subsection.

ArCo Analysis and Problem Statement. ArCo was created by applying Natural Language Processing algorithms to the OCR (Optical Character Recognition) version of printed catalogs. Consequently, even if some of the more technical information was converted into URIs and single nodes in the KG, a great deal of free-text information remains, especially about subjective domains like iconographic readings. Therefore, most of the information regarding iconographical and iconological statements is dumped in a free-text description, not exploiting the full potential of LOD. On the one hand, this puts ArCo in a worse starting position compared to Wikidata, which expresses almost all of the information through URIs and limits the free-text fields. On the other hand, some of the

---

[8] Query last run in December: https://w.wiki/6BZR.

descriptions in ArCo contain detailed interpretations about artworks, even separating pre-iconographic subjects from iconological meanings conveyed by artworks. Additionally, the descriptions have a schematic structure with repeating patterns, especially those related to a series of Italian billboards created in the 20th century. In the current version of ArCo, it is challenging to study the correlations between specific iconographic and pre-iconographic subjects and the cultural event/product they promote (iconological level).

Formulation of Competency Questions for ArCo. Given that the starting point of ArCo is worse compared to Wikidata, only one CQ was formulated, namely:

CQ5. What are the most common iconological meanings associated with Italian Billboards from the 20th century?

The hypothesis is that by transforming the free-text description into structured data following ICON, it will be possible to isolate and then measure the frequency of iconological meanings.

3   IICONGRAPH Development and Release

This section describes how IICONGRAPH was developed and released. Different strategies were adopted for the development according to the issues mentioned in Sect. 2 for the two sources. The main distinction between the two sources is that while Wikidata provides information about the potential relationships between depicted entities (via the qualifiers), requiring a full description using the ICON ontology, ArCo's descriptions are very linear; therefore, only the shortcuts introduced in ICON 2.0 are necessary to describe such information.[9] For both KGs, the generation of the re-engineered LOD was performed in a Python environment via the RDFlib package.[10]

3.1   Wikidata's Conversion

The general pipeline adopted to convert Wikidata was (i) assigning the depicted entities to the classes of ICON, (ii) extracting data about paintings, (iii) aligning them with HyperReal, and then (iv) re-engineering the statements following the ICON ontology. To align Wikidata's depicted entities with ICON classes, we adopted a methodology involving the annotation of the depicted entity types and classes expressed in Wikidata through the properties *instance of* (wdt:P31) and *subclass of* (wdt:P279). Given the impracticality of manually annotating more than 60,000 individual depicted entities, I focused on annotating the top 700 classes and types, ordered by the number of depicted elements assigned to

---

[9] This decision is supported by the work that presents ICON 2.0 [22], in which ArCo's descriptions are a use case example for ICON 2.0.

[10] https://rdflib.readthedocs.io/en/stable/.

them. The top 700 covered more than 85% of the total entities. To ensure objectivity, a no-ambiguity policy guided the single annotator. Each type or class was analyzed on Wikidata using a SPARQL query to verify that all related entities could match the designated ICON class; otherwise, the type or class was discarded. The alignment is not made because of a shared or similar label between the classes of Wikidata and ICON, but rather by choosing the best ICON class to represent the instances of the Wikidata class. For example, the instances of the class *big city* `wd:Q1549591` would be modelled, using ICON, with the `icon:Place` class. Subsequently, all the depictions of big cities will be described in ICON using an `icon:IconographicalRecognition`. At the same time, other classes of Wikidata which have been aligned to `icon:NaturalElement` will make all the elements that belong to classes recognized in ICON via a `icon:PreiconographicalRecognition`. Figure 3 illustrates the distribution of assigned classes and types for pre-iconographical and iconographical elements. After this alignment, the information about the paintings, their depicted elements, the types and classes of the depiction, and their qualifiers were extracted via a SPARQL query. A total of almost 150,000 paintings and their related metadata were extracted. To align Wikidata's entities with HyperReal's symbols for the enhancement, an alignment done in previous work was reused [26]. The conversion of Wikidata yielded more than 29,000,000 triples. More than 3,000,000 symbolic interpretations were inferred, due to the alignment to HyperReal, with an average of around 20 interpretations per painting. For a more detailed description of Wikidata's conversion, refer to the documentation.

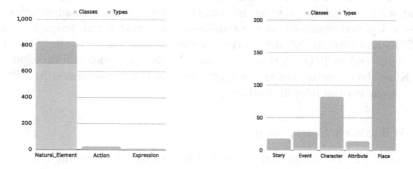

Fig. 3. On the left: manual matching result between Wikidata's types and classes and ICON's classes related to pre-iconographical elements. On the right: manual matching result between Wikidata's types and classes and ICON's classes related to iconographical elements.

3.2   ArCo's Conversion

For the conversion of ArCo, only the shortcut version of ICON was necessary, eliminating the need to assign elements from free-text descriptions to individual ICON classes. Instead, the depicted elements were categorized into the macrogroups of pre-iconographical, iconographical, and iconological. The process involved extracting ArCo's data using a regex pattern to capture "Iconographic Reading:" (in Italian, "Lettura Iconografica:") in artwork descriptions linked via the Dublin Core description property (dc:description). Following the extraction of approximately 23,000 artworks and their descriptions (about 1% of ArCo's total number of artworks), the structure of the descriptions was analyzed to identify other patterns to facilitate the automatization of the conversion. It was noticed that standard descriptions are organized into categories separated by a standard use of punctuation. All descriptions that did not meet this standard were discarded (around 3,000). All iconological meanings, in the context of billboards, were determined to be after the category "Product category/type of event" (in Italian, "Categoria Merceologica/tipo di evento"), where the promotional aspect was described. Ambiguous categories (such as "Names", which included both the people depicted in the billboards but also the CEOs of the companies that were getting promoted) were excluded, and a straightforward approach was employed to distinguish between pre-iconographical and iconographical levels. If an element in the description was written with a capital letter, it was assigned to the iconographic level, otherwise to the pre-iconographical level. Figure 4 visually shows the rationale behind the assignment and parsing of descriptions, exemplified by the artwork available at https://w3id.org/arco/resource/HistoricOrArtisticProperty/0500659063. Before conversion, all descriptions were translated into English using the Google Translate API. Given the simplicity of the texts, this translation did not generate evident errors. Single elements were linked to HyperReal through string matching. In summary, the description from ArCo were translated and then analysed by a simple parser that separates the categories with the punctuation, and then isolates each single element of each description category considering it an iconographical element if written with uppercase or pre-iconographical if lower case. The conversion of ArCo yielded 767,888 triples, which is significantly less than Wikidata because of the difference in number of artworks (150,000 against 20,000), and also because the simplified version of ICON is much less verbose. A total of 457,747 automatic interpretations were generated due to the match with HyperReal.

3.3 IICONGRAPH Release

IICONGRAPH was released according to the FAIR principles [29]. The w3id service was used to obtain persistent URIs for the namespace https://w3id.org/iicongraph/data/, documentation https://w3id.org/iicongraph/docs/ and analysis related to the research case studies https://w3id.org/iicongraph/casestudies/. The same information is accessible via the GitHub repository https://github.com/br0ast/iicongraph/. The prefix *iig*, used in the KG, was registered in http://prefix.cc. The KG is stored in Zenodo, accessible via https://zenodo.org/doi/10.5281/zenodo.10294588. The metadata about the dataset and

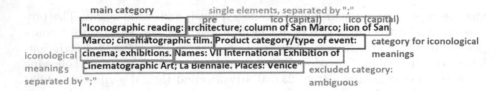

Fig. 4. Visual Example of a standard description in ArCo and the parsing steps applied to it

the provenance of the data is defined in a separate file[11] following the DCAT standard.[12] The ICON ontology used as its schema also respects the FAIR principles, obtaining a score of 90% on the FOOPS tool [11].

4   Quantitative Evaluation

In this section, IICONGRAPH is quantitatively evaluated following the methodology defined by [4]. Three versions of IICONGRAPH will be evaluated, namely IIC-arco, which contains only the re-engineered statements from ArCo, IIC-wikidata, which contains only the re-engineered statements from Wikidata, and IIC-global, containing all the triples. The assessment method considers six criteria, divided into two macro-areas: content and structure. Content considers the evaluation of the correctness of artistic interpretation statements (CR1), and the evaluation on the completeness of artworks interpretations (CR2) (i.e., whether the interpretation mentions, when needed, pre-iconographical, iconographical, and iconological statements). Then, structure addresses the richness of the schema describing the artworks (CR3), the entity linking of artworks with external sources is measured by CR4, CR5 measures how the URIs of the depicted subjects are linked within the same dataset (in technical terms, the outdegree of the subjects' nodes in a graph) and CR6 measures the number of references to external taxonomies of art and culture. All categories are given a weight (CR1,2,3 have a weight of 1, CR4,5 have a weight of 0.6 and CR6 has a weight of 0.8) and the possible scores for each go from 0 to 1. Given the reengineering tasks performed to create IICONGRAPH, this work could only influence the criteria CR2, CR3, CR5 as it does not deal with changing wrong interpretations (CR1), linking artworks between different datasets (CR4), or referring to external taxonomies of art and culture (CR6).

Following the methodology presented in [4], CR2 was calculated by averaging the scores of two annotators that evaluated the description of 100 artworks. The annotators had to decide how many interpretation levels they expected for the artwork. The general guidelines of [4] say that artworks depicting a landscape usually are only interpreted via a pre-iconographical level, most portraits have

---

[11] https://github.com/br0ast/iicongraph/blob/main/data/IICONGRAPH_catalogue.ttl.

[12] https://www.w3.org/TR/vocab-dcat-3/.

both pre-iconographical and iconographical meanings, and allegorical, religious, and culturally relevant scenes (depiction of wars, special events for a country or culture) can usually be described using all levels. After averaging the evaluation, IIC-global obtained 0.92, IIC-arco 0.958 and IIC-wikidata 0.97. CR3 was calculated through a comparison of the ICON ontology structure with the gold standard in [4][13]. Given that the schema behind IICONGRAPH is the ICON ontology, developed to describe all the information mentioned in the gold standard, the score of all the versions of the KG in this category was set at 1. CR5 was computed via SPARQL queries on the data, first counting how many subjects in the data were linked to at least more than 1 artwork, and then dividing this number by the total number of subject recognized. The scores obtained are 0.5771 for IIC-arco, 0.4573 for IIC-wikidata and 0.4337 for IIC-global. Since CR1, CR4, and CR6 were not affected by the changes, IIC-wikidata and IIC-arco maintain their scores of [4], while IIC-global receives an average of the two scores. Table 1 shows the scores compared to the other datasets analyzed in [4]. In Sect. 6 the results are analyzed and discussed. All scripts and queries related to the quantitative evaluation are available in the documentation at https://w3id.org/iicongraph/docs/.

Table 1. Overall results of the quantitative evaluation applied to IIC-global, IIC-wikidata, and IIC-arco compared to the results in the state of the art performed in [4]. UF labeled criteria signal that they were not affected by the changes. Ranking signals only the overall top 3 for each category.

	CR1 UF	CR2	CR3	CR4 UF	CR5	CR6 UF	Content	Rank Cont	Structure	Rank Structure	Overall	Rank overall
IIC-global	0.9023	0.92	1	0.3508	0.4737	0.1404	0.9111	2	0.5357	2	0.7234	2
IIC-arco	0.8278	0.958	1	0.0026	0.5771	0.1238	0.8929	3	0.4823	3	0.6876	3
IIC-wiki	0.9768	0.97	1	0.699	0.4573	0.157	0.9734	1	0.6065	1	0.7899	1
ArCo	0.8278	0.74	0.3333	0.0026	0.172	0.1238	0.7839		0.1790		0.4815	
Wikidata	0.9768	0.74	0.6667	0.699	0.367	0.157	0.8584		0.4773		0.6678	
Fondazione Zeri	0.9925	0.5117	0.1111	0.0005	0.266	0.5449	0.7521		0.2356		0.4939	
Nomisma	0.9768	0.5	0.2222	0	0.749	0.0001	0.7384		0.2239		0.4811	
SARI	0.849	0.3783	0.1111	0.997	0.5	0	0.6136		0.3364		0.475	
Europeana	0.4688	0.236	0.1111	0.0073	0.6122	1	0.3524		0.4276		0.39	
ND_Hungary	0.13	0.5392	0.1111	0	0	0	0.3346		0.037		0.1858	
DBpedia	0.655	0.7242	0.2222	0.994	0.41	0	0.6896		0.3549		0.5222	
Yago	0.99	0.4825	0.1111	1	0.1675	0	0.7362		0.2705		0.5034	

5   Research-Based Evaluation

This section shows how IICONGRAPH can be used to answer the CQs formulated in Sect. 2. Regarding CQ1 and CQ2, the methodology consisted of extracting the data on paintings and their symbolic depictions through a SPARQL query performed on IIC-wikidata. Around 79,000 paintings were associated with

---

[13] In summary, a perfect schema would be able to describe actions, preiconographical elements, stories, allegories, iconographical subjects, symbols, iconological subjects, cultural phenomena, and should be able to be used in combination with a taxonomy or controlled vocabulary of art and culture.

a symbolic meaning shared by more than one symbol. Artwork connections were computed using Python, with an iterative process comparing each depicted element between pairs of paintings. The calculation involved determining how many symbolic meanings were shared between the depicted elements of the pairs. At the end of the calculation, **2,481,489,938 serendipitous connections were exposed**. CQ2 was tackled with a SPARQL query, revealing the top 10 most symbolic paintings. **"Entrance into the Ark" (wd:Q209050) by Jan Brueghel The Elder** tops the list with almost 1,500 associated simulations; the rest of the top 10 are detailed in Table 2. In general, paintings with a multitude of animals and plants were associated with most symbolic meanings. Similarly, simple SPARQL queries facilitated the examination of the distribution of pre-iconographic and iconographic representations in Wikidata (CQ3, CQ4), revealing that **64.86% of the depicted elements belong to the pre-iconographical level**. Among iconographic elements, **Characters are the most recognized, with almost 100,000 occurrences**. The results of this analysis are presented in Table 3. CQ5 followed a similar approach. Through a SPARQL query on IIC-arco, the number of paintings associated with each iconological meaning was determined. The top 10 iconological meanings are presented in Table 4. In particular, **the iconological meaning most referred to in 20th century billboards is the promotion of tourism**. In summary, post-reengineering and enrichment, all CQs formulated in Sect. 2 were effectively answered. All scripts and queries developed to address these CQs are provided at https://w3id.org/iicongraph/casestudies to ensure the transparency and reproducibility of the results.

Table 2. Top 10 of the most symbolic paintings in Wikidata, retrieved by a SPARQL query performed on IICONGRAPH. *wd:* is the prefix for https://www.wikidata.org/wiki/entity/

Painting ID	Painting Label	Sim#
wd:Q66107722	**Entrance into the Ark**	**1,488**
wd:Q18809786	**Entry into Noah's Ark**	**998**
wd:Q321303	**The Garden of Earthly Delights**	**851**
wd:Q27980267	Unknown Title	758
wd:Q2510869	Concert in the Egg	747
wd:Q463392	Paradiesgärtlein	723
wd:Q20170089	The Ark	723
wd:Q18917077	The Garden of Eden and the Creation of Eve	721
wd:Q29656879	Earth or The Earthly Paradise	706
wd:Q18573212	The Animals Entering Noah's Ark	662

Table 3. Distribution of Pre-iconographical and Iconographical statements in Wikidata extracted from IIC-wikidata

Level of interpretation	Total	Unique	Specific Element	Total	Unique
Pre-iconographical	**224,981**	**5,131**	**natural elements**	**220,463**	**4,938**
			actions	4,189	147
			expressions	4,667	65
Iconographical	121,893	37,667	**characters**	**98,354**	**27,847**
			events	817	399
			stories	3,436	3,436
			attributes	791	51
			places	17,050	5,438

Table 4. Top 10 iconological meanings associated with the most artworks in ArCo

Iconological Meaning	Artwork #
iig:promotionOfTourism	**4,572**
iig:promotionOfExhibitions	**3,604**
iig:promotionOfTourismPromotionBodies	**3,380**
iig:promotionOfInformationAndCommunication	2,932
iig:promotionOfFoodIndustry	2,814
iig:promotionOfCulturalEvents	2,219
iig:promotionOfTransport	2,211
iig:promotionOfSport	1,928
iig:promotionOfTrade	1,911
iig:promotionOfAgriculture	1,694

6   Discussion of the Results

After a thorough quantitative evaluation, the performance of IIC-global, along with its subsets IIC-wikidata and IIC-arco, outperforms the rest of the KGs examined in [4] in both structure and content scores. The effectiveness of the re-engineering process is evident in the significant improvements observed, particularly in CR5 (subject intralinking potential) for ArCo, where it experienced an impressive increase (more than 300%) from 0.172 to 0.5771. This increase is due to the generation of more subjects expressed in URIs, which increases the number of connections between artworks that share the same subject (now defereanceable compared to the previous text-only version).

The best-performing KG overall is IIC-wikidata, similarly to when the standard version of Wikidata was the top performer before the re-engineering process. Notably, despite the enhancements, ArCo still falls short in the structure criteria, with an overall structure score of less than 0.5. This limitation is attributed to issues such as references to external taxonomies and the alignment challenges between its artworks and those present in other KGs.

When it comes to the evaluation of research-driven CQs, IICONGRAPH shows great potential for domain-specific analyses, although these results are considered preliminary and show some limitations. In fact, the automatic symbolic interpretations of artwork from a polyvocal point of view (given by Hyper-Real) could be the starting point for more in-depth analysis for art historians, as they only represent potential, creator-agnostic symbolic meanings. Moreover, Table 4 displays elements that could be merged after performing entity disambiguation (i.e., promotion of tourism and promotion of tourism promotion bodies). Despite this, the results underscore the considerable advancement represented by IICONGRAPH and its subgraphs. They not only outperform the state-of-the-art quantitatively but also demonstrate their utility in addressing CQs that were unattainable in the original versions of the KGs. The improvements in both quantitative metrics and research potential underscore the significance of the re-engineering efforts and the enriched representations provided by IICONGRAPH.

7   Related Work

This section provides an overview of the development of artistic KGs or related resources, highlighting differences from IICONGRAPH. Artgraph [7] is a KG developed by combining data from DBpedia and Wikiart, including over 250,000 artworks and associated artists. Its objective is to integrate visual embeddings and graph embeddings from the KG for automated art analysis. However, an examination of Artgraph's properties reveals the same issues found in Wikidata and ArCo, such as the lack of granularity of iconographic and iconological statements due to the absence of interpretative depth. The connection between artworks and subjects relies on a generic "tag" property. Furthermore, the dataset does not incorporate symbolic representation. ICONdataset [3] is a manually annotated KG, containing more than 5,500 art historians' interpretations about more than 400 artworks. It shares with IICONGRAPH the adoption of the ICON ontology as its primary schema. While manual annotation, as employed by ICONdataset, affords complete supervision over the data, ensuring a high degree of accuracy, the inherent drawback lies in its time-consuming nature, evident in the relatively low number of artworks and interpretations. In contrast, IICONGRAPH adopts a semi-automatic approach, resulting in a significant disparity in both the quantity of artworks and interpretations between the two KGs. This distinction emphasizes the scalability and efficiency afforded by a semi-automatic process. Furthermore, IICONGRAPH's incorporation of the HyperReal enrichment introduces an additional layer of symbolic data, augmenting its comprehensiveness, reach, and potentialities in comparison to manually annotated counterparts. MythLOD [18] is an LOD catalog that contains interpretations of more than 4,000 mythological works. It was created by converting a CSV manually populated by domain experts. Its main purpose is to represent in

LOD both the methodology and rationale of the interpretations (iconographic, hermeneutic) and the bibliographic sources which supported the interpretations. However, when it comes to describing the main objects of the interpretations, it relies on the standard Dublin Core[14] subject property (dc:subject), which is extremely limited compared to the possibilities offered by the ICON ontology behind IICONGRAPH. Other datasets, such as [1,8,12,19,20] are not mentioned, as they are compared to IICONGRAPH through the evaluation in Sect. 4.

8   Conclusion and Future Work

This paper presented the development and evaluation of IICONGRAPH, a KG created by re-engineering the iconographic and iconological statements of ArCo and Wikidata. IICONGRAPH, IIC-arco and IIC-wikidata outperformed the state-of-the-art of artistic KGs in both structure and content scores. Furthermore, the results of the requirements evaluation based on the CQs demonstrate the suitability of IICONGRAPH to answer domain-specific artistic inquieres. Future work is divided into two main areas. First, the expansion of IICONGRAPH involves ingestion of additional statements from more artistic KGs. Second, in the realm of Large Language Models (LLMs), IICONGRAPH emerges as a valuable resource for developing question answering and chat-based systems focused on CH, addressing a gap identified in the literature regarding symbolic and iconographic knowledge [10]. Additionally, the descriptions in ArCo and the RDF generated to create IICONGRAPH hold promise as fine-tuning arguments for an LLM capable of autonomously generating intricate iconographic LOD from free-text descriptions via prompts. Despite the narrow focus of IICONGRAPH in the field of iconography and iconology, especially in the context of linked open data, it can have an impact to attract interest in digital humanities initiatives that deal with Semantic Web. One key impact of IICONGRAPH is its potential as a valuable resource for applications dealing with cultural heritage data. With structured data on over 170,000 artworks, IICONGRAPH provides a rich source of information for reuse, facilitating nuanced analyses and interpretations. Moreover, the growing field of digital art history stands to benefit from IICONGRAPH's structured data repository. Museums can leverage this resource to enrich their digital collections; if some of their artworks are already included in Wikidata, they can refer also to the IICONGRAPH version, allowing for more robust and iconographically-centered searches, enhancing the discoverability and interpretive potential of their artworks. Furthermore, IICONGRAPH serves as a model for other underrepresented fields within LOD initiatives. By elevating the discourse surrounding iconography and iconology, it can set a precedent for the inclusion and recognition of other specialized domains, such as symbolism in music or Egyptian iconographic data, fostering innovation and inclusivity within the broader scholarly ecosystem. In conclusion, IICONGRAPH stands as a robust and versatile resource that advances the understanding of artistic interpretation within the domains of art history and digital humanities, and

---

[14] https://www.dublincore.org/specifications/dublin-core/dcmi-terms/.

also presents significant implications for the evolving landscape of LLMs, offering a promising avenue for further exploration and integration into the broader context of CH research.

References

1. Auer, S., Bizer, C., Kobilarov, G., Lehmann, J., Cyganiak, R., Ives, Z.: DBpedia: a nucleus for a web of open data. In: Aberer, K., et al. (eds.) ISWC ASWC 2007. LNCS, vol. 4825, pp. 722–735. Springer, Heidelberg (2007). https://doi.org/10.1007/978-3-540-76298-0_52
2. Barabucci, G., Tomasi, F., Vitali, F.: Supporting complexity and conjectures in cultural heritage descriptions. In: Proceedings of the International Conference Collect and Connect: Archives and Collections in a Digital Age, pp. 104–115. CEUR Workshop (2021). http://ceur-ws.org/Vol-2810/paper9.pdf
3. Baroncini, S., Daquino, M., Tomasi, F.: Exploring iconographical and iconological content in semantic data through art historians' interpretations. In: La memoria digitale. Forme del testo e organizzazione della conoscenza. Atti del XII convegno annuale AIUCD, pp. 9–14. Siena (2023)
4. Baroncini, S., Sartini, B., van Erp, M., Tomasi, F., Gangemi, A.: Is dc:subject enough? A landscape on iconography and iconology statements of knowledge graphs in the semantic web. J. Documentation **79**(7), 115–136 (2023). https://doi.org/10.1108/JD-09-2022-0207
5. Bruno, E., Pasqual, V., Tomasi, F.: Odi and bacodi: a study on destini incrociati by italo calvino with semantic web technologies. In: La memoria digitale. Forme del testo e organizzazione della conoscenza. Atti del XII convegno annuale AIUCD, p. 35. Siena (2023)
6. Carriero, V.A., et al.: ArCo: the Italian cultural heritage knowledge graph. In: Ghidini, C., et al. (eds.) ISWC 2019. LNCS, vol. 11779, pp. 36–52. Springer, Cham (2019). https://doi.org/10.1007/978-3-030-30796-7_3
7. Castellano, G., Digeno, V., Sansaro, G., Vessio, G.: Leveraging knowledge graphs and deep learning for automatic art analysis. Knowl.-Based Syst. **248**, 108859 (2022). https://doi.org/10.1016/j.knosys.2022.108859. https://www.sciencedirect.com/science/article/pii/S0950705122004105
8. Daquino, M., Mambelli, F., Peroni, S., Tomasi, F., Vitali, F.: Enhancing semantic expressivity in the cultural heritage domain: exposing the zeri photo archive as linked open data. J. Comput. Cult. Herit. **10**(4) (2017). https://doi.org/10.1145/3051487
9. Fellbaum, C. (ed.): WordNet: An Electronic Lexical Database. Language, Speech, and Communication, A Bradford Book, Cambridge (1998)
10. Garcia, N., et al.: A dataset and baselines for visual question answering on art. In: Bartoli, A., Fusiello, A. (eds.) ECCV 2020. LNCS, vol. 12536, pp. 92–108. Springer, Cham (2020). https://doi.org/10.1007/978-3-030-66096-3_8
11. Garijo, D., Corcho, O., Poveda-Villalón, M.: FOOPS!: an ontology pitfall scanner for the fair principles. In: Proceedings of the ISWC 2021 Posters, Demos and Industry Tracks: From Novel Ideas to Industrial Practice co-located with 20th International Semantic Web Conference (ISWC 2021). CEUR-WS, Online (2021). https://foops.linkeddata.es/assets/iswc_2021_demo.pdf
12. Isaac, A., Haslhofer, B.: Europeana linked open data – data.europeana.eu. Semant. Web **4**(3), 291–297 (2013)

13. Lodi, G., et al.: Semantic web for cultural heritage valorisation. In: Hai-Jew, S. (ed.) Data Analytics in Digital Humanities. MMSA, pp. 3–37. Springer, Cham (2017). https://doi.org/10.1007/978-3-319-54499-1_1
14. Navigli, R., Ponzetto, S.P.: BabelNet: building a very large multilingual semantic network. In: Proceedings of the 48th Annual Meeting of the Association for Computational Linguistics, pp. 216–225 (2010)
15. Olderr, S.: Symbolism a Comprehensive Dictionary, 2nd edn. McFarland, London (2012)
16. Otto, A.F.: Mythological Japan: The Symbolisms of Mythology in Relation to Japanese Art, with Illustrations Drawn in Japan, by Native Artists - Primar. Bibliolife DBA of Bibilio Bazaar II LLC, Charleston, SC, USA (2014). Google-Books-ID: 0Ki8oAEACAAJ
17. Panofsky, E.: Studies in Iconology: Humanistic Themes in the Art of the Renaissance. Westview Press, Boulder (1972)
18. Pasqual, V., Tomasi, F.: Linked open data per la valorizzazione di collezioni culturali: il dataset mythlod. AIB studi **62**(1), 149–168 (2022). https://doi.org/10.2426/aibstudi-13301. https://aibstudi.aib.it/article/view/13301
19. Rebele, T., Suchanek, F., Hoffart, J., Biega, J., Kuzey, E., Weikum, G.: YAGO: a multilingual knowledge base from Wikipedia, Wordnet, and Geonames. In: Groth, P., et al. (eds.) ISWC 2016. LNCS, vol. 9982, pp. 177–185. Springer, Cham (2016). https://doi.org/10.1007/978-3-319-46547-0_19
20. Sabah, R., Sabah, Z.: Modeling nomisma ontology and comparing solutions for uncertainty. Ph.D. thesis, Goethe University Frankfurt (2022)
21. Sartini, B.: Connecting works of art within the semantic web of symbolic meanings. Ph.D. thesis, Alma Mater Studiorium, University of Bologna (2023). https://doi.org/10.48676/unibo/amsdottorato/11020. http://amsdottorato.unibo.it/id/eprint/11020
22. Sartini, B., Baroncini, S.: A comparative study of simple and complex art interpretations in linked open data using icon ontology. In: Proceedings of the International Workshop on Semantic Web and Ontology Design for Cultural Heritage co-located with the International Semantic Web Conference 2023 (ISWC 2023). CEUR Workshop (2023). https://ceur-ws.org/Vol-3540/paper4.pdf
23. Sartini, B., Baroncini, S., van Erp, M., Tomasi, F., Gangemi, A.: Icon: an ontology for comprehensive artistic interpretations. J. Comput. Cult. Herit. **16**(3) (2023). https://doi.org/10.1145/3594724
24. Sartini, B., van Erp, M., Gangemi, A.: Marriage is a peach and a chalice: modelling cultural symbolism on the semantic web. In: Proceedings of the 11th on Knowledge Capture Conference, K-CAP 2021, pp. 201–208. Association for Computing Machinery, New York (2021). https://doi.org/10.1145/3460210.3493552
25. Sartini, B., Gangemi, A.: Towards the unchaining of symbolism from knowledge graphs: how symbolic relationships can link cultures. In: Book of Extended Abstracts of the 10th National AIUCD Conference, AIUCD, Pisa, pp. 576–580 (2021)
26. Sartini, B., Nesterov, A., Libbi, C., Brate, R., Shoilee, S.B.A., Daniil, S.: Multivocal exhibition: a user-centric application to explore symbolic interpretations of artefacts from different cultural perspectives. In: ExICE - Extended Intelligence for Cultural Engagement Conference, Bologna (2023). https://spice-h2020.eu/conference/papers/posters/ExICE23_paper_7072.pdf
27. Sartini, B., Vogelmann, V., van Erp, M., Gangemi, A.: Comparing symbolism across Asian cultural contexts. In: Digital Humanities 2022 Conference Abstracts,

pp. 358–361. DH2022 Local Organizing Committee (2022). https://dh2022.dhii. asia/abstracts/567

28. Vrandečić, D., Krötzsch, M.: Wikidata: a free collaborative knowledgebase. Commun. ACM **57**(10), 78–85 (2014). https://doi.org/10.1145/2629489

29. Wilkinson, M.D., et al.: The fair guiding principles for scientific data management and stewardship. Sci. Data **3**(1) (2016). https://doi.org/10.1038/sdata.2016.18

30. Zhao, F.: A systematic review of Wikidata in Digital Humanities projects. Digital Scholarship in the Humanities (2022). https://doi.org/10.1093/llc/fqac083

VisionKG: Unleashing the Power of Visual Datasets via Knowledge Graph

Jicheng Yuan[1(✉)], Anh Le-Tuan[1], Manh Nguyen-Duc[1], Trung-Kien Tran[2], Manfred Hauswirth[1,3], and Danh Le-Phuoc[1,3]

[1] Open Distributed Systems, Technical University of Berlin, Berlin, Germany
{jicheng.yuan,anh.letuan,duc.manh.nguyen,manfred.hauswirth,
danh.lephuoc}@tu-berlin.de
[2] Bosch Center for Artificial Intelligence, Renningen, Germany
TrungKien.Tran@de.bosch.com
[3] Fraunhofer Institute for Open Communication Systems, Berlin, Germany

Abstract. The availability of vast amounts of visual data with diverse and fruitful features is a key factor for developing, verifying, and benchmarking advanced computer vision (CV) algorithms and architectures. Most visual datasets are created and curated for specific tasks or with limited data distribution for very specific fields of interest, and there is no unified approach to manage and access them across diverse sources, tasks, and taxonomies. This not only creates unnecessary overheads when building robust visual recognition systems, but also introduces biases into learning systems and limits the capabilities of data-centric AI. To address these problems, we propose the **Vision Knowledge Graph (VisionKG)**, a novel resource that interlinks, organizes and manages visual datasets via knowledge graphs and Semantic Web technologies. It can serve as a unified framework facilitating simple access and querying of state-of-the-art visual datasets, regardless of their heterogeneous formats and taxonomies. One of the key differences between our approach and existing methods is that VisionKG is not only based on metadata but also utilizes a unified data schema and external knowledge bases to integrate, interlink, and align visual datasets. It enhances the enrichment of the semantic descriptions and interpretation at both image and instance levels and offers data retrieval and exploratory services via SPARQL and natural language empowered by Large Language Models (LLMs). VisionKG currently contains 617 million RDF triples that describe approximately 61 million entities, which can be accessed at https://vision.semkg.org and through APIs. With the integration of 37 datasets and four popular computer vision tasks, we demonstrate its usefulness across various scenarios when working with computer vision pipelines.

Keywords: Computer Vision · Knowledge Graph · Linked Data · Ontology · RDF

Resource Type: Datasets/Knowledge Graph
Repository: https://github.com/cqels/vision
Homepage: https://vision.semkg.org
License: MIT

1   Introduction

Computer vision (CV) has made significant advances, with visual datasets emerging as a crucial component in developing robust visual recognition systems (VRSs). The performance of the underlying deep neural networks (DNNs) is influenced not only by advanced architectures but also significantly by the quality of learning data [59]. There exist many open visual datasets, e.g., ImageNet [9], OpenImage [26], and MS-COCO [31], which offer a wide range of visual characteristics in different contexts to support the generalization capabilities of DNNs.

However, a challenge arises as these datasets often come in varied data formats and the quality of their taxonomies and annotations differs significantly. Furthermore, labels used to define objects vary in diverse lexical definitions, from structured lexical definitions, such as WordNet [32], Freebase [4], to unstructured plain text. This often leads to semantic inconsistencies across different datasets [28]. Additionally, the lack of semantic integration not only causes unnecessary overhead in developing robust VRSs but also introduces biases in learning systems, thereby constraining the potential of data-centric AI [45].

Although researchers and practitioners have made efforts to unify visual datasets [18,27,34], a systematic approach to understanding the features and unifying semantics underlying visual datasets is yet to be achieved. For instance, DeepLake [18] can access data from multiple sources in a unified manner, however, it does not bridge the gap in semantics alignments across datasets. Conversely, Fiftyone [34] can partially identify inconsistencies in annotations and analyze data pipeline failures by interlinking metadata manually, while this labor-intensive solution limits the effectiveness of building computer vision pipelines. While these works improve the performance of learning systems in a data-centric manner, training DNNs with high-quality data from multiple sources in a cost-effective way remains a formidable challenge for researchers and engineers [50].

To address the aforementioned data inconsistency problems, leveraging the capabilities of Knowledge Graphs, which offer a flexible and powerful way to organize and represent data that is comprehensible for both humans and machines, we built a knowledge graph for visual data, named VisionKG, to systematically organize and manage data for computer vision. This graph is specifically designed to provide unified and interoperable semantic representations of visual data, seamlessly integrated into computer vision pipelines. Furthermore, VisionKG interlinks taxonomies across diverse datasets and label spaces, promoting a shared semantic understanding and enabling efficient retrieval of images that meet specific criteria and user requirements.

Additionally, our approach enables users to better explore and comprehend relationships between entities using facet-based visualization and exploration powered by a graph data model. Graph queries, facilitated by graph storage, can be employed to create declarative training pipelines from merged computer vision datasets, providing a convenient way to navigate and investigate patterns among interlinked visual datasets such as KITTI [15], MS-COCO [31], and Cityscapes [7]. Moreover, VisionKG enhances flexibility in terms of data representation and organization, ensuring rapid and effortless access to essential visual data information, thereby supporting developers and users in constructing computer vision pipelines conveniently and efficiently.

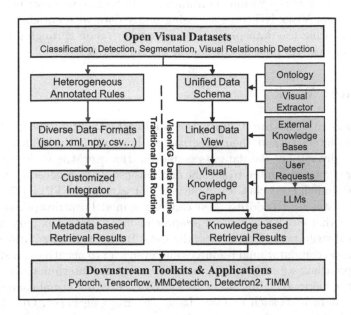

Fig. 1. Differences between VisionKG- and traditional-Data Pipelines

As illustrated in Fig. 1, VisionKG is constructed following the Linked Data principles [3], adhering to the FAIR [51] and open science guidelines [5], and encompasses a large range of data sources. These sources have been defined and maintained by the research community, as they are widely used and have a significant impact on the development of VRSs. Their popularity ensures that they will be updated frequently and extended regularly. This makes VisionKG a valuable resource for researchers and developers who require access to the latest, high-quality image data with enriched semantics. Our main contributions are summarized as follows:

- We provide a unified framework for representing, querying, and analyzing visual datasets. By aligning different taxonomies, we minimize the inconsistencies among different datasets.
- Datasets interlinked in VisionKG are made accessible through standardized SPARQL queries, available via both a web user interface and APIs.
- We demonstrate the advantages of VisionKG through three use cases: composing visual datasets with unified access and taxonomy through SPARQL queries, automating training and testing pipelines, and expediting the development of robust visual recognition systems.
- Currently, VisionKG comprises 617 million RDF triples that describe approximately 61 million entities from 37 datasets, covering four popular computer vision tasks.

The remainder of the paper is structured as follows: Sect. 2 discusses related work. Section 4 presents the detailed steps to enforce the FAIR principles within VisionKG that follow the Linked Data publishing practice. Section 3 describes the infrastructure of the VisionKG framework. In Sect. 5, we describe the example use cases for VisionKG, e.g., accessing image data with enriched semantics, thereby enhancing the data pipeline for computer vision through standardized SPARQL queries. We present our conclusions in Sect. 6.

2 Related Work

Limitations in Existing Computer Vision Datasets: Modern CV models are data-intensive and their effectiveness is significantly influenced by the quality and diversity of the datasets employed. However, the majority of visual datasets are typically limited to specific domains using heterogeneous taxonomies and exhibit imbalanced class distributions, for example, KITTI [15] and MS-COCO [31] datasets. To address these challenges, model-centric approaches, such as [48,57], either employ a domain adapter or incorporate auxiliary models to discern the distribution across diverse datasets. However, these solutions necessitate additional computational resources and even lead to negative transfer. Data-centric approaches, e.g., MSeg [27], manually unify and interlink datasets, albeit at the cost of increased labor intensity. Moreover, existing visual content extractors [39] or data hubs such as Deep Lake [18], Hugging Face[1], OpenDataLab[2] and MetaVD [53] are well-established data infrastructures for organizing datasets from distinct web sources. However, these toolchains primarily rely on metadata, lacking the ability to interlink images and annotations across datasets. In contrast, our framework leverages knowledge graphs and diverse external knowledge bases, and adheres to the FAIR principles [51], enabling VisionKG to interlink and extend visual datasets and tasks with semantically rich relationships.

Knowledge Graph Technologies in Computer Vision: Knowledge graphs can augment real-world visual recognition with background knowledge, capturing semantic relationships in images and videos through external knowledge and facts [8,58]. Approaches such as KG-CNet [13] integrate external knowledge sources like ConceptNet [43] to encapsulate the semantic consistency among objects within images. Similarly, KG-NN [33] enables the conversion of domain-agnostic knowledge, encapsulated within a knowledge graph, into a vector space representation and enhances the model's robustness against domain shift. However, these methods leverage external knowledge during- or post-learning procedure, whereas our solution utilizes not only external knowledge bases but also the knowledge inside interlinked datasets to alleviate the data inconsistency and reduce learning bias. Hence, the enhanced semantics can render fruitful features for integrated datasets benefiting from the interaction between diverse visual features and external knowledge. Similarly, the approach proposed in [14] and

---

[1] https://huggingface.co/docs/datasets/index.
[2] https://github.com/opendatalab/opendatalab-python-sdk.

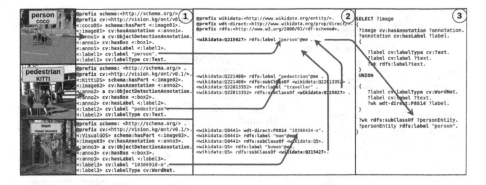

Fig. 2. FAIR for Visual Data Assets

[36] make use of Wikidata [46] to enable and interlink annotations for the ImageNet [25] dataset. Benefiting from that external knowledge and facts, the data
quality has been improved, although these approaches are labor-intensive and
primarily target a specific dataset. The reusability of these approaches with
other extensive visual datasets, such as OpenImages [26] and Objects365 [42],
and knowledge bases like Freebase, have not been investigated so far. Approaches
proposed by [20,21] use WordNet [32] noun hierarchies and bidirectional ontology engineering to integrate pre-existing knowledge resources and the selection
of visual objects within images. In contrast, our VisionKG framework utilizes
diverse knowledge bases including WordNet [32], Wikidata [46], and Freebase [4]
to enrich the semantics at both image-level and instance-level. Additionally,
KVQA [41], another knowledge-based visual dataset employing Wikidata, is
restricted mainly to **person** entities, while our work interlinks various visual
datasets and numerous entities across diverse taxonomies and domains.

3 Unified Access for Integrated Visual Datasets

This section provides an overview of the VisionKG framework and the details
of the integrated visual datasets, and we demonstrate VisionKG's capabilities
in providing unified access to those supported visual datasets with enriched
semantics, ultimately integrating various data sources with different formats
and schemas into CV pipelines seamlessly.

3.1 VisionKG Architecture to Facilitate Unified Access

Figure 3 illustrates the pipeline of creating and enriching the unified knowledge
graph of VisionKG for visual datasets. We start by collecting popular computer
vision datasets from the PaperWithCode platform[3]. Next, we extract their annotations and features across datasets using a *Visual Extractor*. We use the RDF

---

[3] https://paperswithcode.com/datasets.

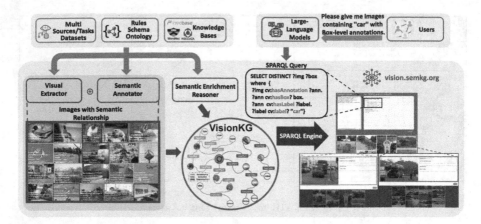

Fig. 3. Overview of VisionKG Platform

Mapping Language (RML) [10] to map the extracted data into RDF. RDF data is generated using a *Semantic Annotator* implemented using RDFizer [19]. To enhance interoperability and enrich semantics in VisionKG, we link the data with multiple knowledge bases, such as WordNet [32] and Wikidata [36]. The *Semantic Enrichment Reasoner* expands the taxonomy by materializing the labels in each dataset using the ontology hierarchy. For instance, categories like `pedestrian` or `man isSubClassOf person` (Fig. 2 ②). Based on the interlinked datasets and with the Semantic Enrichment Reasoner, users can access the data in VisionKG in a unified way (Fig. 2 ③). The SPARQL Engine maintains an endpoint for users to access VisionKG efficiently. To simplify access to the data, we also built a text-to-SPARQL parser into VisionKG's GUI to translate user requests from natural language into SPARQL using OpenAI APIs.

Moreover, VisionKG offers a web interface that allows users to explore queried datasets, such as visualizing their data distribution and their corresponding annotations (https://vision.semkg.org/statistics.html).

3.2 Linked Datasets and Tasks in VisionKG

As of November 2023, VisionKG integrates the 37 most commonly used visual datasets, across the tasks for visual relationship detection, image classification, object detection, and instance segmentation. Table 1 provides an overview of the datasets, images, annotations, and triples integrated into VisionKG. In total, it encompasses over 617 million triples distributed among these visual tasks. To enhance the effectiveness of our framework for image classification, we have integrated both large benchmark datasets, such as ImageNet [9], as well as smaller commonly used datasets, like CIFAR [24]. The diversity of covered datasets enables users to quickly and conveniently validate the effectiveness of learning systems, thus avoiding extra laborious work. As shown in Fig. 4, ImageNet comprises approximately 2.7 million entities across 1.3 million images, dominating

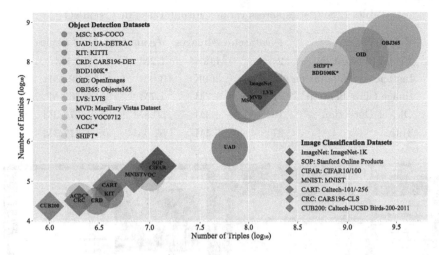

Fig. 4. Statistics of Triples and Entities in VisionKG for Object Detection and Image Classification Datasets. ImageNet [9], SOP [37], CIFAR [24], CART [16], CUB200 [47], MSC [31], UAD [49], KIT [15], CRC [22], BDD100K [55], OID [26], OBJ365 [42], LVS [17], MVD [35], VOC [12], ACDC [40], SHIFT [44]. ∗ presents that synthetic data generated by VisionKG is included.

the distribution of the classification task in VisionKG. Thanks to the interlinked datasets and semantic-rich relationships across visual tasks, users can query images with desired category distributions and contexts to tailor training pipelines for specific scenarios. For object detection, Table 1 reveals that VisionKG includes roughly 576 million triples for 50.8 million box-level annotations primarily derived from large-scale datasets like OpenImages [26] and Objects365 [42]. This variety of visual features enables users to create diverse composite datasets according to specific requirements, such as the size or the density of bounding boxes, which can contribute to mitigating biases inherent in datasets obtained under specific conditions and scenarios, e.g., to enhance the model performance in detecting densely distributed small objects, which are typically challenging to localize and recognize [29,30]. For visual relationship detection, which aims at recognizing object relationships in images, we have integrated datasets such as Visual Genome [23] and Spatial Scene [54], encompassing over 2.1 million triples across 1.2 million annotations for both bounding boxes and object-level relationships. Additionally, VisionKG includes 22.4 million triples for instance segmentation, enabling users to retrieve and reuse masks of all instance-level objects in downstream scenarios.

Table 1. Statistics across various Visual Tasks in VisionKG.

Visual Tasks	#Datasets	#Images	#Annotations	#Triples
Visual Relationship	2	119K	1.2M	2.1M
Instance Segmentation	7	300K	3.9M	22.4M
Image Classification	9	1.7M	1.7M	16.6M
Object Detection	19	4.3M	50.8M	576.2M
Total	37	6.4M	57.6M	617.3M

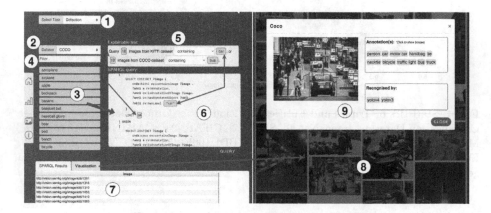

Fig. 5. VisionKG Web Interface

3.3   Visual Dataset Explorer Powered by SPARQL

Organizing multiple datasets, often in heterogeneous formats and with different taxonomies, into a single pipeline is a time-consuming task. To streamline this process, VisionKG offers a GUI for our visual SPARQL frontend, that enables users to access, explore, and efficiently combine data using either the SPARQL query language or natural language, utilizing the text-to-SPARQL parser in VisionKG. This empowers users to specify their requirements or criteria using graph query patterns in an interactive fashion. Figure 5 shows the live-interactive visual datasets explorer in VisionKG: Users can initiate their exploration by selecting a desired task, such as Detection and Classification from a drop-down menu in Fig. 5 ①. Upon task selection, the system will promptly generate a list of all compatible datasets that support the chosen task, as Fig. 5 ② illustrates.

Next, users may choose a dataset, such as MS-COCO [31] or KITTI [15], from the list. This will prompt the system to display all available categories within that dataset in Fig. 5 ③. To filter or select specific categories, users can simply enter a keyword into the text box depicted in Fig. 5 ④. This process is further facilitated by allowing users to drag and drop a category from Fig. 5 ③ to the query box in Fig. 5 ⑥. The system will then auto-generate a SPARQL query, accompanied by an explainable text in Fig. 5 ⑤, designed to select images containing the specified category. It is noteworthy that multiple categories from different datasets can be selected. Users may modify the query by removing categories or adjusting the query conditions by selecting available options from the boxes shown in Fig. 5 ⑤ or Fig. 5 ⑥. Additionally, users can also adjust the number of images to be retrieved.

Once the query is finalized, the user can click the QUERY button, and the results are displayed in a table format as seen in Fig. 5 ⑦. Additionally, users can select the Visualization tab to view the results graphically, as shown in Fig. 5 ⑧. By clicking on an image, users can access additional information, such as meta-data or annotations generated by popular DNNs shown in Fig. 5 ⑨. Overall, VisionKG offers an intuitive and efficient method for users to explore and programmatically query images across diverse datasets, thereby accelerating the data flow in CV pipelines.

4 Enforcing FAIR Principles for Visual Datasets

4.1 Making Visual Data Assets *Findable* and *Accessible*

To ensure the **findability** of visual data assets, VisionKG uses Uniform Resource Identifiers (URIs) to identify resources, including images and their associated metadata. These URIs provide unique and persistent identifiers for each resource, making it easy to find and access specific images or sets of images. Figure 2 ① illustrates one RDF data snippet linking images and their annotations in MS-COCO [31], KITTI [15], and Visual Genome [23]. This enables the use of standardized or popular vocabularies/ontologies, such as schema.org to enrich metadata associated with the content and context of image data as described in Sect. 4.2. These metadata can be used to facilitate searching, filtering, and discovery of visual content based on specific criteria, such as object category, weather condition, or image resolution as demonstrated in Sect. 3.3. In particular, VisionKG links each piece of metadata to a URI for the corresponding image to ensure that metadata clearly and explicitly describes the image they refer to, e.g., containing bounding boxes of a person, a pedestrian or a man in Fig. 2 ①. This not only enables easy retrieval and exploration of target images and their related ones based on their metadata but also ensures that more metadata can be enriched incrementally by simply adding more RDF triples linked to the corresponding image. Such desired features are powered by a triple store for storing, indexing, and querying (cf. Sect. 3).

In this context, VisionKG can significantly improve the **accessibility** of data and metadata by using standardized communication protocols and supporting the decoupling of metadata and data. Its publication practice makes it easier for the targeted user groups to access and reuse relevant data and metadata, even when the original data is no longer available. For instance, several images of ImageNet or MS-COCO were downloaded or extracted from web sources and the metadata will provide alternative sources even if the original sources are no longer accessible.

To push the **accessibility** of VisionKG's data assets even further, users can access VisionKG through a well-documented web interface and a Python API.

Both allow users to explore different aspects of VisionKG, such as the included tasks, images, and annotations with diverse semantic attributes. Additionally, many query examples[4,5] enable users to explore the functionalities of VisionKG in detail and specify queries in SPARQL patterns.

4.2 Ensure *Interoperability* Across Datasets and Tasks

To make VisionKG **interoperable** across different datasets, computer vision tasks, and knowledge graph ecosystems, we designed its data schema as an RDFS ontology as shown in Fig. 6. The schema captures the semantics of the properties of visual data related to computer vision tasks. Our approach makes use of existing and well-established vocabularies such as schema.org. This ensures interoperability and backward compatibility with other systems using these vocabularies and reduces the need for customized schema development.

The key concepts in the computer vision datasets include images, annotations, and labels. To define these concepts, we reuse the `schema.org` ontology by extending its existing classes such as `<schema:ImageObject>`, and `<schema:CreativeWork>`. For example, we extend `<schema:ImageObject>` to the `<cv:Image>` class, `<schema:Dataset>` to the `<cv:Dataset>` class. By doing so, we are able to inherit existing properties, such as `<schema:hasPart>` or `<schema:isPartOf>`, to describe the relationships between datasets and images (Fig. 6 ⓐ). Our newly created vocabulary offers the descriptors to capture the attributes of images that are relevant for training a computer vision (CV) model (Sect. 3.3), such as the image dimensions, illumination conditions, or weather patterns as depicted in Fig. 6 ⓑ.

The concept `Annotation` refers to the labeling and outlining of specific regions within an image. Each type of annotation is used for a particular computer vision task. For instance, bounding boxes are utilized to train object detection models. However, annotations are also reusable for various computer vision tasks. For example, the bounding boxes of object detection annotations can be cropped to train a classification model that does not require bounding boxes. To enable interoperability of annotations across different computer vision tasks, we developed a taxonomy for them using an RDFS ontology as illustrated in Fig. 6 ⓒ. In particular, defining the object detection annotation class as a subclass of the classification annotation enables the machine to understand that object detection annotations can be returned when users query annotations for a classification task. The cropping process can be performed during the preprocessing step of the training pipeline.

Annotations are associated with labels that define the object or relationship between two objects (visual relationship). However, labels use heterogeneous formats, and their semantics are not consistent across datasets. For instance, as shown in Fig. 2 ①, the **pedestrian** in the KITTI dataset or the **man** in the Visual Genome (VG) dataset are annotated as **person** in the MS-COCO dataset.

---

[4] https://vision.semkg.org.
[5] https://github.com/cqels/vision.

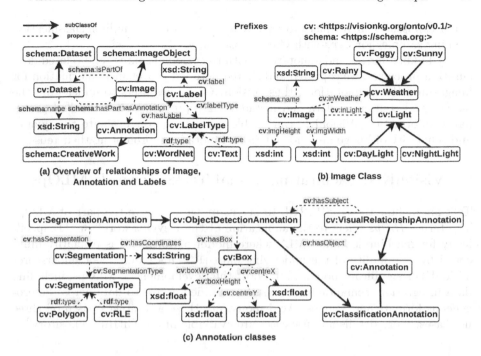

Fig. 6. VisionKG Data Schema

Furthermore, in the VG dataset, WordNet [32] identification is used to describe the label. Such inconsistencies make it unnecessarily challenging to combine different datasets for training or testing purposes. To tackle this issue, we assign a specific label type that indicates how to integrate a dataset with other existing knowledge graphs to facilitate the **semantic interoperability** across datasets. Figure 2 ② and Fig. 2 ③ exemplify how inconsistent labels from three datasets can be aligned using the RDFS taxonomies from WikiData.

4.3 Enhance *Reusability* Through a SPARQL Endpoint

To enhance the reusability of visual data assets, VisionKG provides a SPARQL endpoint[6] to enable users to programmatically discover, combine and integrate visual data assets along with semantic-rich metadata with the vocabularies provided in Sect. 4.2. In particular, users can specify SPARQL queries to automatically retrieve desired data across datasets for various computer vision tasks. More exemplary queries are provided at http://vision.semkg.org/.

Moreover, we annotated VisionKG with licensing information for more than ten types[7] of licenses associated with datasets listed in Sect. 3.2, so that users can filter datasets by their licenses to build their own custom datasets. For example,

---

[6] https://vision.semkg.org/sparql.

[7] List of dataset licenses in VisionKG: http://vision.semkg.org/licences.html.

a user can issue a single query to retrieve approximately 0.8 million classification training samples for `cars` with Creative Commons 4.0 license[8].

By linking images and annotations with the original sources and related data curation processes, we captured and shared detailed provenance information for images and their annotations, thus, VisionKG enables users to understand the history and context of data and metadata. By providing such detailed provenance information, VisionKG can enable users to better evaluate the quality and reliability of image and video data and metadata, promoting their reuse.

5   VisionKG: Facilitating Visual Tasks Towards MLOps

Talk about how to use SPARQL to access images, remove the part of MLOps The term *MLOps* refers to the application of the DevOps workflow [11] specifically for machine learning (ML), where model performance is primarily influenced by the quality of the underlying data [1]. This requirement underscores VisionKG's significant potential to boost the development of MLOps, including data integration, semantic alignment, and unified access to data across heterogeneous formats and sources. We demonstrate these advantages based on three use cases. More details and use cases are available in our GitHub repository[9].

5.1   Composing Visual Datasets in a Unified Taxonomy

Open visual data [9,26], along with their corresponding annotations, often come in a variety of structures and taxonomies. Considering that efficient data management with unified access and expressive query functionalities plays a pivotal role in MLOps, this necessitates a unified approach to organizing those visual corpora. To ensure the efficiency and reliability of developed ML models and the quality and consistency of visual content, as outlined in Sect. 4 and 3, VisionKG, equipped with a SPARQL engine, enables researchers and developers to build composite datasets in graph queries, regardless of the diversity of sources or heterogeneity of annotated formats.

Initially, users can perform queries for a subset or specific categories within a single dataset, such as images containing `car` and `van` from KITTI [15] (Fig. 7 ①). Additionally, benefiting from interlinked datasets in a unified schema, VisionKG supports users to query images from diverse sources with heterogeneous formats, such as images containing `car` from the MS-COCO [31] and `sedan` from UA-DETRAC [49] datasets, despite their differing annotation formats (Fig. 7 ③).

Additionally, inconsistent taxonomies and a vast number of categories, e.g., 1,000 categories in ImageNet-1K [9] based on WordNet [32] and 500 classes in OpenImages [26] using Freebase [4], cause a challenge to construct composite datasets across multiple sources. For instance, in developing a `person` recognition system, diverse features are required to ensure the robust performance

---

[8] https://creativecommons.org/licenses/by/4.0/.
[9] https://github.com/cqels/vision.

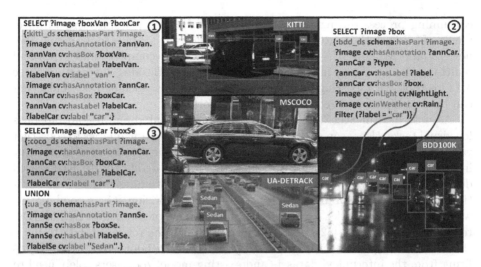

Fig. 7. Retrieving data under various conditions in VisionKG using SPARQL

of learning models. However, there are distinct definitions for the class `person` across different sources and taxonomies: It may defined either as `person` in MS-COCO [31] or `pedestrian` in KITTI [15], or even `man` in Visual Genome [23] (Fig. 2). Hence, unifying labels from distinct taxonomies is not only a time-consuming but also a labor-intensive process. To alleviate it, one approach is to construct a unified taxonomy for these datasets and mitigate the bias introduced by specific domains or similar categories. With VisionKG, we are one step closer to achieving this. Users can carry out this process with the assistance of external knowledge bases, thereby leveraging external knowledge and facts to retrieve interlinked visual content. Additionally, the unified data model that leverages RDF and knowledge graphs, along with the SPARQL endpoint, allows users to conveniently query specific parts of the datasets as desired without the extra effort of parsing and processing the entire large datasets. In this way, VisionKG enables users to query images containing the desired target categories (such as `person`) conveniently (Fig. 2 ③) rather than a more complex query (Fig. 2 ①) that covers all possible cases.

Thanks to the semantic interoperability (Sect. 4.2) of interlinked annotations across diverse label spaces, users can construct datasets from various sources with relevant definitions as desired. Along with the enrichment of semantic relationships, VisionKG provides users with composite visual datasets in a cost-efficient and data-centric manner supporting the data flow in MLOps.

5.2   Automating Training and Testing Pipelines

One of the primary goals of MLOps is to automate the training and testing pipelines to accelerate the development and deployment of ML models [1]. Automated workflows enable rapid iteration and experimentation, avoiding the time-consuming process during model development. However, despite the advancements of MLOps, there are some limitations in current MLOps tools, e.g., Kubeflow [2] and MLflow [1], such as limited support for complex data types and multi-modal data, e.g., images, videos, and audios. Besides, integrating these MLOps tools with existing diverse data infrastructures, such as Deep Lake [18], can be challenging and requires significant effort.

As described in Sect. 3.3, VisionKG boosts automated end-to-end pipelines for visual tasks. Users can start a training pipeline by writing queries to construct various composite visual datasets. As demonstrated in Fig. 3, users can query images and annotations with a few lines of SPARQL code to use RDF-based descriptions to get desired data, such as images containing box-level annotations of `car` and `person` from interlinked datasets in VisionKG. In combination with popular frameworks, e.g., PyTorch, TensorFlow, or toolboxes, e.g., MMDetection [6], Detectron2 [52], users can further utilize the retrieved data to build their learning pipelines with minimal Python code without extra effort. Benefiting from the interlinked datasets and existing model zoo, users solely need to define the model they want to use and the hyperparameters they want to set. Listing 1.1 demonstrates a simplified example code to query VisionKG data and perform training and testing for object detection. More features of automated pipelines using VisionKG are available in our GitHub repository[10].

```
1  # Import VisionKG utilities and integrated training pipeline
2  from vision_utils import semkg_api
3  from torch_model_zoo import utils
4  from torch_model_zoo.train_eval import train_eval_pipeline
5
6  def prepare_vkg_pipeline(query_string):
7      # Execute the query
8      rels = semkg_api.query(query_string)
9      params = utils.prepare_for_training(rels)
10     return params
11
12 # SPARQL query to VisionKG for images with specific objects
13 query_string = ''' SPARQL query for object detection '''
14 params = prepare_vkg_pipeline(query_string)
15 params['MODEL'] = 'fasterrcnn_resnet50_fpn'
16 train_eval_pipeline(params)
```

Listing 1.1. A simplified example of VisionKG pipeline for MLOps

5.3   Robust Visual Learning over Diverse Data-Sources

The increasing demand for robust visual learning systems has led to the need for efficient MLOps practices to handle large-scale heterogeneous data, maintain data quality, and ensure seamless integration between data flow and model development. Moreover, a robust learning system should perform consistently well under varying conditions, such as invariance to viewpoint and scale, stable performance under instance occlusion, and robustness to illumination changes. However, many existing visual datasets are specifically designed and curated for

---

[10] https://github.com/cqels/vision.

particular tasks, often resulting in a limited distribution of image data applicable only in narrowly defined situations [38]. This not only imposes unnecessary burdens but also introduces biases within learning systems and constrains the robustness of VRSs.

As discussed in Sect. 5.1, VisionKG enables users to compose datasets across interlinked data sources and semantic-rich knowledge bases, automating training and testing pipelines starting from SPARQL queries. This paves the way to support the construction of robust learning systems exploiting features from VisionKG. For instance, in developing a robust object detector, besides bounding boxes and annotated categories, other environmental situations should also be considered and incorporated as prior knowledge to improve the robustness of trained detectors, such as weather and illumination conditions. Using VisionKG, as shown in Fig. 7 ②, users can employ fine-grained criteria for retrieving images with annotations, such as querying for "images captured at **night** showing **cars** in **rainy** weather conditions". This extends VisionKG's functionalities further for exploring and constructing datasets, allowing users to retrieve useful visual features and build models that cater to various scenarios robustly, e.g., images captured during adverse weather conditions or at different times of the day. This functionality can assist users in evaluating the capability of models in domain transfer, e.g., if a detector trained on KITTI [15] is robust enough to detect **cars** in **snowy** weather conditions or handle rare categories and long-tail phenomena [56], e.g., query for a composite dataset containing specific categories which are rare in the source dataset to balance the data distribution. These features reduce the bias arising from unrelated samples and enable users to construct scenario-specific datasets covering rich semantics in a convenient fashion. In this way, VisionKG enables users to build robust visual learning systems in a data-centric manner.

6 Conclusions and Future Works

VisionKG **removes** data integration, heterogeneity and format inconsistency problems from datasets intended for vision computing tasks. It **enhances** the integrated datasets with a host of semantic annotations from knowledge bases. It **provides** a unified SPARQL query interface to this integrated dataset and **offers** powerful exploration tools including a human language interface. All these three functionalities significantly **improve** access, efficiency, and usability to visual training data based on the power of semantic technologies and demonstrating how important these technologies are for any kind of data-intensive research and industrial development. The current version of VisionKG includes 617 million RDF triples describing approximately 61 million entities from 37 datasets and four popular computer vision tasks. VisonKG is easily **extensible** and will empower communities to grow around the provided resources. It can serve as a **blueprint** for many digital data resources as the functionalities provided are generic and reusable.

Acknowledgements. This work is supported by the Deutsche Forschungsgemeinschaft, German Research Foundation under grant number 453130567 (COSMO), by the Horizon Europe Research and Innovation Actions under grant number 101092908 (SmartEdge), by the Federal Ministry for Education and Research, Germany under grant number 01IS18037A (BIFOLD) and by the Horizon Europe Research and Innovation programme under grant agreement number 101079214 (AIoTwin).

References

1. Alla, S., Adari, S.K., Alla, S., Adari, S.K.: What is MLOps? Beginning MLOps with MLFlow: Deploy Models in AWS SageMaker, Google Cloud, and Microsoft Azure, pp. 79–124 (2021)
2. Bisong, E., Bisong, E.: Kubeflow and kubeflow pipelines. In: Bisong, E. (ed.) Building Machine Learning and Deep Learning Models on Google Cloud Platform: A Comprehensive Guide for Beginners, pp. 671–685. Apress, Berkeley (2019). https://doi.org/10.1007/978-1-4842-4470-8_46
3. Bizer, C., Heath, T., Berners-Lee, T.: Linked data: the story so far. In: Semantic Services, Interoperability and Web Applications: Emerging Concepts, pp. 205–227. IGI global (2011)
4. Bollacker, K., Cook, R., Tufts, P.: Freebase: a shared database of structured general human knowledge. In: AAAI, vol. 7, pp. 1962–1963 (2007)
5. Budroni, P., Claude-Burgelman, J., Schouppe, M.: Architectures of knowledge: the European open science cloud. ABI Tech. **39**(2), 130–141 (2019)
6. Chen, K., et al.: MMDetection: Open MMLab detection toolbox and benchmark. arXiv preprint arXiv:1906.07155 (2019)
7. Cordts, M., et al.: The cityscapes dataset. In: CVPR Workshop on the Future of Datasets in Vision, vol. 2. sn (2015)
8. Cui, P., Liu, S., Zhu, W.: General knowledge embedded image representation learning. IEEE Trans. Multimed. **20**(1), 198–207 (2017)
9. Deng, J., Dong, W., Socher, R., Li, L.J., Li, K., Fei-Fei, L.: ImageNet: a large-scale hierarchical image database. In: 2009 IEEE Conference on Computer Vision and Pattern Recognition, pp. 248–255. IEEE (2009)
10. Dimou, A., Vander Sande, M., Colpaert, P., Verborgh, R., Mannens, E., Van de Walle, R.: RML: a generic language for integrated rdf mappings of heterogeneous data. Ldow **1184** (2014)
11. Ebert, C., Gallardo, G., Hernantes, J., Serrano, N.: DevOps. IEEE Softw. **33**(3), 94–100 (2016)
12. Everingham, M., Van Gool, L., Williams, C.K.I., Winn, J., Zisserman, A.: The pascal visual object classes (VOC) challenge. Int. J. Comput. Vision **88**(2), 303–338 (2010)
13. Fang, Y., Kuan, K., Lin, J., Tan, C., Chandrasekhar, V.: Object detection meets knowledge graphs. In: International Joint Conferences on Artificial Intelligence (2017)
14. Filipiak, D., Fensel, A., Filipowska, A.: Mapping of ImageNet and Wikidata for knowledge graphs enabled computer vision. In: Business Information Systems, pp. 151–161 (2021)
15. Geiger, A., Lenz, P., Stiller, C., Urtasun, R.: Vision meets robotics: the KITTI dataset. Int. J. Robot. Res. **32**(11), 1231–1237 (2013)
16. Griffin, G., Holub, A., Perona, P.: Caltech-256 object category dataset (2007)

17. Gupta, A., Dollar, P., Girshick, R.: LVIS: a dataset for large vocabulary instance segmentation. In: Proceedings of the IEEE/CVF Conference on Computer Vision and Pattern Recognition, pp. 5356–5364 (2019)
18. Hambardzumyan, S., et al.: Deep lake: a lakehouse for deep learning (2023)
19. Iglesias, E., Jozashoori, S., Chaves-Fraga, D., Collarana, D., Vidal, M.E.: SDM-RDFizer: an RML interpreter for the efficient creation of rdf knowledge graphs. In: Proceedings of the 29th ACM International Conference on Information & Knowledge Management, pp. 3039–3046 (2020)
20. Koeva, S.: Multilingual image corpus: annotation protocol. In: Proceedings of the International Conference on Recent Advances in Natural Language Processing (RANLP 2021), pp. 701–707 (2021)
21. Koeva, S.: Ontology of visual objects. In: Proceedings of the 5th International Conference on Computational Linguistics in Bulgaria (CLIB 2022), pp. 120–129. Department of Computational Linguistics, IBL – BAS, Sofia (2022). https://aclanthology.org/2022.clib-1.14
22. Krause, J., Stark, M., Deng, J., Fei-Fei, L.: 3D object representations for fine-grained categorization. In: 4th International IEEE Workshop on 3D Representation and Recognition (3dRR-13), Sydney, Australia (2013)
23. Krishna, R., et al.: Visual genome: connecting language and vision using crowd-sourced dense image annotations. Int. J. Comput. Vision **123**, 32–73 (2017)
24. Krizhevsky, A., Hinton, G., et al.: Learning multiple layers of features from tiny images (2009)
25. Krizhevsky, A., Sutskever, I., Hinton, G.E.: ImageNet classification with deep convolutional neural networks. In: NeurIPS (2012)
26. Kuznetsova, A., et al.: The open images dataset v4: unified image classification, object detection, and visual relationship detection at scale. Int. J. Comput. Vision **128**(7), 1956–1981 (2020)
27. Lambert, J., Liu, Z., Sener, O., Hays, J., Koltun, V.: MSeg: a composite dataset for multi-domain semantic segmentation. In: Proceedings of the IEEE/CVF Conference on Computer Vision and Pattern Recognition, pp. 2879–2888 (2020)
28. Le-Tuan, A., Tran, T.K., Nguyen, D.M., Yuan, J., Hauswirth, M., Le-Phuoc, D.: VisionKG: towards a unified vision knowledge graph. In: ISWC (Posters/Demos/Industry) (2021)
29. Lin, T.Y., Dollár, P., Girshick, R., He, K., Hariharan, B., Belongie, S.: Feature pyramid networks for object detection. In: Proceedings of the IEEE Conference on Computer Vision and Pattern Recognition, pp. 2117–2125 (2017)
30. Lin, T.Y., Goyal, P., Girshick, R., He, K., Dollár, P.: Focal loss for dense object detection. In: Proceedings of the IEEE International Conference on Computer Vision, pp. 2980–2988 (2017)
31. Lin, T.-Y., et al.: Microsoft COCO: common objects in context. In: Fleet, D., Pajdla, T., Schiele, B., Tuytelaars, T. (eds.) ECCV 2014. LNCS, vol. 8693, pp. 740–755. Springer, Cham (2014). https://doi.org/10.1007/978-3-319-10602-1_48
32. Miller, G.A.: Wordnet: a lexical database for English. Commun. ACM **38**(11), 39–41 (1995)
33. Monka, S., Halilaj, L., Schmid, S., Rettinger, A.: Learning visual models using a knowledge graph as a trainer. In: Hotho, A., et al. (eds.) ISWC 2021. LNCS, vol. 12922, pp. 357–373. Springer, Cham (2021). https://doi.org/10.1007/978-3-030-88361-4_21
34. Moore, B.E., Corso, J.J.: Fiftyone. GitHub (2020). https://github.com/voxel51/fiftyone

35. Neuhold, G., Ollmann, T., Rota Bulo, S., Kontschieder, P.: The mapillary vistas dataset for semantic understanding of street scenes. In: Proceedings of the IEEE International Conference on Computer Vision, pp. 4990–4999 (2017)
36. Nielsen, F.Å.: Linking ImageNet WordNet synsets with Wikidata. In: Companion Proceedings of the the Web Conference 2018, pp. 1809–1814 (2018)
37. Oh Song, H., Xiang, Y., Jegelka, S., Savarese, S.: Deep metric learning via lifted structured feature embedding. In: Proceedings of the IEEE Conference on Computer Vision and Pattern Recognition, pp. 4004–4012 (2016)
38. Paullada, A., Raji, I.D., Bender, E.M., Denton, E., Hanna, A.: Data and its (dis) contents: a survey of dataset development and use in machine learning research. Patterns 2(11), 100336 (2021)
39. Qin, A., Xiao, M., Wu, Y., Huang, X., Zhang, X.: Mixer: efficiently understanding and retrieving visual content at web-scale. Proc. VLDB Endow. 14(12), 2906–2917 (2021)
40. Sakaridis, C., Dai, D., Van Gool, L.: ACDC: the adverse conditions dataset with correspondences for semantic driving scene understanding. In: Proceedings of the IEEE/CVF International Conference on Computer Vision, pp. 10765–10775 (2021)
41. Shah, S., Mishra, A., Yadati, N., Talukdar, P.P.: KVQA: knowledge-aware visual question answering. In: Proceedings of the AAAI Conference on Artificial Intelligence, vol. 33, pp. 8876–8884 (2019)
42. Shao, S., et al.: Objects365: a large-scale, high-quality dataset for object detection. In: Proceedings of the IEEE/CVF International Conference on Computer Vision, pp. 8430–8439 (2019)
43. Speer, R., Chin, J., Havasi, C.: ConceptNet 5.5: an open multilingual graph of general knowledge. In: AAAI (2017)
44. Sun, T., et al.: SHIFT: a synthetic driving dataset for continuous multi-task domain adaptation. In: Proceedings of the IEEE/CVF Conference on Computer Vision and Pattern Recognition, pp. 21371–21382 (2022)
45. Tran, T.K., Le-Tuan, A., Nguyen-Duc, M., Yuan, J., Le-Phuoc, D.: Fantastic data and how to query them. arXiv preprint arXiv:2201.05026 (2022)
46. Vrandečić, D., Krötzsch, M.: Wikidata: a free collaborative knowledgebase. Commun. ACM 57(10), 78–85 (2014)
47. Wah, C., Branson, S., Welinder, P., Perona, P., Belongie, S.: The caltech-UCSD birds-200-2011 dataset (2011)
48. Wang, X., Cai, Z., Gao, D., Vasconcelos, N.: Towards universal object detection by domain attention. In: Proceedings of the IEEE/CVF Conference on Computer Vision and Pattern Recognition (CVPR) (2019)
49. Wen, L., et al.: UA-DETRAC: a new benchmark and protocol for multi-object detection and tracking. Comput. Vis. Image Underst. 193, 102907 (2020)
50. Whang, S.E., Roh, Y., Song, H., Lee, J.G.: Data collection and quality challenges in deep learning: a data-centric AI perspective. VLDB J. 1–23 (2023)
51. Wilkinson, M.D., et al.: The fair guiding principles for scientific data management and stewardship. Sci. Data 3 (2016)
52. Wu, Y., Kirillov, A., Massa, F., Lo, W.Y., Girshick, R.: Detectron2 (2019). https://github.com/facebookresearch/detectron2
53. Yamamoto, Y., Egami, S., Yoshikawa, Y., Fukuda, K.: Towards semantic data management of visual computing datasets: increasing usability of MetaVD. In: Proceedings of the ISWC 2023 Posters, Demos and Industry Tracks (2023)
54. Yang, K., Russakovsky, O., Deng, J.: SpatialSense: an adversarially crowdsourced benchmark for spatial relation recognition. In: Proceedings of the IEEE/CVF International Conference on Computer Vision, pp. 2051–2060 (2019)

55. Yu, F., et al.: BDD100K: a diverse driving dataset for heterogeneous multitask learning. In: Proceedings of the IEEE/CVF Conference on Computer Vision and Pattern Recognition, pp. 2636–2645 (2020)
56. Zhang, Y., Kang, B., Hooi, B., Yan, S., Feng, J.: Deep long-tailed learning: a survey. IEEE Trans. Pattern Anal. Mach. Intell. (2023)
57. Zhou, X., Koltun, V., Krähenbühl, P.: Simple multi-dataset detection. In: Proceedings of the IEEE/CVF Conference on Computer Vision and Pattern Recognition, pp. 7571–7580 (2022)
58. Zhu, C., Chen, F., Ahmed, U., Shen, Z., Savvides, M.: Semantic relation reasoning for shot-stable few-shot object detection. In: Proceedings of the IEEE/CVF Conference on computer vision and Pattern Recognition, pp. 8782–8791 (2021)
59. Zhu, X., Vondrick, C., Fowlkes, C.C., Ramanan, D.: Do we need more training data? Int. J. Comput. Vision **119**(1), 76–92 (2016)

OfficeGraph: A Knowledge Graph
of Office Building IoT Measurements

Roderick van der Weerdt[1]([⊠])[iD], Victor de Boer[1][iD], Ronald Siebes[1][iD],
Ronnie Groenewold[2], and Frank van Harmelen[1][iD]

[1] Vrije Universiteit Amsterdam,
De Boelelaan 1105, 1081 HV Amsterdam, The Netherlands
{r.p.vander.weerdt,v.de.boer,r.m.siebes,frank.van.harmelen}@vu.nl
[2] VolkerWessels iCity, Torenallee 20, 6003, 5617 BC Eindhoven, The Netherlands
RGroenewold@volkerwessels.com

Abstract. In order to support the global energy transition, smart building management provides opportunities to increase efficiency and comfort. In practice, real-world smart buildings make use of combinations
of heterogeneous IoT devices, and a need for (knowledge graph-enabled)
interoperability solutions has been established. While ontologies and synthetic datasets are available, a real-world, large scale and diverse knowledge graph has so far not been available. In this paper, we present Office-
Graph, a knowledge graph expressed in the SAREF ontology containing
over 14 million sensor measurements from 444 heterogeneous devices,
collected over a period of 11 months, in a seven story office building.
We describe the procedure of mapping original sensor measurements to
RDF and how links to external linked data are established. We describe
the resulting knowledge graph consisting of 90 Million RDF triples, and
its structural and semantic features. Several use cases are shown of the
knowledge graph: a) through various realistic data analysis use cases
based on competencies identified by building managers and b) through
an existing machine learning experiment where we replace the original
dataset with OfficeGraph.

Keywords: Knowledge Graph · Dataset · IoT · SAREF · Sensors

1 Introduction

Due to the increasing awareness of climate change, in combination with the rising
energy costs, more interest is being shown towards sustainability and efficiency of
energy usages. One area where sustainability measures can be especially effective
is in office building management, where efficiency gains for large buildings have
large impact, as compared to dealing with one house at a time [7].

To increase the efficiency of office building management, we can use data
produced in such smart office buildings. IoT sensors have become prevalent in
office buildings. Measurements from those sensors can be examined to determine

A. Meroño Peñuela et al. (Eds.): ESWC 2024, LNCS 14665, pp. 94–109, 2024.
https://doi.org/10.1007/978-3-031-60635-9_6

possible sustainability improvements, such as by training a machine learning system to discover behavioral and systematic patterns of occupation density during the week, CO_2 levels and heating values [10].

Open datasets facilitate research opportunities and experiments. Unfortunately, large and heterogeneous datasets of sensor data from office buildings are rarely available publicly. If they are available, they are either small in size or only related to one type of measurement (for example only energy consumption [9] or movement [14]). Some experiments reported in literature are performed on proprietary datasets, restricting evaluation of systems and comparing research.

As smart office buildings typically have a multitude of sensor types, realistic open datasets will contain heterogeneous data since different sensors make different types of measurements (such as temperature, or occupancy). Additionally, a successful data model will need to be able to deal with a varied and sometimes inconsistent use of time intervals. Finally, internal links and links to external data can increase usefulness of said data. Therefore, making office building IoT sensor data available as a knowledge graph addresses these requirements. Ontologies, such as SAREF [3] are already available to represent measurements as knowledge graphs. In summation, the dataset should be a large, heterogenous, and open knowledge graph.

In this paper, we present **OfficeGraph**, a large, real world knowledge graph containing measurements taken by 444 IoT devices, over 11 months, in a seven story office building. The devices are made up of 17 different sensor models, which make measurements of many different *properties*[1]. We first discuss relevant related work, further motivating the resource presented here (Sect. 2). We then describe the original data and the process of converting it to a knowledge graph (Sect. 3). The results and ways of accessing the knowledge graph are described in Sect. 4. In Sect. 5, we demonstrate the usefulness of OfficeGraph through two realistic data analysis use cases provided by building stakeholders. There, we also define and execute a machine learning experiment on the knowledge graph.

2   Related Work

This section describes related research by providing examples of what currently available IoT datasets look like, and what kind of experiments are performed with such datasets. We compare the datasets on the three requirements defined in the introduction: size, heterogeneity and openness.

Arz von Straussenburg et al. created a dataset containing (boolean) measurements of detected movement at desks in an office space, in order to create a desk sharing space [14]. In the experiment the motion sensor measurements were used to classify a desk as occupied, creating a more accurate desk sharing platform for the office occupants. Data was recorded for eleven days. Although the dataset used is open, the measurements are not heterogeneous (only motion)

---

[1] In order to avoid confusion between RDF properties and the property being measured, we will specifically refer to the former as RDF properties, and address the latter as properties.

and it is not large. Motion is also measured in OfficeGraph, and contact sensors show which doors are opened. The experiment from Arz von Straussenburg et al. can be repeated with OfficeGraph by classifying an office as occupied when the door was already opened that day.

Rafsanjani et al. also created a dataset of IoT device data measured in an office environment [10], in order to learn the "energy-use behaviors of the occupants". Occupancy data was used to determine which occupants where using devices in which rooms, to detect who was using what. Data was recorded over a six week period, however the data was not made public. Although the data used in the experiment is heterogeneous, it is not large and not open. OfficeGraph includes occupancy data as well, however since it only includes sensor measurements there is no energy consumption for devices that are used by occupants. Adjustments can be made to the experiment, by changing the energy consumption of devices into the thermostat settings of users, which can yield similar patterns as the original experiment.

The previous two experiments both required one or two datatypes (movement or occupancy and energy consumption), but more heterogeneous datasets have also already been created. Heo et al. created a dataset of 26 different devices, with data recorded for 144 h [5]. They compare various data acquisition scheduling methods for the devices with the goal of keeping the required data collection goals but minimizing the traffic needed for gather it. By scheduling the data acquisition fewer data inquiries need to be performed, therefor saving energy. The dataset has been made available online as downloadable matlab files. Although the data used in the experiment is open and heterogenous, it is not large. Since OfficeGraph also contains heterogeneous data, it can similarly be used to setup a testbed with devices. This would also allow for a longer experiment, because OfficeGraph contains a longer period of measurements.

OfficeGraph is an IoT graph with measurements data from the IoT devices, but there are also different kinds of IoT datasets. An example of such a dataset is created by Ren et al. [11]. This *traffic* dataset does not focus on the measurements made by the IoT devices, but instead it focuses on the traffic that is communicated between the devices. The dataset does not contain the measurements made by the devices, but it contains the "packet headers" of the messages send by 81 devices. Besides recording the measurements being taken by devices for 112 h, this dataset also contains the results from "34,586 experiments" with the communications between the devices, linking different parameter settings to different behaviors from the devices.

With traffic IoT device datasets experiments are performed concerning various aspects like privacy and profiling based on device behavior [2]. Event though this traffic IoT device dataset is available online, it contains different information from the IoT devices then what is collected with OfficeGraph, which puts the emphasis on the measurements made by the IoT devices. Throughout this paper when we refer to an IoT dataset or knowledge graph this will be a IoT measurements dataset or knowledge graph.

A larger dataset that is available online is the OPSD Household data dataset [9]. It contains almost five years of energy consumption information from 68 devices spread out over 11 households in a city in southern Germany. The measurements from the residential households have been used to create a knowledge graph of 36 different devices [16]. However all the information it contains about the devices is energy consumption, limiting the applications of the dataset. Experiments with OPSD that investigate the impact of semantic enrichment on machine learning performance are described in [17]. There, two version of the same knowledge graph are compared, with and without the enrichment. In Sect. 5.2, we describe how we replicate this same experimental setting with OfficeGraph to demonstrate the use of the resource.

3   Converting the Source Data

In order to create the OfficeGraph we construct a pipeline that maps a collection of JSON files to RDF based on the SAREF ontology and perform various enrichments. By making changes to the mapping template described in this section the pipeline is reusable for JSON data from different devices. We did not use any general knowledge graph creation method, such as RML, because due to the size of the dataset general knowledge graph creation methods would require a lot of memory and execution time [6]. The Python scripts used to perform the mapping process can be found on GitHub[2] and were in part based on [17].

3.1   Source Data

The original collection of measurements consists of separate JSON files, one file for each device, stored in three folders which separate the devices based on manufacturer: Airwits, Calumino and Samsung. There are 19 different models in total, Airwits and Calumino both have one type of device model, with the remaining 17 device models being Samsung devices.

All devices are located in a seven story office building in the Dutch city of Eindhoven. Over 200 different companies make use of the building with an average of around 250 people working in the offices. The data was initially collected as part of the InterConnect project[3], which has as its goal to use semantic technologies to facilitate connections between smart devices. By consistently modeling the data in the shared SAREF ontology, any device only needs to map it once, instead of having to translate it to a bi-lateral format for each receiving device.

3.2   Original Data Structure

Each JSON file consists of measurement data originating from one sensor. The objects in the JSON files containing the measurements use a total of 40 different

---

[2] https://github.com/RoderickvanderWeerdt/OfficeGraph
[3] https://interconnectproject.eu

Table 1. Three examples of mapping templates used to create the Officegraph. Bolded variables represent the data from the JSON file, italicized variables are defined elsewhere in the mapping and regular font variables are created for this specific template.

JSON Header	Relevant mapping template
"device_model_description"	*<device>* saref:hasModel **<modeltype>**
"data_room"	*<device>* s4bldg:isContainedIn **<data_room>** **<data_room>** s4bldg:contains *<device>* **<data_room>** rdf:type s4bldg:BuildingSpace.
"data_temp_c"	*<device>* saref:measuresProperty *<property_uri>* *<device>* saref:makesMeasurement <meas_uri> <meas_uri> rdf:type saref:Measurement <meas_uri> saref:hasvalue **<value>** <meas_uri> saref:hasTimestamp *<timestamp>* <meas_uri> saref:isMeasuredIn om:degreeCelsius <meas_uri> saref:relatesToProperty *<property_uri>* *<property_uri>* rdf:type saref:Temperature.

headers. Of these, 24 were identified as containing relevant information for the OfficeGraph, by discussing with experts from the domain to determine which headers contained duplicate information, and by excluding headers that were always left empty. For each of the 24 headers, mapping rules were created that produce triples that capture the data, and structure it correctly in the graph. Three examples of such mapping rules can be seen in Table 1.

3.3 Data Model and Mapping Template

Multiple ontology standards exist for smart device information, such as SSN [1] and WoT Thing Descriptions [15]. OfficeGraph is expressed in SAREF [3], a domain standard ontology specifically created to model measurements of different IoT devices. A comparison and mapping between SAREF and SSN is made in [8].

The main structure we use from SAREF can be seen in Fig. 1, for each individual device the "device template" creates triples for all consistent information about the device, such as the device type and model. For each individual measurement the "measurement template" creates triples to describe the measurement, its value, unit of measurement and timestamp. The device instance and measurement instances are connected in two ways, directly through the `saref:makesMeasurement` property, and indirectly through the `saref:Property` instance. The latter describes what has been measured, such as temperature or humidity.

In addition to the SAREF ontology we use two of its extensions. SAREF4BLDG[4], which provides classes used to describe the relation between devices and rooms, and between rooms and buildings. The other extension is SAREF4ENER[5], which

---

[4] https://saref.etsi.org/saref4bldg/
[5] https://saref.etsi.org/saref4ener/

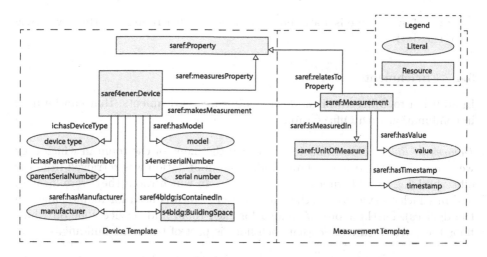

Fig. 1. Visualization of the templates used to create OfficeGraph.

provides additional classes for information about the device. As suggested in the SAREF documentation we use the OM1.8 ontology to represent the units of measure of the measurements [12].

Additionally, the following new instance and six new subclasses of SAREF classes, and two new RDF properties are introduced to enable a more detailed representation of the building data:

new instance of `saref:UnitOfMeasure`:

- `ic:people` is used in the measurement of a number of people, such as a doorcounter which counts the number of passing people.

new subclasses of `saref:Property`:

- `ic:RunningTime` is used in the measurement of time that has passed, such as the time since the last movement was detected.
- `ic:Contact` is a property related to whether or not a sensor is making contact (closed window).
- `ic:BatteryLevel` is a property related to the current percentage of charge left in the device's battery level.
- `ic:CO2Level` is a property related to the current CO_2 level measured by the device.
- `ic:DeviceStatus` is a property related to current status of the device, whether it is active or not.
- `ic:thermostatHeatingSetpoint` is a property related to the current heating setpoint of a thermostat.

new RDF properties to store different information relevant to the device:

- `ic:hasParentSerialNumber` is a property of a device, to store the Parent Serial Number, which is related to the edge device it is connected to.

– `ic:hasDeviceType` is a attribute of the device that represents the devicetype of the device.

3.4 Enrichment

In addition to OfficeGraph we also create three enrichments, that can be used in combination with OfficeGraph.

Devices in Room. Not all devices recorded the name of the room in which they were located in the original data. Additional information was retrieved from the office building to add triples for most devices in which room they were located, and in which "service zone" they are located (which is used for maintenance on the devices). Furthermore, we added for each room and service zone on which floor they were located and that each floor is part of the same building.

Wikidata Days. OfficeGraph is linked to the Wikidata graph, by matching the timestamps to the Wikidata concepts of their corresponding dates. This allows federated queries to be performed, combining information from OfficeGraph and Wikidata. For example, we can query the graphs to determine on which day a measurement is taken.

Graph Learning Enrichment. Previous research has shown that certain semantic enrichments to a knowledge graph can be beneficial for the machine learning on a graph process [17]. These same enrichments are made available for OfficeGraph, in separate files. The enrichments are:

– *Sequence links*, RDF properties that link to the previous and next measurement, taken chronologically.
– *Rounded values*, URI entities of the measurement values, rounded to function as a bucket for all similar values.
– *Timestamp buckets*, This enrichment is slightly different compared to the original semantic enrichment. Where the original was only a URI entity of the timestamp, this time it also serves as a bucket to collect all measurements taken within the same hour.

The results of the mapping process will be discussed in the next section.

4 Description of OfficeGraph

The OfficeGraph consists of 89,599,577 triples describing 14,930,478 measurements measured by 444 devices. Measurements were taken over a period of 11 months, starting March 1st 2022 and ending January 31st 2023. The resulting turtle files have a uncompressed size of 4.5 GB.

The measurements are represented with 11 different properties, which are all shown in Table 2. Additionally, the table shows which properties are measured by which device model and what the distribution of models is for the devices.

Table 2. Distribution of the models from the devices, and properties measured by those device models.

Device model	ic:BatteryLevel	ic:CO2Level	ic:Contact	ic:DeviceStatus	ic:RunningTime	ic:thermostatHeating...	saref:Humidity	saref:Motion	saref:Occupancy	saref:Power	saref:Temperature	Number of devices
Aeon Home Energy Meter				1								1
Fibaro Smoke Sensor	3			3							1	3
Hex Doorcounter Ver 1.0					14				14			14
Qubino Dimmer				1								1
R5		227					227				227	227
SmartPower Outlet				20						13		20
SmartSense Button	3			3							1	3
SmartSense Moisture Sensor	8			8							1	8
SmartSense Motion Sensor	36			36				24			24	36
SmartSense Multi Sensor	93		51	93							62	95
Z-Wave Basic Smoke Alarm	2			2								2
Z-Wave Door/Window Sensor	6		2	6								6
Z-Wave Metering Switch				2								2
Z-Wave Radiator Thermostat	1			1								1
Z-Wave Range Extender				1								1
Z-Wave Switch Secure				4								4
Z-Wave Temp/Light Sensor	2			2								2
Z-Wave Water/Temp/Light Sensor	4			4							2	4
Zigbee Thermostat	14			14		11					11	14
Totals	172	227	53	201	14	11	227	24	14	13	329	444

4.1 Timepoints

The number of timepoints at which measurements were taken differs greatly between devices, as can be seen in Fig. 2. We identified two causes of this difference: (1) some devices take measurements every time a change in the measurement is detected (Samsung and Calumino devices). Which also means devices detecting many changes will generate more measurements than the devices detecting fewer changes, for example a people counter in a busy hallway will make more measurements then a door sensor in a one person office. Other devices (Airwits devices) will make measurements at a given interval, producing a very similar amount of timepoints. (2) Some devices were turned off, or had a low battery, for a period of time, resulting in fewer overall measurements.

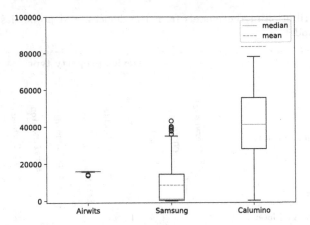

Fig. 2. Boxplots of the number of points in time in which a device has made a measurement. Different update settings result in different distributions of timepoints. One Calumino device outlier is not shown for readability, because it made measurements at 600,000 points in time.

4.2 Graph Structure Metrics

The indegree and outdegree of a knowledge graph provide information concerning the amount of RDF properties of each entities. The outdegree is the number of RDF properties an entity has, the indegree of an entity is the number of entities it is an object of. The indegree and outdegree of a graph can have big effects on algorithms that use graph traversal, such as RDF2Vec [13].

In Fig. 3 we see the indegree and outdegree of OfficeGraph. To compare it with other large knowledge graphs we use the in and outdegree as recorded by Duan et al. [4], where the authors describe multiple characteristics about large knowledge graphs, such as DBpedia or Barton. The average indegree (5.6) and outdegree (6.0) of OfficeGraph is similar to the other knowledge graphs, as is the distribution of the indegree of the entities. However, when we compare the number of entities with an outdegree higher then 10^4, the other knowledge graphs only have two entities with such a high outdegree, while OfficeGraph has hundreds. These high outdegree entities represent the devices and the high outdegree is due to the high number of measurements related to the devices.

4.3 Enrichment

Devices in Room. For 340 devices we are able to add additional room information, which results in a graph containing 2,426 triples.

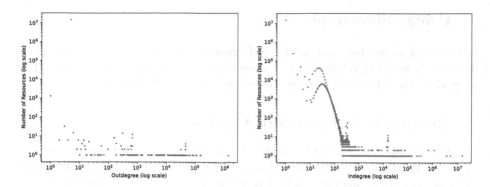

Fig. 3. The indegree and outdegree of entities in OfficeGraph, the axis use logarithmic scale.

Wikidata Days. The Wikidata days enrichment adds 8,088 triples, one triple for every hour in the OfficeGraph. We chose to make the links to Wikidata only for the timebuckets in the graph learning enrichment, since the timestamps in OfficeGraph are literals.

Graph Learning Enrichment. When the enrichment is performed with all devices the graph learning enrichment adds a combined total of 89,581,980 triples. Six new RDF properties are added for each measurement in the OfficeGraph, except for each first and last (chronological) measurement of each device, because those do not have previous or next measurements to link to.

4.4   Accessing the KG

OfficeGraph is accessible under the Creative Commons Attribution 4.0 International license, in three ways: as RDF files on GitHub, a snapshot on Zenodo and through a SPARQL endpoint.

RDF files on GitHub. A zipped version of OfficeGraph is available on GitHub[6]. Instead of one file containing the entire knowledge graph the zipped folder contains a separate file for each individual device. Each file contains all the measurements made by the device. The *devices in room* enrichment is included in a separate file.

Zenodo Snapshot. The same zip file that is available on Github is also made available on Zenodo at: https://zenodo.org/records/10245815.

SPARQL Endpoint. A Cliopatria [18] server has been set up at https://data.interconnect.labs.vu.nl to store the data, and expose it through a SPARQL endpoint. SPARQL queries can be used to retrieve information from the graph. The *devices in room* enrichment is included in the datastore.

---

[6] https://github.com/RoderickvanderWeerdt/OfficeGraph

5   Using OfficeGraph

In this section, we demonstrate the usefulness of OfficeGraph through two realistic use cases: 1) through a data analysis task for building management and 2) by performing a machine learning experiment with the OfficeGraph.

5.1   Building Management Data Analytics

The OfficeGraph can be used to highlight situations where automatization can be of use. By showing that certain situations occur it can be used as an argument for why an automatization can be beneficial. Two competency questions were created in collaboration with the building owners, to assure they are relevant for the office building.

Thermostat and Window Status. The first question relates to occupant behavior: "Is the thermostat turned down when the windows are opened in that same room?". To answer this question we queried the graph for contact sensors, thermostat settings and temperature values, from devices that are located in the same area. The results for one day in one room of these queries are visualized in Fig. 4a, the temperature (grey lines) is measured by multiple devices, each differently colored arrow is a specific window opening (arrow up) and closing (arrow down), and the dots are the thermostat temperature settings. We consider "turning the thermostat down when the windows are opened" to have occurred when the thermostat is turned to a lower value then the current temperature within 30 min after a windows has opened. Using the results from the queries, we can conclude that the answer to the competency question is: no, because the thermostat is never lowered (within 30 min) in an office when an window is opened.

Occupation and Office Climate. The second question relates to the office climate: "Is there a noticeable effect of occupants on the climate of office rooms?". We answer this question by querying the graph for humidity, CO_2 and temperature measurements, over five days: four weekdays and a Saturday. The results for one office are presented in Fig. 4b. The values have been scaled 0–100 to fit in one figure. From the figure we see that in the morning all temperature measurements consistently rise, and lower in the evening, regardless of which day it is. The humidity is not effected by time of day, nor by which day of the week it is. However, the CO_2 values only rise in the morning during the workdays, and stay (relatively) constant during the weekend. Therefor we can answer the question: yes, the office climate is affected by occupants, specifically the CO_2 values.

Jupyter notebooks are available (see footnote 6) that show the code used to create the figures and answer the competency questions.

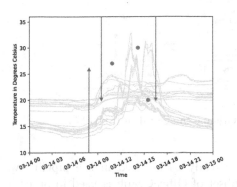 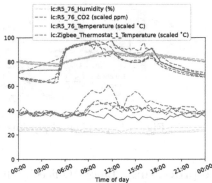

(a) Windows opening (arrow up) and closing (arrow down) with temperature and thermostat setpoints over one day

(b) Scaled measurement changes over four day in one room, dashed lines are workdays, solid line is Saturday

Fig. 4. Plots of measurements from OfficeGraph.

5.2   Machine Learning on OfficeGraph

In this section we demonstrate how OfficeGraph can be used for machine learning experiments. We perform experiments re-using the learning task and learning approach from [17] on OfficeGraph. The goal of the original experiment was to compare the effect of different IoT knowledge graph enrichments on the effectiveness of the embedding method (RDF2Vec) and representativeness of the resulting embeddings.

Experimental Setup. Figure 5 depicts the pipeline used in the experiment. The goal of the experiment is to examine the effect of semantic enrichment on the quality of embeddings learned from a knowledge graph. In Step 1 of the pipeline we have two knowledge graphs, one without the enrichment (Basic Graph) and one with the enrichment (Enriched Graph). The enrichment is described in Sect. 3.4. In Step 2 of the pipeline we train a model to learn embedding representations for both knowledge graphs. Step 3 uses the embeddings to train two classification models. By comparing the accuracy of the classifications we determine whether the semantic enrichment had a (positive) effect on the quality of the embeddings.

The classifier in the original experiment predicted whether the outside temperature at a point in time was warm or cold. This label was created by sorting the timestamps from high to low based on the outside temperature, and labeling the first 50% as warm, and the last 50% as cold. This time the results of the classification model will be based on how well it predicts whether or not a given point in time is a working day (Monday-Friday) between working hours (9–5). All code used in this section is made available through GitHub[7].

---

[7] https://github.com/RoderickvanderWeerdt/semantic-enrichment-of-IoT-graphs

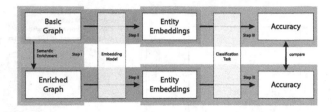

Fig. 5. Experimental pipeline. Original image taken from [17].

Pre-processing. Before OfficeGraph is ready to be used in the pipeline we perform some pre-processing. Only a subset of OfficeGraph is used in order to lower the required compute power to train the embeddings. The subset is created by selecting only the devices located on the 7th floor, which leaves us with 13 devices and a knowledge graph with 3.9 million triples.

We use the graph learning enrichment (as described in Sect. 3.4) in order to use the timestamp uris that bucket the timestamps and allow us to use these uris as entities as input for the pipeline.

We create the *entity file*, the document containing the entities in the graph we want to create an embedding for, and its prediction target (a class or value) by querying the graph.

Classification Task. The classification task we use for the experiment predicts whether a timestamp bucket occurs within working hours. To create the entity file we query the graph to retrieve all timestamp buckets, and use a script to classify each timebucket as occurring within workhours if the day is a weekday, and the hour is between 9 and 17.

Implementation. Since the goal of the experiment is not to get cutting edge results, but to perform the experiment to demonstrate the usability of Office-Graph we use the same preset hyperparameters that the original experiment used. Which means that the RDF2Vec embeddings are made with 25 random walks of length 2. And the classifier is a MLP with one hidden layer of 512 ReLU nodes. The original paper provides additional information [17].

The labels used in the original experiment were made by splitting the dataset in two even halves of warm and cold outside temperatures, therefor when the classifier would exclusively predict one of the classes, the accuracy would be 50%. This is used as a baseline to determine whether the classifier is learning something from the embeddings. For the new experiment the baseline is similarly always predicting the most prevalent class, which in this case is predicting that every hour is not a working hour. This results in a baseline accuracy of 76%.

Results. The results of the experiment can be seen in Table 3. Both the original experiment and the new experiment display the same behavior, the basic graphs score close to the baseline and the enriched graphs score significantly above it.

Table 3. Results of the experiment with OfficeGraph, compared with the results of the original experiment with OPSD.

dataset	baseline	basic graph	enriched graph
Classification (accuracy)			
OPSD [17]	50%	49.8%	**80.7%**
OfficeGraph	76.1%	73.0%	**85.1%**
Value Prediction (MAE)			
OPSD[a]	6.3	6.6	**6.1**
OfficeGraph	2.03	2.01	**1.87**

Value Prediction Task. The experiment can also be performed with a different machine learning task, such as value prediction[8]. For this we replace the accuracy comparison with a mean absolute error (MAE) comparison to evaluate the resulting prediction from the MLP.

The entity file for the value prediction task is created by querying the graph based on the property we want to predict and return all timestamp URIs and values pairs. In the situation where multiple measurements were taken in the timespan of one timestamp bucket, we take the average of those measurements.

Implementation. The MLP structure from the classification experiment is reused, but with a mean squared error loss function instead of the cross entropy loss function. The other change is the evaluation metric. MAE is the average difference between the prediction and the target value. Therefore, when using accuracy a higher value represents a more similar prediction, but with MAE a lower value represents a more similar prediction instead.

In the original experiment the outside temperature was predicted, here we predict the temperature measurements of one specific device. The outside temperature has a bigger range of measurements, with a minimum temperature of -11 °C, maximum temperature of 28 °C and standard deviation of 7.5, compared to a minimum temperature of 15.5 °C, maximum temperature of 27 °C and standard deviation of 2.4 with the new experiments. Therefor the results are expected to differ more then with the classification experiments, however, we still expect the overall behavior, where the model trained with the enriched outperforms the model trained with the basic graph, to occur.

As a baseline we use the average temperature over the entire dataset as the predicted value. This was the same baseline used in the original experiment.

Results. Table 3 shows the results from the value prediction experiment. As with the classification experiment we see that the experiment with the enriched graph outperforms the baseline and basic graph. Because the difference between

---

[8] OPSD results for the value prediction task were not part of the experiments described in [17], but are presented here to compare results.

the MAE results are closer then the classifier results we report the results of a significance test. We performed a t-test which showed that the results from the enriched graph are significantly different from the results with the basic graph ($p < 0.002$). The results with the baseline are not significantly different from the results with the basic graph ($p > 0.5$).

When we compare the results of the new experiment with the original experiment (which used the OPSD dataset) we see that in both cases the enriched graph provides the most similar predictions. The MAE is in all cases much higher for the original experiment, as was expected, due to the bigger variance and range of the outside temperature that is predicted in the original experiment.

6 Conclusion

In this paper we presented OfficeGraph, a knowledge graph containing 11 months of heterogeneous measurements from 444 IoT devices. We described the mapping process, how it applies to this dataset, and made the code available to be adapted and reused for other datasets.

Specifications of OfficeGraph are provided in terms of specific traits: 1) the properties measured by each device, 2) time points: the amount of times a devices records a measurement, 3) outdegree: the high outdegree of the device entities, 4) specific enrichments that can be added to core data of OfficeGraph.

OfficeGraph is accessible in three ways: downloadable via Github or Zenodo, and it can be queried through a SPARQL endpoint.

In order to demonstrate the usability of OfficeGraph, we described how it can be used with python (notebooks), with SPARQL queries and with machine learning experiments.

OfficeGraph is a benchmark set that can be used for future office data experiments, allowing for more representative experiments for sustainability and efficiency of energy usages.

Acknowledgements. This work is part of the InterConnect project (interconnectproject.eu/) which has received funding from the European Unions Horizon 2020 research and innovation program under grant agreement No 857237.

References

1. Compton, M., et al.: The SSN ontology of the W3C semantic sensor network incubator group. J. Web Semant. **17**, 25–32 (2012)
2. Dadkhah, S., Mahdikhani, H., Danso, P.K., Zohourian, A., Truong, K.A., Ghorbani, A.A.: Towards the development of a realistic multidimensional IoT profiling dataset. In: 2022 19th Annual International Conference on Privacy, Security & Trust (PST), pp. 1–11 (2022)
3. Daniele, L., den Hartog, F., Roes, J.: Created in close interaction with the industry: the smart appliances REFerence (SAREF) ontology. In: Cuel, R., Young, R. (eds.) FOMI 2015. LNBIP, vol. 225, pp. 100–112. Springer, Cham (2015). https://doi.org/10.1007/978-3-319-21545-7_9

4. Duan, S., Kementsietsidis, A., Srinivas, K., Udrea, O.: Apples and oranges: a comparison of RDF benchmarks and real RDF datasets. In: Proceedings of the 2011 ACM SIGMOD International Conference on Management of Data, pp. 145–156 (2011)

5. Heo, S., Song, S., Kim, B., Kim, H.: Sharing-aware data acquisition scheduling for multiple rules in the IoT. In: 2020 IEEE Real-Time and Embedded Technology and Applications Symposium (RTAS), pp. 43–55. IEEE (2020)

6. Iglesias, E., Jozashoori, S., Vidal, M.E.: Scaling up knowledge graph creation to large and heterogeneous data sources. J. Web Semant. **75**, 100755 (2023)

7. Jafarpur, P., Berardi, U.: Effects of climate changes on building energy demand and thermal comfort in Canadian office buildings adopting different temperature setpoints. J. Build. Eng. **42**, 102725 (2021)

8. Moreira, J., et al.: Towards IoT platforms' integration semantic translations between W3C SSN and ETSI SAREF. In: SEMANTICS Workshops (2017)

9. Open Power System Data: Data Package Household Data. Version 2020-04-15 (2020). https://data.open-power-system-data.org/household_data/2020-04-15/

10. Rafsanjani, H.N., Ghahramani, A.: Towards utilizing internet of things (IoT) devices for understanding individual occupants' energy usage of personal and shared appliances in office buildings. J. Build. Eng. **27**, 100948 (2020)

11. Ren, J., Dubois, D.J., Choffnes, D., Mandalari, A.M., Kolcun, R., Haddadi, H.: Information exposure from consumer IoT devices: a multidimensional, network-informed measurement approach. In: Proceedings of the Internet Measurement Conference, pp. 267–279 (2019)

12. Rijgersberg, H., Van Assem, M., Top, J.: Ontology of units of measure and related concepts. Semant. Web **4**(1), 3–13 (2013)

13. Ristoski, P., Rosati, J., Di Noia, T., De Leone, R., Paulheim, H.: RDF2Vec: RDF graph embeddings and their applications. Semant. Web **10**(4), 721–752 (2019)

14. Arz von Straussenburg, A.F., Blazevic, M., Riehle, D.M.: Measuring the actual office workspace utilization in a desk sharing environment based on IoT sensors. In: Gerber, A., Baskerville, R. (eds.) DESRIST 2023. LNCS, vol. 13873, pp. 69–83. Springer, Cham (2023). https://doi.org/10.1007/978-3-031-32808-4_5

15. W3C: Web of Things (WoT) Thing Description (2020). https://www.w3.org/TR/2020/REC-wot-thing-description-20200409/

16. van der Weerdt, R., de Boer, V., Daniele, L., Nouwt, B., Siebes, R.: Making heterogeneous smart home data interoperable with the SAREF ontology. Int. J. Metadata Semant. Ontol. **15**(4), 280–293 (2021)

17. van der Weerdt, R., de Boer, V., Daniele, L., Siebes, R., van Harmelen, F.: Evaluating the effect of semantic enrichment on entity embeddings of IoT knowledge graphs. In: Proceedings of the 1st International Workshop on Semantic Web on Constrained Things at ESWC 2023, vol. 3412 (2023)

18. Wielemaker, J., Beek, W., Hildebrand, M., Van Ossenbruggen, J.: ClioPatria: a SWI-prolog infrastructure for the semantic web. Semant. Web **7**(5), 529–541 (2016)

Musical Meetups Knowledge Graph (MMKG): A Collection of Evidence for Historical Social Network Analysis

Alba Morales Tirado[✉][iD], Jason Carvalho[iD], Marco Ratta[iD],
Chukwudi Uwasomba[iD], Paul Mulholland[iD], Helen Barlow, Trevor Herbert[iD],
and Enrico Daga[iD]

The Open University, Milton Keynes, UK
{alba.morales-tirado,jason.carvalho,marco.ratta,chukwudi.uwasomba,
paul.mulholland,helen.barlow,trevor.herbert,enrico.daga}@open.ac.uk

Abstract. Knowledge Graphs (KGs) have emerged as a valuable tool for supporting humanities scholars and cultural heritage organisations. In this resource paper, we present the Musical Meetups Knowledge Graph (MMKG), a collection of evidence of historical collaborations between personalities relevant to the music history domain. We illustrate how we built the KG with a hybrid methodology that, combining knowledge engineering with natural language processing, including the use of Large Language Models (LLM), machine learning, and other techniques, identifies the constituent elements of a *historical meetup*. MMKG is a network of historical meetups extracted from ~33k biographies collected from Wikipedia focused on European musical culture between 1800 and 1945. We discuss how, by providing a structured representation of social interactions, MMKG supports digital humanities applications and music historians' research, teaching, and learning.

Keywords: Knowledge Graph · historical encounters · MEETUPS · Historical Social Network Analysis

Resource Type: Knowledge Graph
License: CC BY 4.0
DOI: 10.5281/zenodo.7924618
URL: https://github.com/polifonia-project/meetups-knowledge-graph
Endpoint: https://polifonia.kmi.open.ac.uk/meetups/sparql/

1 Introduction

The Semantic Web community has been very active in generating knowledge from unstructured sources in domains such as scientific knowledge, social media, and digital humanities. In this regard, Knowledge Graphs (KGs) have emerged as a valuable tool for supporting humanities scholars and cultural heritage organisations [1,3,5,26]. In the EU project Polifonia[1], we study how knowledge graphs can support scholarship in music history. In this paper, we present the Musical Meetups Knowledge Graph (MMKG), a collection of evidence of historical collaborations between personalities relevant to the music history domain. Our resource aims at representing documentary evidence of social interactions in the music history domain, to support the needs of humanities scholars. This includes capturing the evidence text and decorating it with semantic entities, such as type of events, participants, temporal expressions and spatial instances, enabling the exploration of complex *historical meetups*. We build on previous work focused on conceptualising the domain of interest in the Meetups Ontology [21]. Here, we report on the work undertaken to generate a KG extracted from 33,309 biographies collected from Wikipedia focused on European musical culture between 1800 and 1945. Our work provides a structured representation of historical exchanges to enable the discovery of new insights and support music historians' research, teaching, and learning. Therefore, in this paper, we contribute 1. Musical Meetups Knowledge Graph (MMKG), a Knowledge Graph of documentary evidence of musical collaborations from ~33k biographies from Wikipedia 2. A KG generation pipeline, combining Natural Language Processing (NLP), Large Language Models (LLM), Knowledge Engineering, and Knowledge Graph Construction (KGC) techniques. The rest of the paper is structured as follows. We discuss the background and motivation for our work in Sect. 2. In Sect. 3 we illustrate the Meetups Ontology. Section 4 describes the hybrid knowledge graph generation pipeline. We evaluate the knowledge graph in Sect. 5 for its ability to answer key competency questions and via a survey with domain experts. Next, we discuss feedback on the utility and usability of MMKG from two types of stakeholders: domain experts of a Music Department and application developers of Digital Humanities tools (Sect. 6). We report on relevant related work in Sect. 8, before discussing conclusions and future work (Sect. 9).

2   Motivation

Music historians and those involved in the arts and humanities research process rely heavily on information and knowledge contained within historical manuscripts and the biographies of figures from history. A common method used for historical investigation is narrative inquiry [23] in which historical evidence is first organised into a chronicle including evidence of events in temporal order. The evidence is then filtered from the chronicle comprising exchanges with common features of interest, generating, for example, storylines of encounters of a particular location (e.g. London), purpose (e.g. music making) or participant (e.g. Elgar). Such storylines can then be used to investigate comparisons and temporal shifts, for example, why music-making is more common in certain locations during particular periods.

---

[1] http://polifonia-project.eu.

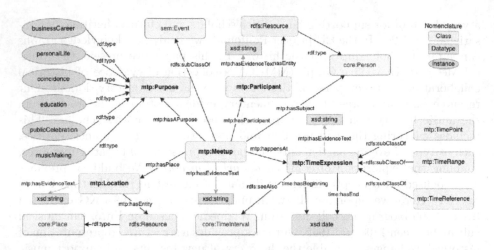

Fig. 1. Meetups Ontology.

Such forms of inquiry are highly resource-intensive in terms of extracting the chronicle of social interactions from source documents and organising them into storylines for further analysis. The development of a knowledge graph comprising the evidence of historical interactions extracted from source documents that can then be queried to create storylines (e.g. the music creation events of a composer or those occurring in a geographic location) would not only enhance the depth of historical analysis but also facilitate a more thorough and nuanced interpretation of the dynamic interplay between music and societal evolution.

A knowledge graph would also open up the possibility for Exploratory Data Analysis (EDA) [25] of storylines to reveal patterns and behaviours that might evade detection during examinations at a smaller scale. By leveraging these techniques, historians can pinpoint temporal and spatial trends, discern correlations between genres and historical periods, and unveil unexpected connections, thus enriching their grasp of the cultural and social contexts surrounding musical encounters.

3   Meetups Ontology

We use as a guiding framework the Meetups Ontology[2] (See Fig. 1) that models the elements of a historical meetup. As presented in previous work [21], the scope of the ontology is the analysis of historical encounters and collaborations of people in the musical world. These knowledge requirements are formalised as Competency Questions (listed in the ontology repository), following good practices in ontology engineering. The ontology considered commonly used vocabularies such as Time Ontology, PROV Ontology, SEM and the Polifonia CORE Ontology.

---

[2] Meetups Ontology repository: https://github.com/polifonia-project/meetups-onto logy.

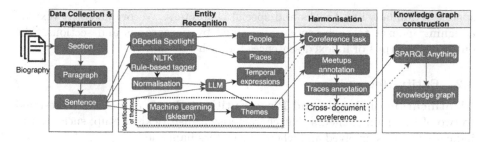

Fig. 2. MMKG construction pipeline.

Here we give a brief description of the main Meetups Ontology classes. A historical meetup – `mtp:Meetup`, is derived from evidence within a biography – `mtp:hasEvidenceText`. Mentions of at least one or more participants and places are represented by the `mtp:Participant` and `mtp:Location` class, respectively. Each mention is an entity (`mtp:hasEntity`) extracted and linked to DBpedia or Wikidata (Sect. 4 gives details on the extraction process). To represent the time when the meetup took place, we use the `mtp:TimeExpression` class. It is composed of start `time:hasBeginning` and end `time:hasEnd` dates as well as the text from where it was compiled. Lastly, the purpose of the encounter is defined by (`mtp:Purpose`) and six different subclasses specified by domain experts. These classes are adjacent but not disjoint and each meetup can be annotated with more than one purpose, namely: `mtp:BusinessCareer`, `mtp:PersonalLife`, `mtp:Coincidence`, `mtp:Education`, `mtp:PublicCelebration` or `mtp:MusicMaking`.

4   Knowledge Graph Generation Pipeline

This section describes the knowledge extraction pipeline developed to build MMKG (see Fig. 2). Our approach focuses on extracting evidence that describes historical meetups according to Meetups Ontology. We apply knowledge extraction techniques and methods for text processing to recognise, classify and link the entities that are part of a historical meetup, particularly: people, places, time expressions and themes. In what follows, we describe in detail the steps taken towards the construction of the KG.

4.1   Data Collection and Preparation

The first step of the pipeline is dedicated to the collection of data. We rely on Wikipedia and its database of open-access biographies. To obtain the list of music personalities, we queried the DBpedia SPARQL endpoint, obtaining all the entities of type `dbo:MusicalArtist`. The biographies of 33,309 personalities were collected[3] in text format[4]. Next, we prepare the text by removing empty

---

[3] Data was collected on January 2022.

[4] Meetups corpus: https://github.com/polifonia-project/meetups_corpus_collection.

spaces, redundant line breaks and special characters. We organise the text by assigning indexes to each sentence, grouped by paragraphs and sections. The output is a corpus of indexed sentences for each biography.

4.2   Entity Recognition

Identification of People and Place Entities. People and places correspond to two of the main elements that characterise a historical meetup; such entities indicate who was involved and where encounters happened.

Therefore, we use the DBpedia Spotlight[5] tool to automatically annotate mentions of people and places linking them to DBpedia resources. Once entities are extracted, we select people and places. For places, we filter the following types: `wikidata:Q41176`, `wikidata:Q486972`, `dbo:Place`, `dbo:Location` or `wikidata:Q6256`. For people, types should be one of `dbo:Person`, `wikidata:Q215627` or `dbo:MusicalArtist`. To solve a data quality issue of DBpedia Spotlight (e.g., errors due to name variation or entity ambiguity [22]), we perform an additional evaluation to verify that the entity is an instance of class `wd:Q5` and has a date of birth on Wikidata. We also filter out people whose date of birth is posterior to the subjects' date of death or whose date of death is before the subject's dob (meaning that they could not have actually met them).

The final output is a bag of entities containing mentions of person and place, grouped by sentence and biography.

Identification and Normalisation of Temporal Expressions. This task is divided into two parts: **(a) identification of temporal expressions and (b) normalisation**. To **(a)** extract temporal expressions from text, we use a rule-base tagger, based on the research by [27] and their implementation of SynTime[6]. The tool is a three-layer system that recognises time expressions using syntactic token types (part-of-speech POS tags) and general heuristic rules. Unlike SynTime, our implementation exploits the NLTK Toolkit and was developed in Python. Importantly, the heuristics rules were revised and expanded adapting them to the Meetups corpus. Furthermore, we classify each expression according to the type of dates they represent, we use the syntactic token types for this classification: *time range* (e.g., from 1959 to 1970), *time point* (e.g., exact date, 23/03/1294), and *time reference* (e.g., usually incomplete dates (19 April), later this year). The result is a list of temporal expressions (a short piece of text), for instance, "2 June 1857" (POS tag "CD NNP CD") for each sentence.

To allow temporal analysis of meetups with SPARQL, we **(b)** normalise temporal expressions into a XSD date time compliant format. We consider time as ranges, with a start and end time point. We follow the ISO8601[7] format (`YYYY-MM-DD`) using two Python libraries (`dateutil`[8] and `approx-dates`[9]). On

---

[5] DBpedia-Spotlight: https://www.dbpedia-spotlight.org/.

[6] SynTime software: https://github.com/zhongxiaoshi/syntime.

[7] ISO8601 International Standard: https://en.wikipedia.org/wiki/ISO_8601.

[8] dateutil library: https://dateutil.readthedocs.io/en/stable/index.html.

[9] approx-dates library: https://pypi.org/project/approx-dates/.

```
You are a tool that extracts time references and returns results in ISO8601 date format. I
 ↪  will provide a sentence and the target text. 1. You should decide if the target text
 ↪  represents a time reference. 2. If the target text is not a specific time reference
 ↪  return "NO". 3. If the target text is a specific time reference then estimate the
 ↪  approximate dates in the context of the sentence. 4. If the information is not enough
 ↪  to calculate a date then use {}'s biography information. 5. Check the results are in
 ↪  ISO8601 format. 6. Return the results in JSON format using two keys: start_date and
 ↪  end_date. Estimate dates after point 4. Don't return fake dates. Sentence {text},
 ↪  temporal expression {}
```

Listing 1: Prompt to normalise temporal expressions

average 65% of temporal expressions (by biography) are normalised automatically. The left 35% corresponds to expressions such as *"the next seven years"* or *"of the twentieth century"*. To cope with these cases, we make use of the LLM tool ChatGPT[10], providing as input context the temporal expression, the sentence where the expression was identified, and the subject of the biography (see Listing 1). We perform dedicated experiments tailoring the prompt to return the best results regarding quality (accurate to the expression) and coverage (number of temporal expressions normalised). By including LLMs in the normalisation process we increase the number of temporal expressions parsed to 82% on average.

The final output is a bag of temporal expressions represented by the textual evidence, start and end date and additional information such as POS tags and the way it was normalised (python library or LLM).

Improving Identification of Meeting Purpose Using LLM tools. The main element of a historical meetup is the reason for the encounter, a type of meetup, which is named as *Purpose* according to the MEETUPS Ontology. As detailed in previous work [21] our pipeline included a Machine Learning approach that follows a semi-supervised classification process, annotating each sentence in the corpus and assigning them one of the meetup types. In [21], we identified that 74% of predictions were correct, and the 26% left were either Partially Correct or Incorrect. Therefore, we explored the use of the LLM tool ChatGPT to increase the accuracy of the automatic classification. We followed a zero-shot learning approach meaning we provided as input the piece of text to analyse, and the list of classes. We ask the tool to return the two classes that better describe the meetup type. The prompt (See Listing 2) was designed having three main elements. First the context of the task (line 1); the expected format output, a JSON response (line 2); and finally instructing the tool on the classification task according to the set list of classes (lines 3 to 6).

For each sentence, we gather the two most probable topics of the text. For instance, the text: *'His father, William Henry Elgar (1821–1906), was raised in Dover and had been apprenticed to a London music publisher.'* will be classified as follows:

---

[10] ChatGPT: https://openai.com/product.

1. "Music making"; the explanation being "The sentence mentions a music publisher, indicating a connection to music making"; and
2. "Personal life"; the given explanation is "The sentence also provides information about the personal life of Elgar's father".

```
1  You are a knowledge classification system that annotates sentences according to their
   ↪ main topic.
2  Respond in json format using the following keys: thm_type_1, thm_type_2,
   ↪ thm_explanation_1 and thm_explanation_2.
3  The value for thm_type_1 is the first most probable topic, use only one of the
   ↪ following keys: ['Music making', 'Business meeting', 'Personal life',
   ↪ 'Coincidence', 'Public celebration', 'Education'].
4  The value for thm_type_2 is the second most probable topic, use only one of the
   ↪ following keys: ['Music making', 'Business meeting', 'Personal life',
   ↪ 'Coincidence', 'Public celebration', 'Education'].
5  The value for thm_explanation_1 should be a short explanation for the topic in
   ↪ thm_type_1. Less than 100 characters.
6  The value for thm_explanation_2 should be a short explanation for the topic in
   ↪ thm_type_2. Less than 100 characters.
```

Listing 2: Prompt to classify sentences according to the meetup type (purpose)

We sampled 83 sentences and asked three annotators to verify the accuracy of the *purpose* generated. We compared these manual annotations with the results of the automatic extraction using the Machine Learning (ML) approach, and the Large Language Model (LLM). Table 1 displays the results in terms of Precision. Using LLM tools leverages the classification of text, increasing its precision to 85% (on average).

Table 1. Classification results. Comparison ML and LLM Precision @ 1 and 2

	# Sentences	Machine Learning (ML) prediction		LLM prediction	
		Precision @ 1	Precision @ 2	Precision @ 1	Precision @ 2
Edward Elgar	56	0.34	0.64	0.45	0.73
Yehudi Menuhin	11	0.36	0.45	0.55	0.82
Clara Butt	16	0.69	0.75	0.88	1
	83	0.46	0.62	*0.62*	*0.85*

The output of this task is a list of sentences grouped by paragraph, each with two of the most probable meetup types. Since we use LLM tools and the API to obtain the results. We decided to keep results from the ML approach when it was not possible to query the tool and obtain an LLM response; this is reflected in the ontology using the `mtp:hasSourcePurpose` attribute.

4.3 Harmonisation

Coreferences. While the entity identification task identifies named entities, there are also mentions of people and places that are not always automatically identified by DBpedia Spotlight, this happens when such mentions are implicit, in the form of noun phrases or pronouns. For example, people referenced in the text as he or she. To maximise the identification of entities we perform a Coreference Resolution (CR) task, finding entities and their coreference mentions [16] and linking them to DBpedia or Wikipedia resources.

We use the spaCy library *coreferee*[11]. The library receives as input a paragraph text, then it identifies the entities' mentions (person or a place) and groups them into chains of mentions. We use the coreference chains to verify that an entity is part of the bag of entities in a sentence. New entities are added when implicit mentions are listed in the chain. The final output is a dataset of sentences, each with an extended bag of entities that now includes coreferent mentions.

Identification of Historical Meetups. At this stage, we have a dataset of sentences, each of them including zero or more entity types (people, place, temporal expressions and meetup type). However, a *historical meetup* can be described in consecutive sentences, having complementary information. In this step, we harmonise the data by joining adjacent sentences representing the same social interaction.

To identify historical meetups, we built an algorithm that traverses adjacent sentences, incrementally (see Listing 3) and applies a set of heuristics. The method checks the sentence being evaluated (A) and the previous sentence (B). The algorithm starts comparing if A has all elements of a meetup: time, place and person (all sentences have a purpose annotation), and then applies the following rules:

- If sentence A does not have time but its place is the same as B's place then sentence A inherits B's time (line 6).
- On the contrary, if sentence A does not have a place but its time is the same as B's time then sentence A inherits B's place (line 7).
- If sentence A does not have a person (participants) but its time is the same as B's, and A's place is the same as B's, then sentence A inherits B's people (line 8).
- Finally, if A does not have time and place, but its person is the same as B's, then A inherits B's entities (line 9).

In any case, the algorithm verifies that whenever an entity type is missing, it can be complemented by the previous sentence given that it complies with having the same participants, place or time accordingly. If A has all the elements, whether complemented by B or not, then it is considered a meetup (line 10).

The second part of the algorithm checks whether sentence B complements sentence A:

---

[11] Coreferee a spaCy library: https://spacy.io/universe/project/coreferee/.

- If all elements of A are the same as B, sentences describe the same evidence and, consequently, can be considered the same meetup (line 11).
- Other cases include when A and B have the same entity, and B lacks the other two: 1. Line 13 describes the case of equal A's and B's time but B lacking person and place, 2. line 14 same person, but B having no time or place, and finally, 3. line 15 the same place but B having no person or time.

For instance, the evidence *"His only formal musical training beyond piano and violin lessons from local teachers consisted of more advanced violin studies with Adolf Pollitzer, during brief visits to London in 1877-78."* has all entity types. People participating (Elgar and Adolf), a location (London) and a date (1877-18), meeting conditions at line 10. We can mention an example of adding context thanks to the coreference task. Sentences (B) *"Dessay had collaborated frequently with Michel Legrand in concerts."* and (A) *"In May 2009, she dedicated two concerts of songs written by him in Toulouse."* represent a meetup. Sentence A satisfies conditions in line 11 (having all the elements of a meetup). And in line 13, B lists the same people but no time or place entities. Therefore, sentences A and B can be joined in a single meetup.

Importantly, when one of the entity types is not present we annotate the evidence as *historical trace*. This type of evidence can be useful to complement social analysis. For example, the sentence *"While in France, he visited his fellow composer Frederick Delius at his house at Grez-sur-Loing."* describes how Edward Elgar and Frederick Delius met in France. However, it does not indicate the date when it took place. This information is still important if we want to answer questions such as the places he visited or the people he met throughout his life.

```
1    A = aSentence() # the current sentence being analysed
2    B = previousSentence() # the previous sentence
3    # place -> all place entities
4    # person -> all people entities
5    # time -> all temporal expressions
6    if [!]A.time & A.place == B.place -> A.time = B.time
7    if [!]A.place & A.time == B.time -> A.place = B.place
8    if [!]A.person & A.time == B.time & A.place == B.place -> A.person = B.person
9    if [!]A.time & [!]A.place & A.person == B.person -> A.time = B.time & A.place = B.place
10   if A.time & A.place & A.person -> A = meetup
11   if A.time = B.time & A.place = B.place & A.person = B.person
12      -> meetup = A + B # sentence A and B have the same entities, can be considered a
         ↪ meetup
13   if A.time = B.time & [!]B.person & [!]B.place or
14      A.person = B.person & [!]B.time & [!]B.place or
15      A.place = B.place & [!]B.person & [!]B.time
16      -> meetup = A + B # A + B have complementary entities and can be considered a
         ↪ meetup
```

Listing 3: Historical meetups identification

The output is a dataset that contains the text (typically a sentence or a set of sentences), and the list of entities that account for a meetup. The results are stored in CSV files, grouped by biographies. This dataset is ready to be transformed into the MMKG in the following step.

4.4 Knowledge Graph Construction

The KG was constructed using the CSV files resulting from the process described so far and applying the Meetups ontology described in Sect. 3. We use SPARQL Anything [2] and design CONSTRUCT mappings, to create triples from each biography. MMKG contains data from 33,309 artists' biographies, 16,748 of which have at least one historical meetup. The KG describes a total of 45,812 historical meetups. The meetups mention 49,170 people involved in different encounters. So far, the historical meetups gathered around 7,107 places and 51,120 time expressions. The KG is currently published in Turtle and N-quads RDF format and available in the MMKG GitHub repository.

5 MMKG Evaluation

We evaluate MMKG by implementing queries to answer the competency questions of the Meetups Ontology and by means of a survey with domain experts.

5.1 Answering CQs

The knowledge requirements, which are the foundation of the Meetups ontology design, were formalised as a list of Competency Questions (CQs) in [21]. In this section, we take as guidelines these CQs (Table 2[12]) and design a series of SPARQL queries[13] to evaluate that the MMKG data meets the knowledge requirements.

Table 2. List of Competency Questions (CQs).

#	Competency Questions	Entity focus
1	What places did musician Z visit in his/her career?	Place
2	Where did musician X and performer Y meet?	where?
3	Why did musician X and performer Y meet?	Purpose /
4	What is the nature of the event (a celebration, a festival, a private event, a performance, accidental)?	Meetup type why?
5	When did musician X and performer Y meet?	Temporal
6	Did musician X and performer Y ever meet?	when?
7	Who other musicians were working at the same time?	Participants
8	What was the composer's network?	who?

---

[12] Due to space constraints, Table 2 displays a summary of the CQs.
[13] Queries and results obtained available in the MMKG repository - queries folder https://github.com/polifonia-project/meetups-knowledge-graph/.

CQs Focus on Place Dimension. One of the main requirements is about the places where people met or visited. We take the example of the German pianist Clara Schumann and build a query (Figs. 3a and 3b) that retrieves the list of places she visited during her life (16 places in total). To answer question 2 we build a query that lists all the places she and Joseph Joachim shared, evidence shows that they met in Germany and the UK.

```
SELECT DISTINCT ?resource ?placeLabel
WHERE {
    VALUES ?subject { <http://dbpedia.org/resource/Clara_Schumann> }
    ?s mtp:hasSubject ?subject ; mtp:hasType ?type .
    FILTER (regex ( str (?type), str ("HM") ) ) .
    ?s  mtp:hasPlace ?aPlaceIRI .
    ?aPlaceIRI mtp:hasEntity ?resource .
    ?resource rdfs:label ?placeLabel . }
```

resource	placeLabel
http://dbpedia.org/resource/Leipzig	Leipzig
http://dbpedia.org/resource/Berlin	Berlin
http://dbpedia.org/resource/Dresden	Dresden
http://dbpedia.org/resource/London	London

(a) Query: Places visited by an artist   (b) Results: Places visited by an artist

Fig. 3. Illustrative example for CQs focused on place entities

CQs Focus on Purpose. Following the previous example, we can expand the queries to include the meetup's purpose and answer questions 3 and 4. Evidence shows that Clara and Joachim's meetings mainly related to "Music Making". For instance, *"In October-November 1857, Schumann and Joachim went on a recital tour to Dresden and Leipzig"*.

CQs Focus on Temporal Expressions. In the previous example, we have textual evidence that indicates the time Clara and Joachim met in 1857. This information is available in the MMKG and can be queried in the form of start and end dates (Figs. 4a and 4b).

```
SELECT DISTINCT ?text ?nrmlsdValueStart ?nrmlsdValueEnd ?timeEvi
WHERE {
    VALUES ?subject { <http://dbpedia.org/resource/Clara_Schumann>
    VALUES ?participant { <http://dbpedia.org/resource/Joseph_Joac
    <https://www.wikidata.org/wiki/Q159976> }
    ?s mtp:hasSubject ?subject ; mtp:hasType ?type .
    FILTER (regex ( str (?type), str ("HM") ) ) .
    ?s mtp:happensAt ?timeExpression_IRI .
    ?timeExpression_IRI a mtp:TimeExpression ;
    OPTIONAL { ?timeExpression_IRI time:hasBeginning ?nrmlsdValu
      time:hasEnd ?nrmlsdValueEnd ; mtp:hasEvidenceText ?timeEvide
```

```
<result>
  <binding name='text'>
    <literal>In October-November 1857, Schumann and Joachim went
      on a recital tour to Dresden and Leipzig.</literal>
  </binding>
  <binding name='nrmlsdValueStart'>
    <literal datatype='http://www.w3.org/2001/XMLSchema#date'>
      1857-01-01</literal>
  </binding>
  <binding name='nrmlsdValueEnd'>
    <literal datatype='http://www.w3.org/2001/XMLSchema#date'>
      1857-12-31</literal>
  </binding>
  <binding name='timeEvidenceText'>
    <literal>1857</literal>
  </binding>
</result>
```

(a) Query: Date of the meetup   (b) Results: Date of the meetup

Fig. 4. Illustrative example for CQs focused on temporal expressions

CQs Focus on Person Dimension. We follow the previous example and build queries that return the list of people Clara met (17 people in total) (Fig. 5a). Importantly, we can expand this query to include all the artists Clara met (a total of 50 people), even if the evidence does not provide data on the time or place they met (a historical trace); results are shown in Fig. 5b.

(a) Query: Meetups and participants	(b) Results: All people she met

Fig. 5. Illustrative example for CQs focused on people

Importantly, we produced SPARQL queries to extract statistics about the top visited places, people met, years of activity and purpose of meetings for each artist. These queries can be found in the MMKG repository[14]

5.2   Feedback Questionnaire from Domain Experts

In a survey with 12 domain experts from the Music Department of our University, we evaluated the value to users of MMKG[15]. Participants were either/or researchers (75%), musicians (33%), educators (33%), and historians (25%), with a significant 91.7% reporting daily engagement with music-related content. All the respondents agreed on the value of documenting musical history encounters, considering them either important (50%) or very important (50%). All respondents reported not being aware of any tool/database to store and organise historical music encounters. We asked about the value of specific elements of the ontology. All respondents rated the importance of documenting the people involved in musical encounters as "very important" (Fig. 6). The place and time of the encounter were rated very important and important by 83.33% and 16.67%, respectively. Responses were varied for the purpose of encounters: 58.34% rated it as "Very Important", 33.33% as "Important", and 8.33% as "Moderately" important.

Business meetings and music-making have been highly valued throughout music history, which received over 83% of the rating as "very important" and "important, respectively". The survey also revealed that 75% of the respondents respectively rated personal life and public celebration as "very important" and "important" purpose for musical encounters. While education and coincidence were rated the same by 66.67%.

In addition, all participants agree on the utility of exploring the geographical, temporal, and thematic proximity of subjects, even outside direct evidence of documented encounters. Finally, the usefulness of knowledge graphs in teaching music history is largely (75%) acknowledged by experts.

---

[14] Stats   queries: https://github.com/polifonia-project/meetups-knowledge-graph/blob/main/queries/top-entities.sparql.

[15] Complete results can be found at this address: https://docs.google.com/document/d/1PGknESmJm4f_-QwSdebTuiHIZ3bMaBrtcs4-9AKLPcc/edit?usp=sharing.

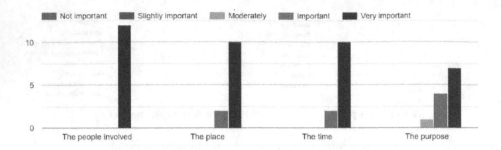

Fig. 6. Dimensions in musical encounters.

6 Using the MMKG

In this section, we discuss the value of the MMKG from the perspective of both domain experts in their research and exploration and developer communities leveraging the data to build novel applications and exploration tools.

6.1 Music Historians and Domain Experts

The MMKG, as described in Sect. 2, offers an exploration of historical information at a macro-scale using EDA principles, in ways not possible when simply studying the biographies of individual musical figures.

This is especially significant for the period before globalisation through broadcasting and recording technologies, when it is often much less obvious how musical ideas and influences were disseminated. The MMKG opens the possibility of identifying points of cultural and musical exchange that have been unsuspected till now, revealing patterns of travel and contact, and intersections of musical figures identified by place and time. For example, from the biography of a composer, the researcher might generate a visualisation that reveals meetings with another musician with whom they were not previously known to have been in contact. This may shed new light on music the composer subsequently wrote, or on a performer's subsequent repertoire choices. Similarly, a previously unknown meeting of a musician with an instrument maker might turn out to be related to the development of a new or modified instrument, or the composition of a new piece for a particular type of instrument. The knowledge graph may also reveal a cluster of meetings in a particular place, prompting the researcher to develop new research questions exploring that place as musically or culturally significant.

Traditional humanities research methods are based on linear investigations in which evidential sources are aligned to research questions and interrogated within predetermined contexts. In providing a non-linear vision of accumulated data capable of stimulating new and often unconsidered ideas, MMKG both complements and expands this process. It offers a different set of perspectives on which to base the evaluation and ordering of data, to shape research questions and to determine the direction and priorities of a research project.

6.2 Developer Communities

In Sect. 2 we give an overview of some of the principles of Exploratory Data Analysis, within the context of the MMKG project. These are facilitated by the use of carefully selected and formatted attributes and annotations that allow developers to leverage and integrate the data into data-driven visualisations and applications. These annotations can be used across various mapping and time-display technologies, libraries, and software. Geolocation data, in particular, enables seamless integration with mapping libraries, Geographical Information System (GIS) software, and advanced geoprocessing routines. Common JavaScript web mapping libraries such as Leaflet[16] or Openlayers[17] can be used to render points or clusters on maps, making use of additional annotations for nuanced visualisations such as colour-coding by theme. The data is also adaptable for integration into GIS software, allowing intricate geoprocessing and geo-analysis tasks such as creating thematic heatmaps, plotting paths, implementing advanced clustering algorithms, and executing task-specific querying and analysis processes. Temporal data offers similar visualisation techniques through the use of timeline displays, frequency distribution analysis, and visual time-based search tools. Again, GIS software can also leverage this temporal information to provide advanced temporospatial geoprocessing.

Beyond academic research, the MMKG offers developers the chance to create applications in other domains such as education, archives, and exploration. MMKG's data can power interactive learning platforms, browsable archive repositories, immersive museum exhibits and exploration tools. This flexibility caters to diverse needs, showcasing KG's potential to transcend disciplinary boundaries.

Accessible through an open SPARQL endpoint, the KG seamlessly integrates into numerous platforms such as mobile apps and desktop applications. Developers can integrate straightforward HTTP calls into their application development and also build intermediary APIs, facilitating efficient data retrieval and reuse of common SPARQL queries. This accessible approach, often using standardised formats like JSON, not only streamlines integration but also promotes collaboration within the developer community, encouraging collective utilisation.

7 Resource Availability, Reusability, Sustainability

Our work on this project has been completed whilst adhering to the FAIR[18] principles. We have built the resource in a number of specific ways to ensure that the outputs are in compliance with the FAIR Guiding Principles for scientific data management and stewardship.

Resource availability for the MMKG is ensured through its presence on GitHub, providing both source data and documentation. Additionally, a permanent SPARQL endpoint is openly accessible on the web, facilitating ease of use

---

[16] https://leafletjs.com/.
[17] https://openlayers.org/.
[18] https://www.go-fair.org/fair-principles/.

and integration into various applications. Furthermore, developers can encapsulate these results as API calls, promoting sharing and collaboration within the developer community. These features contribute to the sustainability of the MMKG, ensuring ongoing accessibility, usability, and collaborative engagement over time.

8 Related Work

Below we consider related work on musical social relationships, the publishing of biographical and prosopographical data, event-based KGs and their application.

Within the musical domain, [6] presents an analysis of musical influence networks for sample-based music. In contrast, [15] analyses the MusicBrainz dataset relationship metadata to uncover how music artists influence one another.

For biographical/prosopographical data, [26] provide a linked data model to integrate biographical and cultural heritage data while [5] presents a KG of biographical information of German academics from the 16th to 18th century. [17] performs similar research but with short textual biographies about Finnish and Swedish academics. [20] extracts information from text about the historical movements of people, focusing on biographies from the first half of the 20th century and [4] presents a relational database of biographies spanning 5,500 years. [11,13,24] and [12] argue towards the adoption of Linked Data practices for the development of databases, applications and Artificial Intelligence systems based on biographies and/or prosopographies.

An Event KG is a graph where the knowledge representation is centred upon dynamic events happening in time rather than entities and relations. While [10] provides a general survey of Event KGs, [19] and [18] research related technical aspects involved in their construction KGs, such as event coreference resolution and temporal knowledge extraction from texts.

In historiography [7] and [9] present an event KG representing 690 thousand events enriched by a timeline generation system representing biographies. In [14] the available archive information of Finland's involvement in WWII is rendered as an event KG.

While relevant resources have been published in the domains as mentioned earlier, there is however evidence (Table 3) of a resource gap when presenting evidence of historical collaborations between personalities relevant to the music history domain. MMKG addresses this gap.

Table 3. Knowledge Graph comparison. P - People, L - Location, T - Time, and R - Reason; e - related to an event only, r - related to a role only.

	P	T	L	R	Description	Size
BiographySampo [13]	✓	e	✓	✗	Finnish Biographies	13.100 biographies
AcademySampo [17]	✓	e	✓	✗	Finnish university student records	27,500 student records
Event KG [8]	✓	e	✓	✗	News, focus on events	18,510 news articles
Early Modern Scholarly Career KG [5]	✓	r	✓	✗	German biographies Professional development	Two sources, # of biographies unknown
Meetups Musical KG	✓	✓	✓	✓	Music personalities	33.300 biographies

9 Conclusions and Future Work

In this resource paper, we introduced MMKG, a knowledge graph of documentary evidence of social interaction for supporting research in music history. Our work shows the potential of hybrid methods for knowledge extraction, combining knowledge engineering with techniques from traditional NLP and current LLMs tools. Future work includes studying how to improve the coverage of the geospatial and temporal annotations of the biographies, for example, tackling implicit, contextual time references. Further research regarding social iterations and network influence (e.g., musical and creative aspects) are natural directions to expand the use of the KG. A user interface for leveraging the potential of MMKG is under development in close collaboration with domain experts. MMKG and the related tools will be applied to teaching and learning content as well as scholarship of the Music Department of the OU.

Acknowledgements. This work was supported by the EU's Horizon Europe research and innovation programme within the Polifonia project (grant agreement N. 101004746).

References

1. Adamou, A., Brown, S., Barlow, H., Allocca, C., d'Aquin, M.: Crowdsourcing linked data on listening experiences through reuse and enhancement of library data. Int. J. Digit. Libr. **20**(1), 61–79 (2019)
2. Asprino, L., Daga, E., Gangemi, A., Mulholland, P.: Knowledge graph construction with a façade: a unified method to access heterogeneous data sources on the web. ACM Trans. Internet Technol. **23**(1), 1–31 (2023)
3. de Berardinis, J., et al.: The polifonia ontology network: building a semantic backbone for musical heritage. In: Payne, T.R., et al. (eds.) ISWC 2023. LNCS, vol.

14266, pp. 302–322. Springer, Cham (2023). https://doi.org/10.1007/978-3-031-47243-5_17

4. Beytía, P., Schobin, J.: Networked pantheon: a relational database of globally famous people. Available at SSRN 3255401 (2018)

5. Blanke, J., Riechert, T.: Towards an RDF knowledge graph of scholars from early modern history. In: 2020 IEEE 14th International Conference on Semantic Computing (ICSC), pp. 471–472. IEEE (2020)

6. Bryan, N.J., Wang, G.: Musical influence network analysis and rank of sample-based music. In: ISMIR, pp. 329–334 (2011)

7. Gottschalk, S., Demidova, E.: EventKG: a multilingual event-centric temporal knowledge graph. In: Gangemi, A., et al. (eds.) ESWC 2018. LNCS, vol. 10843, pp. 272–287. Springer, Cham (2018). https://doi.org/10.1007/978-3-319-93417-4_18

8. Gottschalk, S., Demidova, E.: EventKG - the hub of event knowledge on the web - and biographical timeline generation (2019). http://arxiv.org/abs/1905.08794

9. Gottschalk, S., Demidova, E.: EventKG+BT: generation of interactive biography timelines from a knowledge graph. In: Harth, A., et al. (eds.) ESWC 2020. LNCS, vol. 12124, pp. 91–97. Springer, Cham (2020). https://doi.org/10.1007/978-3-030-62327-2_16

10. Guan, S., et al.: What is event knowledge graph: a survey. IEEE Trans. Knowl. Data Eng. (2022)

11. Hyvönen, E.: Using the semantic web in digital humanities: shift from data publishing to data-analysis and serendipitous knowledge discovery. Semant. Web 11, 187–193 (2020)

12. Hyvönen, E., et al.: Linked data–a paradigm change for publishing and using biography collections on the semantic web. Biograph. Data Digit. World (2022)

13. Hyvönen, E., et al.: BiographySampo – publishing and enriching biographies on the semantic web for digital humanities research. In: Hitzler, P., et al. (eds.) ESWC 2019. LNCS, vol. 11503, pp. 574–589. Springer, Cham (2019). https://doi.org/10.1007/978-3-030-21348-0_37

14. Koho, M., Ikkala, E., Leskinen, P., Tamper, M., Tuominen, J., Hyvönen, E.: WarSampo knowledge graph: Finland in the second world war as linked open data. Semant. Web 12(2), 265–278 (2021)

15. Kopel, M.: Analyzing music metadata on artist influence. In: Nguyen, N.T., Trawiński, B., Kosala, R. (eds.) ACIIDS 2015. LNCS (LNAI), vol. 9011, pp. 56–65. Springer, Cham (2015). https://doi.org/10.1007/978-3-319-15702-3_6

16. Lata, K., Singh, P., Dutta, K.: Mention detection in coreference resolution: survey. Appl. Intell. (2022). https://doi.org/10.1007/s10489-021-02878-2

17. Leskinen, P., Hyvönen, E.: Using the AcademySampo portal and data service for biographical and prosopographical research in digital humanities. In: ISWC-Posters-Demos-Industry 2021 International Semantic Web Conference (ISWC) 2021: Posters, Demos, and Industry Tracks. CEUR-WS. org (2021)

18. Liu, Y., Hua, W., Zhou, X.: Temporal knowledge extraction from large-scale text corpus. World Wide Web 24, 135–156 (2021)

19. Lu, J., Ng, V.: Event coreference resolution: a survey of two decades of research. In: IJCAI, pp. 5479–5486 (2018)

20. Menini, S., Sprugnoli, R., Moretti, G., Bignotti, E., Tonelli, S., Lepri, B.: RAMBLE ON: tracing movements of popular historical figures. In: Proceedings of the Software Demonstrations of the 15th Conference of the European Chapter of the Association for Computational Linguistics, pp. 77–80 (2017)

21. Morales Tirado, A., Carvalho, J., Mulholland, P., Daga, E.: Musical meetups: a knowledge graph approach for historical social network analysis. In: SEMMES 2023: Semantic Methods for Events and Stories Workshop co-located with 20th European Semantic Web Conference (ESWC 2023) (2023). https://ceur-ws.org/Vol-3443/ESWC_2023_SEMMES_Meetups-CR.pdf
22. Olieman, A., Azarbonyad, H., Dehghani, M., Kamps, J., Marx, M.: Entity linking by focusing DBpedia candidate entities. In: Proceedings of the first international workshop on Entity recognition & disambiguation - ERD 2014, pp. 13–24 (2014). https://doi.org/10.1145/2633211.2634353
23. Polkinghorne, D.E.: Narrative Knowing and the Human Sciences. SUNY Press (1988)
24. Tamper, M., Leskinen, P., Apajalahti, K., Hyvönen, E.: Using biographical texts as linked data for prosopographical research and applications. In: Ioannides, M., et al. (eds.) EuroMed 2018. LNCS, vol. 11196, pp. 125–137. Springer, Cham (2018). https://doi.org/10.1007/978-3-030-01762-0_11
25. Tukey, J.W., et al.: Exploratory data analysis, vol. 2. Reading (1977)
26. Tuominen, J.A., Hyvönen, E.A., Leskinen, P.: Bio CRM: a data model for representing biographical data for prosopographical research. In: Proceedings of the Second Conference on Biographical Data in a Digital World 2017 (BD2017). CEUR Workshop Proceedings (2018)
27. Zhong, X., Sun, A., Cambria, E.: Time expression analysis and recognition using syntactic token types and general heuristic rules. In: Proceedings of the 55th Annual Meeting of the Association for Computational Linguistics (2017)

Generate and Update Large HDT RDF Knowledge Graphs on Commodity Hardware

Antoine Willerval[1,2]([envelope]) [iD], Dennis Diefenbach[2] [iD], and Angela Bonifati[1] [iD]

[1] CNRS, LIRIS UMR 5205, University of Lyon, Lyon, France
angela.bonifati@univ-lyon1.fr
[2] The QA Company SAS, Saint-Étienne, France
{antoine.willerval,dennis.diefenbach}@the-qa-company.com

Abstract. HDT is a popular compressed file format to store, share and query large RDF Knowledge Graphs (KGs). While all these operations are possible in low hardware settings (i.e. a standard laptop), the generation and updates of HDT files come with an important hardware cost especially in terms of memory and disk usage.

In this paper, we present a new tool leveraging HDT, namely k-HDTDiffCat, that allows to a) reduce the memory and disk footprint for the creation of HDT files and to b) remove triples from an existing HDT file thus allowing updates.

We show that in a system with 8 times less memory, we can achieve HDT file generation in almost the same time as existing methods. Moreover, our system allows to remove triples from an HDT file catering for updates. This operation is possible without the need to uncompress the original data (as it was the case in the original HDT file) and by keeping low memory consumption.

While HDT was suited for storing, exchanging and querying large Knowledge Graphs in low hardware settings, we also offer the novel functionality to generate and update HDT files in these settings. As a side effect, HDT becomes an ideal indexing structure for large KGs in low hardware settings making them more accessible to the community.

In particular, we show that we can compress the whole Wikidata graph, which is the largest knowledge graph currently available, on a standard laptop with 16 GB of RAM as well as generate Wikidata indexes that are at most 24 h behind the live Wikidata endpoint.

Keywords: HDT · HDTq · HDTCat · HDTDiff · LUBM · Wikidata · Update

1 Introduction

RDF Knowledge Graphs (KGs) are growing in size, storing and querying them becomes increasingly challenging. For example, the amount of triples in the Wikidata KG increased from 18 billion to 19.2 billion in the last year. Moreover,

A. Meroño Peñuela et al. (Eds.): ESWC 2024, LNCS 14665, pp. 128–144, 2024.
https://doi.org/10.1007/978-3-031-60635-9_8

serving large graphs can easily become expensive in terms of hardware resources, making them inaccessible for consumers in low hardware settings, thus impeding the democratization of the Web.

To overcome this problem, the HDT file format was created [10]. HDT uses succinct data structures [13] to store RDF graphs. The aim of succinct data structures is to compress the underlying dataset as much as possible while preserving the query capabilities. In the case of HDT, it is possible to compress RDF graphs to similar sizes as a GZIP compressed NTriple file while allowing to search for triple patterns at a speed that is in the same order of magnitude of common triple stores. As a concrete example, it is possible to compress the whole Wikidata KG to an HDT file of 300 GB and have a triple pattern access that is equal or faster then the one of the public Wikidata query service.

This explains why HDT is used as the backbone of past projects where scalability becomes a problem. For instance in the LOD laundromat [2] in order to expose datasets in the LOD cloud, for question-answering engines [3] and as an indexing structure of Linked Data Fragments [18]. HDT was also used to store the 28 billion triples dump of the LOD cloud called LOD-a-lot [8].

HDT is used to provide large data, for example in LOD laundromat, providing an infrastructure to clean and serve all datasets in the LOD cloud and LOD-a-lot [8], an index of the whole Linked Open Data cloud published as HDT. For the question answering system WDAqua-core1 [5], a question answering system that allows to query some of the largest datasets in the LOD cloud, namely: DBpedia, Wikidata, MusicBrainz and DBlp. But HDT is mostly use for triple stores and RDF graph querying like Linked Data Fragments [18] to query the Web of data on Web-scale by moving the query load from servers to clients, qEndpoint [19] a SPARQL endpoint that uses HDT as an underlying index and OSTRICH [17], a hybrid archiving approach for RDF (Resource Description Framework) graphs. It is designed to provide efficient triple pattern queries for different versioned query types while keeping storage requirements reasonable.

The key contribution of the paper is k-HDTDiffCat, a new method to combine and delete triples from one or multiple HDT files into a new one. Unlike HDTCat [4], a method to combine two HDT files into one HDT file, our method allows to combine an arbitrary number of HDT files while keeping a small time overhead per added HDT file. It allows to create big HDT files by splitting the HDT generation into small HDT files. The small HDT files are then merged with k-HDTDiffCat into one HDT file. Moreover k-HDTDiffCat allows also to eliminate triples from already generated HDT files.

With provide experiments showing the efficiency of our method compared with previous implementation in systems with few resources.

While storing, exchanging and querying HDT files is easy in low hardware settings, this is not the case for the generation and updates. The tool presented in this paper fills exactly this gap, i.e. allowing to efficiently generate and update HDT files in low hardware settings. The paper is organized as follows.

We will first explain the HDT internals in Sect. 2, in Sect. 3 we discuss the related works, in Sect. 4 we present our tool, in Sect. 5 we present our experimental results and within Sect. 6 a presentation of the open source repository where to find our tool with a command line to use it.

2   HDT Internals

Before describing the related works and our contribution, we describe on a high level the internals of a HDT file. HDT [10,11] is a file format to compress an RDF graph while keeping the ability to query over it by triple patterns, it is composed of 3 components. The header component, the dictionary component and the triples component.

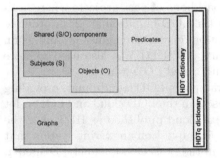

Fig. 1. The different HDT and HDTq components in the dictionary part.

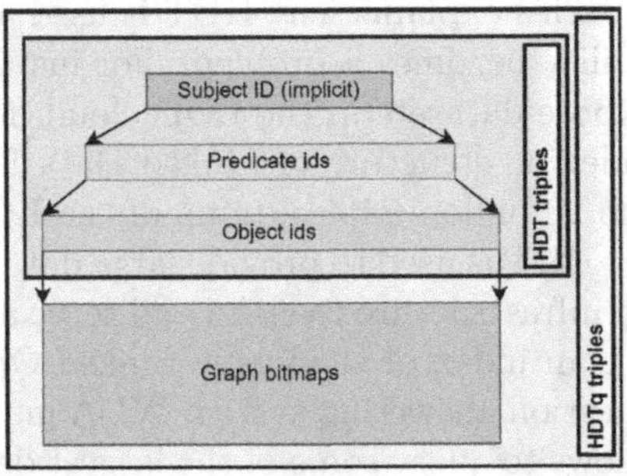

Fig. 2. The different HDT and HDTq components in the triples part.

Header. It contains metadata information about the HDT file like the number of RDF terms, the raw size, the number of distinct subjects, etc. Due to the trivial aspect of this component, we won't consider it in the future sections.

Dictionary (Fig. 1). It contains a mapping between the terms in the RDF graph (i.e. URIs, Literals and Blank Nodes) and numerical IDs.

The default dictionary is called Four Section Dictionary (FSD), previous HDT Dictionary [10] is composed of four sections: Shared (SH), Subjects (S), Predicates (P) and Objects (O). The Shared section contains all terms that appear both as a subject and as an object inside the graph. The subject section contains terms that appear exclusively in the subject position. Similarly with the object section, only containing the term appearing at the object position. The predicate section contains all terms contained in the predicate position. In each section the terms are sorted lexicographically and compressed using Front-Coding [21] which is a technique based on differential compression over the string prefixes.

Other dictionary implementations exist called Multiple Section Dictionaries (MSD) [16]. These versions are based on the FSD above, but are splitting the literals in the object section by data-types or language. This saves space by grouping the literals with the same datatypes and allows quick retrieval of the literals of a given datatype or language while allowing a fast lookup of a datatype or language using the literal numerical ID.

Triples (Fig. 2). It contains the triples encoded with the above IDs using adjacency lists. On a high level these are lists of triples sorted by subject-predicate-object (i.e. an SPO index). These are stored in a compressed format using two bitmaps and two sequences. The shared section terms are represented by adding to non-shared subject/object terms the count of shared terms. If the ID is lower than the shared terms count, it means the ID is representing the position inside the shared section. If the ID is greater than the shared terms count, it means the ID is representing a subject or an object.

Overall one can summarize HDT contains two components, the Dictionary component and the Triples component that use a global ordering to store and compress the data.

2.1 HDTq

HDTq [9] is an extension of HDT to allow the storage of named graphs or quads.

In the dictionary, it adds another sorted section to store the named graphs. (HDTq dictionary part of Fig. 1).

In the triples component, this new section of n named graphs is reflected with n bitmaps that have a length corresponding to the number of triples. Each bitmaps indicates with 1 if the corresponding triple is in the named graph associated with the bitmap. These bitmaps are compressed using Roaring bitmaps [15]. (HDTq triples in Fig. 2).

Another version of HDTq exists using one bitmap per triple instead of one bitmap per named graph. We do not consider this version because it was getting worse results than the one bitmap per named graph version.

3 Related Work

We first describe the current methods to compress an RDF file into HDT and then describe general RDF graph indexing methods. There are currently 3 methods to compress an RDF file to HDT. *rdf2hdt* [11], is the original implementation used to compress an RDF file to HDT. This implementation is fully in memory. It basically performs a lexicographic sorting of the terms (URIs, Literals, blank nodes) for the dictionary and of the IDs in SPO order in the triples. *HDT-MR* [12], is an implementation using a MapReduce setup to compress large dataset into HDT. This algorithm can only be executed on a MapReduce cluster. This requirement is a hard stop for users having access only to commodity hardware. *HDTCat* [4], is an algorithm to merge 2 HDT files together without the need to uncompress the data. This method was used to compress large HDT files by creating small HDT files and combine them recursively into one big HDT file. There are no methods to delete triples from an existing HDT file without uncompressing the dataset.

Besides methods to compress RDF graphs to HDT, the most related works include triple store indexing strategies. In these cases the RDF graph is stored into some internal indexing structure that is subsequently used to query it via SPARQL. Typical indexing structures are:

- B+-trees like Blazegraph[1], Apache Jena[2] or RDF4J Native Store[3].
- Storing the graph into a SQL database, like Virtuoso [6].
- Custom binary structure, for example inside QLever [1] using a read-only compressed data structure.

Overall these indexing strategies are memory intensive making it difficult to run them on commodity hardware.

4   Contribution

In this paper, we present k-HDTDiffCat, a new tool that allows to merge and update multiple HDT files. In combination with an indexing algorithm, it can be used to compress and update large HDT files in low hardware settings. More precisely, we provide the following contributions:

1. Allow to combine multiple HDT files together at the same time.
2. Allow to subtract triples from HDT files.
3. Extend these algorithms also for named graphs.

4.1   k-HDTCat

While all functionalities are integrated in the same tool, we first describe the functionality of k-HDTCat, i.e. merging together mutliple HDT files.

Dictionary Generation. An HDT dictionary is composed of multiple sorted sections. Inside each section the RDF terms respect multiple properties,

1. An RDF term is unique in its section. (No duplicated term)
2. If an RDF term is used as a subject and as an object, it is inside the shared section and doesn't appear inside a subject or an object section.
3. An RDF term is represented by its position or index in the section.

We describe in the following how we merge multiple HDT files named $HDT_1 \ldots HDT_k$ with Shared, Subject, Object and Predicate sections named respectively $SH_1 \ldots SH_k$, $S_1, \ldots S_k$, $O_1, \ldots O_k$ and $P_1, \ldots P_k$.

As all sections are sorted, we create iterators over each section type. it_{SH} is an iterator over all shared sections $(SH_1, \ldots SH_k)$ that returns all terms of the shared sections sorted without duplicates using a merge join. Analogously we

---

[1] https://blazegraph.com.
[2] https://jena.apache.org/index.html.
[3] https://rdf4j.org/.

create it_S for subjects, it_O for objects and it_P for predicates. By comparing it_S and it_O we can compute the terms that need to be moved into the new shared section SH_{new} with the already shared terms from it_{SH}. All terms that are not moved to this section will remain in the S_{new}, O_{new} sections respectively. With that, we respect the properties 1 and 2.

Added to this method, we keep track of the original term index with the origin HDT IDs and sections, so when we compute the end section S_{new}, O_{new}, SH_{new} and P_{new}, we have both the old and new IDs of each term. Using them, we create 4 arrays $M_{Sec,HDT}$, one per HDT file and section $Sec \in \{S, O, P, SH\}$, $HDT \in \{HDT_1, \ldots HDT_k\}$. We call them "maps" and we fill them using the origin term location i.e. ID/Section/HDT file as the index and the new location and if the term is shared for the value. $M_{Sec,HDT}[OldID] = (NewID, IsShared)$.

With this task done, we have now access to the new sections for the dictionary with a mapping between the old and the new term's indexes.

Triples Component Generation. The dictionary being created, we need to build the triples component, for this part, we extended the HDTCat [4] algorithm to handle multiple triples by using a merge join. First we read the triple ids from the HDT files into multiple stream mapped using $M_{Sec,HDT}$, the arrays created during the dictionary creation. Before merging them, we need to take into consideration that a subject or object term can become a shared term leading to our ids in our streams to be unsorted due to the shared IDs representation defined in the triples paragraph in Sect. 2.

To fix that we split our streams into two different streams. A stream with the triples with shared subjects and a stream with the triples with non-shared subjects. Once this is done, we use a merge join to create two streams from all the streams, removing the duplicated terms at the same time.

This solves the unsorted problem for the subject terms, not for the object terms. To sort again the objects, we can use the fact that our triples are sorted by subjects and predicates, so if we peek from our stream all the triples with the same subject and predicate, we can retrieve all the unsorted objects for a given (subject, predicate) couple. This number of objects is usually small compared to the triples count, so we can sort them in memory and stream the sorted results.

The result streams being sorted, we can create our triple component.

Large File Indexing Using k-HDTCat. Using this new algorithm version, we can combine multiple HDT files into one. Removing the overhead added by the generation of the HDT file, but inducing the overhead of reading multiple HDT files at once. We made the hypothesis that this added overhead isn't as big as the one removed from the original HDTCat. This can be used to index big HDT files by first chunking the data and indexing smaller HDT files and then combining them to create a bigger HDT file using k-HDTCat. A comparison with existing methods is available in Sect. 5.2 (Fig. 3).

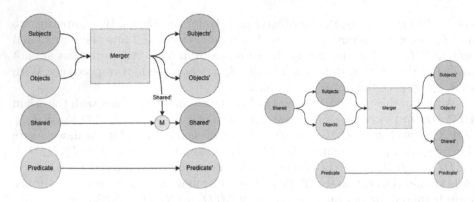

Fig. 3. k-HDTCat Merge streams   **Fig. 4.** k-HDTDiffCat Merge streams

4.2   k-HDTDiffCat

The main drawback of HDTCat is the fact that it is only providing the addition on datasets, but not the ability to remove triples from datasets. To do it, one is forced to reindex the dataset without the unwanted triples.

To overcome this missing part, we created k-HDTDiffCat, a modified version of k-HDTCat to remove triples from one or multiple HDT files into one HDT file. It is built on top of k-HDTCat.

Dictionary Generation. Unlike k-HDTCat, during a diff, an RDF term can be removed from the dictionary of a HDT file, leading to 3 cases,

1. The term is still used at least once in the same section, in which case nothing should be done.
2. The term was a shared term, but now it is only an object or a subject, then we need to consider its sharedness loss.
3. The term isn't used anywhere in the dictionary, then we need to completely remove it.

To mark a triple to be deleted, we are using a bitmap per HDT file. If the bit at the index i is set to 1, it means that the triple at the index i will be removed from this HDT file.

To compute the deleted triples, we first create one bitmap per section per HDT file, a bit set to 1 in a bitmap represents if an term is used inside the section. We then fill the bitmaps by reading the triples for each HDT file while ignoring the ones with the same position as a 1 in the triples bitmap for this HDT.

With these bitmaps, when we are reading a section, we only have to check first if this term should be read or ignored.

Due to the property 2, we need to check if a shared element is still shared after the diffcat. To do that, as represented in Fig. 4, we are merging the shared

Data: it_S, it_O two sorted iterators of respectively subjects and objects terms.

Result: it'_S, it'_O, it'_{SH}, three sorted iterators of the final subjects, objects and
  shared terms.

$it'_S \leftarrow \emptyset \ it'_O \leftarrow \emptyset \ it'_{SH} \leftarrow \emptyset$

SharedLoop: **while** $it_S \neq \emptyset$ and $it_O \neq \emptyset$ **do**

> $NewSubject \leftarrow \text{Next}(it_S) \ NewObject \leftarrow \text{Next}(it_O)$
>
> **while** $NewSubject \neq NewObject$ **do**
>
> > **if** $NewSubject < NewObject$ **then**
> >
> > > $it'_S \leftarrow it'_S \cup \{NewSubject\}$
> > >
> > > **if** $it_S = \emptyset$ **then**
> > >
> > > > | break SharedLoop
> > >
> > > $NewSubject \leftarrow \text{Next}(it_S)$
> >
> > **else**
> >
> > > $it'_O \leftarrow it'_O \cup \{NewObject\}$
> > >
> > > **if** $it_O = \emptyset$ **then**
> > >
> > > > | break SharedLoop
> > >
> > > $NewObject \leftarrow \text{Next}(it_O)$
>
> $it'_{SH} \leftarrow it'_{SH} \cup \{NewSubject\}$

while $it_S \neq \emptyset$ **do**

> | $it'_S \leftarrow it'_S \cup \{\text{Next}(it_S)\}$

while $it_O \neq \emptyset$ **do**

> | $it'_O \leftarrow it'_O \cup \{\text{Next}(it_O)\}$

Algorithm 1: Split subject/object iterators into subject/object/shared iterators

term iterator it_{SH} with both the subjects it_S and the objects it_O iterators. As described in Algorithm 1, by comparing the two iterators in a merged way, k-HDTDiffCat is able to recompute the shared terms with the subjects/objects when merging the HDT files by comparing when two elements in the iterators are equal.

We then run the k-HDTCat method to compute the dictionary without using it_{SH} at the end because it was already used at the start.

Triples Generation. Like in the dictionary generation, we are reusing the k-HDTCat method to compute the triples, we add to the triple reading and mapping part a check reading the input delete bitmap to see if the read triple is deleted or not. If it is deleted we ignore the triple, otherwise we continue the k-HDTCat method. The k-HDTCat method already taking care of the sharedness "loss" with the same strategy as the sharedness "gain".

Complexity. The k-HDTDiffCat method being close to HDTCat [4], it is reflected with a same time and space complexity. In HDTCat, for n, m the number of triples in the two input HDT files, the time complexity is $O((n + m) \log(n + m))$ with at best $O(n + m)$ and the space complexity is $O(n + m)$. Unlike HDTCat, we don't have a constant amount of input HDT files. We denote the complexities using n, the number of all triples in the input HDT files and we add to the definition m, the number of all RDF terms in the input HDT file dictionaries. We will first explain the time complexity for the triples generation, then the time complexity for the dictionary generation and the space complexity.

The input dictionaries being already sorted, computing the union of them is done using a merge fashion and thus, giving a complexity of $O(m)$.

The triples generation is done by grouping the triples with the same subject-predicate couple and then sort these groups. The worst case scenario is only one group giving a time complexity of $O(n \log n)$. In the best scenario, where all the groups are containing a constant amount of triples, the time complexity is $O(n)$. By combining both the dictionary and triples generation, the time complexity is $O(m + n \log n)$.

The space complexity is given by the space required to store the new HDT file sections, which is $O(m)$ for the dictionary and $O(n)$ for the triples. The combined space complexity is $O(m + n)$.

4.3   HDTq Integration

To integrate HDTq inside these two methods, we need to consider the new graph section and the graph bitmaps inside the triples (or quads) section.

The graph section is compressed like all the other sections and isn't merged with a shared section, so we can apply our merge join with or without the section delete bitmaps depending on if we are deleting triples or not using k-HDTDiffCat.

For the quads, in k-HDTDiffCat, we are already sorting in memory the objects ids by grouping them by (subject, predicate) because the memory impact is low. But we can also notice that the memory impact for grouping the quads ids by (subject, predicate) is also low so we can extend the triples generation of k-HDTCat to sort the graphs with the objects.

The main issue comes with the deletion bitmap, HDTq files not being based on a triple list, but on a quad list, we now consider our delete bitmap as a 2D matrix (i, j) instead of a 1D list (i), the i staying the triple id, but we add the j to denote the graph id. To construct this matrix, like in HDTq [9], we used Roaring bitmaps [15] to avoid having to have full matrix lines with only few bits because named graphs are only containing few triples.

5   Experiments

To evaluate HDTDiffCat we run four different experiments. Their codes are available on Github[4].

1. This experiment aims to determine the best value of k when compressing a dataset using k-HDTCat.
2. In this experiment we compare our compression methods with the existing ones, i.e. rdf2hdt [11], *HDT-MR* [12] and HDTCat [4].
3. This experiment compares the compression process we propose with other compression methods, using as an example the Wikidata dataset.
4. This experiment shows how it is possible to use k-HDTDiffCat to create an up to date HDT file of Wikidata with a max delay of 24 h.

---

[4] https://github.com/ate47/kHDTGenDiskBenchmark.

5.1   Experiment: Experimentally Determine a Good Value of k in k-HDTCat

This first experiment was made using the LUBM benchmark [14]. LUBM is a benchmark for SPARQL that allows to generate synthetically an RDF graph with different sizes. The size is generally indicated by the number of universities contained in the graph. We use a small LUBM dataset of 1000 universities, giving us a dataset with 133.5 million RDF triples. We then split this dataset into small datasets of 1 million triples converted into HDT files, giving us $n = 134$ HDT files. We then run k-HDTCat in a k-way merge fashion to create one HDT file from all the 134 HDT files by using different k. We run our experiments on a KVM virtual machine with 16GB of RAM with 1TB of SSD with 4 vcpu Intel(R) Xeon(R) CPU E5-2667 v4 3.20GHz in a University server. The results are reported in the Table 1.

Table 1. Time in function of the k and the number of layers

k	layers	cats	time (s)	average (s)
2	8	132	2264	2264
4	4	44	1245	1245
8	3	19	987	971
10		14	955	
12	2	12	849	854
20		7	805	
28		5	840	
36		4	890	
44		4	884	
134	1	1	1135	1135

We used 4 different metrics, the number of k-HDTCat (cats) used obtained with $\lceil \frac{n-1}{k-1} \rceil$, the number of layers in the k-ways tree, obtained with $\lceil \log_k(n) \rceil$, the time to create the HDT file for a given k value and the average time for a given layer count. We notice that the time to merge the HDT files can be divided by 2 with a good k choice. We can also see that the time is linked with the number of layers during the k-ways merge, a large number of layers is increasing the time, the results for $k = 10$ and $k = 12$ is also showing that the number k-HDTCat has less impact than the number of layers. We can also see that, after a certain point the higher the number of HDT file is, the slower the method is, the HDT files being mapped from disk, the higher the number is, the higher the number of file pointer is, reducing the speed.

In our future experiments, we will set $k = 20$, this k being the one with the best time.

5.2   Experiment: Comparison with Existing HDT Compression Methods

To compare our approach with existing methods for compressing HDT file, we follow the same procedure as in the HDTCat and HDT-MR papers. The idea is to measure the time to compress different sizes of the data generated in the LUBM benchmark [14]. Following existing evaluations we try to generate an HDT file for the LUBM dataset with a university count of 1000, 2000, 3000, ..., 8000 (i.e. with a step of 1000 universities), then from 8.000, 12.000, 16.000, ..., 40000 (i.e. with a step of 4.000 universities). This gives us different datasets with sizes from 130 million triples to 5.3 billion triples. For the other approaches we do no replicate the results but report the results from the previous papers. We run our experiments on the same machine as the one described in the previous experiment in Sect. 5.1. Each experiment was run 3 times and reported using the average and standard deviation. The results are reported in Table 2. We see that despite using only a 16 GB RAM machine we are outperforming the original HDTCat implementation running on both a machine with 16 GB and 128 GB of RAM. The map reduce setup is still more competitive by 65% but uses a map reduce cluster with 8 times more memory. Overall we can see that we are able to compress big datasets on commodity hardware using only one machine.

Table 2. Comparison in seconds (s) between methods to serialize RDF graphs into HDT using HDTCat [4], HDT-MR [12] and k-HDTCat

LUBM		128GB		16GB		
Univ.	Triples	HC128	HMR	HC16	kHC Avg	SD
1k	0.13B	1856	936	8082	1305	74
2k	0.27B	2257	1706	11622	2878	36
3k	0.40B	3695	2498	15616	4791	377
4k	0.53B	5285	3113	19928	6041	173
5k	0.67B	7058	4065	24400	7556	168
6k	0.80B	8960	4656	30235	9046	39
7k	0.93B	11018	5338	-	10501	83
8k	1.07B	13308	6020	-	11955	149
12k	1.60B	19777	9499	-	19355	1057
16k	2.14B	26825	13229	-	26078	1480
20k	2.67B	34486	15720	-	32777	1959
24k	3.20B	42789	26492	-	43006	550
28k	3.74B	51807	36812	-	50116	1362
32k	4.27B	61366	40633	-	57736	1727
36k	4.81B	72161	48322	-	65641	1706
40k	5.32B	84633	55471	-	73110	2081

HC: HDTCat, HMR : HDT-MR, kHC : k-HDTCat, Avg : average, SD : standard deviation.

5.3   Experiment: Indexing Wikidata

In this section, we want to show how we compare with respect to indexing strategies of other SPARQL endpoints.

To do this, we want to see how our approach behaves on indexing the whole Wikidata dump. This is seen as a challenging problem. As reported in [7] there is only a limited number of successful attempts to index the whole of Wikidata on existing triple stores since most do not scale to KGs of this size (even with large hardware configurations). In the year 2020 the Wikidata dump surpassed 13B triples. Since then only 6 triple stores have been reported to be capable of indexing the whole dump, namely: Virtuoso [6], Stardog[5], Apache Jena[6], QLever [1] and Blazegraph. We report in Table 3 the loading times, the number of indexed triples, the amount of needed RAM, the final index size and the documentation for indexing Wikidata.

Table 3. Wikidata Index characteristics for different endpoints.

System	Loading Time	#Triples	RAM	Index size	Doc
Apache Jena	9d 21h	13.8 B	64 GB	2TB	https://wiki.bitplan.com/index.php/ WikiData_Import_2020-08-15.
Virtuoso	"several days"[a] (preprocessing) + 10 h	11.9 B	378 GB	NA	https://community.openlinksw.com/t/ loading-wikidata-into-virtuoso-open- source-or-enterprise-edition/2717.
Blazegraph	~5.5d	11.9 B	128 GB	1.1 T	https://addshore.com/2019/10/your-own- wikidata-query-service-with-no-limits/.
Stardog	9.5 h	16.7 B	256 GB	NA	https://www.stardog.com/labs/blog/ wikidata-in-stardog/.
QLever	14.3 h	17 B	128 GB	823 GB	https://github.com/ad-freiburg/qlever/ wiki/Using-QLever-for-Wikidata.
qEndpoint	57 h	**19.2 B**	16 GB	**340 GB**	https://github.com/the-qa-company/ qEndpoint/wiki/Use-qEndpoint-to-index- a-dataset.

[a] The precise number of days for the preprocessing is not indicated in the documentation.

Using k-HDTCat we were able to index the Wikidata public dump from February 2024 with 19.2 billion triples[7]. The experiment was run on a 16 GB desktop computer with a 12 cores AMD Ryzen 5 5600 3.50 GHz CPU and 1 TB of SSD. The experiment was repeated two times, the average time and standard deviation are used as a metric. The compression time was 52 h. The compression time is the third best between the reported once. On the other hand, this compression was achieved on a commodity hardware with 16 GB of RAM which is from 8 to 23 smaller than other approaches. The final index size of 340 GB is the smallest between the reported ones.

We measured the total time for the different generation steps. The k-HDTCat generation steps are *dict* for merging and writing the dictionaries, *triples* for

---

[5] https://www.stardog.com/.

[6] https://jena.apache.org.

[7] https://dumps.wikimedia.org/wikidatawiki/entities/.

merging and writing the triples and *save* to write the end HDT file. This results are reported in Table 4.

Table 4. Time split per part during WD compression

Method	Section	Time (s)	Time SD	Percent.	Total (s)	Total SD	Percent.
HDT file Generation	–				104449	1124	59,68 %
k-HDTCat	dict	18964	478	26.87 %	70582	1498	40,32 %
	triples	42767	1092	60.6 %			
	save	8837	73	12.52 %			
Total	–				175032	378	100 %

SD = Standard deviation

We can see that most of the time is used to compress the small HDT files.

5.4   Experiment: k-HDTDiffCat to Keep Up to Date Datasets

Table 5. Times per part to compute HDTDiff over a Wikidata Truthy HDT file with 371M changed triples.

Step	Diff only time (s)	Cat only time (s)	DiffCat time (s)
Diff bitmap	501	–	462
Dictionary	2121	2155	2206
Triples	4446	3401	4352
Total	7068	5556	7020

A way to keep RDF graphs up to date, is by using buffer updates, i.e. adding and deleting the changes over time in a buffer and by applying all of them at the same time. In this experiment we are using the Wikidata recent changes API[8] to fetch the recent changes from the Wikidata dataset [20] and combine them with an HDT dump of the Wikidata dataset.

For our experiment, we are using a Wikidata truthy dump from 2023-10-28 00:40 (CET) and the recent changes changes from the dump date to the 2023-11-06 14:00. This accounts for $2,509,863$ Wikidata entity changes. We create a bitmap for the HDT triples, when an entity e is changed, we mark as removed by a 1 in the bitmap all the triples matching the pattern $(e, ?, ?)$. We put in a new HDT file the triples with e as a subject by getting them from Wikidata. This gives us 371.278.906 added triples inside what we call the "Delta" HDT file.

---

[8] https://www.mediawiki.org/wiki/API:RecentChanges.

Table 6. Times (s) per part to compute k-HDTDiffCat over a Wikidata Truthy HDT file with 371M changed triples using different counts. The added time is compared with the time to compute a k-HDTDiffCat with 2 HDT files.

Step	1	2	3	4	5	6	7
Diff bitmap	581	553	530	525	550	552	548
Dictionary	2873	3006	3219	3371	3615	3739	3959
Triples	6157	6416	6863	7149	7661	8083	8161
Total	9611	9975	10612	11045	11826	12374	12668
Added time	–	+4%	+10%	+14%	+23%	+28%	+32%

Using these datasets, we did four experiments to test the efficiency of k-HDTDiffCat, they were done on a 16GB laptop with 200GB of SSD available.

The first one was to only apply the HDTDiff part on the Truthy Wikidata HDT file with the delete bitmap. This allows to see the speed of only the diff part. A second test is made by running the HDTCat part on the HDTDiff result with the delta graph. Giving a time on how fast the HDTCat part is working, it is not made on the first Truthy Wikidata HDT file to avoid duplicated terms. The third is to run both algorithms to compare how fast is the couple k-HDTDiffCat vs HDTCat + HDTDiff. The results of these experiments are available in Table 5. In the table, the time to compute each HDT section is mentioned with the total time to run the method, the diff bitmap building is omited in the cat because we aren't running a diff method.

The results of these three experiments are available in Table 5. We can see that HDTDiff is adding an overhead to HDTCat, we believe that it is due to the bitmap reading to test if an term is in the result HDT file. Another result is the time difference between HDTDiff only + HDTCat only and k-HDTDiffCat, showing that it is pertinent to use k-HDTDiffCat instead of HDTDiff and then HDTCat when building a new HDT file.

A fourth experiment is done to understand how the increasing count of HDT files is affecting our method. To do that, we first split our delta HDT file into 7 pieces and we run the k-HDTDiffCat on the truthy HDT file and i pieces, with $i = \{1, \ldots 7\}$. The results of this experiment are available in Table 6. The diff being only done on the input HDT file, the time to compute the diff bitmap is the same for all the steps. We then notice an increase in time for each added HDT file between 4 and 9 percents added to the time to compute two k-HDTDiffCat.

6   Code

k-HDTDiffCat and its HDTq support are part of the qEndpoint core repository[9]. A fork of the Java HDT library[10]. It is used in qEndpoint, a SPARQL endpoint

---

[9] https://github.com/the-qa-company/qEndpoint/tree/master/qendpoint-core.
[10] https://github.com/rdfhdt/hdt-java.

based on HDT and RDF4J. The code is released under the *Lesser General Public License*. The tool is available as a command line interface[11] together with existing tools like rdf2hdt, hdt2rdf, hdtInfo, hdtVerify. The new tool can be used as:

```
hdtDiffCat <input files> -diff <delta file> <output HDT file>
```

The input files are the HDT files to combine, an additional HDT file can be added to tell which triples to delete.

It can also be used as a lightweight library without the endpoint for more specific operations.

7 Conclusion

HDT is an RDF file format that allows to store, share and query large RDF Knowledge Graphs on commodity hardware. In this paper, we presented a new tool, k-HDTDiffCat, a generalization of HDTCat to combine multiple HDT files and to remove some of the existing triples.

It is available online as a command line interface or by using our Java library in the qEndpoint repository[12] under the *Lesser General Public License*. We have shown how this tool can be used to compress HDT file and how it compares with respect to existing methods. We have also compared the HDT compression with the indexing strategies of other performant SPARQL endpoints. Finally, we have seen how they can be used to maintain an up-to-date Wikidata index. To conclude, k-HDTDiffCat allows generating and update HDT files on commodity hardware, something that was not possible before. This is particularly important since now all operations in the HDT life-cycle can be carried out on commodity hardware. As a consequence HDT becomes an ideal indexing structure for large KGs in low hardware settings allowing the community to manipulate these graphs more easily.

References

1. Bast, H., Buchhold, B.: QLever: a query engine for efficient SPARQL+ text search. In: Proceedings of the 2017 ACM on Conference on Information and Knowledge Management, pp. 647–656 (2017)
2. Beek, W., Rietveld, L., Bazoobandi, H.R., Wielemaker, J., Schlobach, S.: LOD laundromat: a uniform way of publishing other people's dirty data. In: Mika, P., et al. (eds.) ISWC 2014. LNCS, vol. 8796, pp. 213–228. Springer, Cham (2014). https://doi.org/10.1007/978-3-319-11964-9_14
3. Diefenbach, D., Both, A., Singh, K., Maret, P.: Towards a question answering system over the semantic web. Semant. Web **11**(3), 421–439 (2020)

---

[11] https://github.com/the-qa-company/qEndpoint/wiki/qEndpoint-CLI-commands.
[12] https://github.com/the-qa-company/qEndpoint/tree/master/qendpoint-core.

4. Diefenbach, D., Giménez-García, J.M.: HDTCat: let's make HDT generation scale. In: Pan, J.Z., et al. (eds.) ISWC 2020. LNCS, vol. 12507, pp. 18–33. Springer, Cham (2020). https://doi.org/10.1007/978-3-030-62466-8_2
5. Diefenbach, D., Singh, K., Maret, P.: WDAqua-core1: a question answering service for rdf knowledge bases. In: Companion Proceedings of the The Web Conference 2018, WWW 2018, pp. 1087–1091. International World Wide Web Conferences Steering Committee, Republic and Canton of Geneva, CHE (2018)https://doi.org/10.1145/3184558.3191541
6. Erling, O., Mikhailov, I.: RDF support in the virtuoso DBMS. In: Pellegrini, T., Auer, S., Tochtermann, K., Schaffert, S. (eds.) Networked Knowledge - Networked Media. Studies in Computational Intelligence, vol. 221, pp. 7–24. Springer, Berlin, Heidelberg (2009). https://doi.org/10.1007/978-3-642-02184-8_2
7. Fahl, W., Holzheim, T., Westerinen, A., Lange, C., Decker, S.: Getting and hosting your own copy of Wikidata. In: 3rd Wikidata Workshop @ International Semantic Web Conference (2022). https://zenodo.org/record/7185889#.Y0WD1y0RoQ0
8. Fernández, J.D., Beek, W., Martínez-Prieto, M.A., Arias, M.: LOD-a-lot: a queryable dump of the LOD cloud. In: d'Amato, C., et al. (eds.) ISWC 2017, Part II. LNCS, vol. 10588, pp. 75–83. Springer, Cham (2017). https://doi.org/10.1007/978-3-319-68204-4_7
9. Fernández, J.D., Martínez-Prieto, M.A., Polleres, A., Reindorf, J.: HDTQ: managing RDF datasets in compressed space. In: Gangemi, A., et al. (eds.) ESWC 2018. LNCS, vol. 10843, pp. 191–208. Springer, Cham (2018). https://doi.org/10.1007/978-3-319-93417-4_13
10. Fernández, J.D., Martínez-Prieto, M.A., Gutiérrez, C., Polleres, A., Arias, M.: Binary RDF representation for publication and exchange (HDT). J. Web Semant. **19**, 22–41 (2013). https://doi.org/10.1016/j.websem.2013.01.002, https://www.sciencedirect.com/science/article/pii/S1570826813000036
11. Fernández García, J.D., et al.: Binary RDF for scalable publishing, exchanging and consumption in the web of data (2013)
12. Giménez-García, J.M., Fernández, J.D., Martínez-Prieto, M.A.: HDT-MR: a scalable solution for RDF compression with HDT and MapReduce. In: Gandon, F., Sabou, M., Sack, H., d'Amato, C., Cudré-Mauroux, P., Zimmermann, A. (eds.) ESWC 2015. LNCS, vol. 9088, pp. 253–268. Springer, Cham (2015). https://doi.org/10.1007/978-3-319-18818-8_16
13. Gog, S., Beller, T., Moffat, A., Petri, M.: From theory to practice: plug and play with succinct data structures. In: Gudmundsson, J., Katajainen, J. (eds.) SEA 2014. LNCS, vol. 8504, pp. 326–337. Springer, Cham (2014). https://doi.org/10.1007/978-3-319-07959-2_28
14. Guo, Y., Pan, Z., Heflin, J.: LUBM: a benchmark for owl knowledge base systems. J. Web Semant. **3**(2–3), 158–182 (2005)
15. Lemire, D., et al.: Roaring bitmaps: implementation of an optimized software library. Softw.: Pract. Exp. **48**(4), 867–895 (2018)
16. Martínez-Prieto, M.A., Fernández, J.D., Cánovas, R.: Compression of rdf dictionaries. In: Proceedings of the 27th Annual ACM Symposium on Applied Computing, SAC 2012, pp. 340–347. Association for Computing Machinery, New York (2012). https://doi.org/10.1145/2245276.2245343
17. Taelman, R., Mahieu, T., Vanbrabant, M., Verborgh, R.: Optimizing storage of RDF archives using bidirectional delta chains. Semant. Web **13**(4), 705–734 (2022)
18. Verborgh, R., et al.: Triple pattern fragments: a low-cost knowledge graph interface for the web. J. Web Semant. **37–38**, 184–206 (2016). https://doi.org/10.1016/j.websem.2016.03.003, http://linkeddatafragments.org/publications/jws2016.pdf

19. Willerval, A., Bonifati, A., Diefenbach, D.: qEndpoint: a Wikidata SPARQL endpoint on commodity hardware. In: Companion Proceedings of the ACM Web Conference 2023, pp. 119–122 (2023)
20. Willerval, A., Diefenbach, D., Maret, P.: Easily setting up a local Wikidata SPARQL endpoint using the qEndpoint (2022)
21. Witten, I.H., et al.: Managing Gigabytes: Compressing and Indexing Documents and Images. Morgan Kaufmann (1999)

SMW Cloud: A Corpus of Domain-Specific Knowledge Graphs from Semantic MediaWikis

Daniil Dobriy[1]([⊠])(iD), Martin Beno[1](iD), and Axel Polleres[1,2](iD)

[1] Vienna University of Economics and Business, Vienna, Austria
{daniil.dobriy,martin.beno,axel.polleres}@wu.ac.at
[2] Complexity Science Hub, Vienna, Austria

Abstract. Semantic wikis have become an increasingly popular means of collaboratively managing Knowledge Graphs. They are powered by platforms such as Semantic MediaWiki and Wikibase, both of which enable MediaWiki to store and publish structured data. While there are many semantic wikis currently in use, there has been little effort to collect and analyse their structured data, nor to make it available for the research community. This paper seeks to address this gap by systematically collecting structured data from an extensive corpus of Semantic-MediaWiki-powered portals and providing an in-depth analysis of the ontological diversity (and re-use) amongst these wikis using a variety of ontological metrics. Our paper aims to demonstrate that semantic wikis are a valuable and extensive part of Linked Open Data (LOD), and in fact may be considered an own active "sub-cloud" within the LOD ecosystem, which can provide useful insights into the evolution of small and medium-sized domain-specific Knowledge Graphs.

Keywords: Semantic MediaWiki · Linked Open Data · Ontology · Ontology Metrics · Ontology Links

Resource accessibility

The resource is made openly available with the necessary access information provided below. Section 5.3 provides a sustainability plan, and details further implemented access modalities for the resource.

Resource Type: Dataset
DOI: 10.5281/zenodo.7920174
License: Creative Commons Attribution 4.0 International[1]
URL: https://semantic-data.cluster.ai.wu.ac.at/smwcloud/

© The Author(s), under exclusive license to Springer Nature Switzerland AG 2024
A. Meroño Peñuela et al. (Eds.): ESWC 2024, LNCS 14665, pp. 145–161, 2024.
https://doi.org/10.1007/978-3-031-60635-9_9

1   Introduction

With the advent of Large Language Models (LLMs), unconventional approaches for extracting rich Linked Data from collaborative platforms and knowledge hubs are gaining attention among researchers, including in the Semantic Web community [5]. First introduced in 2005, Semantic MediaWiki[2] (SMW) is an extension for the MediaWiki platform that enables semantic annotations of wiki pages [19], making it a collaborative Knowledge Graph management platform. It is also a precursor that majorly inspired Wikidata, and therefore Wikibase (WB), which uses select code from SMW for common tasks [28]. Yet, SMW has been available for a longer time and is indeed more broadly used than WB by various projects to manage their structured data. Indeed, following the approach described in Sect. 2, we could discover 1458 active Semantic MediaWiki instances, compared to a lower number of 327 Wikibase instances. The two platforms differ insofar that SMW stores its data as part of its textual page content and has a less complicated data model [28]: SMW's simple subject-predicate-object statement structure known as a *semantic facts* corresponds straightforwardly to RDF triples, where subjects are commonly single wiki pages, properties (predicates) are defined by special syntax in pages or via templates and forms enabled through additional extensions, and objects can be of different datatypes[3] (e.g. numbers, dates, pages etc.). Therefore, SMW serves as a flexible tool to collaboratively create and maintain domain-specific KGs, along with their own vocabularies.

RDF/SPARQL Access. The SMW platform allows to generate full RDF dumps[4] of its structured data. Additionally, although semantic facts are stored in a relational database by default, RDF triples can also be optionally exported/synced with a triplestore or a SPARQL endpoint via a special extension.[5] However, in practice, SMW instances rarely publish periodical dumps of their data, nor do they typically make their data available via SPARQL endpoints.[6] This significantly decreases the effective semantic interoperability and accessibility of KGs provided and maintained through SMW. So far, to the best of our knowledge – *an in-depth analysis of the RDF data made available through SMW instances on the Web is missing.*

Linkage and Ontology Re-use. The re-use of external URLs is in principle possible in semantic facts in SMW, as well as the import of external RDF vocabularies[7] and ontologies[8]; yet, semantic linkage to other KGs is not directly incen-

---

[2] https://www.semantic-mediawiki.org/.

[3] https://www.semantic-mediawiki.org/wiki/Help:Datamodel.

[4] https://www.semantic-mediawiki.org/wiki/Help:Maintenance_script_dumpRDF.php.

[5] In principle, this integration also supports adding additional RDF with SPARQL Updates, cf. https://www.semantic-mediawiki.org/wiki/Help:Using_SPARQL_and_RDF_stores, but herein we focus solely on the RDF data exportable from SMW pages directly.

[6] We note that also there is no "best practice" to detect whether an SMW instance hosts a SPARQL endpoint, as it is not exposed by the SMW API.

[7] https://www.semantic-mediawiki.org/wiki/Help:Import_vocabulary.

[8] https://github.com/TIBHannover/ontology2smw.

tivised within SMW, or respectively, *it is an open question in how far these features are being used*, i.e., in how far the KGs provided by SMW instances *(a) re-use existing ontologies* and *(b) create links to related RDF from other authorities*.

A commonly cited shortcoming of the Linked Open Data (LOD) infrastructure is the lack of a single aggregation point [8,13]. To this end, our approach, SMW Cloud, aims at solving this data accessibility issue by aggregating all publicly available SMWs into a single corpus, addressing the above-mentioned gaps by making the following concrete contributions:

- we systematically track (for now) 1458 Semantic MediaWiki instances, extract their page RDF data when technically feasible, and aggregate it to a Linked Data corpus, following a similar approach as the CommonCrawl[9] and WebDataCommons [21] projects,
- we make this corpus available as an HDT [12] dump, in an accessible, scalable and available, easy to (re-)use and cost-effective manner, following the LOD-a-LOT approach [13] and make calculated metrics for the corpus available in a SPARQL endpoint.
- we provide an extensive analysis of our corpus in terms of (a) ontology metrics, following the Neontometrics approach [24] and (b) LOD metrics, following the LODStats approach [7,8].

As such, we strive to obtain a comprehensive picture of the current state of Linked Data stored in SMWs, evaluating the quality and internal structure, thereby tracking the evolution of a significant, previously unexplored part of the LOD ecosystem. Note that we may hypothesise that the domain-specific, small and medium-sized KGs, represented by SMW instances, closely reflect Enterprise Knowledge Graphs (EKGs), for which there is no publicly available corpus. Analysing our corpus, in comparison with the "classic" KGs making up the LOD Cloud[10], but also in comparison with Wikidata, will therefore gain insights into the possible different parameters to be found in EKGs.

The remainder of this paper is structured as follows: In Sect. 2, we describe the architecture and our approach to collecting the SMW corpus. Section 3 introduces the methods used for further corpus analysis. Corpus statistics and results of our analyses, including a comparison with similar metrics applied to the "traditional" LOD Cloud and Wikidata, are summarized in Sect. 4, before we close with a discussion and outlook to future work in Sect. 5.

2   Methods for Collecting the Corpus

Our overall corpus collection approach is illustrated in Fig. 2. In first step, we discover Semantic MediaWiki instances in a three-fold manner:

---

[9] https://commoncrawl.org.
[10] http://lod-cloud.net.

- We filter the *BuiltWith* MediaWiki collection[11] for SMW instances.
- We query *WikiApiary*[12] – a "meta-wiki" collecting information about public MediaWiki instances – for instances that have the SMW extension installed.
- Lastly, we follow the approach utilized by the web platform discovery tool Crawley[13] and use Search Engine APIs (such as the BingAPI, but also by manual usage of other Search Engines) to discover SMW instances by specific text excerpts or HTML elements commonly found on SMW-powered websites: e.g., "powered by SMW" text snippets).

Following this approach, we collect an extensive list of 1458 SMW instances, for details on the numbers of instances per source, we refer to Fig. 1.

For each found SMW instance, we further retrieve basic statistics directly available via SMW, such as numbers of pages, numbers of users, creation and last modified dates, in order to assess how long the wikis have been operational and how active they are, and the pagelist. Next, we attempt to crawl RDF by querying the pagelist, using the MediaWiki API.[14] Frequent problems encountered in the process of collecting the corpus, such as non-standard behaviours of MediaWiki and SMW platforms, access restrictions, as well as a number of parsing errors, limit technical feasibility of collecting RDF from each instance. Table 1 gives an overview of such issues. Apart from the RDF representation we also crawl the versioning history to identify all changes per page for future analysis.[15] In the last step, we aggregate[16] the RDF by wiki instance to create our corpus. Apart from creating a single HDT file per crawled instance containing all RDF triples, we add metadata per wiki KGs using the VoID [2] and DataCube [10] vocabularies to include more complex statistics and metrics discussed in detail in Sect. 3 below, in the HDT headers.

As an additional item in this metadata aggregation, we collect and classify wikis per "topics", similar to the LOD Cloud topics[17]. Our approach to classify wikis into "LOD Cloud topics" works by, whenever available, fetching metainformation collected by WikiApiary (manually assigned topics) and BuiltWith (SEO-related keywords), plus the textual information from the respective wiki's main page, a random sample of up to 100 page titles and the name of the wiki. We then feed GPT-4 with this textual information[18] to assign it one of the LOD Cloud topics – this current naive approach serves mainly for illustration, cf. Figure 4 below.

---

[11] https://trends.builtwith.com/websitelist/MediaWiki.
[12] https://wikiapiary.com.
[13] http://purl.org/crawley.
[14] https://www.mediawiki.org/wiki/API:Query.
[15] Cf. Sect. 5, we plan to also extract and analyse the *evolution* of the RDF KGs per SMW instances as future work.
[16] Given the absence of Blank Nodes within instances, skolemization is unnecessary.
[17] https://lod-cloud.net/.
[18] Roughly, our GPT prompt is: *"Given the text "[WIKINAME+MAINPAGETEXT+ PAGETITLES+METAINFO]", tell me the best fitting topic among [LODCLOUD-Topiclist]".*

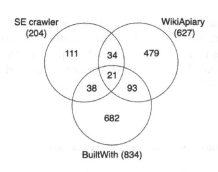

Fig. 1. Venn Diagram of Collected SMWs (1458 in Total) and Their Sources

Table 1. Breakdown of Collection and Processing Losses

SMWs	Description
1458	all active SMW instances
-108	malformed API response
-107	API endpoint unavailable
-55	server-terminated connection
-31	non-standard encoding scheme
1157	instances for which the full pagelist and page RDF could be collected
-51	XML wrongly declared
-36	malformed XML/mismatched tags
-5	non-compliant IRIs
-36	other processing errors
1029	SMW instances for which HDTs could be aggregated

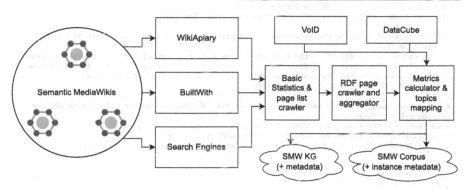

Fig. 2. Architecture of the SMW Crawler and Metrics Processor

2.1   Corpus Provision

Our SMW corpus is registered on Zenodo[19] and is available under a permanent URL[20] and directly on the open data repository of the institute[21] we provide both separate RDF HDT [12] dumps per SMW instance, as well as in a single HDT file for the whole corpus. A SPARQL endpoint, serving the VoID & DataCube metadata in a queryable form, is available at: https://smwcloud-sparql.cluster.ai.wu.ac.at/. The resource including all calculated metrics are provided under the Creative Commons Attribution 4.0 International License.[22]. The canonical citation for the SMW Cloud is:

Dobriy, D., Beno, M., & Polleres, A. (2023). SMW Cloud: A Corpus of Domain-Specific Knowledge Graphs from Semantic MediaWikis. Retrieved from http://purl.org/SMWCloud.

---

[19] 10.5281/zenodo.7920175.
[20] http://purl.org/SMWCloud.
[21] https://semantic-data.cluster.ai.wu.ac.at/smwcloud/.
[22] https://creativecommons.org/licenses/by/4.0/.

Comprehensive documentation for the resource is available at: https://github. com/semantisch/smwcloud. For illustration, we provide the VoID metadata and selected DataCube entries available through our endpoint (and as part of the respective HDT header) for "Wien Geschichte Wiki", an SMW instance providing historical information about Vienna [18] in Turtle syntax in Fig. 3.

```
@prefix smwcloud: <http://purl.org/smwcloud/> .

smwcloud:7f5cb281-76f8-4d16-aee1-a4ad7c660eec void:inDataset <http://purl.org/smwcloud/> .

smwcloud:7f5cb281-76f8-4d16-aee1-a4ad7c660eec a void:Dataset ;
  foaf:homepage <https://www.geschichtewiki.wien.gv.at/Wien_Geschichte_Wiki>;
  foaf:page <https://www.geschichtewiki.wien.gv.at/api.php>;

  dcterms:title "Wien Geschichte Wiki";
  dcterms:source <https://www.geschichtewiki.wien.gv.at>;
  dcterms:modified "2023-05-05"^^xsd:date;
  dcterms:license <https://www.geschichtewiki.wien.gv.at/Impressum>;

  # The dcterms:description was generated by summarising the wikis main page text using GPT:
  dcterms:description
    "\"Wien Geschichte Wiki\" is the historical knowledge platform of the city of Vienna, based
    on the "Historical Lexicon of Vienna" by Felix Czeike, which brings together expertise from
    city administration and the public and currently has over 48,000 contributions,
      279,000 addresses, and 15,000 images.";

  # The dcterms:subject topic was assigned one of the LODCloud categories using using GPT:
  dcterms:subject "Government";
  void:feature <http://purl.org/HDT/hdt#HDTv1>;
  void:dataDump <ACTUAL_URL_FOR_SINGLE_WIKI_HDT_DUMP> ;
  void:uriSpace "https://www.geschichtewiki.wien.gv.at/";

  # Void observations:
  void:triples 5236436;
  void:entities 1038817;
  void:classes 245;
  void:properties 256;
  void:distinctSubjects 436147;
  void:distinctObjects 401053;
  void:documents 328141;

# A DataCube observation:
smwcloud:7f5cb281-76f8-4d16-aee1-a4ad7c660eec/sameIndividualsAxioms/2023-05-05 a qb:Observation ;
    qb:dataSet smwcloud:7f5cb281-76f8-4d16-aee1-a4ad7c660eec ;
    smwcloud:referenceDate "2023-05-05"^^xsd:date ;
    smwcloud:sameIndividualsAxioms 7491 .
```

Fig. 3. Metadata for "Wien Geschichte Wiki"

3   Methods for Analysing the Corpus

Due to their topical diversity, data and schemas differ considerably among SMW instances, but also we hypothesize that the RDF data from SMW instances has fundamentally different characteristics than other Linked Data corpora, such as the LOD Cloud datasets, or Wikidata. In order to verify these assumptions, a comprehensive characterization of our corpus requires two things: (1) a fundamental understanding of each dataset, and (2) an overview of all available data

Table 2. Related Work and Implemented Metrics

Paper \ Use case	Fernandez et al.[13]	Ermilov et al. [8][9][7]	Nogalez et al. [22]	Reiz et al. [24]	Abedjan et al. [1]	Haller et al. [17]	Rietveld et al. [26]
Basic graph metrics	X	X	X	X	X	X	X
Basic ont. metrics			X	X		X	X
Quality analysis	X		X	X		X	
Vocabulary re-use	X	X				X	
Dataset interlinkage	X					X	
Languages analysis	X	X					

Paper	Eval. dimensions
Ermilov et al. [7]	Basic graph metrics
Reiz et al. [24]	Basic ontology metrics[a]
Haller et al. [17]	Instance, ontology links
Yao et al. [31]	Cohesion
Yang et al. [30]	Complexity
Fernandez et al. [14]	Coverage, structure
Duque-Ramos et al. [6][25]	SQuaRE[b] -based quality
Gangemi et al. [15]	Structure, functionality, usability
Tartir et al. [27]	Populated ontology (instances, schema)
Orme et al. [23]	Quality, completeness, and stability

[a] Basic ontology metrics can be used a building block for calculation of quality frameworks.
[b] https://www.iso.org/standard/64764.html

[3]. Therefore, we perform our analyses both on the single wiki datasets as well as on the corpus as a whole in terms of commonly used metrics.

In order to establish a foundation for comparative analysis, we review related LOD analysis studies in Table 2. This allows us to discern and categorize the prevailing analytical themes. The most common analyses within these studies are performed on *Basic graph metrics*, *Basic ontology metrics*, and *Quality*. In addition to the aforementioned themes, other forthcoming analyses encompass *Vocabulary re-use*, *Dataset interlinkage* and *Language usage*.

General graph metrics give a comprehensive and comparable characterization of the corpus [7]. Additionally, we calculate *basic ontology metrics* to assess the used schemata/ontologies of the individual SMW instances in a comparable manner, and evaluate the corpus on the basis of established *quality analysis* frameworks to gain a better understanding of quality characteristics. Explicitly including ontology metrics and common ontology quality frameworks in our analyses through the implementation of the Neontometrics calculation engine [24], we address the lack of metric validation for real-world data [24], especially in *small KGs*: we perceive SMW instances as a publicly available pendant/proxy for enterprise KGs with their own characteristics.

Table 2 briefly summarizes the various metrics and quality frameworks we have calculated for the SMW corpus: as for calculating the basic graph and ontology metrics, we use the Neontometrics OPI (Ontology Programming Interface).

Afterwards, we apply these metrics to calculate common quality frameworks: Cohesion Metrics [31], Complexity Metrics [30], Fernandez et al. [14], OQuaRE [6,25], Gangemi et al. [15], OntoQA [27] and Orme et al. [23]. Please refer Table 2 for a summary of their respective dimensions.

4   Results and Corpus Statistics

In this section, we provide a brief overview of the insights into the corpus based on the collected statistics. We excluded the datasets causing processing errors as described in Table 1, resulting in 1029 datasets which collectively form the corpus and the basis for analyses.

4.1   Basic RDF Metrics

Table 3 gives a distilled overview of of the corpus dimensions. Notably, the absolute numbers we report for SMW Cloud fall short of the statistics for the number of statement reported by the instances themselves: totalling 1,012,521,773 statements and 206,997 unique properties, calculated by aggregating statistics reported by individual SMWs. At the same time, the SMW Cloud dimensions are comparable to that of LODStats [8], which totals 192,230,648 triples. Though Wikidata has grown considerable in the last 5 years, from 3b triples in 2018 to more than 17b in 2022, exceeding SMW Cloud in size considerably [11]. Nevertheless, despite its comparatively smaller size in terms of total number of statements, the SMW Cloud exhibits a significantly broader range of unique properties, exceeding both Wikidata and LODStats, as well as suggesting limited vocabulary re-use in SMW Cloud.

For a better overview of the characteristics of individual datasets comprising the corpus, we refer to Table 4. There, we compare their parameters to the individual LOD Cloud datasets [8]. Though LOD Cloud datasets are significantly larger on average (2,180,651 triples to 186,813 for SMWs), the majority of LOD datasets are smaller (median 2,486 vs 12,596 for SMWs) implying more uniform sizes of the SMWs. Another key characteristic of SMWs is the higher number of properties and classes per datasets as well as the higher number of properties per entity, suggesting a more granular and detailed data modeling approach in SMWs and a user-centric, bottom-up nature of ontology creation. The lack of class and property depth suggests a flat ontology structure in the SMW instances. We attribute this to the a) user communities with rich domain knowledge and limited expertise in ontology management, b) ad-hoc nature of ontology creation and c) decentralized ontology development in SMWs. Other characteristics regarding high numbers of labeled subjects and large median typed and untyped string lengths for Literals further differentiate user-centric SMWs from LOD datasets.

Table 3. SMW Cloud summary statistics

Dataset	#Triples	#Subjects	#Predicates	#Objects	#Literals
LODStats [8]	192,230,648	Not reported	49,916	Not reported	90,261,655
SMW Cloud	236,505,705	24,010,566	52,670	66,052,823	160,108,216
Wikidata 2021[a]	17,662,800,665	1,625,057,179	38,867	Not reported	Not reported
LOD-a-lot [13]	28,362,198,927	3,214,347,198	1,168,932	3,178,409,386	1,302,285,394

[a] http://gaia.infor.uva.es/hdt/wikidata/wikidata20210305.hdt.gz

Table 4. SMW Cloud and LOD Cloud comparison

Metric	SMW Cloud				LOD Cloud [8]			
	Mean	Min	Max	Median	Mean	Min	Max	Median
Triples p. dataset	186,813	0	31,582,870	12,595.6	2,180,651	2	247,620,294	2,486
Entities	14,828	0	5,036,913	1,281.0	390,325.95	0	63,494,920	106.5
Literals	54,076	0	18,514,040	3,304.0	790,000.57	0	88,315,872	127.0
Blanks					484,540.68	0	202,745,495	0.0
Blanks (subjects)	0.04	0	14	0	399,680.75	0	166,901,812	0.0
Blanks (objects)	0.02	0	6	0	143,005.6	0	50,803,539	0.0
Subclasses	0.14	0	46	0	14.07	0	2,000	0.0
Typed subjects	13,068.83	0	44,374.58	1,047.0	109,790.35	0	25,848,850	22.0
Labeled subjects	2,241.23	0	760,619	267.0	28,652.13	0	11,588,129	0.0
Properties p. entity	6.22	0.88	12.32	4.10	2.86	0	27.27	2.54
String length (typed)	9.32	0	476.05	9.51	9.5	0	1,854.0	0.0
String length (untyped)	72.43	0	369.77	73.12	38.24	0	2,688.0	20.0
Class hierarchy depth	0.009	0	2	0.0	1.63	0	6	0.0
Property hierarchy depth	0	0	0	0.0	1.04	0	5	0.0
Classes	356.52	0	113,270	27.0	20.09	1	1,328	5.0
Properties	155.01	0	45,209	38.0	30.36	1	885	20.0

4.2 Topical Analysis

Semantic MediaWikis capture a variety of highly-specialized domain knowledge, as visualized in Fig. 4 reusing the LOD Cloud categories:[23] 16% wikis specialize on publishing/annotating *media*, 10% are *life science* wikis, 6% *geography*-oriented, 5% *government*-related, 4.3% *language*-related. Still, about half of all wikis (48%) could not be classified under one of the categories (i.e. summarized under *user generated other*), hinting at the topic diversity and high degree of specialization of SMWs.

Manual coding of a randomly selected sample of 100 wikis (as partially represented in Table 5) has shown that the chosen topics represent the wiki well, overlap and are similar in meaning (87% similarity) with WikiApiary tags and BuildWith verticals. Therefore, as a result, we characterize each wiki by 3 independently created tag/domain collections which promotes discoverability and an automatically generated description.

We further analyse the distribution of specialized domains in the corpus with freely annotated tags, see Fig. 5. The big components of the hitherto unclassified wikis are therefore: *gaming* with 134 instances in total, *technology* (115), *education* and *community*. The 101 unclassified wikis indeed can hardly be classified

---

[23] https://lod-cloud.net.

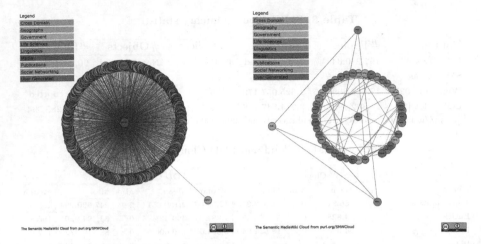

Fig. 4. Connected SMW Cloud instances with and without semantic-mediawiki.org

Table 5. Examples of SMW domain annotations

SMW	LOD Cloud classification[a]	Free classification	Description	Topic (WikiApiary)	Topic (BuiltWith)
geschichtewiki.wien.gv.at -	history (government, geography)	Vienna, Austria	*The Wien Geschichte Wiki is an encyclopedia of historical, geographic, and cultural information related to the city of Vienna and its surrounding regions.*	city wiki, history, vienna	Art And Entertainment
bacid.eu	government	public administration	*BACID Wiki contains information about decentralized governance, capacity building, and public administration initiatives in the Danube region.*	–	Business And Industrial
korrekt.org	publications (media, user generated)	knowledge-based systems	*Korrekt.org is a wiki focused on the research and publications of Professor Markus Krötzsch, covering topics such as description logic, semantic wikis, and knowledge-based systems.*	homepage, semantic mediawiki	Science
www.gardenology.org	life sciences	plants, gardening, encyclopedia	*A comprehensive wiki encyclopedia covering plants and gardening, featuring detailed entries and photographs.*	–	–

[a] Classifications enclosed within parentheses are also produced by the model, serving as alternatives.

because of the lack of investigated content (see Sect. 2). While we see that common LOD Cloud topics are well suited for classifying about half of SMW Cloud, other significant topics emerge: SMW Cloud has a rich number of technology, education and community wikis not prominently featured in LOD Cloud.

4.3 Ontological Analysis

A number of metrics has been been proposed for the analysis of KGs and ontologies. Since a KG comprises both A-Box as well as T-Box statements, we consider

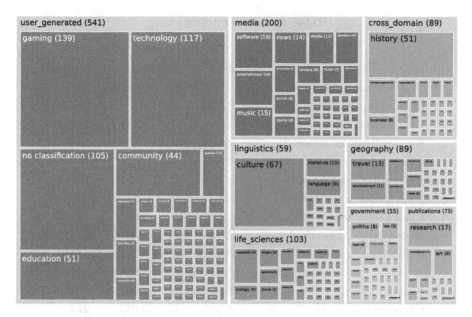

Fig. 5. Prevalent Topics Across SMW Cloud Instances

both metrics for characterizing KGs and ontologies as suitable for analysing KG with notable limitations applying to ontology metrics discussed separately.

Reiz et al. [24] proposes an ontology describing common metrics used to characterize Knowledge Graphs and also introduces an open source tool automating the calculation of a broad variety of metric and quality analyses calculations[24]. The website of the tool also includes a Metric Explorer with metric overviews and descriptions. For SMW Cloud, Table 6 summarizes the basic ontology metrics for SMWs. We have also calculated all quality analyses based on these basic ontology metrics suggested by the Neontometrics engine (see Table 8).

Ontologically, SMW do contain a large number of class and property assertion axioms, same individual assertions as well as individual, class and property annotations. Notably, although SMW technically allows the use of RDFS and OWL concepts, only a total of 5 SMWs[25] implement class hierarchies (via *rdfs:subClassOf*) and no SMW instance implements property hierarchies (via *rdfs:subPropertyOf*) in practice, while 5 SMW instances use *owl:equivalentProperty* definitions, some of which seem redundant.[26] A closer analysis of the RDF(S) and OWL vocabulary used in 1029 crawled SMW instances in terms of Description Logics expressivity (testable again through the Neontometrics tool) is illustrated in Table 7: here, the concrete RDF(S)+OWL

---

[24] http://neontometrics.com/.

[25] Specifically: *wiki.spell-plattform.de*, *wiki.fablab.is*, *wiki.attraktor.org*, *spiele.j-crew.de* and *dotawiki.de*.

[26] E.g., a triple *dcterms:isPartOf owl:equivalentProperty dcterms:isPartOf* in *pool. publicdomainproject.org*.

Table 6. Basic ontology metrics

Metric	SMW Cloud			
	Mean	Min	Max	Median
Class assertion axioms	12,782.75	0	540,701	530.0
Object property assertion axioms	21,735.10	0	1,169,337	635.5
Data property assertion axioms	55,397.72	0	3,144,162	1,793.0
Same individuals axioms	346.05	0	18,512	10.0
General annotation axioms	1,759.55	0	49,391	172.0
Annotation assertion axioms	5,065.86	0	374,185	508.0
Data property annotations	6.92	0	178	6.0
Class annotations	3.25	0	374	2.0
Object property annotations	15.58	0	374	5.0
Individual annotations	5,004.62	0	374,116	439.0
Axioms	95,654.59	0	5,236,436	3,951.5
Logical axioms	90,308.68	0	4,861,744	3,297.5
Classes(See footnote 27)	195.57	0	9,082	22.5
Classes with individuals	188.06	0	9,074	14.5
Object properties	30.83	0	1,500	21.0
Data properties	48.80	0	1,249	32.0
Individuals	12153.97	0	728,482	650.5

constructs being used in each DL expressivity class are analysed, which reveals that only a small fraction of RDFS' and OWL's statements are being used in SMW instances. Indeed, for instance, neither *rdfs:domain* and *rdfs:range* definitions, nor *owl:equivalentClass*, with one exception, hardly any multi-triple OWL axioms are being used in SMW instances: under-use of complex OWL constructs, not even mentioning OWL2, can therefore be also observed on the SMW ecosystem, in a similar and even more pronounced form than already observed more than 10 years ago for the LOD Cloud [16]. Also, due to the sparse use of subclassing and sub- or equivalent properties, further analysis does not further focus on ontology metrics and quality framework metrics, which emphasize schema depth/inheritance richness [27], see also Footnote[27] in Table 6.

In our metric processing, we calculate all Quality Frameworks indicated in Table 2. Although it is not feasible to discuss the evaluation of frameworks in full, we demonstrate the OQueRe framework in Table 8, examplified by metrics receiving the best score and the worst score suggesting a more in-depth analysis as subject of future work capitalizing on the resource established in this work.

---

[27] Due to the observed lack of hierarchical structure, the *number of classes* is equivalent with the number of *root classes*, *paths to leaf classes*, *absolute leaf cardinality* and *absolute depth*, so we do not provide these metrics separately..

Table 7. Use of the RDF(S)+OWL and DL expressivity of SMW instances

Number of SMW instances:	$\mathcal{AL}$ (99)	$\mathcal{AL}$(D) (165)	$\mathcal{ALO}$(D) (708)	$\mathcal{ALEO}$(D) – (50)	$\mathcal{ALHO}$(D) – (3)	(1029)
rdf:type	10206194	217002	18593506	1807	69973	29088482
rdfs:isDefinedBy	1829566	35365	2987260	665	3336	4856192
rdfs:label	1829657	35365	2988428	666	3336	4857452
rdfs:seeAlso	–	–	2	–	–	2
rdfs:subClassOf	–	51	16	–	–	67
rdfs:comment	–	–	255	–	–	255
owl:imports	1430995	26574	2065990	443	3065	3527067
owl:Ontology	1430995	26574	2065990	443	3065	3527067
owl:Class	136758	3934	193832	39	7175	341738
owl:DatatypeProperty	8043	3027	35345	17	216	46648
owl:ObjectProperty	8377	1232	19169	24	82	28884
owl:sameAs	450445	–	358972	76	164	809657
owl:differentFrom	–	–	16	–	–	16
owl:equivalentProperty	–	–	–	–	5	5
owl:intersectionOf	–	–	–	3	–	3
owl:Restriction	–	–	–	3	–	3
owl:onProperty	–	–	–	3	–	3
owl:hasValue	–	–	–	3	–	3
rdf:first	–	–	–	6	–	6
rdf:rest	–	–	–	6	–	6
rdf:nil	–	–	–	3	–	3

Table 8. OQueRE Metrics and Scores

Metric	Mean	Min	Max	Median	Score
Mean number of annotations per class	37.96	0.65	710.16	14.29	1 (excellent)
Mean number of attributes per class	1.05	0.01	2.67	0.77	1 (excellent)
Weighted Method Count: Mean number of properties per class [6]	345.37	0.70	55439.4	35.19	5 (unsatisfactory)

5   Conclusion and Future Work

This paper presented and characterized the SMW Cloud corpus, an extensive collection of RDF data collected from Semantic MediaWiki instances. We demonstrate, with a focused crawling pipeline, that we can identify and collect data from over 1000 SMW instances, some of which have been in existence and active use for over 15 years, which demonstrates the considerable interest of relevant communities and SW technology users of this largely unobserved part of the Semantic Web.

To promote interoperability and ease of use, the SMW corpus is made available as HDT and the corpus' metadata is queryable via a SPARQL endpoint, in line with the FAIR data principles [29]. We plan to update the SMW Cloud regularly and extend it by discovering and crawling RDF from new SMW instances as they appear.

Following the same approach, we recommend that Semantic MediaWiki developers 1) enable RDF dump generation by default rather than requiring administrators to manually make use of a maintenance script to create a dump (or us to crawl the RDF data per page) 2) when a SPARQL-enpoint is available, make it discoverable through SMW API and 3) consider adopting HDT as a compact format for publishing regular dumps as we have demonstrated that it is highly compact format for SMW data (achieving a Data Compression Ratio of 17,5 for SMW Cloud compared to NTriples, more efficiently that for other benchmarks evaluated [20]).

In terms of evaluation and benchmarking as a field of interest of the Semantic Web Community [4], SMW Cloud provides a novel and distinct dataset with unique characteristics that introduces variety into the field of LOD sources investigated so far; we have demonstrated these unique characteristics in terms of a variety of common basic graph and ontology metrics, that illustrate significant differences of RDF usage within SMW instances and the rest of the LOD Cloud. We expect the SMW Corpus to enable previously unexplored approaches in LOD and EKG research.

5.1 Limitations

Statistics calculated by us can not be directly integrated back into individual SMWs, creating a discoverability problem. To this end, it is planned to introduce an SMW extension that will 1) schedule regular RDF dump generation, 2) notify the proposed architecture of the Wiki, and 3) fetch calculated statistics from the SMW Corpus and integrate them into the Wiki.

5.2 Future Work

As future work we think that the SMW corpus can also provide a basis for longitudinal analysis, link analysis [17], etc. This will enable a better understanding of dynamics and evolution of vocabularies. It is our goal to create profiling tools and resources *enabling users to create an assessment of the data at hand* [3]. Finally, as noted in Sect. 1, Wikibases are the second most widely used semantic wiki platform to date. Therefore, crawling efforts and analyses of Wikibase instances following a similar methodology are a prioritised part of future work.

5.3 Sustainability Plan

To account for the updates in the SMW Cloud, which particularly concerns the introduction of new SMW instances, but also general changes to already accounted SMWs, we plan to release new versions of SMW Cloud at least annually. The sustainability plan includes further extension of the automatic metric calculation in the frame of future work and other continuing research as well as tight collaboration with other researchers and users with regards to its further development and maintenance, as well as use case documentation.

We are commited to sustainably host and maintain the corpus thought our institute that already hosts various widely adopted Semantic Web resources for several years now and promote the sustainability strategy within ongoing community activities such as the "Distributed Knowledge Graphs" COST Action[28], which as one of its activities aims at aligning and sustaining community services and tools.

The Resource is made Accessible in Following Ways:

1. The aggregated SMW Cloud dataset is made available via the institutional repository.[29]
2. The SMW Cloud corpus containing individual SMW datasets is also made available via the institutional repository.[30]
3. The calculated metrics for the corpus are available via a public SPARQL endpoint.[31]

Acknowledgements. The authors would like to express their profound gratitude and give special acknowledgment to Alexandra Hager for her invaluable, expert and time-critical support, Thomas Seyffertitz for expert advice in the area of research data management and Gary Brewer, BuiltWith, for providing an extensive MediaWiki collection. This work is part of a project funded by the *WU Anniversary Fund of the City of Vienna.*

References

1. Abedjan, Z., Gruetze, T., Jentzsch, A., Naumann, F.: Profiling and mining RDF data with ProLOD++. In: 2014 IEEE 30th International Conference on Data Engineering, pp. 1198–1201. IEEE, Chicago, IL, USA, March 2014. https://doi.org/10.1109/ICDE.2014.6816740, http://ieeexplore.ieee.org/document/6816740/
2. Alexander, K., Cyganiak, R., Hausenblas, M., Zhao, J.: Describing linked datasets. In: LDOW (2009)
3. Bohm, C., et al.: Profiling linked open data with ProLOD. In: 2010 IEEE 26th International Conference on Data Engineering Workshops (ICDEW 2010), pp. 175–178. IEEE, Long Beach, CA, March 2010. https://doi.org/10.1109/ICDEW.2010.5452762, http://ieeexplore.ieee.org/document/5452762/
4. Boncz, P., Fundulaki, I., Gubichev, A., Larriba-Pey, J., Neumann, T.: The linked data benchmark council project. Datenbank-Spektrum **13**(2), 121–129 (2013)

---

[28] https://cost-dkg.eu/.
[29] https://semantic-data.cluster.ai.wu.ac.at/smwcloud/.
[30] https://semantic-data.cluster.ai.wu.ac.at/smwcloud/corpus/.
[31] https://smwcloud-sparql.cluster.ai.wu.ac.at/.

5. Burns, A., et al.: A suite of generative tasks for multi-level multimodal webpage understanding. arXiv preprint arXiv:2305.03668 (2023)
6. Duque-Ramos, A., Fernández-Breis, J.T., Stevens, R., Aussenac-Gilles, N.: OQuaRE: a SQuaRE-based approach for evaluating the quality of ontologies. J. Res. Pract. Inf. Technol. **43**(2) (2011)
7. Ermilov, I., Demter, J., Martin, M., Lehmann, J., Auer, S.: Lodstats–large scale dataset analytics for linked open data. Under review in ISWC (2013)
8. Ermilov, I., Lehmann, J., Martin, M., Auer, S.: LODStats: the data web census dataset. In: Groth, P., et al. (eds.) ISWC 2016. LNCS, vol. 9982, pp. 38–46. Springer, Cham (2016). https://doi.org/10.1007/978-3-319-46547-0_5
9. Ermilov, I., Martin, M., Lehmann, J., Auer, S.: Linked open data statistics: collection and exploitation. In: Klinov, P., Mouromtsev, D. (eds.) KESW 2013. CCIS, vol. 394, pp. 242–249. Springer, Heidelberg (2013). https://doi.org/10.1007/978-3-642-41360-5_19
10. Escobar, P., Candela, G., Trujillo, J., Marco-Such, M., Peral, J.: Adding value to linked open data using a multidimensional model approach based on the RDF data cube vocabulary. Comput. Stand. Interfaces **68**, 103378 (2020)
11. Fahl, W., Holzheim, T., Westerinen, A., Lange, C., Decker, S.: Getting and hosting your own copy of wikidata. In: Wikidata Workshop @ ISWC 2022 (2022). https://ceur-ws.org/Vol-3262/paper9.pdf
12. Fernández, J.D., Martınez-Prieto, M.A., Gutiérrez, C., Polleres, A., Arias, M.: Binary RDF representation for publication and exchange (HDT). J. Web Semant. **19**(2) (2013). https://doi.org/10.1016/j.websem.2013.01.002, http://www.polleres.net/publications/fern-etal-2013-HDT-JWS.pdf
13. Fernández, J.D., Beek, W., Martínez-Prieto, M.A., Arias, M.: LOD-a-lot. In: d'Amato, C., et al. (eds.) ISWC 2017. LNCS, vol. 10588, pp. 75–83. Springer, Cham (2017). https://doi.org/10.1007/978-3-319-68204-4_7
14. Fernández, M., Overbeeke, C., Sabou, M., Motta, E.: What makes a good ontology? A case-study in fine-grained knowledge reuse. In: Gómez-Pérez, A., Yu, Y., Ding, Y. (eds.) ASWC 2009. LNCS, vol. 5926, pp. 61–75. Springer, Heidelberg (2009). https://doi.org/10.1007/978-3-642-10871-6_5
15. Gangemi, A., Catenacci, C., Ciaramita, M., Lehmann, J.: Modelling ontology evaluation and validation. In: Sure, Y., Domingue, J. (eds.) ESWC 2006. LNCS, vol. 4011, pp. 140–154. Springer, Heidelberg (2006). https://doi.org/10.1007/11762256_13
16. Glimm, B., Hogan, A., Krötzsch, M., Polleres, A.: OWL: yet to arrive on the web of data? In: WWW2012 Workshop on Linked Data on the Web (LDOW2012). Lyon, France, April 2012. http://www.polleres.net/publications/glim-etal-2012LDOW.pdf
17. Haller, A., Fernández, J.D., Kamdar, M.R., Polleres, A.: What are links in linked open data? A characterization and evaluation of links between knowledge graphs on the web. J. Data Inf. Qual. **12**(2), 1–34 (2020)
18. Krabina, B.: Building a knowledge graph for the history of Vienna with semantic MediaWiki. J. Web Semant. **76**, 100771 (2023)
19. Krötzsch, M., Vrandečić, D., Völkel, M.: Semantic MediaWiki. In: Cruz, I., et al. (eds.) ISWC 2006. LNCS, vol. 4273, pp. 935–942. Springer, Heidelberg (2006). https://doi.org/10.1007/11926078_68
20. Martínez-Prieto, M.A., Arias Gallego, M., Fernández, J.D.: Exchange and consumption of huge RDF data. In: Simperl, E., Cimiano, P., Polleres, A., Corcho, O., Presutti, V. (eds.) ESWC 2012. LNCS, vol. 7295, pp. 437–452. Springer, Heidelberg (2012). https://doi.org/10.1007/978-3-642-30284-8_36

21. Meusel, R., Petrovski, P., Bizer, C.: The webdatacommons microdata, RDFa and microformat dataset series. In: Mika, P., et al. (eds.) ISWC 2014. LNCS, vol. 8796, pp. 277–292. Springer, Cham (2014). https://doi.org/10.1007/978-3-319-11964-9_18
22. Nogales, A., Angel Sicilia-Urban, M., García-Barriocanal, E.: Measuring vocabulary use in the linked data cloud. Online Inf. Rev. **41**(2), 252–271 (2017)
23. Orme, A.M., Yao, H., Etzkorn, L.H.: Indicating ontology data quality, stability, and completeness throughout ontology evolution. J. Softw. Maint. Evol. Res. Pract. **19**(1), 49–75 (2007)
24. Reiz, A., Sandkuhl, K.: Neontometrics–a public endpoint for calculating ontology metrics. In: Proceedings of Poster and Demo Track and Workshop Track of the 18th International Conference on Semantic Systems co-located with 18th International Conference on Semantic Systems (SEMANTiCS 2022), vol. 13, pp. 22–15. CEUR-WS, Vienna (2022)
25. Reiz, A., Sandkuhl, K.: Harmonizing the OQuaRE quality framework:. In: Proceedings of the 24th International Conference on Enterprise Information Systems, pp. 148–158. SCITEPRESS - Science and Technology Publications, Online Streaming (2022). https://doi.org/10.5220/0011077200003179, https://www.scitepress.org/DigitalLibrary/Link.aspx?doi=10.5220/0011077200003179
26. Rietveld, L., Beek, W., Hoekstra, R., Schlobach, S.: Meta-data for a lot of LOD. Semant. Web **8**(6), 1067–1080 (2017)
27. Tartir, S., Arpinar, I.B.: Ontology evaluation and ranking using ontoqa. In: International Conference on Semantic Computing (ICSC 2007), pp. 185–192. IEEE (2007)
28. Vrandečić, D., Krötzsch, M.: Wikidata: a free collaborative knowledgebase. Commun. ACM **57**(10), 78–85. ACM, New York, NY, USA (2014)
29. Wilkinson, M.D., et al.: The FAIR guiding principles for scientific data management and stewardship. Sci. Data **3**(1), 160018 (2016). https://doi.org/10.1038/sdata.2016.18, https://www.nature.com/articles/sdata201618, number: 1 Publisher: Nature Publishing Group
30. Yang, Z., Zhang, D., Ye, C.: Ontology analysis on complexity and evolution based on conceptual model. In: Leser, U., Naumann, F., Eckman, B. (eds.) DILS 2006. LNCS, vol. 4075, pp. 216–223. Springer, Heidelberg (2006). https://doi.org/10.1007/11799511_19
31. Yao, H., Orme, A.M., Etzkorn, L.: Cohesion metrics for ontology design and application. J. Comput. Sci. **1**(1), 107–113 (2005)

SousLeSens - A Comprehensive Suite for the Industrial Practice of Semantic Knowledge Graphs

Claude Fauconnet[1]([envelope]) [iD], Jean-Charles Leclerc[2] [iD], Arkopaul Sarkar[3] [iD],
and Mohamed Hedi Karray[4] [iD]

[1] SousLeSens, Paris, France
claude.fauconnet@gmail.com
[2] TotalEnergies, Paris, France
[3] Knowledge Graph Alliance, Brussels, Belgium
[4] Université de Technologie de Tarbes, Tarbes, France

Abstract. Over recent decades, the advancement of semantic web technologies has underscored the increasing importance of tools dedicated to developing and managing the foundational components of the semantic web stack. Addressing the evolving needs, a variety of tools have emerged from the research and development projects from academia as well as commercial software vendors. These tools offer a diverse range of services tailored to the management of various aspects of semantic knowledge graphs. Despite this proliferation, feedback from stakeholders involved in public and privately funded projects has highlighted notable shortcomings in existing tools. These gaps become evident in two key areas: firstly, the user experience struggles to scale up to meet industrial-level data practices and knowledge engineering methodologies. Secondly, a lack of interoperability and compatibility among the existing task-specific tools leads to elevated costs and efforts. This paper introduces a novel semantic knowledge management ecosystem embodied in a suite of tools collectively known as 'SousLeSens'. Unlike its counterparts, SLS not only provides comprehensive coverage of typical knowledge engineering tasks while adhering to best practices for ensuring quality but also boasts a purely visual (no to minimum-code) interface. This feature is particularly well-suited for handling large-scale, industry-grade semantic data models. The paper delves into the establishment of requirements for knowledge engineering tools and services, derived from recent stakeholder surveys. It proceeds to present the SLS toolkit, elucidating its architecture and operational protocols. Finally, the paper validates the toolkit's capabilities by comparing it with existing tools against predefined requirements and illustrating various use cases.

Keywords: ontology editor · knowledge graph · SousLeSens ·
protege · semantics

A. Meroño Peñuela et al. (Eds.): ESWC 2024, LNCS 14665, pp. 162–177, 2024.
https://doi.org/10.1007/978-3-031-60635-9_10

1 Introduction

In the evolving landscape of semantic web engineering tools, there exists a pressing need for solutions that can seamlessly navigate the intricacies of constructing and managing the foundational elements of the semantic web stack. Despite the emergence of various tools from both academic and commercial spheres, feedback from stakeholders has consistently highlighted notable shortcomings [1]. These deficiencies manifest themselves primarily in the struggle to scale user experiences to meet industrial-level data practices and the lack of interoperability among existing, task-specific tools, resulting in increased costs and efforts.

Against this backdrop, this paper introduces 'SousLeSens' (SLS), a collaborative semantic knowledge management (KM) ecosystem specifically designed to address the identified gaps in the current tool landscape. Unlike its counterparts, SLS not only comprehensively covers many typical knowledge engineering tasks, but also lets users to use a visually driven, minimal-code interface tailored for handling large-scale, industry-grade semantic data models. The Semantic Labeling System (SLS) was developed as part of the TotalEnergies Semantic Framework (TSF) project [7] to address the need for a set of tools that comply with the best practices in knowledge engineering while also being user-friendly and easy to learn for professionals in the industry.

In this paper, we first identified the requirements of a comprehensive KM tool by exploring both the past literature and industrial expectations in Sect. 2. Afterwards, in Sect. 3, the methodological principle and technical architecture of SLS is presented. In Sect. 4, three industrial use cases are presented to demonstrate the capabilities of SLS. Finally, a comparative analysis of SLS against other similar products is presented in Sect. 5.

2 State-of-the-art

The realm of KM tools is diverse, mirroring the variety of methods, languages, and formats for knowledge management. The aim of the section is however not to analyse these tools individually but to identify the requirements for a comprehensive KM tool from the past surveys and industrial feedback. SLS gathered these requirements from two sources: 1) review of the existing KM tools and feedback from users of these tools as described in Sect. 2.1 and 2) industrial needs identified through various initiatives and projects as described in Sect. 2.2.

2.1 Existing Knowledge Engineering Tools

In ontology engineering, while many tools address specific phases, only a few provide comprehensive solutions. A recent EU Horizon2020 OntoCommons survey [11] categorized tools, including competency questions for requirement specification, Linked Open Vocabulary (LOV) and IndustryPortal for ontology reuse and publication, Chowlk and Menthor editor for conceptual modelling, various reasoners, e.g., Pellet, Hermit, Fact++, and consistency checkers, e.g., OOPS!, all of which has targeted focus in some of the activities along the ontology engineering lifecycle. In contrast, a comprehensive KM tool facilitates many KM activities, such as ontology implementation, covering drafting, source editing, evaluation, ontology matching, maintenance, issue management, and usage as well as managing large data volumes. Past surveys [3,8,9,12,13] on ontology editing tools mention comprehensive tools such as SWOOP, Protégé, WebODE, TopBraid Composer, OntoPic Fluent editor, OWLGrEd, OntoEdit, Anzo platform, Cameo modeller, and PoolParty, which comply to the most popular and de facto standards for knowledge engineering, such as OWL and RDF. It can also be observed that ontology editing and knowledge graph management are distinct activities, and the mentioned tools have varied support for both. Graph database systems such as Neo4J, GraphDB, AllegroGraph, Stardog, and RDFox often include dedicated data transformation tools along with a triplestore as their main offering.

The primary aspects of evaluating these tools are their features and usability; the former covers the functionalities, architecture, and support to various activities of ontology engineering and the latter covers various types of user experience. Past evaluations [5,9,11,13] mention many common features that ontology and knowledge graph editors typically support. These are expressivity, language, modularisation and reusing, consistency check, reasoning and inference, merging, mapping, encoding and storage, visualisation, data transformation, query, and third-party support. As Islam and Sheikh [6] noted, there is no standard approach to evaluate the usability of ontology editors. Still, some of the usability criteria that can be found in the small number of past surveys are user experience and visual abstraction, collaboration, multi-lingual support, performance and scalability, methodological guidance, practicality, help and documentation, and exception handling. Easy access and deployment of the tool, along with its openness and extensibility also play a big role in ensuring its usability. The OntoCommons survey [11] collected 77 responses from the major knowledge engineering tool developers using online questionnaires that include a list of common requirements for knowledge engineering tools: collaboration of multiple stakeholders, visualisation, debugging, validation, quality assurance and analytics, API support, OWL support, ontology import, user-friendliness, connected ontologies, tool integration, modularisation, search and reuse ontology, ontology correlations, ontology deployment and document generation, and ontology conceptualisation, understandability of GUI labels. Although the basic features for a comprehensive ontology editor can be found by surveying the existing tools, the development of SLS prioritised those features that can fulfil the requirements gathered from community surveys as mentioned above.

2.2   Industrial Feedback

The introduction of a new process and working method requires the support of new types of tools, as described in the OntoCommons roadmap [1]. The Knowledge Translator report [4] emphasizes the need for easy on-boarding and training for the transition from a human-centric paper standard to a data-centric and model-centric approach, exemplified by initiatives such as CFIHOS[1], allowing the analysis of digital requirements, source coherence and internal knowledge sharing with external partners.

In 2020 and 2021, TotalEnergies collaborated with stakeholders of the International Association of Oil & Gas Producers[2] (IOGP) and the World Economic Forum (WEF) to formalize the conditions for better data exchanges in the world's energy industries. It is evident in the industrial outlook that sharing reliable information requires addressing the big data challenges (volume, value, variety, velocity, and veracity) and a common way of structuring and exchanging knowledge. The IOGP working group identified not only the fundamentals for common semantics for data structuring and exchange but also a set of recommendations for a suitable KM tool, including web (HTTP protocol) compliance, following the motto: 'Everything is available to everyone and everywhere at any time', open code practice, publishing vocabulary definitions with IRI, obligatory common schema definition, compliance to RDF/OWL formalism, and interactive functional web-applications for query/extraction of information. The industrial stakeholders of the above-mentioned initiatives realised that existing tools for supporting these semantic web requirements often have a high learning curve, necessitating a new kind of tool for easy onboarding and upskilling. In the following sections, we describe how SLS addresses these requirements from the perspective of its core architectures and various tools dedicated to critical KM tasks.

3   Specification of SLS

Developed within the TSF project, SousLeSens[3] (SLS) is a suite of web tools designed to facilitate the creation of semantic knowledge graphs using ontologies. It functions as an adaptable set of tools and a cohesive suite that aims to demystify the complexities associated with the Semantic Web. By offering a user-friendly interface, SLS makes it possible for individuals, including those in industrial sectors, who may not specialize in these technologies, to leverage Semantic Web capabilities. This accessibility is crucial for meeting industrial requirements, particularly in managing data and knowledge, developing digital twins, and supporting decision-making processes.

3.1   Methodological Foundations

The initial requirements for a knowledge graph management tool were chartered by the TSF project in January 2021, as shown in Fig. 1. The SLS development team facilitated the creation of initial prototypes that were periodically reviewed to progressively develop the versatile TSF tool suite. Over time, the support

---

[1] https://www.jip36-cfihos.org/cfihos-standards/.
[2] https://www.iogp.org/.
[3] https://sls.kg-alliance.org/.

for W3C-recommended formats in a cohesive data management framework provided a flexible solution to TSF for predefined data interoperability in several use cases. This allowed the immediate reuse of internal technical references, expressed in SKOS, by converting them into RDF and OWL formats within TSF. The code and interface integrated methodological governance, ensuring conformity to common structuring principles. This orchestration aligned company activities with semantic knowledge graphs, serving as domain ontologies for reference data domains.

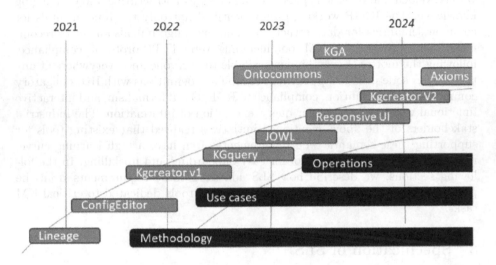

Fig. 1. Timeline of SousLeSens evolution.

The SLS toolset (purposes of various tools under SLS are summarised in Fig. 2) is designed to facilitate the continuous onboarding and upskilling of internal members of TotalEnergies by mirroring the exploration process of the semantic web for newcomers. However, the responsive and interactive design principles of SLS are poised to benefit all users in learning semantic web technologies, addressing common inquiries throughout the learning curve. For example: 1) **Discovering, Comparing, and Choosing Ontologies**: SLS's visualization and manipulation of graphs under the tool Lineage simplifies understanding essential ontology notions, allowing users to explore, mix, and compare different ontologies with visually driven capabilities. 2) **Building Ontology**: SLS provides a user-friendly interface for creating classes, establishing semantic relationships, and respecting constraints. The tool automates SPARQL queries within triplestore databases based on the type of ontology being built. 3) **Associating an Ontology with Data**: SLS aids in generating mappings between ontology objects and data model elements, especially for tabular data. The tool allows users to express, save, and graphically represent mappings for validating their relevance. 4) **Building a Semantic Knowledge Graph (SKG)**: SLS transforms data from relational databases or CSV files into a knowledge graph using pre-established mappings. The tool is evolving to support the RML standard in its roadmap. 5) **Using SKG**: SLS supports two distinct uses of semantic knowledge graphs, enabling queries through APIs or exploration mode. In exploration mode, users can interact with graphical representations, simplifying queries based on ontology concepts. 6) **Collaborative Work**: SLS's internet-native architecture promotes collaborative work by providing secure user management, data source control, and read-write rights. Metadata addition helps trace modifications and qualify their status. 7) **Combining Tools**: SLS's layered, modular architecture, combined with technical standards, allows it to offer integrated services and act as a client or third-party service provider, facilitating seamless combination with other tools.

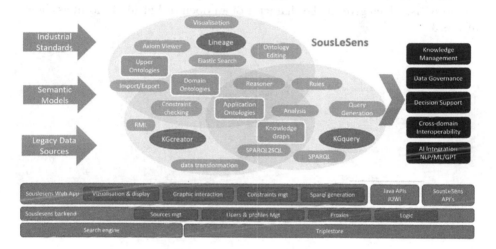

Fig. 2. Overview of SLS mapping different usage of its tools (Lineage, KGCreator and KGQuery) along with the technical stack (at the bottom).

In this context, the technical architecture of SLS was designed based on the following pillars: 1) Rigorous management of semantics included in upper-level ontologies, encoding the constraints in reference languages, such as RDF, RDFS, and OWL; 2) A graphical visual representation, utilizing nodes and edges as a global metaphor for an RDF graph, captures the expressive richness of the triples graph while ensuring understandability; filtering and navigation capabilities within the network elements, coupled with the graph spatialization engine, aid users in comprehending complexity, coherence, inconsistency, and multiple relationships by accommodating the limitations of simultaneous information apprehension by the human eye. 3) Alternative mode of interaction and manipulation based on the generalization of a three-step process: translation of user actions into SPARQL queries, execution of queries on a triplestore internal to SLS or other in reading as well as in writing modes, and representation of query results either in graph mode or in table mode.

3.2 Software Architecture

The organic design of SLS evolved by gradually aggregating functionalities around the central core concept of visualizing and manipulating graphs. Technical solutions, implementing some original codebases, reflect this development. Notably, the client bears the majority of processing, enabling rich interactions with the graph without frequent server calls-a key for the performance of SLS. The choice of untyped JavaScript, used on both the client and server sides (node.js) was based on its agility in seamlessly moving code between them. Type-Script, a typed form of JavaScript, was not used due to its heavy constraints on typing, which were deemed impractical for our frequently evolving code needs. The architecture of SLS is centered on its NodeJs web server which essentially acts as a flow distributor between its different peripheral components through secure APIs, which gives it the character of an open technical platform as shown in Fig. 3.

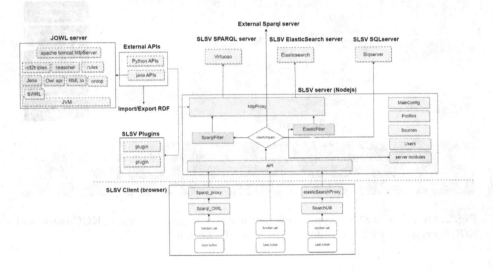

Fig. 3. Technical architecture of SLS

In the following, various core components of SLS are described based on the architecture.

1. **Security and access management**: Each user of the SLS web interface or API is authenticated. Several authentication systems are supported but only one is active within an instance. In addition, requests made to the internal TripleStore or the search engine are filtered according to the user's rights.
2. **Administration and configuration module**: As a collaborative application, SLS rigorously manages the access of different users to different resources and allows very flexible management of access to resources ranging from public sources visible to all to private sources, having restricted write rights for

only a few users. For this purpose, SLS has developed an administrative management module composed of the objects: Users, having different roles and permissions, Source, identifying different KGs, and Profiles, maintaining access rights by mutual association.

3. **Storage layer**: The RDF graphs manipulated by SLS are stored either in its internal triplestore (Virtuoso) or in other triple stores referenced and accessible in SLS depending on the configuration.

4. **Application server layer**: This layer powered by Node.js communicates via APIs in HTTP(S) mode with the user interface and with external clients while respecting the access rules applicable to each client. Requesting APIs triggers various calls, e.g., execution of queries on SPARQL or SQL servers, specific internal commands, and access to third-party APIs (python, java, etc.) depending on the case, always checked in terms of access rights.

5. **The web client layer (browser)** locally manages most of the actions carried out by the user (business logic) and limits the interactions with the server layer for reading data or specific processing. For example, the construction of SPARQL or SQL queries in response to user actions is done dynamically on the client side, unlike the practices of many other applications. SLS incorporates common UI components, such as the *SourceSelector*, for user-authorized source selection, the *jsTreeWidget*, facilitating tree representation and node control actions, and the *NodeInfos* dialogue, displaying predicates of a node, including the ability to add or remove predicates based on user rights and experimental visualization of axioms. These components streamline various interactions within the interface across multiple contexts.

6. **Visual representation of knowledge graphs** stands out in SLS by prioritizing graph drawing and manipulation, a central feature that distinguishes it from similar tools. It utilizes the vis.js[4] JavaScript library, offering a robust API for graph visualization and interaction. Vis.js provides various spatialization algorithms, optimizing graph representation based on factors like the number of relationships each node has, with central nodes having more connections. For example, the configuration for the BarnesHut layout algorithm, which is a quadtree-based gravity model and the fastest non-hierarchical solver. Graph stabilization is achieved through successive iterations, which can be manually interrupted by users. Before graph drawing in SLS, SPARQL queries select triples from the store, transformed into nodes and edges using vis.js API. As RDF graphs in OWL ontologies or SKGs can be intricate, different triplet filtering strategies, detailed in Sect. 3.3, are implemented for clear and useful representations. Once represented on the screen it is possible to interact via the mouse with the nodes and edges of the graph in order either to obtain information to navigate in the graph or to create new predicates.

7. **Plugins**: SLS has a system of plugins allowing users to create specific applications, including their web app, that can be used like other tools and take advantage of the entire environment. The open architecture of SLS supports

---

[4] https://github.com/visjs.

interaction with external libraries, such as JOWL[5] -a Java web application with REST APIs developed in 2023. This integration allows the execution of OWLAPI and SWRL (reasoner and rules) Java methods within SLS. Additionally, an integrated Python API enables users to choose import/export formats for triplestores and, soon, to interact with SLS-referenced graphs from a Jupyter or other Python environment while respecting user access rights.

8. **Deployment**: SLS's technical environment is deployed through diverse Docker images, including a node.js web server with SLS code and APIs[6], a Virtuoso triplestore, an ElasticSearch search engine, an SQL server (and soon Postgres SQL) database, a Python environment, and optional third-party components and specific SLS plugins.SLS can be downloaded freely from its GitHub repository[7] under an MIT license. SLS releases follow a standard versioning system. Supporting the easy onboarding, a documentation website[8] (currently containing 'quick start' and many video tutorials) is also made available.

3.3   Tools in SLS

Lineage in SLS facilitates the simultaneous representation and manipulation of graph representations of different ontologies. It enables the selection, editing, evaluation, and comparison of ontologies, allowing users to generate overviews or details for specific tasks. Key features include selecting source ontologies, transforming triples into interactive graph drawings, random navigation on the whiteboard, creation of classes and individuals, visualization of predicates and axioms, drag-and-drop relationship creation, advanced SPARQL query generation, representation of label similarities, label-based graph searches, and object properties selection and presentation. The UI components of Lineage displaying an example ontology shown in Fig. 4. Lineage being a versatile ontology editor, it supports constraints on class and properties in a variety of expressivity, from simple subsumption and transitivity suitable of RDF graph to domain, range, existential, and universal constraints to support full Description Logic (DL) formalism. The graph-drawing complexity is balanced by providing the option to export information displayed in tabular form (CSV) for users accustomed to spreadsheets and relational databases. As SLS is integrated into IndustryPortal [2], users may search for a FAIR ontology from the portal for easy reuse.

KGCreator can be used to simplify the transform complex industrial data into a semantic knowledge graph by serving as a user-friendly alternative to RML or R2ML-based tools. Its straightforward structure, depicted in Fig. 5, proves

---

[5] https://github.com/souslesens/jowl.
[6] https://sls.kg-alliance.org/api/v1/.
[7] https://github.com/souslesens/souslesensVocables.
[8] http://souslesens.org/index.php/tools/.

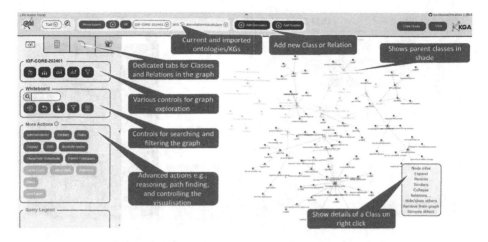

Fig. 4. Lineage tool displaying an ontology with upper ontologies in its import and various UI controls for users to manage, view and edit the ontology.

effective for even non-specialist operators. While KGCreator facilitates interoperability with standards by easily translating to RML, it offers features such as access to tabular data schemas, graphical exhibition of the ontology for column/class associations, detailed mapping for enriched associations, visualization of mappings' completeness and consistency, and simulation of generated triplets for previewing and corrections before storing in the triple store. Additionally, KGCreator supports functions and transformations for data line processing and table mapping, ensuring flexibility in adjusting data structures and avoiding errors. Resource identifiers in KGCreator can take various forms, including real URIs and blank nodes associated with random numbers. Triplet Generation Engine, a backend processing program, utilizes mappings and associated data to generate the knowledge graph in the triple store, offering an API for regenerating the entire sub-graph from previous mapping.

KGQuery allows the use of SKG in exploration mode without having to master the SPARQL language and know the complex structure of the graph, the KGQuery tool offers an interactive query-able abstraction of the KG, which allows users to automatically generate queries by graphically selecting the classes, as shown in Fig. 6. KGQuery is also able to apply filters and perform queries on multiple graphs. The visual manipulation of knowledge graphs through queries relies on correct data typing and predicate construction in alignment with ontology constraints during graph construction. The queryable abstraction of the KG is derived from the actual classes and predicates present in the graph, maintaining fidelity. The graph traversal algorithm, based on shortest path calculations using adjacency matrices, facilitates automatic SPARQL query construction, with results presented in tabular form - following the usual expectations of data users - along with group queries and set operations.

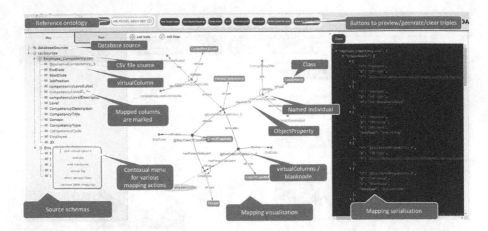

Fig. 5. KGCreator interface to create and manage mapping from heterogeneous sources (e.g., database, CSV) to ontology and generate triples using these mappings.

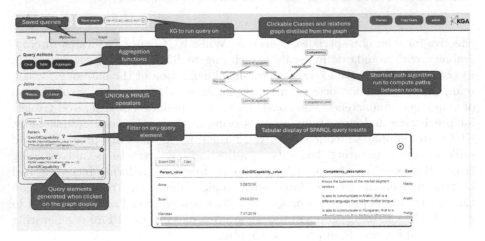

Fig. 6. Example of automatic SPARQL query generation using the graphical interface of KGQuery.

4   Validation

In this section, we first provide three industrial use cases to demonstrate the practical use of SLS in semantic modelling and exploitation of data. Furthermore, we discussed the essential capabilities of SLS in comparison to other tools against the scope, coverage, and requirements identified in Sect. 2.

4.1   Case Studies

As a fundamental tool, SLS supports many data activities in TSF. The following sections present three use cases where SLS plays major roles in standardising industrial data for cross-organisation exchange, supporting business decisions, and valorising geoscience data by integrating AI tools for oil discovery.

Lineage for Reusing Semantic Standards for Industrial Data. Onto-Commons Roadmap [1] identifies industrial needs for enhanced data standards, such as logic-based formats, integration of cross-cutting standards, and multi-domain stakeholder involvement. The development of the CFIHOS RDL[9] proto-type during the READI JIP[10] in Norway (2018-2022), aligned with the Industrial Domain Ontology[11] (IDO) structure, exemplifies progress in this area, fostering major industry adoption under ISO standardization. The lack of interoperability among standardized ontologies and the demand for clear presentations of CFI-HOS RDL values emphasize the importance of semantization, providing benefits like easier accessibility and flexibility for extensions. Lineage proves valuable in facilitating collaboration in ontology setup and validation phases through its filtering capabilities and visual representations, aiding in the detection of defaults. TotalEnergies leverages Lineage for digital technical data interoperability and NLP processing for noise reduction and enhancing machine learning confidence in used labels, based on application ontologies in the Geosciences and Reservoir Well domain, which are built following ISO 23726 standard family for ontology and ISO/IEC 81346 standard for managing digital data. Lineage's key applications include versatile source comparisons, collaborative work on a writable semantic layer, ensuring coherence in the domain knowledge graph, developing a collaborative CFIHOS vocabulary in IDO through SLS, and facilitating easy integration of business applications with reference domain ontologies across the organization.

KGCreator and KGquery for Business Decision Support. KGCreator and KGQuery play a pivotal role in TotalEnergies' business decision support, particularly in addressing challenges during major installation shutdowns, as showcased in the Dalia asset's life cycle extension project. In this project, SLS, equipped with KGCreator and KGQuery, optimized planning sequences by considering criteria from various Information Systems like SAP, Document Management System, and Primavera planning tool. The digital approach transformed the project by facilitating real-time insights across disciplines and systems, with a key strength in linking each Work Breakdown Structure item with pertinent data sources for efficient categorization and filtering. The application of KGCreator and KGQuery within SLS resulted in streamlined decision making, efficient change management, simplified project reviews, automated compliance checks, and impact analysis, bringing tangible benefits such as reduced standby risks, improved operational efficiency, comprehensive documentation, and continuity preservation.

---

[9] https://www.jip36-cfihos.org/cfihos-standards/.
[10] https://readi-jip.org/.
[11] https://www.iso.org/standard/87560.html.

SLS for AI-Powered Oil Discovery and Ocean Exploration. TotalEnergies' pilot study integrates SLS and advanced AI tools like NLP, GPT, and LLM with the well domain ontology (see Sect. 4.1) to revolutionize oil discovery and ocean exploration. NLP addresses challenges in managing complex informational portfolios, while GPT enriches the knowledge graph with additional facts. The experiment focuses on SLS for metadata management, entity reconciliation, and acculturation support to enhance data value and mitigate challenges in processing data labels and business objects across contexts. The proposed demonstrator, leveraging diverse databases while preserving semantics, aims to rationalize source databases, enhance data usage, and virtualise data access. For generative AI projects, SLS provides a reference vocabulary-based semantic guidance and automated verification by reasoning as an essential service to address interoperability challenges and inaccurate data. An SLS python API facilitates easy access to SLS RDF graphs and third-party AI tool libraries in the Jupiter python environment. In conclusion, the modular elements of SLS offer a comprehensive approach to combine generative AI and ontologies for data and industrial engineering document valorisation. The proposed benchmarking initiative will emphasize knowledge graphs' role in enhancing LLMs' accuracy for question answering on enterprise SQL databases, as posited by Sequeda et al. [10].

5   Comparative Analysis

SLS aims to be one of the most widely used modern ontology editors that supports OWL and RDF. It therefore includes tools that span various stages of ontology engineering, notably Lineage for ontology implementation and KGCreator and KGQuery for ontology maintenance and use. This combination of features within a single ecosystem is uncommon among other tool systems, with the exception of TopBraid and PoolParty. Notably, Protégé, in its standard offering, does not include knowledge graph management. Various features of Lineage, such as the visual whiteboard for conceptual to formal drafting of ontology, mapping, matching and comparison facility for handling ontology import stack in a modular fashion, along with in-place guidance to help users build coherent ontologies typical to the other ontology editors, SLS stands out from other editors, e.g., Protege, TopBraid Composer, WebODE, SWOOP, OntoPic and Fluent with its unique feature of purely visual, no to minimal code environment for ontology editing - although many of them provide ad hoc graph visualisation. This purely visual design becomes a more distinguishable feature of SLS in terms of KGCreator and KGQuery, considering no comprehensive knowledge management system contains such a novel interface. Collaboration is a primary feature of SLS and covers every knowledge engineering activity under its support. Although collaboration is also provided by some of the other editors, e.g., WebProtege, TopBraid, Anzo, SWOOP, and OntoEdit, the user experience for these editors will be vastly different in comparison to SLS's multi-user simultaneous manipulation of visual knowledge graphs. Lastly, in past and ongoing projects, SLS's visual abstraction of many complexities of end-to-end knowledge engineering has proven to be particularly suitable for industrial users in

Table 1. Comparison of tools. Columns: A - coverage of KM activities (e - editing ontology, r - reasoning KG, v - visualizing KG, p - population of data in KG, q - query, u - use), B - modularisation/import resolution, C - search and reuse ontology, D - Consistency check, E - reasoning/inference, F - rules, G - mapping, H - model repository, I - conceptualisation, J - data transformation, K - visual query, L - collaboration, M - methodological guide, N - User-friendliness (no-code environment, ease of learning, third-party integration)

Tools	A	B	C	D	E	F	G	H	I	J	K	L	M	N
Protégé	e,r,v	Y	N	Y	Y	Y	N	N	N	N	N	N	Y	N
WebProtege	e,r,v	Y	N	Y	N	Y	N	Y	N	N	N	Y	Y	N
OntoPic	p,q,v	N	N	N	N	N	Y	N	N	Y	N	Y	N	Y
TopBraid	e,r,v,p,q	Y	Y	Y	Y	Y	Y	N	N	Y	N	Y	N	N
Fluent	e,r,v	Y	N	Y	Y	Y	Y	N	N	N	N	N	Y	N
OWLGrEd	e,v	Y	Y	N	N	N	N	Y	Y	N	N	N	N	N
OntoEdit	e,r	Y	Y	Y	Y	N	N	N	N	N	N	N	N	N
Anzo	p,q,v,u	Y	Y	Y	N	N	Y	Y	N	Y	N	Y	N	Y
PoolParty	e,v,p,u	Y	Y	N	Y	N	Y	Y	Y	Y	N	Y	N	Y
SLS	e,r,v,p,q,u	Y	Y	Y	Y	Y	Y	Y	Y	Y	Y	Y	Y	Y

co-modelling, co-creating and co-analysing vast amounts of data for common understanding, system-wide integration and exchange, supporting practical benefits in decision support driven by SLS's easy integration with other AI-based tools.

In Table 1, we provided a comparative analysis of the SLS against the requirements identified in Sect. 2, considering only the default configuration, i.e., without any plug-in for every product. As described in Sect. 2, the requirements are derived from two sources: 1) user surveys on existing tools, and 2) industrial feedback. The tools presented in Table 1 include many other features, which are sometimes unique to them. These features are not included for them not being part of baseline requirements. Therefore, the comparison matrix in Table 1 is not an evaluation of the overall efficacy of the tools, as each one of them is built with its purpose and serves its users with some unique features. Moreover, the comparison is conducted by the authors conjointly with some industrial stakeholders and users, which lacks the critical mass of a typical survey. We want to conduct a wide survey to compare several existing tools against SLS in the future.

SLS being more focused on ease of use for industrial operators, it does not yet provide some of the more rigorous language supports that are available in other tools. e.g., Protégé. These languages and grammars, including Manchester Syntax Format for writing complex axioms, SWRL, DataLog, or SPIN rules for rule-based inference, and SHACL for data validation. The mappings created by KGCreator is also not exchangeable in standardised formats such as RML and SSSOM. We plan to include these features in the future versions of SLS.

6   Conclusion

This paper introduced SousLeSens (SLS) as a solution that addresses practical industrial needs and facilitates easy onboarding of industries into semantic web technologies, especially at a time when traditional data technologies are no longer sufficient to manage present and future data challenges. SLS, born out of industry necessity, now aspires to foster broad adoption of semantic KM practices. The future work will focus on key areas for improvement and expansion, including collaboration support, enhanced graphic axiom creation tools, specific ontology creation tools, reasoner capabilities for KGcreator mappings validation, refining the virtual SQL query system in KGquery, and reshaping the user interface for better ergonomics and a responsive design. Looking ahead, SLS envisions growing its user community to drive its development roadmap, along with fostering collaboration between academic and industrial perspectives through its open-source initiatives. The establishment of a dedicated working group within the Knowledge Graph Alliance[12] (KGA) will play a pivotal role in achieving these goals and ensuring the continuous evolution of SLS to meet the evolving needs of its user base[13].

Acknowledgment. This work was funded by the EU H2020 Ontology-driven Data Documentation for Industry Commons (OntoCommons) under grant agreement no. 958371 and was supported by TotalEnergies and SousLeSens. We would like to thank Karim Ounnoughi from Akkodis Group, Xavier Garnier and Nicolas Chauvat, from Logilab, Amine Karoui from UTTOP, and Pierre Jallais from TotalEnergies for their valuable technical contributions to this work.

References

1. Adamovic, N., et al.: Ontocommons roadmap v1, January 2023. https://doi.org/10.5281/zenodo.7544509
2. Amdouni, E., Sarkar, A., Jonquet, C., Karray, M.H.: IndustryPortal: a common repository for FAIR ontologies in industry 4.0. In: The 22nd International Semantic Web Conference. Athens, Greece (2023)
3. Buraga, S.C., Cojocaru, L., Nichifor, O.C.: Survey on web ontology editing tools. Trans. Autom. Control Comput. Sci. **NN**(ZZ), 1–6 (2006)
4. Goldbeck, G., et al.: The Translator in Knowledge Management for Innovation - A Semantic Vocation of Value to Industry (2023)
5. Gyrard, A., Datta, S.K., Bonnet, C.: A survey and analysis of ontology-based software tools for semantic interoperability in IoT and WoT landscapes. In: IEEE World Forum on Internet of Things, WF-IoT 2018 - Proceedings, vol. 2018-Janua, pp. 86–91 (2018). https://doi.org/10.1109/WF-IoT.2018.8355091
6. Islam, N., Sheikh, G.S.: A review of techniques for ontology editor evaluation. J. Inf. Commun. Technol. **9**(2), 104–114 (2015)

---

[12] https://www.kg-alliance.org/.
[13] https://ontocommons.eu.

7. Leclerc, J.C., Tetard, G., Keraron, Y., Fauconnet, C.: Use of ontologies to structure and manage digital technical data of industrial assets: first steps towards an ecology of knowledge in multi-energies industry. In: CEUR Workshop Proceedings, vol. 3240 (2022)

8. Rahamatullah Khondoker, M., Mueller, P.: Comparing ontology development tools based on an online survey. In: WCE 2010 - World Congress on Engineering 2010, vol. 1, pp. 188–192 (2010)

9. Rastogi, N., Verma, P., Kumar, P.: Analyzing ontology editing tools for effective semantic information retrieval. Int. J. Eng. Sci. Res. Technol. **6**(5), 40–47 (2017). http://www.ijesrt.com

10. Sequeda, J., Allemang, D.T., Jacob, B.: A Benchmark to Understand the Role of Knowledge Graphs on Large Language Model's Accuracy for Question Answering on Enterprise SQL Databases. ArXiv **abs/2311.0** (2023). https://api.semanticscholar.org/CorpusID:265150432

11. Skjæveland, M.G., Slaughter, L.A., Kindermann, C.: OntoCommons D4.3 - Report on Landscape Analysis of Ontology Engineering Tools, April 2022. https://doi.org/10.5281/zenodo.6504670

12. Slimani, T.: Ontology development: a comparing study on tools, languages and formalisms. Indian J. Sci. Technol. **8**(24) (2015). https://doi.org/10.17485/ijst/2015/v8i1/54249

13. Youn, S., Arora, A.: Survey about Ontology Development Tools for Ontology-based Knowledge Management. University of ..., pp. 1–26 (2009). http://suanpalm3.kmutnb.ac.th/teacher/FileDL/supot22255310501.pdf

MLSea: A Semantic Layer for Discoverable Machine Learning

Ioannis Dasoulas[(✉)] [iD], Duo Yang [iD], and Anastasia Dimou [iD]

KU Leuven – Leuven.AI – Flanders Make@KULeuven, Leuven, Belgium
{ioannis.dasoulas,duo.yang,anastasia.dimou}@kuleuven.be

Abstract. With the Machine Learning (ML) field rapidly evolving, ML pipelines continuously grow in numbers, complexity and components. Online platforms (e.g., OpenML, Kaggle) aim to gather and disseminate ML experiments. However, available knowledge is fragmented with each platform representing *distinct* components of the ML process or *intersecting* components but in different ways. To address this problem, we leverage semantic web technologies to model and integrate ML datasets, experiments, software and scientific works into **MLSea**, a resource consisting of: (i) **MLSO**, an ontology that models ML datasets, pipelines and implementations; (ii) **MLST**, taxonomies with collections of ML knowledge formulated as controlled vocabularies; and (iii) **MLSea-KG**, an RDF graph containing ML datasets, pipelines, implementations and scientific works from diverse sources. MLSea paves the way for improving the search, explainability and reproducibility of ML pipelines.

Keywords: Machine Learning · Ontologies · Knowledge Graphs · Semantic Web · Big Data Management

Resource Type: Ontology, Taxonomies and Knowledge Graph.
MLSea: https://w3id.org/mlsea.
MLSO Ontology: https://w3id.org/mlso.
DOI: 10.5281/zenodo.10286868 | **License:** CC BY 4.0.
MLSea-KG: https://w3id.org/mlsea-kg.
DOI: 10.5281/zenodo.10287349 | **License:** CC BY 4.0.

1 Introduction

As the field of Machine Learning (ML) continues to evolve, ML pipelines have grown in complexity, incorporating numerous systems, algorithms, datasets and hyper-parameters. Therefore, creating ML pipelines necessitates extensive research and a significant number of experiments to assess potential configurations, leading to expensive testbeds in terms of available resources and time [69].

To facilitate the construction of ML pipelines, several *general-purpose* (e.g., OpenML [46,68], Papers with Code [50] or Kaggle [34]) and *type-specific* (e.g., Hugging Face [27] and TensorFlow [65] which focus on deep learning) platforms and repositories catalogue ML experiments. Yet these platforms not only exhibit variations in their data representations, access interfaces and search functionalities, but they also cover diverse aspects of ML pipelines. Hence, obtaining a holistic view of the entire ML pipeline process can be challenging, further hindering the already time-consuming and resource-intensive nature of the task and heightening the raising concerns about a reproducibility crisis in AI [23, 28].

The searchability of ML pipelines can be improved by semantically enhanced representations that capture the entire spectrum of the ML process and embrace their diversity. This way, the discovery of ML knowledge can be facilitated by complementing ML knowledge across platforms. Efficient ML pipelines can then be achieved by discovering relevant datasets, publications, parameters and design choices from past experiments, without browsing over multiple platforms.

While past works have tried to model the various aspects of the ML process [16, 37, 49, 54], they do not represent all aspects of the ML pipelines. Every framework is designed to model distinct data sources or aspects of the ML process, resulting in a scarcity of datasets and services that combine publicly accessible ML knowledge from a variety of sources.

To tackle these challenges, this work studies the ML pipeline, dataset attributes and software characteristics available in online repositories (e.g., OpenML, Kaggle, Papers with Code), and integrates their ML experiment data and metadata, resulting in our resource, **MLSea**, which makes these contributions:

(i) The **Machine Learning Sailor Ontology (MLSO)** that reuses and extends state-of-the-art ontologies to describe ML workflows, configurations, experimental results, models, datasets, and software implementations.

(ii) The **Machine Learning Sailor Taxonomies (MLST)**: 8 Simple Knowledge Organization System (SKOS) [43] taxonomies of ML-related concepts (e.g., task types, evaluation measures) with a combined total of 4532 SKOS concepts.

(iii) The **Machine Learning Knowledge Graph (MLSea-KG)**, a declaratively constructed and regularly updated KG with more than 1.44 billion RDF triples of ML experiments, regarding datasets used in ML experiments, tasks, implementations and related hyper-parameters, experiment executions, their configuration settings and evaluation results, code notebooks and repositories, algorithms, publications, models, scientists, and practitioners.

This resource provides a large-scale KG built from diverse sources related to ML pipelines descriptions, datasets attributes, and software implementations, accompanied by novel ML concepts taxonomies. MLSea provides a resource for sharing ML knowledge, potentially supporting the ML community in experiment documentation and reproducibility. This resource can be leveraged by ML and semantic web researchers and practitioners to discover ML workflows and metadata from a large source of ML experiments, conduct analyses and draw conclusions over ML experiments and their results, support ML recommendation systems, and complement Automated ML (AutoML) software systems.

In the next sections, we discuss motivating examples leading to the development of this resource (Sect. 2), related work (Sect. 3), the MLSO and MLST (Sect. 4), the construction process and use cases of MLSea-KG (Sect. 5), the potential impact of our resource (Sect. 6), and future work (Sect. 7).

2   Motivating Examples

Currently, the acquisition and discovery of multifaceted ML information require users to browse different ML repositories and platforms, where data are fragmented and disconnected from each other. We provide two motivating examples:

Example 1. *Find a dataset & its relevant code notebooks & scientific papers.* A user may search for the image dataset "CIFAR-10"[1] in OpenML [46], view its statistics and ML tasks defined on it. Yet, conducting a sole search on OpenML would not uncover the ML code notebooks on Kaggle [34] for this dataset[2] which can assist the users in programming their own ML projects. More, the user would not find scientific papers that introduced or referenced this dataset, as the ones included in Papers with Code[3], accompanied with code repositories. Such papers would enable the users to understand the scientific questions that can be tested with the dataset and the details of the ML pipeline. To gather information on various aspects of the ML process related to a specific dataset, multiple searches across different online repositories are needed.

Example 2. *Find a pipeline & its scientific papers, algorithms & parameters.* A user may search for implementations of the "Bagging" ensemble learning method in Papers with Code[4] and discover related scientific papers along with algorithms they may leverage. However, there also exist implementations in OpenML using this method that additionally provide hyper-parameters they are using, their descriptions and values[5]. The hyper-parameters can help users understand the configurations they would have to make and their different options when implementing this kind of pipeline.

3   Related Work

Semantic web technologies are regularly used to support data mining and ML systems in different stages of their pipeline [6,56]. ML systems leverage large knowledge graphs (KGs) to enhance their performance [8] and provide explanations regarding the models' decisions [31], taking advantage of the semantics and relationships captured within the KGs. In addition, semantic web technologies

---

[1] https://www.openml.org/d/40927.
[2] https://www.kaggle.com/datasets/pankrzysiu/cifar10-python/code.
[3] https://www.cs.toronto.edu/~kriz/learning-features-2009-TR.pdf.
[4] https://paperswithcode.com/paper/bagging-provides-assumption-free-stability.
[5] https://www.openml.org/f/2058.

are regularly deployed to model ML pipelines, their different stages and components [16,37,48,54], in an effort to describe and document the ML lifecycle and the rich metadata that are associated with it.

Knowledge Graphs. Researchers have used semantic representations to better track, describe, and encode ML pipelines. In **Bosch** [72], formally encoded ML knowledge and solutions are translated to executable scripts, for external systems to leverage. **SemML** [73] enables the reuse and generalisation of ML pipelines for condition monitoring relying on ontology templates for ML task negotiation and data and feature annotation. **Venkataramanan et al.** [69] propose a knowledge-infused recommender system that utilizes metadata of executed ML pipelines from open repositories to recommend pipelines based on the users' queries. **AssistML** [70] collects and pre-processes metadata of existing ML solutions, to recommend alternatives for ML implementations. Regarding the tracking of ML publications, **Linked Papers with Code** [18] is a KG that provides information about ML publications from Papers with Code [50] with related metadata such as their datasets, tasks, and evaluations. Similarly, **SWeMLS-KG** [14] is a KG that contains workflows and machine-actionable metadata of 470 papers regarding systems that combine semantic web resources and ML components. To track ML datasets, **KGLac** [25] captures metadata and semantics of datasets to construct a KG that interconnects relevant datasets.

Despite the progress in encoding ML knowledge, there is an absence of large and openly available resources with ML knowledge from multiple sources and stages of the ML pipeline due to the complexity and diversity of the various ML repositories. While domain-specific KGs are commonly used in other areas, e.g., scientific work organization [4], publication tracking [19], and healthcare [39,57], the ML field lacks large resources describing and inter-connecting ML workflows.

Ontologies. Several ontologies have been curated to model ML systems, experiments, and pipelines. **EXPO** [63], one of the earlier attempts to model scientific experiments, formalizes the generic concepts of experiment design, methodology, and results representation and **Exposé** [67] focuses on describing ML experiments and components. **OntoDM** [48] provides generic representations and descriptions of the data mining domain and **DMOP** [37] describes data mining tasks, data, algorithms, hypotheses, and workflows, in an effort to support decision-making during the data mining process. **MEX Vocabulary** [16] and **PROV-ML** [64] describe ML experiments, with a strong focus on data provenance between stages of the ML lifecycle. **Task Ontologies** [72] model executable KGs of ML pipelines, describing pipelines as series of data, methods, and tasks. **ML-Schema** [54] is a collaborative effort from the W3C Machine Learning Schema Community Group[6], developed to align existing ML ontologies and serve as the foundation for more specific ontologies and applications.

These ontologies provide a solid foundation for describing the fundamental components within the ML domain. However, they are not integrated with other domain-specific ontologies. For instance, they are not aligned with ontologies about dataset and data catalogs description (e.g., DCAT Vocabulary [40], daQ

---

[6] https://www.w3.org/community/ml-schema/.

Ontology [11]), software systems and characteristics (e.g., SWO [41], SDO [22]), and scientific works (e.g., FaBiO [51]). More, there are no taxonomies covering pivotal ML concepts, such as algorithms, task types, fields, evaluation measures, and dataset characteristics. Whenever such taxonomies do exist within the ontologies (e.g., MEX Vocabulary [16]), they are limited in scope, and embedded within the ontologies as class taxonomies. This lack of modularity makes existing ML taxonomies hard to manage and integrate with other works, while future updates and additions may require extensive changes to the ontology structure.

ML Platforms. **Kaggle** [34] is a data science competition platform and online community of data scientists and ML practitioners. It contains numerous ML datasets, along with statistical analyses and code used to conduct ML experiments with them. **Papers with Code** is a community-driven platform which encompasses ML-related research papers together with their code, datasets, methods, and evaluation tables. **OpenML** [46, 68] is an open platform for sharing datasets, algorithms, and experiments. It contains datasets along with ML tasks and pipelines in which they were employed. Additionally, it provides statistical metadata for the dataset characteristics and pipeline performance, and experiment configurations. **Hugging Face** [27] and **TensorFlow** [65] are popular platforms for collaboration in ML applications, focusing on the sharing of ML datasets and development of ML models.

4   The MLS Ontology and Taxonomies

The **Machine Learning Sailor Ontology (MLSO)** and the **Machine Learning Sailor Taxonomies (MLST)** provide a flexible schema to represent ML pipelines, datasets, implementations, and experiments. They are developed based on an in-depth analysis of ML experiment-related data from prominent online repositories, such as OpenML [46], Kaggle [34], and Papers with Code [50]. MLSO extends and enriches existing ontologies, such as ML-Schema [54], DCAT [40], SDO [22], and FaBiO [51] to model the ML pipeline. MLST consist of SKOS [43] controlled taxonomies to organize ML concepts. MLSO and MLST are available at https://github.com/dtai-kg/mlso/ and published at https://w3id.org/mlso/. A summary of their namespaces is available at Table 1.

Table 1. MLS Modules

Module	Description	Namespace
MLSO	Machine Learning Sailor Ontology	http://w3id.org/mlso/
MLSO-DC	Dataset Characteristic Taxonomy	http://w3id.org/mlso/vocab/dataset_characteristic/
MLSO-FC	Feature Characteristic Taxonomy	http://w3id.org/mlso/vocab/feature_characteristic/
MLSO-EM	Evaluation Measure Taxonomy	http://w3id.org/mlso/vocab/evaluation_measure/
MLSO-EP	Estimation Procedure Taxonomy	http://w3id.org/mlso/vocab/estimation_procedure/
MLSO-LM	Learning Method Taxonomy	http://w3id.org/mlso/vocab/learning_method/
MLSO-ALGO	Algorithm Taxonomy	http://w3id.org/mlso/vocab/ml_algorithm/
MLSO-F	Machine Learning Field Taxonomy	http://w3id.org/mlso/vocab/ml_field/
MLSO-TT	Task Type Taxonomy	http://w3id.org/mlso/vocab/ml_task_type/

4.1   MLS Development Methodology and Maintenance

The development of MLSO and MLST follows the Linked Open Terms (LOT) methodology [52]. The four major stages of LOT are: **Requirements Specification, Implementation, Publication** and **Maintenance**. We defined the ontology *requirements* based on the scope of the ontology, i.e. the discovery of ML knowledge from diverse platforms. The ontology was conceptualized using the draw.io [13] diagram generation tool and *implemented* in OWL2 [42] using Protegé [45]. To evaluate the ontology, SPARQL [24] queries[7] and the OOPS! validator [53] are used and its documentation is generated with Widoco [21].

Availability and Maintenance. For at least a ten-year period, KU Leuven will *maintain* the ontology and taxonomies with new requirements, error corrections, and gathering of recommendations, using the GitHub issue tracker of the ontology repository[8], where everyone can contribute and raise issues. We anticipate that this collaborative approach will foster the creation of a community around the ontology, that will take part in the ontology's further growth and development. Since we plan to add new knowledge and data from more platforms to our system, such as Hugging Face [27], the ontology will need to be carefully revised as newer versions will be published.

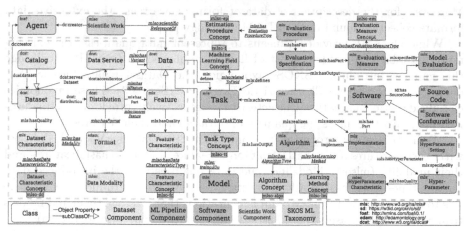

Fig. 1. MLSO and MLST Overview (Color figure online)

4.2   MLSO: The Machine Learning Sailor Ontology

The ontology's elements are grouped into four components: the **Dataset components** representing ML datasets along with their statistical and generic metadata; the **ML Pipeline components** representing the fundamental concepts of

---

[7] https://github.com/dtai-kg/MLSea-KGC/tree/main/sparql_examples.
[8] https://github.com/dtai-kg/MLSO.

the ML pipeline, such as the ML task and experiment; the **Software components**, representing software characteristics of the described implementations; and the **Scientific Work components**, representing ML peer-reviewed publications. The primary focus of the ontology lies in interconnecting these components to create a cohesive framework for modeling ML processes, extending already established standards. MLSO's core elements are shown in Fig. 1.

Dataset Components (yellow in Fig. 1) represent the concepts inherent to datasets utilized in ML processes. They describe the structural composition of datasets, along with other traits such as generic and statistical metadata. These concepts include: datasets, catalogs, data services, dataset distributions, formats, modalities, characteristics, dataset features, and feature characteristics.

To articulate the generic traits of dataset entities, such as their language, creators, and licences, we reuse the following general-purpose ontologies: the Data Catalog (DCAT), Friend Of A Friend (FOAF) [7], Provenance Ontology (PROV-O) [38], and Dublin Core (DC) [71]. While these ontologies capture the generic aspects of datasets, they do not provide statistical metadata crucial for ML processes or for defining ML tasks relevant to the datasets. To address this limitation we align DCAT and ML-Schema, and use ML-Schema to describe data qualities of datasets and dataset features, as well as ML tasks based on datasets. Moreover, for the description of dataset formats, we reuse the extensive data formats collection found in the EDAM Ontology [32].

While OpenML provides a means to represent data qualities[9], the existing representation is limited to a list of literals published on OpenML. To bridge this gap, we introduce 2 SKOS taxonomies: the Dataset Characteristic Taxonomy and the Feature Characteristic Taxonomy (Sect. 4.3). These taxonomies classify dataset and feature characteristics, respectively, providing a standardized approach to express the qualities of datasets and their features.

We introduce new properties to connect datasets (mlso:hasVariant), datasets with their features (mlso:hasDefaultTargetFeature and mlso:hasIdFeature) and their modality (mlso:hasModality), and data qualities with the introduced data quality types (mlso:hasDataCharacteristicType). We also introduce new properties to connect datasets and ML implementations that leverage them and models trained on these datasets (mlso:hasRelatedImplementation, mlso:trainedOn).

Last, the reused ontologies do not include a way to connect datasets with peer-reviewed publications that reference them or software that leverages them. Therefore, we added new properties to link datasets with relevant publications (mlso:hasScientificReference) and software using them (mlso:hasRelatedSoftware), such as code notebooks or large-scale software applications. We also include other dataset attributes, e.g., their data loader locations (mlso:hasDataLoaderLocation), as well as the cache format of their platform version (mlso:hasCacheFormat).

ML Pipeline Components (blue in Fig. 1) serve as a comprehensive representation of the fundamental concepts integral to the ML pipeline. They focus on describing the characteristics of ML experiments, their hyper-parameters, set-

---

[9] https://www.openml.org/search?type=measure.

tings, and evaluation results. The concepts include: ML tasks, runs, implementations, implementation characteristics, algorithms, hyper-parameters, hyper-parameter settings, experiments, models, model evaluations, model characteristics, evaluation measures, evaluation specifications, and evaluation procedures.

We reuse and extend ML-Schema to represent the fundamental concepts of ML pipelines, such as the tasks they address, their implementations and executions, and their inputs and outputs. While ML-Schema captures the fundamental concepts of the ML process, it does not include the details and characteristics of software used in these processes. To address this, we align ML-Schema and SDO, an ontology for describing software components, including their metadata and their inputs, outputs and variables. SDO enriches the representations of ML pipelines with their software characteristics and requirements.

ML-Schema offers descriptions of estimation procedures, evaluation measures, algorithms, and tasks. However, these are represented as literals without systematic classification or categorization. To more efficiently classify and document these concepts, we introduce 4 SKOS taxonomies; the Estimation Procedure, Evaluation Measure, Task Type, and Algorithm Taxonomies (Sect. 4.3), allowing for the classification of estimation procedures, evaluation measures, algorithms, and tasks, enriching the ontology with a categorized representation. More, we introduce 2 new taxonomies: the Machine Learning Field Taxonomy to classify ML fields of research that tasks belong to and the Learning Method Taxonomy to categorize learning methods used in ML pipelines (Sect. 4.3).

To explicitly assign types and categories to ML-Schema classes, we introduce new properties linking ML tasks to ML task categories (mlso:hasTaskType) and ML fields they relate to (mlso:relatedToField). We link ML algorithms with algorithm types (mlso:hasAlgorithmType) and types of ML learning method they may include (mlso:hasLearningMethodType). We also link evaluation measures and estimation procedures with their types (mlso:hasEvaluationProcedureType) and evaluation types (mlso:hasEvaluationMeasureType. Last, we introduce a new property (mlso:hasScientificReference) to link ML models or pipelines and the scientific works related to them or referencing them.

Software Components (orange in Fig. 1) encapsulate fundamental software concepts related to the execution of ML experiments, the settings and the requirements they have. These concepts include: software, software configuration, and software source code. We reuse SDO to describe the software characteristics and requirements of software used in ML pipelines. MLSO leverages these already established descriptions to augment the linkage between ML experiments and their software components. We introduce new properties to interconnect software components with scientific works (mlso:hasScientificReference), datasets (mlso:hasRelatedSoftware), and with ML fields of research (mlso:relatedToField).

Scientific Work Components (pink in Fig. 1) represent peer-reviewed publications related to developments in the field of ML. We reuse the FaBiO and FOAF vocabularies to describe publications, authors. MLSO extends FaBiO to connect ML publications with datasets they leverage or reference, ML experiments they conduct, models they create and publish, and the software they use. We introduce new properties to enrich the ML research works descriptions, connecting them with datasets and software they leverage (mlso:hasScientificReference, mlso:hasRelatedSoftware), and ML fields of research (mlso:relatedToField).

4.3 MLST: Machine Learning Sailor Taxonomies

MLSO is complemented by MLST, a series of SKOS taxonomies, formulated as RDF vocabularies, to provide a flexible and standardized framework for managing large controlled collections of ML knowledge. These taxonomies serve as comprehensive thesauri, offering a structured overview of essential ML concepts.

The taxonomies were developed by systematically studying and integrating data from three primary sources. Firstly, data were gathered from online ML repositories that provide organised data collections, such as the OpenML data qualities collection[10] and the Papers with Code ML methods collection[11]. Secondly, information was sourced from smaller pre-existing collections formalized as vocabularies, such as the MEX vocabulary [16]. Lastly, categorizations were extracted from peer-reviewed publications that systematically consolidate ML knowledge, predominantly from ML surveys and scholarly works.

MLST include the following 8 ML-focused taxonomies:

(i) **Dataset Characteristic Taxonomy**, a collection of qualities used to characterize datasets (e.g., entropy, number of classes). It is based on the OpenML data qualities collection(see footnote 10) and contains 127 dataset characteristics.

(ii) **Feature Characteristics Taxonomy**, a collection of qualities to describe dataset features (e.g., data-type, maximum value). It is based on the OpenML data qualities collection(see footnote 10) and contains 55 feature characteristics.

(iii) **Evaluation Measure Taxonomy**, a collection of measures for the evaluation of ML experiments. It is based on the OpenML evaluation measures collection[12] and contains 86 evaluation measures (e.g., accuracy, recall).

(iv) The **Estimation Procedure Taxonomy**, a collection of data-splitting techniques to evaluate ML models based on the OpenML evaluation procedures collection[13] containing 5 estimation procedures (e.g., cross validation, holdout).

(v) The **Learning Method Taxonomy**, a collection of methods of learning and training in ML, based on the learning approach and the type of data they input and output. The taxonomy reuses MEX vocabulary learning method classes, learning methods found in Papers with Code ML tasks and literature review [59]. It contains 33 learning methods (e.g., supervised learning, transfer learning).

---

[10] https://www.openml.org/search?type=measure&measure_type=data_quality.

[11] https://paperswithcode.com/methods.

[12] www.openml.org/search?type=measure&measure_type=evaluation_measure.

[13] www.openml.org/search?type=measure&measure_type=estimation_procedure.

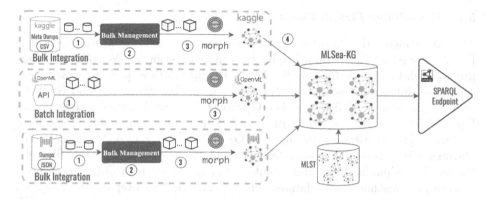

Fig. 2. MLSea-KG Construction Process Overview

(vi) The **Algorithm Taxonomy**, a collection of 2321 algorithms used in different stages of the ML process (e.g., Adam, Dropout). The taxonomy re-uses MEX vocabulary algorithm classes, the Paper with Code methods collection(see footnote 11), and ML surveys that organize ML algorithms from diverse ML fields [1,3,5,9,17,20,36,44,55,58,60–62,66].

(vii) The **Machine Learning Field Taxonomy**, a collection of areas of study in the ML domain. It is based on MEX vocabulary ML context classes and literature review [33] and contains 30 fields (e.g., computer vision, bioinformatics).

(viii) The **Task Type Taxonomy**, a collection of 1875 ML task types, defined based on the problem they try to solve (e.g., object detection, colorization). The taxonomy is based on MEX vocabulary ML context classes and task types found in OpenML tasks and Papers with Code datasets, methods, and publications.

The modular design and availability of the taxonomies aim to empower the ML community, allowing researchers and practitioners to propose new entries, suggest modifications, and redefine the hierarchy of terms via GitHub issues. This collaborative approach aims to sustain a resource that evolves in line with the dynamic landscape of ML, ensuring the taxonomies remain up-to-date.

5   MLSea-KG: Construction, Publication and Usage

We applied our MLSO ontology to create **MLSea-KG**, a KG for discovering ML data containing more than 1.44 billion triples (Fig. 2). We discuss the population and update methodology we follow for declaratively constructing and preserving MLSea-KG which is available at http://w3id.org/mlsea-kg. In this section, we showcase MLSea-KG's key statistics, availability and usage examples.

5.1   Knowledge Graph Construction Process

The KG construction process starts with the data collection step (**Step 1**, Fig. 2) for each of the examined publicly available platforms. We collected **Kaggle's** [34] data as CSV files via the **Meta Kaggle** dataset [35], a public repository containing metadata about Kaggle datasets, kernels, users, and competitions, updated on a daily basis. For **OpenML** [46], we iteratively collected all OpenML datasets, tasks, flows, runs, and their related metadata, in the form of Pandas [47] dataframes, through the **OpenML Python API** service[14]. For **Papers with Code** [50], we collected the platform's data, as JSON files, via the platform's public dump files[15] that contain metadata regarding papers, code repositories, methods, and datasets of the platform. To prepare the collected data, pre-processing modules filter out problematic data, such as faulty OpenML URLs, new-line characters in literals, and non-escaped backslashes, as well as ML pipeline-unrelated data, such as Kaggle forum messages, as we do not include platform-specific data to the MLSea-KG that are not directly related to ML.

The RDF graph is constructed by applying the MLSO and MLST to the retrieved data. We leverage the RDF Mapping Language (RML) [12,30] to map the heterogeneous data (Pandas DataFrames from OpenML, CSV files from Kaggle and JSON files from Papers with Code) to RDF triples. To define the RML mapping rules, we leverage the human-friendly serialization YARRRML [26] and the Yatter [29] tool which converts YARRRML mapping rules to RML rules.

To efficiently process large data sources, such as the Meta Kaggle and the Papers with Code metadata datasets, with RML processors we extract a batch of the complete initial dataset each time (**Step 2**, Fig. 2). We employ platform-specific custom *sampling strategies* to ensure that pertinent data are consistently grouped together within each batch. For example, when constructing an RDF graph from a batch of Kaggle datasets metadata, we also extract related Kaggle code notebooks metadata for code notebooks based on the datasets of the batch, and as a result contain useful information for the datasets' RDF graph.

We leverage Morph-KGC [2] and its extension for in-memory RDF generation [10] to declaratively generate the RDF triples for each extracted batch (**Step 3**, Fig. 2). The generated RDF batches are compressed into .gz archives, to facilitate data management and reduce the total storage. Each RDF batch is then imported into our Virtuoso triple store [15], hosted on an Ubuntu 22.04.3 LTS server with Intel(R) Xeon(R) CPU E5-2650 v2 and 128 GB RAM (**Step 4**, Fig. 2). The 3 RDF graphs, 1 for each platform, comprise the MLSea-KG.

---

[14] https://www.openml.org/apis.
[15] https://paperswithcode.com/about.

Table 2. MLSea-KG core entities, number of instances & triples per dataset & type.

Entity Type	Instance Count				Triples Count			
	OpenML	Kaggle	PwC	Total	OpenML	Kaggle	PwC	Total
Datasets	5.4K	277.4K	11.1K	295.9K	49.7M	4.2M	163.2K	54.1M
Tasks	47.2K	–	2.1K	49.3K	642.3K	–	8.5K	650.8K
Pipelines	16.7K	–	26.9K	43.6K	1.3M	–	1.2M	2.6M
Algorithms	–	–	2.1K	2.1K	–	–	–	19.4K
Runs	10.1M	–	26.9K	10.1M	1.36B	–	524.7K	1.36B
Models	-	–	26.9K	26.9K	–	–	214.6K	214.6K
Notebooks	–	940.4K	–	940.4K	–	9.3M	-	9.3M
Repositories	–	–	146.2K	14.2K	–	–	955.2K	955.2K
Publications	308	–	407.4K	407.4K	1.2K	–	6.8M	6.8M
Agents	1.4K	360.1K	433.5K	407K	4.3K	1.0M	1.3M	2.3M
Total	10.1M	1.5M	1.0M	12.6M	1.41B	14.5M	11.1M	**1.44B**

Continuous Integration. MLSea-KG is updated using an automatic procedure. The updated Meta Kaggle dataset and the Papers with Code dump files are
downloaded and compared with their previous versions to identify new entries,
while the latest data of the OpenML are downloaded through its API. Then, the
same KG construction process is followed to update MLSea-KG.

Statistics of MLSea-KG. As of November 2023, MLSea-KG consists of 5.4K
datasets, 47.2K ML tasks, 16.7 flows (descriptions of ML pipelines), 10.1M runs
(executions, settings, and evaluations of ML experiments), 308 publications, and
1.4K agents (scientists and practitioners) from OpenML; 277K datasets, 940K
ML code notebooks and 360.1K agents from Kaggle; 11.1K datasets, 2.1K ML
tasks, 2.1K algorithms, 407K ML publications, 146K ML code repositories, 26.9K
ML models, accompanied by experiment metadata and related evaluations, and
433K researchers from Papers with Code, all complemented with rich metadata.
A total count of the instances of MLSea-KG, along with the total number of
triples by instance, is exhibited in Table 2. Along with all metadata, the total
triples count of MLSea-KG exceeds 1.44 billion, with the majority of the RDF
triples originating from OpenML, which contains a plethora of ML-related metadata, from detailed characteristics for each dataset to numerous ML experiment
configuration settings and results. Kaggle and Papers with Code focus more on
generic metadata and can be, thus, represented with less RDF triples.

Availability and Maintenance. Our resource's landing page (http://w3id.
org/mlsea) provides pointers to the public SPARQL endpoint of MLSea-KG
(http://w3id.org/mlsea-kg), the Zenodo repository for the RDF snapshots of
MLSea-KG, and the GitHub repository with the RML mapping rules for KG
construction and the source code employed for metadata collection and sampling, and KG construction. The webpage summarizes how MLSea-KG was con-

structed leveraging MLSO and MLST. For at least a ten-year period, KU Leuven will *maintain* MLSea-KG, applying the continuous integration process on a monthly basis to incorporate the latest updates from all ML repositories. The KG population scripts and RML mapping rules will also be regularly updated.

5.2   Use Case Examples

The MLSea-KG allows users to search for ML datasets, tasks, implementations, models, experiments, software, and scientific works. They can view the characteristics of these components and navigate through their intricate relationships. The search over the data of the different platforms is facilitated as a user can find all relevant information with a single query. In this section, we look back at the motivating examples (Sect. 2) and demonstrate how the users can take advantage of MLSea to address the same use cases.

Example 1. *Find a dataset & its relevant code notebooks & scientific papers.* In this example, a user searches for a dataset, its code notebooks, and scientific papers over the 3 platforms simultaneously, as it was described in Sect. 2.

As opposed to this manual task, a user can retrieve the same information by leveraging MLSea. The SPARQL query of this search over MLSea-KG for the "CIFAR-10" is shown in Listing 5.1 and an excerpt of the results is shown in Table 3. The complete set of results is returned within 12 secs.

Listing 5.1. Query for CIFAR-10 dataset locations, tasks, code and publications.

```
PREFIX mlso: <http://w3id.org/mlso/>
PREFIX mls: <http://www.w3.org/ns/mls#>
#... dcterms, rdfs, dcat, prov, schema and skos are omitted
SELECT ?datasetTitle, ?datasetLocation, (GROUP_CONCAT(DISTINCT COALESCE
(?omlTask, ?pwcTask);separator=',\n') AS ?task), (GROUP_CONCAT(DISTINCT
COALESCE(?codeNotebook, ?codeRepo);separator=',\n') AS ?code),
(GROUP_CONCAT(DISTINCT ?publication; separator=',\n') AS ?introducedIn)
WHERE {
  ?dataset a mls:Dataset;
     dcat:landingPage ?datasetLocation; dcterms:title ?datasetTitle.
  OPTIONAL{?dataset dcterms:description ?label}
  OPTIONAL{?dataset rdfs:label ?label}
  FILTER(CONTAINS(?label, "CIFAR-10")||CONTAINS(LCASE(?label), "cifar-10"))
  OPTIONAL{?dataset mlso:hasRelatedSoftware ?softwareID.
    ?softwareID schema:codeRepository ?codeNotebook.}
  OPTIONAL{?taskId mls:definedOn ?dataset; prov:atLocation ?omlTask.}
  OPTIONAL{?dataset mlso:hasTaskType ?taskType.
    ?taskType skos:prefLabel ?pwcTask.}
  OPTIONAL{?dataset mlso:hasScientificReference ?publicationID.
    ?publicationID dcterms:source ?publication.}
  OPTIONAL{?dataset mlso:hasScientificReference ?publicationID.
    ?publicationID mlso:hasRelatedSoftware  ?softwareID.
    ?softwareID schema:codeRepository ?codeRepo.}
}GROUP BY ?datasetTitle ?datasetLocation
```

Table 3. Query results for CIFAR-10 dataset locations, tasks, code & publications.

dataset Title	dataset Location	task	code	introducedIn
CIFAR-FS	paperswithcode.com/dataset/cifar-fs	Few-Shot Image Classification, ...	github.com/bertinetto/r2d2	arxiv.org/pdf/1805.08136v3
CIFAR-10	kaggle.com/datasets/ayush1220/cifar10	–	kaggle.com/code/alphapii/knn-cvpr	–
CIFAR_10 small	api.openml.org/data/v1/download/16797612/ CIFAR_10_small.arff	openml.org/t/294086	–	–

Listing 5.2. Query for Bagging implementations, publications & hyper-parameters.

```
PREFIX mls: <http://www.w3.org/ns/mls#>
#... dcterms, rdfs, dcat, prov, schema and skos are omitted
SELECT (STR(COALESCE(?label, ?title)) AS ?implementation),
(GROUP_CONCAT(DISTINCT ?publication; separator=',\n') AS ?publications),
(GROUP_CONCAT(DISTINCT ?algorithm; separator=',\n') AS ?algorithms),
(GROUP_CONCAT(DISTINCT ?hyperP; separator=',\n') AS ?hyperParameters)
WHERE{
    {?implemId a mls:Implementation; rdfs:label ?label.
    FILTER(CONTAINS(LCASE(?label), ''bagging''))}
    UNION{?implemId a mls:Implementation; dcterms:description ?desc;
    dcterms:title ?title. FILTER(CONTAINS(LCASE(?desc), "bagging"))}
    OPTIONAL{?pubId mlso:hasRelatedImplementation ?implemId;
    rdf:type mlso:ScientificWork; dcterms:source ?publication.}
    OPTIONAL{?implemId mls:implements ?algoId. ?algoId rdfs:label ?algorithm.}
    OPTIONAL{?implemId mls:hasHyperParameter ?hyperPID.
    ?hyperPID dcterms:description ?hyperP_desc; dcterms:title ?hyperP_title.
    BIND(CONCAT(STR(?hyperP_title),'': '', str(?hyperP_desc)) as ?hyperP)}
}GROUP BY ?label ?title
```

***Example* 2.** *Find a pipeline & its papers, algorithms & parameters.* In this example, a user manually searches for a pipeline over the 3 platforms to find scientific papers, algorithms, and hyper-parameters, as described in Sect. 2.

As opposed to this manual task, a user can retrieve the same information by leveraging MLSea. The SPARQL query of this search over MLSea-KG is shown in Listing 5.2, where publications, algorithms, and hyper-parameters about the popular "Bagging" ensemble method are retrieved. An excerpt of the query results is shown in Table 4; the complete results are returned within 6 secs.

6   Impact of the Resource

This resource can be of interest and have impact for the ML and the Semantic Web community offering abundant prospects for future research and adoption. Practitioners can immediately use it for ML artifacts search, such as dataset

Table 4. Query results for Bagging implementations, publications & hyper-parameters.

implementation	publications	algorithms	hyperParameters
Internal node bagging	arxiv.org/pdf/1805.00215v5.pdf	Dropout	–
weka.Bagging_REPTree(22)	--	–	L: Maximum tree depth, ...
BagBERT	arxiv.org/pdf/2111.05808v1.pdf	Adam, BERT, ...	–

and model search, while researchers can leverage it for analyzing ML metadata, discover ML insights and trends, and develop ML recommendation systems.

Searchability. MLSea's immediate impact lies on the ML knowledge discovery opportunities it facilitates with the MLSea-KG and the MLST that organize ML knowledge. Researchers and practitioners can now navigate the prominent repositories (OpenML, Kaggle, and Papers with Code), by formulating precise SPARQL queries and immediately get integrated answers. They can retrieve ML datasets and view their statistical and feature characteristics, ML pipelines, their inputs, hyper-parameter settings and results, ML tasks and related implementations that attempt to solve them, ML peer-reviewed publications, code notebooks, and ML models, precisely tailored to their needs.

This semantic layer has the potential to accelerate the progress of ML projects by facilitating more efficient searches through previous works and enabling their reuse. For example, users can reuse or augment datasets, identify optimal hyper-parameter settings for a specific task or leverage pre-trained models, via transfer learning. Likewise, the integration of the taxonomies (MLST) with the MLSea-KG can enhance the search capabilities over MLSea-KG. For instance, users can query MLSea-KG for a task with a specific type from the ML Task Type taxonomy.

MLSea does not only facilitate individual platform searches, but also enables combined searches over platforms. The diverse data that the resource provides offer new capabilities for fostering a more comprehensive understanding of ML experiments, by connecting fragmented information. For instance, discovering a dataset from Papers with Code and subsequently locating relevant code notebooks in Kaggle enhances cross-platform connectivity, promoting a deeper and more complete understanding of the available ML resources.

Reproducibility. Utilizing MLSea to model and store ML pipelines significantly enhances documentation and has the potential to increase the repeatability, reproducibility, traceability, and explainability of ML pipelines. It promotes a standardized approach to sharing experiments, enhancing knowledge exchange among practitioners and interoperability amongst ML online repositories. Simultaneously, MLST function as a dynamic thesaurus, offering a structured repository for organizing ML knowledge in a modular way.

Data Analysis. By leveraging MLSea-KG, new data analysis and insights opportunities emerge. Through innovative techniques, such as graph embeddings, users can derive significant insights, such as hidden patterns and trends, from connections prevalent in the graph. Users can investigate relationships between dataset characteristics, the impact of different hyper-parameter settings on model performance, or discover correlations between specific algorithms and successful experiments. These potential explorations can lead to a better understanding of best practices, optimizations, and success factors within ML projects.

Recommendations. MLSea provides an extensive data source for ML recommendation systems to be based on by harnessing past successful experiments and user requirements to recommend suitable datasets, pre-trained models, hyper-parameter settings, and algorithms. These recommendation systems could complement AutoML systems in providing solutions to ML practitioners. For instance, a recommendation system could analyze experiment outcomes, and propose related datasets, effective models or algorithms for a given context.

7 Conclusions and Future Work

This work leverages semantic web technologies to meticulously model diverse ML information and encompass a large corpus of ML datasets, experiments, software and scientific publications. The introduced MLSO and MLST extend and combine past ontologies and W3C recommendations to provide a versatile schema that describes different facets of the ML process.

We applied this schema to 3 prominent ML platforms (OpenML, Kaggle, and Papers with Code), using their metadata related to ML processes to generate RDF graphs, ultimately creating MLSea-KG, a large-scale KG for ML, boasting over 1.44 billion RDF triples. We discuss MLSea-KG's construction and update, its characteristics, use cases, and potential impact for the ML community, highlighting its usefulness for practitioners and researchers on a variety of levels.

In the future, we plan to continue updating the resources, integrating the latest data of the examined platforms. We also plan to extend our resources, by modeling and incorporating metadata from additional ML repositories, thus encompassing an even broader picture of the ML landscape. Furthermore, we aim to enhance specificity in representing deep learning components and experiments, fostering a more detailed layer of deep learning semantic descriptions. Finally, we intend to explore further potential of our resource, examining its use as a source for data analysis, insights discovery, and ML recommendation systems.

Acknowledgements. This research was partially supported by Flanders Make (REX-PEK project), the strategic research centre for the manufacturing industry and the Flanders innovation and entrepreneurship (VLAIO – KG3D project).

References

1. AlMahamid, F., Grolinger, K.: Reinforcement learning algorithms: an overview and classification. In: 2021 IEEE Canadian Conference on Electrical and Computer Engineering (CCECE), pp. 1–7 (2021). https://doi.org/10.1109/CCECE53047.2021.9569056
2. Arenas-Guerrero, J., Chaves-Fraga, D., Toledo, J., Pérez, M.S., Corcho, O.: Morph-KGC: scalable knowledge graph materialization with mapping partitions. Semant. Web (2022). https://doi.org/10.3233/SW-223135
3. Arulkumaran, K., Deisenroth, M.P., Brundage, M., Bharath, A.A.: Deep reinforcement learning: a brief survey. IEEE Signal Process. Mag. **34**(6), 26–38 (2017). https://doi.org/10.1109/MSP.2017.2743240
4. Auer, S., Kovtun, V., Prinz, M., Kasprzik, A., Stocker, M., Vidal, M.E.: Towards a knowledge graph for science. In: Proceedings of the 8th International Conference on Web Intelligence, Mining and Semantics, pp. 1–6 (2018). https://doi.org/10.1145/3227609.3227689

5. Bielza, C., Larrañaga, P.: Discrete Bayesian network classifiers: a survey. ACM Comput. Surv. **47**(1) (2014). https://doi.org/10.1145/2576868
6. Breit, A., et al.: Combining machine learning and semantic web: a systematic mapping study. ACM Comput. Surv. **55**(14s) (2023). https://doi.org/10.1145/3586163
7. Brickley, D., Miller, L.: FOAF Vocabulary Specification 0.99 (2014). http://xmlns.com/foaf/spec/
8. Castellano, G., Digeno, V., Sansaro, G., Vessio, G.: Leveraging knowledge graphs and deep learning for automatic art analysis. Knowl.-Based Syst. **248**, 108859 (2022). https://doi.org/10.1016/j.knosys.2022.108859
9. Charbuty, B., Abdulazeez, A.: Classification based on decision tree algorithm for machine learning. J. Appl. Sci. Technol. Trends **2**(01), 20–28 (2021). https://doi.org/10.38094/jastt20165
10. Dasoulas, I., Chaves-Fraga, D., Garijo, D., Dimou, A.: Declarative RDF construction from in-memory data structures with RML. In: Proceedings of the 4th International Workshop on Knowledge Graph Construction co-located with 20th Extended Semantic Web Conference ESWC 2023, vol. 1613, p. 0073 (2023)
11. Debattista, J., Lange, C., Auer, S.: daQ, an ontology for dataset quality information. In: LDOW (2014)
12. Dimou, A., Vander Sande, M., Colpaert, P., Verborgh, R., Mannens, E., Van de Walle, R.: RML: a generic language for integrated RDF mappings of heterogeneous data. In: Bizer, C., Heath, T., Auer, S., Berners-Lee, T. (eds.) Proceedings of the 7th Workshop on Linked Data on the Web. CEUR Workshop Proceedings, vol. 1184. CEUR (2014)
13. Draw.io: Security-first diagramming for teams. https://www.drawio.com. Accessed 28 Nov 2023
14. Ekaputra, F.J., et al.: Describing and organizing semantic web and machine learning systems in the SWeMLS-KG. In: Pesquita, C., et al. (eds.) The Semantic Web. ESWC 2023. LNCS, vol. 13870, pp. 372–389. Springer, Cham (2023). https://doi.org/10.1007/978-3-031-33455-9_22
15. Erling, O., Mikhailov, I.: Virtuoso: RDF support in a native RDBMS. In: de Virgilio, R., Giunchiglia, F., Tanca, L. (eds.) Semantic Web Information Management, pp. 501–519. Springer, Berlin, Heidelberg (2009). https://doi.org/10.1007/978-3-642-04329-1_21
16. Esteves, D., et al.: MEX vocabulary: a lightweight interchange format for machine learning experiments. In: Proceedings of the 11th International Conference on Semantic Systems, pp. 169–176. SEMANTICS '15, Association for Computing Machinery, New York, NY, USA (2015). https://doi.org/10.1145/2814864.2814883
17. Fahad, A., et al.: A survey of clustering algorithms for big data: taxonomy and empirical analysis. IEEE Trans. Emerg. Top. Comput. **2**(3), 267–279 (2014). https://doi.org/10.1109/TETC.2014.2330519
18. Färber, M., Lamprecht, D.: Linked papers with code: the latest in machine learning as an RDF knowledge graph. In: ISWC 2023 Posters and Demos: 22nd International Semantic Web Conference, 6–10 November 2023, Athens, Greece (2023). https://doi.org/10.48550/arXiv.2310.20475
19. Färber, M., Lamprecht, D., Krause, J., Aung, L., Haase, P.: SemOpenAlex: the scientific landscape in 26 billion RDF triples. In: Payne, T.R., et al. (eds.) The Semantic Web – ISWC 2023. ISWC 2023. LNCS, vol. 14266, pp. 94–112. Springer, Cham (2023). https://doi.org/10.1007/978-3-031-47243-5_6, https://doi.org/10.48550/arXiv.2308.03671

20. Fürnkranz, J., Kliegr, T.: A brief overview of rule learning. In: Bassiliades, N., Gottlob, G., Sadri, F., Paschke, A., Roman, D. (eds.) RuleML 2015. LNCS, vol. 9202, pp. 54–69. Springer, Cham (2015). https://doi.org/10.1007/978-3-319-21542-6_4

21. Garijo, D.: WIDOCO: a wizard for documenting ontologies. In: d'Amato, C., et al. (eds.) ISWC 2017. LNCS, vol. 10588, pp. 94–102. Springer, Cham (2017). https://doi.org/10.1007/978-3-319-68204-4_9

22. Garijo, D., Osorio, M., Khider, D., Ratnakar, V., Gil, Y.: OKG-Soft: an open knowledge graph with machine readable scientific software metadata. In: 15th International Conference on eScience (eScience), pp. 349–358 (2019). https://doi.org/10.1109/eScience.2019.00046

23. Gundersen, O.E., Shamsaliei, S., Isdahl, R.J.: Do machine learning platforms provide out-of-the-box reproducibility? Futur. Gener. Comput. Syst. **126**, 34–47 (2022). https://doi.org/10.1016/j.future.2021.06.014

24. Harris, S., Seaborne, A.: SPARQL 1.1 Query Language. Recommendation, World Wide Web Consortium (W3C), March 2013. https://www.w3.org/TR/sparql11-query/

25. Helal, A., Helali, M., Ammar, K., Mansour, E.: A demonstration of KGLac: a data discovery and enrichment platform for data science. Proc. VLDB Endow. **14**(12), 2675–2678 (2021). https://doi.org/10.14778/3476311.3476317

26. Heyvaert, P., De Meester, B., Dimou, A., Verborgh, R.: Declarative rules for linked data generation at your fingertips! In: The Semantic Web: ESWC 2018 Satellite Events: ESWC 2018 Satellite Events, Heraklion, Crete, Greece, 3–7 June 2018, Revised Selected Papers 15 (2018)

27. Hugging Face: Hugging Face – The AI community building the future. https://huggingface.co. Accessed 28 Nov 2023

28. Hutson, M.: Artificial intelligence faces reproducibility crisis (2018). https://doi.org/10.1126/science.359.6377.725

29. Iglesias-Molina, A., Chaves-Fraga, D., Dasoulas, I., Dimou, A.: Human-Friendly RDF graph construction: which one do you chose? In: Garrigós, I., Murillo Rodríguez, J.M., Wimmer, M. (eds.) Web Engineering. ICWE 2023. LNCS, vol. 13893, pp. 262–277. Springer, Cham (2023). https://doi.org/10.1007/978-3-031-34444-2_19

30. Iglesias-Molina, A., et al.: The RML ontology: a community-driven modular redesign after a decade of experience in mapping heterogeneous data to RDF. In: Payne, T.R., et al. (eds.) The Semantic Web – ISWC 2023. ISWC 2023. LNCS, vol. 14266, pp. 152–175. Springer, Cham (2023). https://doi.org/10.1007/978-3-031-47243-5_9

31. Ismaeil, Y., Stepanova, D., Tran, T.K., Saranrittichai, P., Domokos, C., Blockeel, H.: Towards neural network interpretability using commonsense knowledge graphs. In: Sattler, U., et al. (eds.) The Semantic Web – ISWC 2022. ISWC 2022. LNCS, vol. 13489, pp. 74–90. Springer, Cham (2022). https://doi.org/10.1007/978-3-031-19433-7_5

32. Ison, J., et al.: EDAM: an ontology of bioinformatics operations, types of data and identifiers, topics and formats. Bioinformatics **29**(10), 1325–1332 (2013). https://doi.org/10.1093/bioinformatics/btt113

33. Jordan, M.I., Mitchell, T.M.: Machine learning: trends, perspectives, and prospects. Science **349**(6245), 255–260 (2015). https://doi.org/10.1126/science.aaa8415

34. Kaggle: Kaggle: Your Machine Learning and Data Science Community. https://www.kaggle.com. Accessed 28 Nov 2023

35. Kaggle: Meta Kaggle - Kaggle's public data on competitions, users, submission scores, and kernels. https://www.kaggle.com/datasets/kaggle/meta-kaggle. Accessed 28 Nov 2023
36. Kaur, J., Madan, N.: Association rule mining: a survey. Int. J. Hybrid Inf. Technol. **8**(7), 239–242 (2015)
37. Keet, C.M., et al.: The data mining optimization ontology. J. Web Semant. **32**, 43–53 (2015). https://doi.org/10.1016/j.websem.2015.01.001
38. Lebo, T., et al.: PROV-O: The PROV Ontology. Recommendation, World Wide Web Consortium (W3C), April 2013. https://www.w3.org/TR/prov-o/
39. Li, L., et al.: Real-world data medical knowledge graph: construction and applications. Artif. Intell. Med. **103**, 101817 (2020). https://doi.org/10.1016/j.artmed.2020.101817
40. Maali, F., Erickson, J.: Data Catalog Vocabulary (DCAT). Recommendation, World Wide Web Consortium (W3C), January 2014. https://www.w3.org/TR/vocab-dcat/
41. Malone, J., et al.: The software ontology (SWO): a resource for reproducibility in biomedical data analysis, curation and digital preservation. J. Biomed. Semant. **5**(1), 1–13 (2014). https://doi.org/10.1186/2041-1480-5-25
42. McGuinness, D.L., Van Harmelen, F., et al.: Owl web ontology language overview. W3C Recommendation (2004)
43. Miles, A., Bechhofer, S.: SKOS Simple Knowledge Organization System Reference. Recommendation, World Wide Web Consortium (W3C), August 2009. https://www.w3.org/TR/skos-reference/
44. Moradi, R., Berangi, R., Minaei, B.: A survey of regularization strategies for deep models. Artif. Intell. Rev. **53**, 3947–3986 (2020). https://doi.org/10.1007/s10462-019-09784-7
45. Musen, M.A.: The Protégé project: a look back and a look forward. AI Matters **1**(4), 4–12 (2015). https://doi.org/10.1145/2757001.2757003
46. OpenML: OpenML: a worldwide machine learning lab. https://www.openml.org
47. pandas: Pandas - A fast, powerful, flexible and easy to use open source data analysis and manipulation tool, built on top of the Python programming language. https://pandas.pydata.org. Accessed 28 Nov 2023
48. Panov, P., Džeroski, S., Soldatova, L.: OntoDM: an ontology of data mining. In: 2008 IEEE International Conference on Data Mining Workshops, pp. 752–760. IEEE (2008). https://doi.org/10.1109/ICDMW.2008.62
49. Panov, P., Soldatova, L., Džeroski, S.: OntoDM-KDD: ontology for representing the knowledge discovery process. In: Fürnkranz, J., Hüllermeier, E., Higuchi, T. (eds.) DS 2013. LNCS (LNAI), vol. 8140, pp. 126–140. Springer, Heidelberg (2013). https://doi.org/10.1007/978-3-642-40897-7_9
50. Papers with Code: Papers With Code: The latest in Machine Learning. https://paperswithcode.com. Accessed 28 Nov 2023
51. Peroni, S., Shotton, D.: FaBiO and CiTO: ontologies for describing bibliographic resources and citations. J. Web Semant. **17**, 33–43 (2012). https://doi.org/10.1016/j.websem.2012.08.001
52. Poveda-Villalón, M., Fernández-Izquierdo, A., Fernández-López, M., García-Castro, R.: LOT: an industrial oriented ontology engineering framework. Eng. Appl. Artif. Intell. **111**, 104755 (2022). https://doi.org/10.1016/j.engappai.2022.104755
53. Poveda-Villalón, M., Gómez-Pérez, A., Suárez-Figueroa, M.C.: OOPS! (OntOlogy Pitfall Scanner!): an on-line tool for ontology evaluation. Int. J. Semant. Web Inf. Syst. (IJSWIS) **10**(2), 7–34 (2014). https://doi.org/10.4018/ijswis.2014040102

54. Publio, G.C., et al.: ML-Schema: Exposing the Semantics of Machine Learning with Schemas and Ontologies. arXiv preprint arXiv:1807.05351 (2018). https://doi.org/10.48550/arXiv.1807.05351

55. Ravishankar, N., Vijayakumar, M.: Reinforcement learning algorithms: survey and classification. Indian J. Sci. Technol. **10**(1), 1–8 (2017). https://doi.org/10.17485/ijst/2017/v10i1/109385

56. Ristoski, P., Paulheim, H.: Semantic web in data mining and knowledge discovery: a comprehensive survey. J. Web Semant. **36**, 1–22 (2016). https://doi.org/10.1016/j.websem.2016.01.001

57. Rotmensch, M., Halpern, Y., Tlimat, A., Horng, S., Sontag, D.: Learning a health knowledge graph from electronic medical records. Sci. Rep. **7**(1), 5994 (2017). https://doi.org/10.1038/s41598-017-05778-z

58. Ruder, S.: An overview of gradient descent optimization algorithms (2017).https://doi.org/10.48550/arXiv.1609.04747

59. Sah, S.: Machine learning: a review of learning types. Int. Res. J. Mod. Eng. Technol. Sci. (2020). https://doi.org/10.20944/preprints202007.0230.v1

60. Saxena, A., et al.: A review of clustering techniques and developments. Neurocomputing **267**, 664–681 (2017). https://doi.org/10.1016/j.neucom.2017.06.053

61. Sharma, H., Kumar, S., et al.: A survey on decision tree algorithms of classification in data mining. Int. J. Sci. Res. (IJSR) **5**(4), 2094–2097 (2016)

62. Shrestha, A., Mahmood, A.: Review of deep learning algorithms and architectures. IEEE Access **7**, 53040–53065 (2019). https://doi.org/10.1109/ACCESS.2019.2912200

63. Soldatova, L.N., King, R.D.: An ontology of scientific experiments. J. R. Soc. Interface **3**(11), 795–803 (2006). https://doi.org/10.1098/rsif.2006.0134

64. Souza, R., et al.: Provenance data in the machine learning lifecycle in computational science and engineering. In: 2019 IEEE/ACM Workflows in Support of Large-Scale Science (WORKS), pp. 1–10. IEEE (2019). https://doi.org/10.1109/WORKS49585.2019.00006

65. TensorFlow: An end-to-end open source machine learning platform for everyone. https://www.tensorflow.org. Accessed 28 Nov 2023

66. Tian, Y., Zhang, Y.: A comprehensive survey on regularization strategies in machine learning. Inf. Fusion **80**, 146–166 (2022). https://doi.org/10.1016/j.inffus.2021.11.005

67. Vanschoren, J., Blockeel, H., Pfahringer, B., Holmes, G.: Experiment databases: a new way to share, organize and learn from experiments. Mach. Learn. **87**, 127–158 (2012). https://doi.org/10.1007/s10994-011-5277-0

68. Vanschoren, J., Van Rijn, J.N., Bischl, B., Torgo, L.: OpenML: networked science in machine learning. ACM SIGKDD Explor. Newsl. **15**(2), 49–60 (2014). https://doi.org/10.1145/2641190.2641198

69. Venkataramanan, R., Tripathy, A., Foltin, M., Yip, H.Y., Justine, A., Sheth, A.: Knowledge graph empowered machine learning pipelines for improved efficiency, reusability, and explainability. IEEE Internet Comput. **27**(1), 81–88 (2023). https://doi.org/10.1109/MIC.2022.3228087

70. Villanueva Zacarias, A.G., Reimann, P., Weber, C., Mitschang, B.: AssistML: an approach to manage, recommend and reuse ML solutions. Int. J. Data Sci. Anal. 1–25 (2023). https://doi.org/10.1007/s41060-023-00417-5

71. Weibel, S.L., Koch, T.: DCMI metadata terms. Technical report, Dublin Core Metadata Initiative (2012). http://dublincore.org/documents/dcmi-terms/

72. Zheng, Z., et al.: Executable knowledge graphs for machine learning: a Bosch case of welding monitoring. In: Sattler, U., et al. (eds.) The Semantic Web – ISWC 2022. ISWC 2022. LNCS, vol. 13489, pp. 791–809. Springer, Cham (2022). https://doi.org/10.1007/978-3-031-19433-7_45

73. Zhou, B., et al.: SemML: facilitating development of ML models for condition monitoring with semantics. J. Web Semant. **71**, 100664 (2021). https://doi.org/10.1016/j.websem.2021.100664

Enabling Social Demography Research Using Semantic Technologies

Lise Stork[1]([✉]) [iD], Richard L. Zijdeman[2] [iD], Ilaria Tiddi[1] [iD],
and Annette ten Teije[1] [iD]

[1] Vrije Universiteit Amsterdam, Amsterdam, The Netherlands
l.stork@uva.nl
[2] International Institute of Social History, Amsterdam, The Netherlands

Abstract. A shift in scientific publishing from paper-based to knowledge-based practices promotes reproducibility, machine actionability and knowledge discovery. This is important for disciplines like social demography, where study indicators are often social constructs such as race or education, hypothesis tests are challenging to compare due to their limited temporal and spatial coverage, and research output is presented in natural language, which can be ambiguous and imprecise. In this work, we present the MIRA resource, to aid researchers in their research workflow, and publish FAIR findings. MIRA consists of: (1) an ontology for social demography research, (2) a method for automated ontology population by prompting Large Language Models, and (3) a knowledge graph populated in terms of the ontology by annotating a set of research papers on health inequality. The resource allows researchers to formally represent their social demography research hypotheses, discovering research biases and novel research questions.

Keywords: Scientific Knowledge Graphs · Social Demography · Hypothesis Representation · Health Inequality · Information Extraction

Resource type: Ontology, Knowledge Graph
License: CC BY 4.0 International
DOI: https://doi.org/10.5281/zenodo.10286846
URL: http://w3id.org/mira, http://w3id.org/mira/ontology/

1 Introduction

Research on social demography focuses on the statistical study of human populations, with the aim of understanding and predicting social, cultural and economic trends across populations. Since the first known census taken by the Babylonian Empire in 3500 BCE [25], demographers have involved themselves with the task of explaining aggregate statistics of a population [14]. Specifically, the research cycle of a social historian consists of analysing observational data about society to form novel hypotheses and theories about societal mechanisms (see left side of Fig. 1). However, such studies tend to be restricted to specific time periods and regions, making comparison of hypothesis tests across the vast array of research papers difficult. Moreover, demographers test research hypotheses in which variables are often social constructs such as intelligence, ownership, or nationality. Unclarity and ambiguity reporting research findings in natural language complicates their precise understanding. Due to these complexities, demographers often describe rather than explain demographic phenomena [14], whereas causal explanations could help shape better policies for the future. Below we describe a common motivating scenario.

Example 1. *A social historian aims to analyse a population census from the Netherlands between 1850–1922—consisting of certificates (births and marriages), occupational and survival data[1]—to better understand mechanisms of social inequality. For this, the historian has to carefully survey the literature for known theories and the datasets and statistics that support them.* What was the evidence for a specific hypothesis? How did they measure social stratification? What were the outcomes? Which societal factors, that are (not) in my dataset, can moderate the effect between my study variables? *The historian may find it challenging to discover relevant papers or interpret research findings precisely.*

To address such challenges, the paradigm of scientific publishing is seeing a shift from document-oriented publishing to knowledge-based publishing [1,20], with the aim of making the infrastructure for scientific publication of research output more FAIR (Findable, Accessible, Interoperable, and Reusable). Semantic technologies have been successfully employed in various domains to accommodate such a shift. Notable examples are the Open Science Knowledge Graph [1, 31], the Unified Medical Language System (UMLS) [2], or Biomedical knowledge graphs such as [17], but many other examples exist [4,7,8,10,21,22,32,33]. These sources promote reusability of research findings, as well as the machine-aided design of novel research questions. Moreover, by adopting formal representations of knowledge, such resources promote transparency and explainability.

In social demography, work has been done formally describing observational data, such as census data hosted as linked data at the International Institute of Social History (IISH)[2] [24]. To the best of our knowledge, no studies formalise knowledge such as *hypotheses* and *findings* on social demography–and very few from social sciences in general [22,32], whereas these are important in each of the steps of the scientific workflow of a social historian (see Fig. 1). The research process, hypotheses and findings are mostly written up in scientific documents in natural language, which can be ambiguous and imprecise. Such fields can thus benefit from adopting the FAIR data principles, to reduce unclarity and ambiguity in the research workflow of a social demographer.

In summary, there is a need for the improvement of the digital infrastructure underlying scientific publication in social demography and social history research, to stimulate a deep understanding, and reuse of existing hypotheses, methods and findings. To address this need, this work provides:

---

[1] for example: https://datasets.iisg.amsterdam/dataverse/HSNDB-HSN.

[2] https://iisg.amsterdam/en.

1. The *MIRA ontology*, which includes a set of classes, properties and axioms for capturing research findings (*observations, comparisons and explanations*) on social demography, as well as SHACL shapes following data quality criteria of [5], for data validation.
2. A Knowledge Graph Construction (KGC) method, based on: (i) prompting a Large Language Model to annotate paper abstracts using the ontology, (ii) mapping concepts to terms from NCBO BioPortal ontologies and GeoNames, and (iii) refining the final graph by a set of SHACL constraints, developed according to data quality criteria.
3. The *MIRA-KG*, a knowledge graph of machine-annotated paper abstracts on social health inequality in terms of the MIRA ontology. Annotations are linked to Linked Open Data. The resource is published on the druid datalegend database infrastructure[3], maintained by the international institute of social history (IISH) and Triply[4].

In general, this work (i) supports the shift towards knowledge-based scientific publishing by contributing a novel method for KGC construction that can easily be adapted to accommodate other application domains, and (ii) contributes to a more FAIR infrastructure for social demography research.

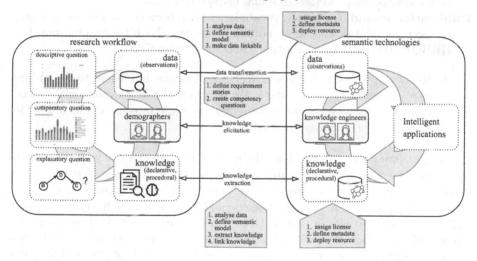

Fig. 1. The social demography research workflow. Blue boxes contain components of FAIR data management (e.g. for social history), which would enable social historians to make their research more FAIR. (Color figure online)

2   Related Work

Ontologies and Vocabularies for Scientific Knowledge. Below we discuss examples of ontologies developed for various types of scientific knowledge:

---

[3] https://druid.datalegend.net/.
[4] https://triply.cc/.

Upper-level science ontologies. Examples of upper-level ontologies for scientific research are the Modern Science (ModSci) ontology [10], an upper ontology for modern science branches and related entities, and the Semanticscience Integrated Ontology (SIO) [9], a simple integrated ontology for rich description of scientific concepts and processes.

Hypothesis representations. Work has been done on formalising research hypotheses, and notable examples are the SuperPattern ontology [4], which allows researchers to write up the main claims of scientific articles as statements in formal logic; the nanopublication model [15], which aims at publishing "core scientific statements with associated context", or the DISK Hypothesis Evolution ontology [12], which captures the evolution of hypotheses over time. Many other representations exist, of which [12] provides an extensive comparative overview. An example of a domain-specific scientific ontology is the PICO ontology (for Population, Intervention, Comparator, Outcome) for synthesis and querying of clinical trial experiments [23].

Data representations. The RDF Data Cube vocabulary[5] allows researchers to publish their multi-dimensional data, and an example of a domain-specific model for publishing datasets is the Data Scopes model [3,18], which captures how datasets are processed in social history research.

Publication metadata. Lastly, vocabularies have been created to capture publication metadata. The most notable ones are the bibliographic ontology (BIBO)[6], the PRISM vocabulary[7], and the Dublin Core[8].

In this work, we formalise research hypotheses and link them to data representations and publication metadata. We do so for the domain of social demography, which has not been done before, and make use of some of the ontologies and vocabularies enumerated above.

Scientific Knowledge Graphs. Knowledge Graphs that capture scientific knowledge have been created from unstructured texts such as research papers, in various domains like Computer Science and Artificial Intelligence [6–8], social science [29], biomedicine [17], plant sciences [21], social and behavioural sciences [22], or scientific articles in general [1,30,31]. Resources such as these support a variety of tasks that aid researchers in the development of their research questions and methods. Our work is most related to the work of [29] and [22], but instead proposes a semantic model of social demography hypotheses and findings, and a knowledge graph construction (KGC) method that does not rely on the knowledge-intensive task of expert semantic annotation and links extracted knowledge to other linked open data (LOD).

---

[5] https://www.w3.org/TR/vocab-data-cube/.
[6] https://www.dublincore.org/specifications/bibo/bibo/bibo.rdf.xml.
[7] https://www.w3.org/submissions/2020/SUBM-prism-20200910/psv-over.html.
[8] https://www.dublincore.org/.

3   Knowledge Graph Construction

This section describes the knowledge graph construction pipeline (see Fig. 2 for the entire pipeline). *Ontology creation* is discussed in Sect. 3.1, the resulting ontology in Sect. 3.2, *ontology population* in Sect. 3.3, and the resulting KG in Sect. 3.4.

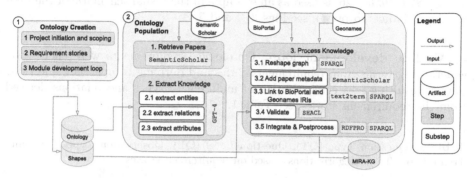

Fig. 2. The knowledge graph construction pipeline. Coloured artifacts are novel contributions; non-coloured artifacts represent external repositories. (Color figure online)

3.1   Ontology Creation

Below, we describe ontology creation process (see ① of Fig. 2). We follow the eXtreme Design (XD) method for ontology development [27], a collaborative, incremental, iterative method for pattern-based ontology design. We followed the main steps of the XD methodology: (i) project scoping, (ii) creation of requirement stories, (iii) a module development loop.

1. Project initiation and scoping. A first interview was set up with a domain expert on social history and humanities research from the International Institute of Social History (IISH)[9]. The outcome of the interview was used to define the task context, get a better understanding of the challenges, and write out a first list of ontology requirements (inspired by how a hypotheses is represented in DISK [12,13]): *Article metadata* (**RQ1**), *Hypothesis classification* (**RQ2**), *Hypothesis statement* (**RQ3**), *Hypothesis context* (**RQ4**), *Hypothesis qualifier* (**RQ5**), and *Hypothesis evidence* (**RQ6**). For **RQ2–6**, we collected requirement stories.

2. Requirement stories. Within this project, requirement stories were collected based on insights retrieved during the project scoping phase about hypothesis types and their elements. We show one requirement story below (Example 2), which shows an explanatory question (asking whether economic developments can explain differences in socioeconomic inequality).

---

[9] https://iisg.amsterdam/en.

Example 2. *"Is the influence of ascription on education larger than the influence of achievement, and is the effect moderated by economic developments?"*

After a first elicitation round, academic papers were used as requirement stories. An example annotation, based on the paper *"Industrialization and inequality revisited: Mortality differentials and vulnerability to economic stress in Stockholm, 1878–1926"* [26] is used as an example in the visual schematic of the final ontology (indicated by ■), see Figs. 3, 4 and 5.

3. Module development loop.

Ontological requirements were elicited by generalising terms from requirement stories and deriving competency questions (CQs), resulting in a categorisation of main entity types and relations derived from the requirement stories, see Table 1.

Table 1. Question Type (QT), Question Level (QL), Observation Type (OT), and Trend Type (TT) categorisations, based on requirement stories.

QT	QL	OT	TT
Descriptive Describing phenomena, e.g. *temperature is rising over time*	Micro *Individuals Human populations*	Longitudinal *Observations over time*	Temporal trend *Comparison of time intervals*
Comparative Comparisons between sample means, trends, or effects, e.g. *did temperature rise more after industrialisation?*	Meso *Social groups, Organisations*	Intergenerational *Observations over generations*	Spatial trend *Comparison of regions*
Explanatory Defining a potential cause of the outcome of a comparison, e.g. *did human emission cause the rise of temperature?*	Macro *Geographical regions*	Intersectional *Observations from a single point in time*	Socioeconomic trend *Comparison of distribution across social classes*

Moreover, contextual statements (CSs), and reasoning requirements (RRs) were derived. CSs informed the creation of SHACL constraints for validation, and RRs informed the creation of OWL[10] axioms. A collaborative environment in the form of a Wiki was set up to gather the CQs, CSs, RRs and other outcomes. A dump of the Wiki is published on Zenodo together with the dataset.

Ontology Reuse. For representing article metadata (**RQ1**), we use BIBO, PRISM and Dublin Core. To classify hypotheses (**RQ2**), we use the classification (QT) from Table 1. Moreover, to write up hypothesis statements (**RQ3**) and their context (**RQ4**, based on (QL) from Table 1) we utilise the structure and properties of the SuperPattern Ontology [4]. However, we represent instances of the SuperPattern as individuals instead of classes. As in social demography, evidence often

---

[10] https://www.w3.org/TR/owl-syntax/.

comes from specific time periods and regions, future work will explore the use of class axioms to collect all evidence belonging to a claim. We additionally reuse classes and properties from the Semanticscience Integrated Ontology (SIO) [33] (e.g. trend line `sio:SIO_000527` or human population `sio:SIO_001062`). For qualifiers (**RQ5**), we reuse qualifier categories from [16], as results can be translated to effect sizes. Lastly, to link hypotheses to their evidence (**RQ6**), we reuse the *RDF Data Cube Vocabulary*[11], furthering reproducibility and machine actionability.

Design Pattern (ODP) Reuse. Scientific hypotheses and claims often consist of complex relations between variables, relations, and findings, and as such there are various ways of modeling them. One typical way is to reify the relation-holding context as a node with binary relations for the subject, object and property, and a fourth binary relation indicating the context [11]. A downside of such a representation is that the Web Ontology Language (OWL)[12] does not support reification. Some Ontology Design Patterns such as the Content Slices ODP[13] address the issue, but such modeling hampers easy integration with paper metadata. Therefore, we choose for *reification* with the idea that the reified hypotheses can later be transformed to binary relations, should OWL reasoning be required.

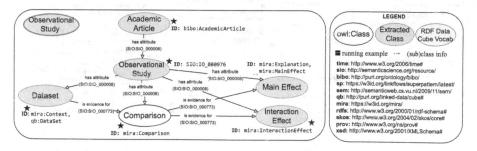

Fig. 3. Main classes of the MIRA ontology. A ★ points to the IRI of the class(es) or superclass. Elements retrieved from paper abstracts during the ontology population process (see Sect. 3.3) are indicated in blue. Commonly, paper abstracts from social demography do not contain statistical data and precise findings. (Color figure online)

3.2 The MIRA Ontology

The main concepts, relations and their domains and ranges of the MIRA Ontology are created in light of our requirements and categorisations (Table 1)[14]. These are shown in Fig. 3. Figure 4 unfolds the *comparison* branch of the MIRA

---

[11] http://www.w3.org/TR/vocab-data-cube/.

[12] https://www.w3.org/TR/owl-ref/.

[13] http://ontologydesignpatterns.org/wiki/Submissions:Context_Slices.

[14] Some categorisations (such as OT and CT) are omitted as these can be derived by querying dataset information (the `qb:sliceStructure` of a `qb:Slice`).

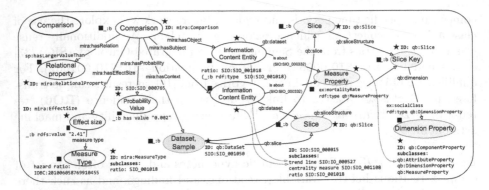

Fig. 4. The **Comparison** class and its links to the RDF Data Cube Vocabulary. Comparisons compare information content entities such as trend lines, centrality measures, and ratios, which are based on slices over multidimensional data cubes. Example instances and literals are based on the article *"Industrialization and inequality revisited: Mortality differentials and vulnerability to economic stress in Stockholm, 1878–1926"*, and indicated with ■ [26] (Color figure online)

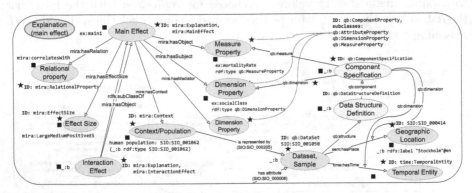

Fig. 5. The **Explanation (Main Effect)** class and its links to the RDF Data Cube Vocabulary. Explanations describe measured effects of dimensions in the dataset (such as `ex:socialClass`, instance of `qb:DimensionProperty`) on measurements in the dataset (instances of `qb:MeasureProperty` such as `ex:mortalityRate`). These properties can then be linked to concepts from ontologies using `qb:concept` (for example `ex:mortalityRate qb:concept STATO:STATO_0000414`). The `mira:correlatesWith` property is used as a subproperty of `mira:RelationalProperty`. No causal link is yet stated, since more evidence from various regions and periods is required to state a causal relationship. **Interaction Effects** are subclasses of main effects. They are modeled in the same way, with the following exceptions: the range of `mira:hasObject` is an instance of `mira:MainEffect`; the range of `mira:hasProperty` is `mira:moderates`. (Color figure online)

ontology. Descriptive statistics (such as ratios) can be compared, and are linked to their respective data cube slices. Figure 5 unfolds the *explanation* (main effect and interaction effect) branch of the MIRA ontology.

From the CSs and RRs enumerated during the ontology design process, we developed a set of OWL axioms and SHACL constraints for validation, which describe the semantic requirements of the hypotheses. An example of an OWL statement and axiom are: *is evidence for* is an `owl:transitiveProperty`, and `mira:InteractionEffect owl:subClassOf mira:Explanation` respectively. Examples of SHACL constraints are the use of `sh:minCount` and `sh:maxCount` to ensure that each paper has at least one study, each study has at least one explanation, each explanation has as exactly one context, subject, object, relation and qualifier.

3.3 Ontology Population

Below, we describe the ontology population process from scientific papers (See ② of Fig. 2). Our method is related to other KGC methods such as [6], but explores prompt-based triple extraction as a single extraction step allows for fewer errors to be propagated to subsequent steps. Future work will compare such a method with other established KGC methods. As a use case, we focus on articles related to health inequality.

1. Retrieve papers. Papers included were retrieved from Semantic Scholar using the Semantic Scholar API, and selected by the following steps:

- retrieving papers between 2020–2023, based on the keywords: $\in$ {*social, inequality, disparities, mortality, population, socioeconomic, demographic, study*}, and the fields of study $\in$ {*Economics, History, Sociology*}. These keywords were terms encountered in the titles of the five papers used as requirement stories;
- filtering papers based on:
  - i *citation count:* removing articles with lower impact, with ≤ 10 citations;
  - ii *journal:* removing articles published in non peer-reviewed journals;
  - iii *abstract length:* including articles with abstract length $l = \mu - \sigma > l > \mu + \sigma$ (within plus-or-minus 1 standard deviation) as we found that it was easier to extract hypotheses from texts that were not too long nor too short due to conciseness and lack of information, respectively;
  - iv *doi:* whether or not articles included a Digital Object Identifier (DOI).

2. Extract Knowledge. In social demography, the abstract of a paper commonly includes the explanatory question and the time period and location of the population sample. We thus annotate paper abstracts with these parts of the ontology (see the blue classes in Figs. 3, 4 and 5). In order to extract the relevant entities, relations and attributes in terms of the ontology, we prompt GPT-4 (OpenAI, 2023), see Table 2. Large Language Models can learn multiple tasks without any explicit supervision [19,28] and can therefore take on the task normally performed through human annotators via crowdsourcing, without any training. Retrieved annotations were extracted directly as triples of the form $< subject, predicate, object >$ using the Resource Description Framework[15].

---

[15] https://www.w3.org/RDF/.

Table 2. Prompt used to retrieve structured abstract annotations using GPT-4. Each prompt consisted of the paper abstract, the ontology (domains and ranges), and some instructions for formatting of individuals.

Prompt template
< *abstract* >
Describe the claim of the abstract above only using RDF (the turtle syntax),
and using the following ontology:
< *property* >< *domain* >< *range* >
< *instructionnumber* >< *instruction* >< *example* >
Only return proper RDF, no free text comments

Instruction example	Answer
Instruction: use rdfs:label to describe all blank nodes, also the geographic region. Use short descriptions, pieces of text verbatim from the abstract, and add language tags to all labels. *Example*: [] :hasSubject [rdfs:label "social class"@en].	[ ] :hasSubject [rdfs:label "residential patterns and nutrition"@en]
Instruction: for instances of the class gn:Feature, find the URI for the place name in GeoNames (uri = https://www.geonames.org/<code>) *Example*: [] gn:locatedIn <uri>	[] gn:locatedIn <http://sws.geonames.org/2673730/>

3. Process Knowledge. After extracting a set of triples (a subgraph) from a paper abstract, we: (i) **reshape** the subgraph, as we prompted GPT-4 to return annotations in a somewhat simpler structure to avoid structural errors, (iii) **add paper metadata** by transforming paper metadata retrieved from SemanticScholar (abstract, DOI, citations, publication date, authors) to RDF, (ii) **link** study variables in the subgraph to Linked Open Data from BioPortal and GeoNames, (iii) **validate** the subgraph using the SHACL shapes, and (iv) **integrate** the subgraph with the MIRA-KG, and **postprocess** the merged graph by removing redundant entities.

Specifically, in the **link** step, instances of qb:ComponentProperty are linked to concepts from BioPortal[16] using qb:concept. Prior to linking, a manual mapping study was performed (output can be found in the Zenodo repository) to see which BioPortal ontologies contained most of the useful study variables. Selected ontologies were HHEAR[17], SIO[18], IOBC[19] and MESH[20]). Subsequently,

---

[16] https://bioportal.bioontology.org/.
[17] https://bioportal.bioontology.org/ontologies/HHEAR/.
[18] https://www.ebi.ac.uk/ols/ontologies/sio.
[19] https://purl.bioontology.org/ontology/IOBC.
[20] https://purl.bioontology.org/ontology/MESH.

we retrieve location metadata from GeoNames[21] through FactForge[22], as the knowledge extraction step already retrieves GeoNames IRIs. Location coordinates, for instance, can aid researchers in discovering regional biases, or temporal trends. For the **validate** step, SHACL shapes are used to check for schema and ontological correctness. One of the SHACL shapes, for instance, checks for syntactic validity of dates, by ensuring `sh:datatype xsd:date`, and by checking for ontological correctness (begin before end-date, see SHACL shapes). For the **integrate** and **postprocess** steps, the subgraph is merged with the MIRA-KG. After processing all paper subgraphs, we remove duplicate BioPortal concepts and their labels via `owl:sameAs` smushing using RDFpro[23].

The time it took to process a single paper abstract was 1 min and 11 s (MacBook M1 Chip, 8 cores, 8 gb RAM). A fully annotated paper abstract as machine-readable data can be found in the Github repository.

3.4   The MIRA-KG

Table 3 shows statistics of the final knowledge graph, formalising 398 paper abstracts. We remove paper metadata functional properties from this view (for example `dcterms:created`), as these counts are equal to the instance count for `bibo:AcademicArticle`. We present the average degree with and

Table 3. Statistics of the MIRA-KG: Class instance count, property count, number of nodes and edges, and average degree.

Classes	Instances	Properties	Count
`time:Instant`	948	`bibo:cites`	13496
`qb:DimensionProperty`	701	`qb:concept`	4041
`skos:Concept`	587	`rdfs:label`	3133
`mira:Explanation`	582	`dcterms:contributor`	1176
`SIO:SIO_000414` (geographic region)	524	`SIO:SIO_000008` (has attribute)	1065
`SIO:SIO_001050` (sample)	477	`time:inXSDDate`	946
`time:TemporalEntity`	474	`mira:hasSubject`	607
`qb:MeasureProperty`	477	`mira:hasContext`	607
`SIO:SIO_000976` (observational study)	469	`SIO:SIO_000205` (is represented by)	607
`SIO:SIO_001062` (human population)	408	`mira:hasObject`	602
`bibo:AcademicArticle`	398	`mira:hasEffectSize`	589
`gn:Feature`	114	`mira:hasRelation`	583
`mira:InteractionEffect`	105	`sem:hasPlace`	479
`SIO:SIO_000012` (organisation)	12	`time:hasTime`	477
		`gn:locatedIn`	454
Dataset statistics		`wgs84_pos:long`	172
Number of Nodes	24281	`wgs84_pos:lat`	172
Number of Edges	32359	`gn:name`	114
Av. Degree	1.59	`mira:hasMediator`	77
Av. Degree (no types)	1.33	`SIO:SIO_000061` (located in)	2

---

[21] https://www.geonames.org/.
[22] http://factforge.net.
[23] https://github.com/dkmfbk/rdfpro.

without types, as these are naturally densely connected hubs. More interesting are the densely connected papers via citations or BioPortal concepts and locations with high in-degrees. Nodes with the highest in-degree that were not classes of the MIRA ontology were: economics/economy (`MESH:D004467`, `IOBC:200906008393315870`, 222), mortality rate (`MESH:D009026`, 188), hygiene (`MESH:D006920`, 91), the United States (`geonames:6252001`, 90) health (`MESH:D006262`, 90), age (`MESH:D006262`, 83) and income (`MESH:D007182`, 47).

4   Evaluation

In this section, we first evaluate the ontology (Sect. 4.1), and then the whole knowledge graph via a use case and data quality measures (Sect. 4.1).

4.1   Ontology Evaluation

Here, we show one of the competency questions as a SPARQL query (for brevity we omit prefixes, but these can be found in Fig. 3): The **CQ** retrieves a claim with a specific dependent variable and a potential mediator.

```
PREFIX ...
select distinct ?ind_lab ?ind_var ?qual
                ?med_var ?med_lab where {
?exp mira:hasSubject/qb:concept/rdfs:label ?ind_lab;
     #what is the subject of the explanation
     mira:hasSubject/qb:concept ?ind_var;
     #the object is COVID-19 mortality
     mira:hasObject/qb:concept mesh:D000086382,
                               MESH:D00902;
     #what is the effectSize of the association
     mira:hasEffectSize ?effectSize .
     #which variables mediate the association
OPTIONAL{?exp mira:hasMediator ?med_var;
              mira:hasMediator/rdfs:label ?med_lab .}
}
```

ind_lab	med_lab
1 Residential Segregation	
2 Economics	
3 Ethnicity	
4 Occupation	Ability
5 Occupation	Home

effectSize
1 mira:largeMediumNegativeES
2 mira:largeMediumPositiveES
3 mira:largeMediumPositiveES
4 mira:smallPositiveES
5 mira:smallPositiveES

(a) The SPARQL query for the **CQ**

(b) The result for the **CQ** (first five rows)

Fig. 6. CQ1: *Have associations been found between a socioeconomic variable and COVID-19, and which explanations can be found for the inequality?*

Figure 6b shows the output of the query for the **CQ** (first five rows). It indicates that residential segregation, economics and ethnicity were all correlated with COVID-19 mortality. The association between COVID-19 and occupation was specifically mediated by the ability to work from home (*ability, home*). The rest of the competency questions can be found as SPARQL queries in the Github repository. They could all be answered using SPARQL queries over the MIRA ontology, although some limitations were discovered during ontology creation, see Sect. 4.2 below.

Limitations. The sessions with the expert showed that within papers there are various reformulations of the same hypothesis, which are at times not semantically the same. Such variations cannot be covered entirely without overly complicating the ontology, and cannot always be fully understood without access to the data and experiments. Moreover, effect sizes are often not clearly reported in the paper abstracts, hampering the quality of the extracted effectsizes.

4.2   Knowledge Graph Evaluation

In this section, we evaluate the use of the MIRA-KG via a use case, and its quality via a set of data quality criteria.

Use Case: Geographic Biases of Hypotheses and Findings. A researcher is studying the effect of income on mortality rates. They aim at discovering whether there is a geographic study bias for the research question, and whether the strength of the association differs among geographic regions. The researcher queries the MIRA-KG for all studies researching the influence of income (MESH:D007182) on mortality (MESH:D00902).

```
PREFIX ...
select ?long ?lat ?locName ?es ?geoId where {
#the subject of the explanation is income
?exp mira:hasSubject/qb:concept MESH:D007182 ;
    #the object of the exp. is mortality
    mira:hasObject/qb:concept MESH:D00902 ;
    #what is the effect size of the explanation
    mira:hasEffectSize ?es ;
    #what is the context of the explanation
    mira:hasContext ?pop .
#which sample is used to represent the population.
?pop sio:SIO_000205 ?sample .
#where is the sample collected
?sample sem:hasPlace ?location .
#what is the GeoNamesId of the location
?location gn:locatedIn ?geoId .
?geoId rdf:type gn:Feature ;
    #what is the name of the location
    gn:name ?locName ;
    #what is the longitude
    wgs84_pos:long ?long ;
    #what is the latitude
    wgs84_pos:lat ?lat . }
```

long	lat	locName
1 17.64	59.85	Uppsala
2 8.05	47.4	Aarau
3 24.93	60.17	Finland
4 -52.0	-13.84	Brazil

geoId	es
1 gn:2666199	largeMediumNegativeES
2 gn:2661881	largeMediumPositiveES
3 gn:660013	largeMediumPositiveES
4 gn:3469034	largeMediumPositiveES

(a) The SPARQL query for the **use case**

(b) The query result for the **use case** (first four rows)

Fig. 7. Use case: *A social historian queries the MIRA-KG for metadata of all studies researching the influence of income (MESH:D007182) on mortality (MESH:D00902)*

The output of the SPARQL query (first four rows shown in Fig. 7b) is visualised on a world map (see Fig. 8), and shows a bias of research studies towards American samples for the specific correlation. Moreover, by aggregating the results, the historian notices that four studies that are based on American population samples measure a negative correlation, and four a positive.

Fig. 8. Density plot for the **use case** query, showing a bias towards studies based on American population samples.

Data Quality Evaluation. We use the RDF data quality criteria as defined by [5] to, on the one hand, validate the MIRA-KG as well as the KGC pipeline, and, on the other hand, refine the graph. We summarise the most important ones for our case below.

Accuracy. Accuracy in terms of Linked Data deals with *syntactic* and *semantic* validity, as well as *duplicate entries. Syntactic validity:* the `DatatypeConstraintComponent` catches data type violations, such as the use of `rdf:XMLLiteral` where `xsd:date` should have been used. Furthermore, Table 3 shows all retrieved GeoNames identifiers were correct identifiers, as metadata was retrieved for all of them from FactForge. *Semantic validity:* The `LessThanConstraintComponent` measures logical temporal violations (begin date before end date). *Duplicate entries:* from Table 4 we see that with eight violations, these were annotated with high logical accuracy (98.3%). Lastly, duplicate BioPortal entities were handled during the postprocessing step of the KGC pipeline, as described in Sect. 3.3.

Table 4. Left: SHACL constraint violations for the MIRA-KG. **Right**: LLM retrieval errors for 20 research articles.

Constraint violation	Count	LLM retrieval error (20 articles)	Count
sh:LessThanConstraintComponent	8	Study variables	3
sh:DatatypeConstraintComponent	23	Location	2
sh:ClassConstraintComponent	38	Context	1
sh:MinCountConstraintComponent	122	Time period	7
sh:MaxCountConstraintComponent	4	Effect size	1
sh:XoneConstraintComponent	27		

Trustworthiness. This dimension is defined as the degree to which the information is accepted to be correct, true, real and credible. As the MIRA-KG was created automatically using GPT-4, we analyse the first twenty hypotheses (annotations can be found on Zenodo). Errors with respect to the retrieval are shown in Table 4. *Study variables:* in case study variables were incorrect, GPT-4 used related terms (such as *time* instead of *age* as independent variable). *Time period:* most common errors were incorrectly retrieved dates. However it should be mentioned that, in most cases, dates were incorrectly extracted when no dates were mentioned in the abstract.

Even though errors appear, most terms appear to be retrieved correctly, even for quite complicated hypotheses such as: *In the context of a human population, "Social inequality", mediated through "Health-services structure", is correlated with "COVID-19 mortality" with a largeMediumPositiveES. "Governmental response to COVID-19" moderates this correlation. Evidence comes from "São Paulo residents", from "São Paulo" between the years "2020-03-01" and "2020-09-30".*

Consistency. Semantic consistency is the extent to which a collection uses the same values for conveying the same meanings throughout. SHACL constraints were applied to enforce schema-correctness (such as a hypothesis has at least one independent variable). Constraint violations can be found in Table 4 (`sh:Class`, `sh:MinCount`, `sh:MaxCount` and `sh:Xone-ConstraintComponent`). By looking at the exact violations, we see that common errors were errors in structure, such as a context which was linked to a study instead of an explanation, resulting in violations of both the `Class` as well as the `MinCount` constraint components. The graph was queried to retrieve and dissolve these common errors to further consummate the entire graph.

Limitations. Due to the limitations mentioned in Sect. 4.1 (underspecification, ambiguity, and unclarity), it is challenging to extract hypotheses from scientific papers in a precise manner. The ontology will, however, allow researchers to publish their findings in a machine-readable manner alongside paper publication. Second, representing complex concepts, such as 'the ability to work from home', is non-trivial, as these are not always defined in ontologies or vocabularies and can be described in many different ways. For querying, linking such a variable to the concepts 'ability' as well as 'home' would suffice, but if precise reasoning is required, other solutions need to be considered (e.g. OWL axioms).

5   Conclusions

Studies in (historical) social sciences, such as social demography, tend to be restricted to specific time periods and regions, making comparison of hypothesis tests across the vast array of research papers difficult. To assist social historians and demographers in the scientific process, this study describes MIRA, a method knowledge graph construction, and a resource consisting of a ontology and knowledge graph to capture hypotheses and findings in social demography.

This study shows that the MIRA ontology allows researchers to formulate their key questions, and research results in a structured and semantically sound way. Moreover, using over 400 abstracts from the field of social demography, our knowledge graph construction pipeline demonstrates that the knowledge-intensive task of semantic annotation can be (semi-)automated when employing a Large Language Model, even without any training, validating data quality after automated annotation.

Future work will focus on dealing with variations in natural language, and on expanding the MIRA-KG by application of the MIRA ontology on a larger set of studies in order for the field to reorganize itself, for instance by motivating researchers to publish their findings in a machine-readable manner.

Acknowledgements. This work was funded by the European MUHAI project (Horizon 2020 research and innovation program) under grant agreement number 951846. We thank Tobias Kuhn, Frank van Harmelen, and Inès Blin for the insightful discussions that contributed to this work.

References

1. Auer, S., Kovtun, V., Prinz, M., Kasprzik, A., Stocker, M., Vidal, M.E.: Towards a knowledge graph for science. In: Proceedings of the 8th International Conference on Web Intelligence, Mining and Semantics, pp. 1–6 (2018)
2. Bodenreider, O.: The unified medical language system (UMLS): integrating biomedical terminology. Nucleic Acids Res. **32**(suppl_1), D267–D270 (2004)
3. de Boer, V., Bonestroo, I., Koolen, M., Hoekstra, R.: A linked data model for data scopes. In: Garoufallou, E., Ovalle-Perandones, M.A. (eds.) MTSR 2020. CCIS, vol. 1355, pp. 345–351. Springer, Cham (2021). https://doi.org/10.1007/978-3-030-71903-6_32
4. Bucur, C.I., Kuhn, T., Ceolin, D., Van Ossenbruggen, J.: Expressing high-level scientific claims with formal semantics. In: K-CAP 2021 - Proceedings of the 11th Knowledge Capture Conference, pp. 233–240 (2021). https://doi.org/10.1145/3460210.3493561
5. Candela, G., Escobar, P., Carrasco, R.C., Marco-Such, M.: Evaluating the quality of linked open data in digital libraries. J. Inf. Sci. **48**(1), 21–43 (2022)
6. Dessí, D., Osborne, F., Recupero, D.R., Buscaldi, D., Motta, E.: SCICERO: a deep learning and NLP approach for generating scientific knowledge graphs in the computer science domain. Knowl.-Based Syst. **258**, 109945 (2022). https://doi.org/10.1016/j.knosys.2022.109945
7. Dessí, D., Osborne, F., Reforgiato Recupero, D., Buscaldi, D., Motta, E.: CS-KG: a large-scale knowledge graph of research entities and claims in computer science. In: Sattler, U., et al. (eds.) ISWC 2022. LNCS, vol. 13489, pp. 678–696. Springer, Cham (2022). https://doi.org/10.1007/978-3-031-19433-7_39
8. Dessì, D., Osborne, F., Reforgiato Recupero, D., Buscaldi, D., Motta, E., Sack, H.: AI-KG: an automatically generated knowledge graph of artificial intelligence. In: Pan, J.Z., et al. (eds.) ISWC 2020, Part II. LNCS, vol. 12507, pp. 127–143. Springer, Cham (2020). https://doi.org/10.1007/978-3-030-62466-8_9
9. Dumontier, M., et al.: The Semanticscience Integrated Ontology (SIO) for biomedical research and knowledge discovery. J. Biomed. Semant. **5**, 1–11 (2014)
10. Fathalla, S., Lange, C., Auer, S.: An upper ontology for modern science branches and related entities. In: Pesquita, C., et al. (eds.) ESWC 2023. LNCS, vol. 13870, pp. 436–453. Springer, Cham (2023). https://doi.org/10.1007/978-3-031-33455-9_26

11. Gangemi, A., Presutti, V.: A multi-dimensional comparison of ontology design patterns for representing *n*-ary relations. In: van Emde Boas, P., Groen, F.C.A., Italiano, G.F., Nawrocki, J., Sack, H. (eds.) SOFSEM 2013. LNCS, vol. 7741, pp. 86–105. Springer, Cham (2013). https://doi.org/10.1007/978-3-642-35843-2_8
12. Garijo, D., Gil, Y., Ratnakar, V.: The DISK hypothesis ontology: capturing hypothesis evolution for automated discovery. In: K-CAP Workshops, pp. 40–46 (2017)
13. Gil, Y., et al.: Towards continuous scientific data analysis and hypothesis evolution. In: Proceedings of the AAAI Conference on Artificial Intelligence, vol. 31 (2017)
14. Graham, E.: Theory and explanation in demography: the case of low fertility in Europe. Popul. Stud. **75**(sup1), 133–155 (2021)
15. Groth, P., Gibson, A., Velterop, J.: The anatomy of a nanopublication. Inf. Serv. Use **30**(1–2), 51–56 (2010)
16. de Haan, R., Tiddi, I., Beek, W.: Discovering research hypotheses in social science using knowledge graph embeddings. In: Verborgh, R., et al. (eds.) ESWC 2021. LNCS, vol. 12731, pp. 477–494. Springer, Cham (2021). https://doi.org/10.1007/978-3-030-77385-4_28
17. Himmelstein, D.S., et al.: Systematic integration of biomedical knowledge prioritizes drugs for repurposing. Elife **6**, e26726 (2017)
18. Hoekstra, R., Koolen, M.: Data scopes for digital history research. Hist. Methods: A J. Quant. Interdisc. Hist. **52**(2), 79–94 (2019)
19. Kojima, T., Gu, S.S., Reid, M., Matsuo, Y., Iwasawa, Y.: Large language models are zero-shot reasoners. In: Advances in Neural Information Processing Systems, vol. 35, pp. 22199–22213 (2022)
20. Kuhn, T., et al.: Decentralized provenance-aware publishing with nanopublications. PeerJ Comput. Sci. **2**, e78 (2016)
21. Larmande, P., Todorov, K.: AgroLD: a knowledge graph for the plant sciences. In: Hotho, A., et al. (eds.) ISWC 2021. LNCS, vol. 12922, pp. 496–510. Springer, Cham (2021). https://doi.org/10.1007/978-3-030-88361-4_29
22. Magnusson, I.H., Friedman, S.E.: Extracting fine-grained knowledge graphs of scientific claims: dataset and transformer-based results. In: EMNLP 2021 - 2021 Conference on Empirical Methods in Natural Language Processing, Proceedings, pp. 4651–4658 (2021). https://doi.org/10.18653/v1/2021.emnlp-main.381
23. Mavergames, C., Oliver, S., Becker, L.: Systematic reviews as an interface to the web of (trial) data: using PICO as an ontology for knowledge synthesis in evidence-based healthcare research. SePublica **994**, 22–6 (2013)
24. Meroño-Peñuela, A., Ashkpour, A., Guéret, C., Schlobach, S.: CEDAR: the Dutch historical censuses as linked open data. Semant. Web **8**(2), 297–310 (2017)
25. Missiakoulis, S.: Cecrops, King of Athens: the first (?) recorded population census in history. Int. Stat. Rev. **78**(3), 413–418 (2010)
26. Molitoris, J., Dribe, M.: Industrialization and inequality revisited: mortality differentials and vulnerability to economic stress in Stockholm, 1878–1926. Eur. Rev. Econ. Hist. **20**(2), 176–197 (2016)
27. Presutti, V., Daga, E., Gangemi, A., Blomqvist, E.: Extreme design with content ontology design patterns. In: Proceedings of the Workshop on Ontology Patterns, pp. 83–97 (2009)
28. Radford, A., Wu, J., Child, R., Luan, D., Amodei, D., Sutskever, I., et al.: Language models are unsupervised multitask learners. OpenAI Blog **1**(8), 9 (2019)
29. Spadaro, G., et al.: The Cooperation Databank: machine-readable science accelerates research synthesis. Perspect. Psychol. Sci. **17**(5), 1472–1489 (2022)

30. Stocker, M., et al.: SKG4EOSC-scholarly knowledge graphs for EOSC: establishing a backbone of knowledge graphs for fair scholarly information in EOSC. Res. Ideas Outcomes **8**, e83789 (2022)

31. Stocker, M., et al.: FAIR scientific information with the open research knowledge graph. FAIR Connect **1**(1), 19–21 (2023)

32. Tiddi, I., Balliet, D., ten Teije, A.: Fostering scientific meta-analyses with knowledge graphs: a case-study. In: Harth, A., et al. (eds.) ESWC 2020. LNCS, vol. 12123, pp. 287–303. Springer, Cham (2020). https://doi.org/10.1007/978-3-030-49461-2_17

33. Viet, S.M., et al.: Human Health Exposure Analysis Resource (HHEAR): a model for incorporating the exposome into health studies. Int. J. Hyg. Environ. Health **235**, 113768 (2021)

SCOOP All the Constraints' Flavours for Your Knowledge Graph

Xuemin Duan[1]([📧])[ID], David Chaves-Fraga[2,1][ID], Olivier Derom[1], and Anastasia Dimou[1][ID]

[1] KU Leuven – Flanders Make@KULeuven – Leuven.AI, Leuven, Belgium
{xuemin.duan,anastasia.dimou}@kuleuven.be
[2] Grupo de Sistemas Intelixentes, Universidade de Santiago de Compostela, Santiago de Compostela, Spain
david.chaves@usc.es

Abstract. Creating SHACL shapes for the validation of RDF graphs is a non-trivial endeavor. Automated shape extraction systems typically derive SHACL shapes from RDF graphs, and thus, their effectiveness is inherently influenced by the size and complexity of the RDF graph. However, these systems often overlook the constraints imposed by individual artifacts, although RDF graphs are often constructed by applying ontology terms to heterogeneous data. Only a few systems extract SHACL shapes from either the data schema or the ontology, leading, in either case, to limited or incomplete constraints. We propose SCOOP, a framework that exploits all artifacts associated with the construction of an RDF graph, i.e. data schemas, ontologies, and mapping rules, and integrates the SHACL shapes extracted from each artifact into a unified shapes graph. We applied our approach to real-world use cases and experimental results showed that SCOOP outperforms systems that extract SHACL shapes from RDF graphs, generating more than double the types of constraints than those systems, and effectively identifying missing and erroneous RDF triples during the validation process.

Resource type: Software Framework — **License**: Apache-2.0
DOI: https://doi.org/10.5281/zenodo.10280346
URL: https://github.com/dtai-kg/SCOOP

Keywords: SHACL · Shape integration · Knowledge graph validation

1 Introduction

Creating SHACL shapes for the validation of RDF graphs is a non-trivial endeavor. Shapes Constraint Language (SHACL) [27], the W3C recommendation for validating RDF graphs, has gained increasing popularity, which has further prompted a growing number of endeavors in automating shape extraction. However, a notable proportion of users in industry and academia still favor creating shapes manually [13,32], indicating the practical limitations of existing works.

Currently, automated shape extraction broadly falls into two categories: RDF-based and non-RDF-based systems. The cost and performance of systems

© The Author(s), under exclusive license to Springer Nature Switzerland AG 2024
A. Meroño Peñuela et al. (Eds.): ESWC 2024, LNCS 14665, pp. 217–234, 2024.
https://doi.org/10.1007/978-3-031-60635-9_13

extracting shapes from *RDF* graphs [16–18,28,33,38] are inherently contingent upon the scale and intricacy of the RDF graph, frequently leading to a limited subset of constraints [31], e.g., not covering value range (e.g., sh:minExclusive) or string-based constraints (e.g., sh:minLength). Besides, these systems also overlook the constraints imposed by an RDF graph's individual artifacts.

Non-RDF systems can be further delineated into extraction systems mining shapes from either ontologies, mappings, or raw data schemas, i.e. the artifacts from which RDF graphs are constructed. However, extracting shapes only from *ontologies* [5,23] often results in redundant shapes, as the shapes frequently encompass a broader spectrum of classes and properties than those in the target RDF graph. Extracting shapes from *raw data schemas*, e.g., SQL schema [39], XML Schema Definitions (XSD) [12,21] or JSON Schema [6], always results in the misalignment between the extracted shapes and the classes and properties within the target RDF graph [12]. Extracting shapes from *mappings* [9] covers only a limited set of constraints [9]. This singular input source often results in limited or incomplete constraints. To date, no research has been undertaken to integrate shapes from multiple relevant sources into a unified shapes graph, alleviating the drawbacks of individual systems and bolstering overall robustness.

We present **SCOOP**, a framework that exploits all artifacts associated with the construction of an RDF graph: data **SC**hemas, **O**nt**O**logies, and ma**P**pings. SCOOP integrates the SHACL shapes extracted from each artifact into a unified shapes graph. To achieve this, SCOOP comprises three modules: (i) *post-adjustment* to align schema-driven shapes with the target RDF graph; (ii) *equivalences identification* to align shapes from diverse sources, and (iii) *integration and inconsistencies resolution* to prevent unsatisfiable shapes. We implement SCOOP as an open-source system[1] which incorporates RML2SHACL [8,9], Astrea [4,5], and XSD2SHACL [11,12] to integrate shapes from mappings in RML [10,25], ontologies in OWL [2], and raw data schemas in XSD [15].

We compare SCOOP with state-of-the-art systems in a real-world use case. The performance experiments show that SCOOP has a significantly lower maximum memory usage compared to the RDF-based system. Addtionally, its running time is independent of the data size and faster than the RDF-based system when the RDF graph exceeds 3.30 GB in size. The coverage experiments reveal that SCOOP excels in generating accurate shapes to target classes and properties, outperforming state-of-the-art systems, and generates more than twice the types of constraints compared to RDF-based systems. SCOOP is an extensible framework that can seamlessly integrate more sources as additional shape extraction systems emerge, e.g., other raw data schemas or mapping languages.

The remaining paper is organized as follows: Sect. 2 describes related works and preliminaries; Sect. 3 discusses the challenges during shape integration; Sect. 4 describes our methodology and implementation to address these challenges. Section 5 provides the evaluation of SCOOP in real-world use cases. Section 6 concludes this paper and outlines possible future directions.

---

[1] https://github.com/dtai-kg/SCOOP.

2   Preliminaries and Related Work

In this section, we introduce RDF validation (SHACL) and RDF construction (RML), and then outline related work regarding shape extraction.

2.1   Preliminaries

This subsection summarizes the concepts required to understand the paper.

KG Validation with SHACL. To validate nodes in the RDF graph, the Shapes Constraint Language (SHACL) was recommended by W3C [27]. The *shapes graph* refers to a collection of shapes containing constraints expressed in RDF format, while the *data graph* pertains to the target RDF graph undergoing validation. A *node shape* typically specifies constraints on the focus node, where the focus node represents the node in the RDF graph being validated (e.g., all instances of :Student, Fig. 2). The *focus node* can be directly designated by *target declaration* (e.g., :NS sh:targetClass :Student), indirectly specified through reference relationships (e.g., :NS sh:node :NS2), or explicitly fed to the SHACL processor with nodes to be validated. In cases where RDF graphs are to be validated automatically without explicit extra specification, shapes lacking target declarations become invalid as they do not trigger validation. A property shape primarily serves to define the property value reached from the focus node through a property path (e.g., :PS sh:path :grade). Therefore, reference relationships between shapes (e.g., :NS sh:property :PS) are crucial, as they delineate how the SHACL processor traverses from the focus node to the property value.

KG Construction with RML. To map heterogeneous data to RDF graphs, the RDF Mapping language was proposed in [10,25] generalizing R2RML [7], the W3C recommendation to construct RDF graphs from relational databases. The triples map describes how to map a data source, comprised by a logical source, a subject map, and multiple predicate-object maps. The logical source defines information about the mapped data source, including data location (e.g., "student.xml" in Fig. 2), reference formulation (e.g., ql:XPath in Fig. 2), and an optional iterator (e.g., "/student" in Fig. 2). The subject map defines how the subjects of triples are generated (e.g., "http://example.com/{@id}" in Fig. 2), and the predicate-object map defines how the corresponding predicate (e.g., :grade in Fig. 2) and object (e.g., "/grade" in Fig. 2) are generated. The reference is used to directly specify the original data source, while the template is used to build strings with the data source, which can be a single-component template or a multi-component template (e.g., "http://example.com/{@id}_{grade}").

2.2   Related Work

Prior research on SHACL shape extraction primarily focuses on deriving shapes graphs from *RDF graphs*; but also *ontologies, raw data schemas*, and *mapping rules*. However, no system integrates multiple shapes into a unified shape.

RDF Graphs-Driven. Numerous efforts were proposed to extract shapes and constraints from *RDF graphs* but the computational burden is contingent upon the scale of the RDF graphs and the covered constraints are limited [31]. **QSE** [33] mines shapes from large RDF graphs and avoids spurious shapes by calculating the support and confidence scores of extracted shapes; **SHACTOR** [34] provides a graphical user interface based on QSE. **SHACLGEN** [1] implements a query-based system, which loads the whole RDF graph in memory restricting its capacity to handle large RDF graphs. **SheXer** [17,18] mines and filters feature for constraints according to the frequency of occurrence, but the implementation lacks support for N-Quads. **ABSTAT** [38] employs a summarization model to mine shapes by summarizing triple patterns extracted from the semantic profile of RDF graphs. **ShapeInduction** [28] proposes an RDF graph profiling approach using machine learning techniques by transforming the regression problem into a classification problem. **SHACLearner** [22] utilizes the inverse open path (IOP) to infer potential constraints in shape fragments for a given target. Last, **ShapeDesigner** [3] extracts shapes using a query language.

Ontology-Driven. Deriving SHACL shapes from *ontologies* is independent of data scale, yet limited to constraints exclusively defined by the ontology, and frequently derives redundant shapes as the RDF graph may only involve a subset of the ontology. **Astrea** [5] derives SHACL shapes from ontologies by executing a set of pre-defined SPARQL queries to retrieve ontology elements and derive corresponding shapes and constraints. **SHACLGEN** also supports extracting shapes from ontologies and **Harshvardhan et al.** [23,29] reuse the Ontology Design Pattern (ODP) axioms to extract equivalent SHACL shapes.

Schema-Driven. Extracting SHACL shapes from *raw data schemas* eliminates the dependencies on the RDF graph scale, akin to ontology-driven systems. However, the extracted shapes resort to a default namespace, causing a misalignment with their targeted RDF graphs. For XML, **XSD2SHACL** [12] mines SHACL shapes based on a set of correspondences between XSD and SHACL, while **XMLSchema2ShEx** [21] mines ShEx shapes, but partially covers XSD.

Mapping-Driven. Deriving shapes from *mapping rules* [9] captures the implied constraints within the mapping rules, but it is limited to the constraints that can be described by the mapping language. **RML2SHACL** [9] is the only system that derives SHACL shapes from RML mapping rules [10] based on a set of proposed correspondences. Its coverage is limited to constraints of a more basic nature, as RML does not offer the same scope of support for rich constraints found in SHACL, such as value range constraints (e.g., sh:minExclusive).

As opposed to the aforementioned, **SCOOP** integrates SHACL shapes extracted from the raw data schema, the ontology, and the mapping rules, taking advantage of all aspects that contributed to the construction of an RDF graph.

3   Shape Integration Challenges

Integrating SHACL shapes from mapping rules, ontologies, and raw data schemas is not straightforward, as challenges may arise during the integration process.

(C1) Misalignments. Misalignment arises inevitably during the integration of shapes extracted from raw data schemas and those extracted from ontology or mappings. The shapes derived from mappings and ontologies are swiftly applicable for validation purposes, as they inherently align with the defined classes and properties within the RDF graph (e.g., sh:targetClass of stu:Student).

However, the shapes from raw data schemas cannot be directly aligned with the SHACL shapes extracted from the mappings and ontologies. Due to the absence of classes and properties information specific to the target RDF graphs, the extracted shapes resort to default namespaces pre-defined by the extraction systems. As shown in Fig. 2, the *XSD-driven* shapes opt for ex:student as target class (instead of stu:Student as in the target RDF graph). Moreover, constraints extracted from the raw data schema may be superseded or become invalid during the RDF construction. For instance, the id originally defined as a string in *XSD-driven* shapes may be used to create an IRI according to the mappings.

(C2) Inequivalences. The basis of the shape integration lies in the consolidation of constraints encapsulated within equivalent shapes, i.e. shapes validating the same node, which cannot be solely ascertained through uniform target declarations or property paths due to the flexibility of SHACL syntax. For instance, a node shape specified with sh:targetClass :Student is deemed equivalent to a shape that defines the same target declaration. However, it may also be considered equivalent to another node shape referenced by a shape sharing the same target declaration (e.g., sh:targetClass :Student) through sh:node, even if the latter node shape lacks the same target declaration.

(C3) Inconsistencies. Integrating shapes from different sources may lead to constraint inconsistencies, potentially rendering the unsatisfiable shape, i.e., a shape that can never be conformed. Two distinct types of inconsistencies are identified: one type adheres to SHACL syntax without violation, while the other type poses a risk to the well-formedness of the resulting shape. As an illustrative scenario, consider the construction of an RDF graph from two distinct raw data sources, each is adhering to dissimilar grading systems. One source specifies a passing grade range spanning from 8 to 20 points and the student id should be IRI, while the other designates that from 60 to 100 and the id should be a string. Direct integration of constraints of sh:nodeKind sh:IRI and sh:datatype :string will lead to inconsistency, i.e. it does not violate syntax but will cause the shape to never be satisfied. The simultaneous presence of two distinct passing grade constraints sh:minInclusive and two sh:maxInclusive can be categorized as an inconsistency, which arises from the restriction that a shape incorporates at most one sh:minInclusive constraint and one sh:maxInclusive constraint.

4 SCOOP

We propose SCOOP, an open-source framework[1] designed to integrate existing shape extraction systems targeting diverse sources into a unified and comprehensive shapes graph. The current version of SCOOP supports SHACL core [27].

The integration workflow (Fig. 1) can be delineated into three principal modules: (1) **post-adjustment** of shapes extracted from raw data schema to ensure

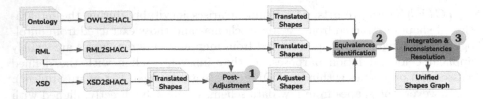

Fig. 1. The workflow of SCOOP.

alignment with the target RDF graph (Fig. 1–**1**), overcoming (C1); (2) **equivalences identification** among extracted shapes from diverse sources to identify equivalent shapes (Fig. 1–**2**), overcoming (C2); (3) **integration and inconsistencies resolution** for identifying inconsistent constraints within equivalent shapes (Fig. 1–**3**) to make integration decisions based-on three configurations, SCOOP-All, SCOOP-Prior, and SCOOP-Prior-R, overcoming (C3). The modules are explained in detail in Subsect. 4.1, 4.2, and 4.3 respectively.

4.1 Post-adjustment

We mitigate the misalignment between preliminary shapes extracted from raw data schemas and target RDF graphs by leveraging the RML mappings during **post-adjustment**. Given that the most mature systems to extract shapes from the raw data schema are focused on XML, we demonstrate our methodology for XML Schema but the same should hold for other schemas as well.

The post-adjustment (Fig. 2) is structured into three steps: (a) **SHACL parsing** to compute the implicit XPath within each shape (e.g., /student/grade) (Fig. 2–**A**); (b) **RML parsing** to extract the XPath alongside the corresponding classes and properties (e.g., the property stu:grade is related to objects constructed with the values of the elements matching the /student/grade XPath expression) (Fig. 2–**B**); (c) shape **adjustment** based on the outcomes of the parsing process (e.g., adjust ex:grade to stu:grade) (Fig. 2–**C**).

SHACL Parsing. We compute the XPath for each *XSD-driven* shape based on shape identifiers and the referencing relationships among shapes by utilizing a depth-first search (DFS) algorithm. The identifier for shapes (e.g., http://example.com/PropertyShape/studentType/grade) generated by XSD2SHACL is the concatenation of the names of element declarations (e.g., grade), attribute declarations (e.g., id), and global complex type definitions (e.g., studentType) within the XSD. It encapsulates the path from the global declaration or definition (e.g., studentType) to the corresponding XSD component (e.g., grade). Nevertheless, the identifier cannot be swiftly extracted as an XPath due to the potential truncation of the XPath (e.g., /student/studentType and /studentType/grade) in the identifier. Thus, the entire shapes graph needs to be traversed to compute the complete XPath (e.g., student/grade).

We convert the shapes into a reversed directional acyclic graph of identifiers and employ a DFS algorithm to traverse it, then compute the complete XPath for each shape by considering all relevant shapes. We initiate

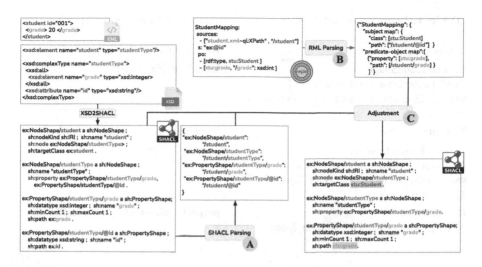

Fig. 2. An example of **post-adjustment**. RML in YARRRML serialisation.

the process by reversing the relationships of identifiers referenced through sh:property and sh:node to construct a graph. Shapes that reference other shapes but are not referenced by any shape are transformed into leaf nodes (e.g., http://example.com/NodeShape/student). Then we traverse the graph using DFS to calculate the paths leading to all potential leaf nodes commencing from each node. We can distinguish the segments within identifiers that are not elements or attributes names (e.g., studentType), as complex type definitions do not require the target declarations creation in XSD2SHACL (e.g., http://example.com/NodeShape/student/studentType). Ultimately, we obtain an XPath for each shape by concatenating the path fragments found within each path list (e.g., /student and /grade), while eliminating any fragments corresponding to complex type definitions (e.g., studentType). An example outcome of SHACL parsing can be found in Fig. 2.

RML Parsing. We parse the RML mappings to extract the XPath (e.g., student/grade) corresponding to the associated classes or properties (e.g., stu:grade) as Fig. 2 shows. For each triples map (e.g., :StudentMapping), we identify all relevant classes (e.g., stu:Student) and associate them with the XPath extracted from a template (e.g., id from http://example.com/@id) or reference in the subject map and concatenate it with the iterator (e.g., /student). Similarly, for each predicate-object map, we correlate the property (e.g., stu:grade) defined by the predicate map with the XPath (e.g., /student/grade) extracted also from the object map, as described previously. Simultaneously, in cases of multiple components templates (e.g., http://example.com/{@id}_{name}) where multiple XPaths are implicated and multiple shapes are involved, we manage them as a list (e.g., [/student/@id, /student/name]) for future adjustment.

Adjustment. We adjust the classes, properties, and constraints within the preliminary shapes to align with the target RDF graph based on parsing outcomes

Table 1. Focus node and property value extraction for equivalences identification.

Extraction	Resultant mapping
?S a sh:NodeShape ?S sh:targetClass | sh:targetNode | sh:targetSubjectsOf | sh:targetObjectsOf ?node	focusNode[S]=node
?S sh:node* ?S2	focusNode[S2]+=focusNode[S]
?S a sh:PropertyShape ?S sh:targetClass | sh:targetNode | sh:targetSubjectsOf | sh:targetObjectsOf ?fn ?S sh:path ?node	propertyValue[S]=(?fn,?node)
if focusNode[S]: ?S sh:property ?PS ?PS sh:path ?node	propertyValue[PS]=(focusNode[S],?node)

from both RML and SHACL, and showcase the example in Fig. 2. For each class and property (e.g., stu:grade) associated with the XPath (e.g., /student/grade) within the RML parsing results, we look for the corresponding shape identifier (e.g., http://example.com/PropertyShape/studentType/grade) that shares the same XPath in the SHACL parsing results. If found, we update the target declaration (i.e. sh:targetClass) or property path (i.e. sh:path) with the class or property (e.g., stu:grade) defined in RML. Ultimately, we eliminate shapes that remain unadjusted and are not referenced by the adjusted shapes.

In addition to aligning classes and properties, we specifically create a new shape for templates with multiple references to the raw data schema (e.g., http://example.com/{id}_{name}). As that template involves multiple shapes derived from the raw data schema, one for each XPath expression in the template, the constraints originally present in individual shapes may no longer be valid. For instance if, on the one hand, we have string-based constraints (e.g., sh:pattern) and, on the other hand, the sh:datatype is an integer, not both constraints may be retained. After parsing the RML mappings, the XPath list is retrieved.

Moreover, in the presence of cardinality constraints (e.g., sh:minCount 2 and sh:minCount 3) across all pertinent shapes, these constraints are multiplied to calculate the cardinality constraint (e.g., sh:minCount 6) for the merged shape. Similarly, if length constraints are present in all relevant shapes (e.g., sh:minLength 3 for id and sh:minLength 1 for name in the template above), the cumulative sum (e.g., sh:minLength 24), considering the length of the string outside the component in the template (e.g., length of 20 for http://example.com/_), is added.

4.2 Equivalences Identification

To determine the constraints within shapes that should be integrated, we identify the equivalent shapes, i.e. the shapes designated for validating either the same focus node or the identical property value reached via the same focus node.

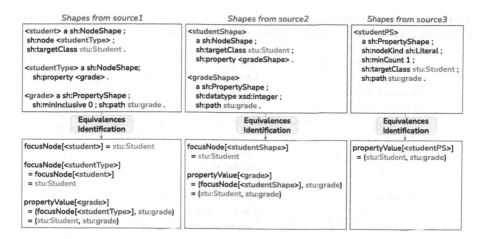

Fig. 3. An example process of the **equivalences identification** module. Identifiers of the same color refer to equivalent shapes.

We traverse the shapes from diverse sources that are intended for integration, sequentially evaluating the following four scenarios, as delineated in Table 1, to ascertain equivalency: (i) the present focus nodes of the node shape that defines the target declaration; (ii) the cumulative focus nodes of shapes referenced through sh:node by other shapes that possess focus nodes; (iii) the directly defined property path with focus nodes; and (v) the property path of the property shape referenced by the node shape with focus nodes through sh:property. Utilizing these outcomes, shapes sharing identical focus nodes or property values, derived from disparate sources, are recognized as equivalent shapes.

Figure 3 presents an example of equivalences identification, emphasizing the necessity of considering four scenarios. The first scenario's equivalences calculation facilitates the determination of the focus nodes directly defined by node shapes (e.g., <student> sh:targetClass stu:Student). The second scenario's equivalence calculation prevents the oversight of focus nodes indirectly defined through sh:node reference relationships (e.g., <student> sh:node <studentType>). The third scenario assists in identifying the focus node and property value pair that is directly defined within the same property shape (e.g., <studentPS> sh:targetClass stu:Student, sh:path stu:grade). The fourth scenario aids in determining the property value reached through the sh:property reference relationship from the focus node (e.g., <studentShape> sh:property <gradeShape>).

4.3   Integration and Inconsistencies Resolution

To provide a variety of integration possibilities, we devised three approaches: SCOOP-All, SCOOP-Prior, and SCOOP-Prior-R. *All* aims to integrate all constraints from all equivalent shapes, *Prior* aims to integrate constraints from lower-priority shapes that are not inconsistent with higher-priority equivalent

Table 2. The inconsistent combination of constraints slated for addition and the corresponding constraints within the presently integrated shape.

Constraints to be added	Inconsistent constraints
sh:datatype	sh:nodeKind *isnot* sh:Literal
sh:nodeKind *is* (sh:IRIOrLiteral *or* sh:IRI *or* sh:BlankNodeOrLiteral *or* sh:BlankNode *or* sh:BlankNodeOrIRI)	sh:datatype *or* sh:languageIn *or* sh:minExclusive *or* sh:minInclusive *or* sh:maxExclusive *or* sh:maxInclusive
sh:minCount	> sh:maxCount
sh:maxCount	< sh:minCount
sh:minExclusive	sh:nodeKind *isnot* sh:Literal *or* ≥ sh:maxExclusive *or* ≥ sh:maxInclusive
sh:minInclusive	sh:nodeKind *isnot* sh:Literal *or* ≥ sh:maxExclusive *or* > sh:maxInclusive
sh:maxExclusive	sh:nodeKind *isnot* sh:Literal *or* ≤ sh:minExclusive *or* ≤ sh:minInclusive
sh:maxInclusive	sh:nodeKind *isnot* sh:Literal *or* ≤ sh:minExclusive *or* < sh:minInclusive
sh:minLength	sh:nodeKind *isnot* sh:Literal *or* > sh:maxLength
sh:maxLength	sh:nodeKind *isnot* sh:Literal *or* < sh:minLength

shapes based on defined source priority, and R is designed to filter out redundant shapes from the ontology based on higher-priority shapes. We also introduce the inconsistencies resolutions for *All* and *Prior* to harmonize all constraints within equivalent shapes to be integrated, mitigating inconsistencies in the final shape.

SCOOP and Resolution. For all algorithms, we initialize an empty graph S to store the final unified shapes. We consider the current shape s as the shape to be added and the current constraint c as the constraint to be added. The constraints defined for shapes equivalent to s in S are denoted as $C(s)$. For SCOOP-All, we sequentially add s translated from different sources. If an equivalent shape does not exist in S, we directly add s to S. Otherwise, we perform constraint checks on $C(s)$ and c (explained in detail below). In cases where no inconsistencies are found, we add c directly to $C(s)$. Conversely, we reconstruct and integrate inconsistent constraints using sh:or. For SCOOP-Prior, we traverse and add s into S based on the user-defined priorities of different sources. Similarly, if an equivalent shape does not exist in S, we directly add s to S, otherwise, we conduct an inconsistencies check. However, in cases of finding an inconsistency, we refrain from adding c. Unlike SCOOP-Prior, SCOOP-Prior-R refrains from adding s that is translated from ontology to S if there is no equivalent shape in S.

Inconsistencies Check. We perform two types of constraint checks: (i) internal checks based on the SHACL specification [26], determining whether adding c violates the constraint's cardinality restriction (e.g., a shape cannot have two sh:minLength), and (ii) external checks based on Table 2, verifying if there are inconsistencies between $C(s)$ and c (e.g., $C(s)$ contains sh:nodeKind sh:IRI while c defines sh:datatype xsd:string). Specifically, we categorized the core constraints into those constraints permitting at most one appearance in a shape and those allowing multiple occurrences. We consider it an inconsistency if there is a constraint in $C(s)$ same as c that allows only one occurrence. All cases are outlined in Table 2.

4.4 Implementation

Algorithm 1: SCOOP implementation.

---

1 **Function** SCOOP(*rml_files* $= \emptyset$, *owl_files* $= \emptyset$, *xsd_files* $= \emptyset$,
   priority $= [\text{"}rml\text{"}, \text{"}owl\text{"}, \text{"}xsd\text{"}]$, *mode* $= [\text{"}All\text{"}, \text{"}Prior\text{"}, \text{"}Prior\_R\text{"}]$):
2   *shapes_inorder*, $S \leftarrow \emptyset$, Graph()
3   **for** *source in priority* **do**
4   **if** *source is rml* **and** *rml_files* **then**
5   *shapes* $\leftarrow$ **RML2SHACL**(*rml_files*)
6   **else if** *source is owl* **and** *owl_files* **then**
7   *shapes* $\leftarrow$ **OWL2SHACL**(*owl_files*)
8   **else if** *source is xsd* **and** *xsd_files* **then**
9   *xsd_shapes* $\leftarrow$ **XSD2SHACL**(*xsd_files*)
10   **if** *rml_files* **then**
11   *xsd_shapes* $\leftarrow$ **Post_adjustment**(*shapes*, *rml_files*)
12   *shapes_inorder*.add(*shapes*)
13     $S \leftarrow$ *shapes_inorder*[0]
14   **for** *shape_next in shapes_inorder[1:]* **do**
15   *parseResults_current* $\leftarrow$ **Equivalences_identification**(*S*)
16   *parseResults_next* $\leftarrow$ **Equivalences_identification**(*shape_next*)
17   **for** *parseResult in parseResults_next* **do**
18   **if** *parseResult* **can be found in** *parseResults_current* **then**
19                 $S \leftarrow$ **Inconsistencies_resolution_integration**(*S*, *shape_next*,
                   parseResult, *parseResults_current*) // Check for inconsistencies
                   that may caused by constraints to be added and resolve them
20
21   **else if** *mode is not Prior_R* **then**
22                 $S \leftarrow$ addConstraints(*shape_next*, *parseResult*) // Direct add the
                   corresponding shape with constraints since there is no equivalent
                   shape that may raise inconsistencies found in the current shape
23
24   **return** S

SCOOP integrates RML2SHACL [8], Astrea [4], and XSD2SHACL [11] to extract shapes from the mappings, ontology, and XSD respectively, implements the post-adjustment, equivalences identification, and integration and inconsistencies resolution modules in the workflow (Fig. 1) as outlined in Algorithm 1, and provides configuration options with SCOOP-All, SCOOP-Prior, and SCOOP-Prior-R. SCOOP accepts files from diverse sources as input, with default user-defined priority that accords precedence to mappings over ontology and over XSD, ultimately yielding a unified shapes graph. Besides, the SCOOP framework can be expanded to incorporate shapes from supplementary sources, such as CSVW and JSON Schema. The code and usage instructions for SCOOP are available online on the GitHub repository: https://github.com/dtai-kg/SCOOP.

5   Evaluation

We performed a comprehensive analysis, encompassing both performance and coverage aspects, to evaluate the effectiveness of SCOOP in addressing real-world use cases and compared it with current state-of-the-art systems.

Systems. We selected a state-of-the-art system from each of the *RDF graphs*, *ontologies*, *mappings*, and *raw data schemas*-based systems for extracting SHACL shapes to serve as a point of comparison. For the *RDF graphs*-based system, we considered the available systems, including SHACLGEN [1], SheXer [19], and QSE [30], ultimately opting for QSE. This selection was influenced by QSE's broader coverage of constraints compared to other systems [31]. For the *ontologies*-based system, our considerations encompass Astrea [4] and the OWL2SHACL conversion rules [20]. We finally selected Astrea due to the availability of detailed information on its implementation and performance [5], which is absent for OWL2SHACL. For the systems based on *mapping rules* and *raw data schemas*, we opted for RML2SHACL [8] and XSD2SHACL [11].

Datasets. To demonstrate our framework's potential, we leverage the real-world use case RINF [35], the railway infrastructure register published by each country, containing the infrastructure parameters applied to the railway system. RINF includes raw XML data from 30 countries, 28 RML files[2], an ERA ontology from version 3.0.0 [14], and an XSD from version 1.5 [36]. We arrange the XML data from 30 countries in ascending order of size and progressively construct RDF graphs using the RML mapping rules and the RMLMapper [24]. The minimum RDF graph (0.003 GB) comprises solely the smallest XML dataset, while the largest RDF graph (8.52 GB) incorporates data from all countries. The constructed RDF graphs serve as input for QSE.

Experimental Setup. We conduct all experiments on a Rocky 8.8 Linux based system with Intel(R) Xeon(R) Gold 6140 CPUs running at 2.30 GHz, configured with 128 GB RAM and 32 cores. We experimented with SCOOP v1.0.0 in its different configurations (i.e. SCOOP-All, SCOOP-Prior, and SCOOP-Prior-R) under different input combinations. We executed the RML2SHACL v1.0.0, Astrea v1.2.1, and XSD2SHACL v1.0.0 systems as per the instructions outlined in their repositories. Regarding QSE (*pvldb* release), we ran QSE-Exact with confidence $\geq 25\%$ and support $\geq 100\%$, and QSE-Approx with confidence $\geq 25\%$, support $\geq 100\%$, sampling percentage of 50%, and reservoir size of 5000.

Performance Analysis. We evaluated the running time and maximum memory usage of different systems (average of 5 runs) in the RINF use case across diverse data sizes. Figure 4 illustrates the running time and maximum memory usage of different systems, with both figures including only one QSE-Exact and one SCOOP-Prior-R due to negligible differences between the various approaches. Figure 4b shows QSE and SCOOP exclusively, as the results for other systems align closely with those of SCOOP.

---

[2] The mapping rules will be publicly available soon by ERA (era.europa.eu/).

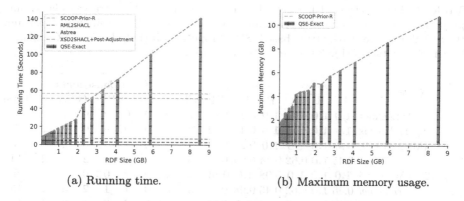

(a) Running time.   (b) Maximum memory usage.

Fig. 4. (a) Running time and (b) Maximum memory usage comparison across various systems on the RINF use case.

Our experiments demonstrate that the memory usage of the QSE increases approximately linearly with the size of the RDF graph, and the maximum memory usage of QSE is higher than SCOOP in all experiments. The running time of QSE is higher than all non-RDF-based systems without post-adjustment when the RDF graph's size exceeds 0.10GB; is higher than XSD2SHACL with post-adjustment when the graph size exceeds 2.73GB; and is higher than SCOOP when the RDF graph's size exceeds 3.30GB. The running time of SCOOP is primarily influenced by the post-adjustment phase, while the triggering and integration of shapes incur relatively less time. SCOOP's memory usage is independent of the RDF graph's size. SCOOP uses lower memory usage than QSE throughout all experiments, and surpasses QSE in terms of running time when the RDF graph's size exceeds 3.30 GB, ensuring scalability for larger RDF graphs.

Coverage Analysis. We conducted a statistical analysis of the extracted shapes concerning targeting sufficient classes and properties and generating rich constraints. We extracted the involved 21 classes and 223 properties of the largest RDF graph (8.52 GB), which includes all raw data as the ground truth. We also chose the shapes produced by QSE on this RDF graph for comparison.

We compared the classes defined by the sh:targetClass and the properties defined by the sh:path referenced by shapes containing target declarations in the extracted shapes with the ground truth to calculate precision (P), recall (R), and F1 score. We also assessed the richness of constraints within shapes. Following the SHACL specification [27], we categorized SHACL core constraints into eight categories: Value Type (VT), Value Range (VR), String-based (SR), Property Pair (PP), Logical (LG), Shape-based (SA), Other (OT) which also includes sh:name and sh:description, and analyze the coverage for each category. Table 3 show that SCOOP-Prior-R performs comparably to XSD2SHACL with our post-adjustment module, and surpasses all other systems in defining sufficient classes and properties. SCOOP-All generates the richest constraints, and all SCOOP systems surpass QSE by generating more than twice the types of constraints.

Table 3. The precision (P), recall (R), and F1 score on the extracted classes and properties, and the coverage of constraints: Value Type (VT), Cardinality Constraint (CD), Value Range (VR), String-based (SR), Property Pair (PP), Logical (LG), Shape-based (SA), Other (OT). *PA* refers to the post-adjustment.

Systems	Classes			Properties			Core Constraints								
	P	R	F1	P	R	F1	VT	CD	VR	SR	PP	LG	SA	OT	Total
QSE-Exact	**1.0**	**1.0**	**1.0**	**1.0**	0.44	0.61	2	1	0	0	0	0	1	2	7
QSE-Approx	**1.0**	**1.0**	**1.0**	**1.0**	0.44	0.61	2	1	0	0	0	0	1	2	7
RML2SHACL	**1.0**	**1.0**	**1.0**	**1.0**	0.26	0.41	2	0	0	1	0	0	2	0	5
Astrea	0.45	**1.0**	0.62	0.44	0.94	0.60	3	1	0	1	1	2	4	2	14
XSD2SHACL+*PA*	**1.0**	**1.0**	**1.0**	0.98	**1.0**	**0.99**	2	2	0	2	0	0	2	1	9
SCOOP All — *rml+owl*	0.45	**1.0**	0.62	0.45	0.98	0.62	**3**	1	0	1	1	2	**5**	2	15
SCOOP All — *rml+xsd*	**1.0**	**1.0**	**1.0**	0.98	**1.0**	**0.99**	2	2	0	3	0	1	2	1	11
SCOOP All — *rml+owl+xsd*	0.45	**1.0**	0.62	0.45	**1.0**	0.62	**3**	**2**	0	3	1	2	**5**	2	**18**
SCOOP Prior — *rml+owl*	0.45	**1.0**	0.62	0.45	0.98	0.62	**3**	1	0	1	1	1	**5**	2	14
SCOOP Prior — *rml+xsd*	**1.0**	**1.0**	**1.0**	0.98	**1.0**	**0.99**	2	2	0	3	0	0	2	1	10
SCOOP Prior — *rml+owl+xsd*	0.45	**1.0**	0.62	0.45	**1.0**	0.62	**3**	**2**	0	3	1	1	**5**	2	17
SCOOP Prior-R — *rml+owl*	**1.0**	**1.0**	**1.0**	**1.0**	0.26	0.41	**3**	1	0	1	0	0	**5**	2	12
SCOOP Prior-R — *rml+xsd*	**1.0**	**1.0**	**1.0**	0.98	**1.0**	**0.99**	2	2	0	3	0	0	2	1	10
SCOOP Prior-R — *rml+owl+xsd*	**1.0**	**1.0**	**1.0**	0.98	**1.0**	**0.99**	**3**	**2**	0	3	0	0	**5**	2	15

Coverage Analysis in Classes. Examining the outcomes for the targeted classes, QSE and systems involving RML demonstrate the capability of perfectly targeting classes. The exceptional performance of QSE in class extraction is foreseeable, given its input is the target RDF graph. Among the non-RDF-systems, RML2SHACL benefits from RML, aligning perfectly with the target RDF graph's classes. Our implemented post-adjustment helps XSD2SHACL to capture information from RML, thereby achieving full scores across all metrics. However, Astrea exhibits lower precision, a common issue in systems extracting shapes from ontologies, because ontologies cover the entire domain but the target RDF graph may only involve a subset, resulting in many unnecessary shapes. In the case of the SCOOP-All and SCOOP-Prior, the inclusion of the entire ontology negatively impacts the precision where SCOOP-Prior-R is specifically designed to mitigate the issue of redundant shapes generated by ontologies. The results demonstrate that SCOOP-Prior-R achieves full scores across all metrics for all input combinations, indicating its stronger robustness.

Coverage Analysis in Properties. In terms of targeted properties, SCOOP exhibits superior overall performance compared to other systems. The low recall scores of QSE indicate that they omit many properties during the shape extraction process. We attribute this to their novel extraction method based on support and confidence score, which, in an attempt to filter out spurious shapes, also filter out some properties present in the RDF graph. The low recall values observed in RML2SHACL can be attributed to instances where certain property shapes lack references from target declarations. This is attributed to implicit class definitions in our RML use case, where multiple triples maps are involved, with only one explicitly defining the class, while the others imply its existence using the same subject map. However, RML2SHACL fails to capture this implicit definition, resulting in the oversight of certain reference relationships. In contrast, our post-adjustment module combined with XSD2SHACL performs well and does not encounter this issue because we considered implicit class definitions when parsing RML, and the precision of 0.98 suggests that the generated RDF graph may not have produced some expected triples due to missing raw data. In addition, Astrea's lower precision score in property extraction is ascribed to the ontology's broader coverage of properties. The performance of all SCOOP approaches with RML and XSD as inputs overcomes all other systems.

Coverage Analysis in Constraints. The analysis of core constraints confirms the outstanding performance of SCOOP in terms of constraint richness. The shapes extracted by SCOOP-All encompass a total of 18 distinct constraints, slightly surpassing SCOOP-Prior, SCOOP-Prior-R, and Astrea, marginally higher than XSD2SHACL, and markedly superior to both QSE and RML2SHACL. Furthermore, with regard to the SCOOP-All, we conducted a fine-grained analysis of the contributions of different sources to the final constraints. Among the 18 final constraints, 5 originate from RML, 14 from the ontology, and 9 from XSD. In particular, the ontology covers property pair constraints (e.g., sh:equals) and logical constraints (e.g., sh:not) not covered by other sources.

Practical Implications on Validation. We assessed the effectiveness of SCOOP to extract valid SHACL shapes by validating an RDF graph using those shapes. We used the pySHACL validator [37] to validate the smallest RDF graph (0.003 GB, 1620 triples) constructed from RINF. Due to violations of SHACL syntax in shapes generated by QSE, e.g., multiple occurrences of sh:in, and Astrea, e.g., missing sh:path, we could not directly use their shapes for validation.

The validation results indicated that the target RDF graph conformed to all shapes generated by RML2SHACL but violated shapes generated by other systems. Specifically, the shapes extracted by XSD2SHACL revealed 738 missing triples and 540 error triples (e.g., sh:maxLength, sh:datatype, and sh:nodeKind). We analyzed the additional violations found by XSD2SHACL, attributing them to lingering issues from mismatched versions of XSD and RML. SCOOP-Prior and SCOOP-R, incorporating the mapping rules, ontology, and XSD, discovered 738 missing triples and 972 error triples (involving sh:class and sh:maxLength). We attribute this to the introduction of constraints from the ontology, distinguishing it from XSD2SHACL. SCOOP-All, including all sources, also identified 738 missing triples but labeled 864 error triples (involving only sh:class), slightly fewer than SCOOP-Prior. This was reasonable as SCOOP-All's strategy of adding sh:or introduces more lenient constraints to the RDF graph. In summary, this experiment demonstrates that our SCOOP framework strictly adheres to SHACL syntax, and provides users with effective RDF validation results.

6 Conclusion

In this paper, we propose SCOOP, an open-source framework designed to integrate existing shape extraction systems targeting diverse sources into a unified and comprehensive shapes graph. SCOOP consists of three modules and devises three integration approaches to provide diverse choices. The implementation of SCOOP includes the incorporation of RML2SHACL, Astrea, and XSD2SHACL. SCOOP exhibits significantly lower memory usage compared to RDF-based systems, performs faster when the RDF graph exceeds 3.30 GB in size, and outperforms state-of-the-art systems in extracting effective node and property shapes and generating richer constraints.

SCOOP is an extensible framework that goes beyond current sources and systems, including ontologies, mapping rules, and raw data schemas. The methodology is transferable to any SHACL shapes extraction work, therefore, seamless integration with other systems can be easily achieved. In the future, we will extend SCOOP to a broader range of sources, e.g., CSVW, JSONSchema, etc.

SCOOP enables users to extract SHACL shapes effortlessly, without even having to construct the RDF graphs using hardware with limited resources. It is expected that this framework will have a high impact on the Semantic Web community as most RDF graphs nowadays are constructed from various data.

Acknowledgement. Xuemin Duan and Anastasia Dimou are partially supported by Flanders Make, the research centre for the manufacturing industry, and the Flanders innovation and entrepreneurship (VLAIO) through the KG3D project. David Chaves-Fraga is funded by the Galician Ministry of Education, University and Professional Training and the European Regional Development Fund (ERDF/FEDER program) through grants ED431C2018/29 and ED431G2019/04. The resources and services used in this work were provided by the VSC (Flemish Supercomputer Center), funded by the Research Foundation - Flanders (FWO) and the Flemish Government.

References

1. Arndt, N.: SHACLGEN. https://github.com/AKSW/shaclgen. Accessed 20 Sept 2023
2. Bock, C., et al.: OWL 2 Web Ontology Language – Structural Specification and Functional-Style Syntax, 2nd edn. Recommendation, World Wide Web Consortium (W3C) (2012). http://www.w3.org/TR/owl2-syntax/
3. Boneva, I., Dusart, J., Fernández Alvarez, D., Gayo, J.E.L.: Shape designer for ShEx and SHACL constraints. In: Proceedings of the ISWC 2019 Satellite Tracks (Poster & Demonstrations, Industry, and Outrageous Ideas), vol. 2456, pp. 269–272. CEUR (2019)
4. Cimmino, A.: Astrea. https://github.com/oeg-upm/astrea. Accessed 20 Sept 2023
5. Cimmino, A., Fernández-Izquierdo, A., García-Castro, R.: Astrea: automatic generation of SHACL shapes from ontologies. In: Harth, A., et al. (eds.) ESWC 2020. LNCS, vol. 12123, pp. 497–513. Springer, Cham (2020). https://doi.org/10.1007/978-3-030-49461-2_29

6. Comelli, T.: JS2SHACL - JSON schema to SHACL conversor. https://github.com/ThiagoCComelli/JS2SHACL-JSON-Schema-to-SHACL-conversor. Accessed 20 Sept 2023

7. Das, S., Sundara, S., Cyganiak, R.: R2RML: RDB to RDF mapping language. Working group recommendation, World Wide Web Consortium (W3C) (2012). http://www.w3.org/TR/r2rml/

8. Delva, T.: RML2SHACL. https://github.com/RMLio/RML2SHACL. Accessed 20 Sept 2023

9. Delva, T., Smedt, B.D., Min Oo, S., Assche, D.V., Lieber, S., Dimou, A.: RML2SHACL: RDF generation taking shape. In: Proceedings of the 11th on Knowledge Capture Conference, pp. 153–160. ACM (2021). https://doi.org/10.1145/3460210.3493562

10. Dimou, A., Vander Sande, M., Colpaert, P., Verborgh, R., Mannens, E., Van de Walle, R.: RML: a generic language for integrated RDF mappings of heterogeneous data. In: Proceedings of the 7th Workshop on Linked Data on the Web, vol. 1184. CEUR Workshop Proceedings (2014)

11. Duan, X.: XSD2SHACL (2023). https://doi.org/10.5281/zenodo.8318452. Accessed 20 Sept 2023

12. Duan, X., Chaves-Fraga, D., Dimou, A.: XSD2SHACL: capturing RDF constraints from XML schema. In: Proceedings of the 12th Knowledge Capture Conference 2023, K-CAP 2023, pp. 214–222. Association for Computing Machinery (2023). https://doi.org/10.1145/3587259.3627565

13. Ekaputra, F.J., et al.: Describing and organizing semantic web and machine learning systems in the SWeMLS-KG. In: Pesquita, C., et al. (eds.) ESWC 2023. LNCS, vol. 13870, pp. 372–389. Springer, Cham (2023). https://doi.org/10.1007/978-3-031-33455-9_22

14. European Union Agency for Railways: ERA_vocabulary. https://data-interop.cra.europa.eu/era-vocabulary/. Accessed 20 Sept 2023

15. Fallside, D., Walmsley, P.: XML Schema Part 0: Primer Second Edition. Recommendation, W3C (2004). https://www.w3.org/TR/xmlschema-0/

16. Felin, R., Faron, C., Tettamanzi, A.G.B.: A framework to include and exploit probabilistic information in SHACL validation reports. In: Pesquita, C., et al. (eds.) ESWC 2023. LNCS, vol. 13870, pp. 91–104. Springer, Cham (2023). https://doi.org/10.1007/978-3-031-33455-9_6

17. Fernández-Álvarez, D., García-González, H., Frey, J., Hellmann, S., Gayo, J.E.L.: Inference of latent shape expressions associated to DBpedia ontology. In: Proceedings of the ISWC 2018 Posters & Demonstrations, Industry and Blue Sky Ideas Tracks Co-Located with 17th International Semantic Web Conference (ISWC 2018), vol. 2180. CEUR Workshop Proceedings (2018)

18. Fernandez-Álvarez, D., Labra-Gayo, J.E., Gayo-Avello, D.: Automatic extraction of shapes using sheXer. Knowl.-Based Syst. 238, 107975 (2022). https://doi.org/10.1016/j.knosys.2021.107975

19. Fernández-Álvarez, D.: sheXer. https://github.com/DaniFdezAlvarez/shexer. Accessed 10 Nov 2023

20. Francart, T.: OWL2SHACL. https://github.com/sparna-git/owl2shacl. Accessed 10 Nov 2023

21. Garcia-Gonzalez, H., Labra-Gayo, J.E.: XMLSchema2ShEx: converting XML validation to RDF validation. Semant. Web 11(2), 235–253 (2020)

22. Ghiasnezhad Omran, P., Taylor, K., Rodríguez Méndez, S., Haller, A., et al.: Towards SHACL learning from knowledge graphs. In: Proceedings of the ISWC

2020 Demos and Industry Tracks: From Novel Ideas to Industrial Practice Co-Located with 19th International Semantic Web Conference (ISWC 2020), vol. 2721, pp. 94–99. CEUR Workshop Proceedings (2020)

23. Pandit, H.J., O'Sullivan, D., Lewis, D.: Using ontology design patterns to define SHACL shapes. In: 9th Workshop on Ontology Design and Patterns (WOP 2018), vol. 2195, pp. 67–71. CEUR-WS, Monterey (2018)

24. Heyvaert, P., Meester, B.D., et al.: RMLMapper-Java. https://github.com/RMLio/rmlmapper-java. Accessed 20 Sept 2023

25. Iglesias-Molina, A., et al.: The RML ontology: a community-driven modular redesign after a decade of experience in mapping heterogeneous data to RDF. In: Payne, T.R., et al. (eds.) ISWC 2023, Part II. LNCS, vol. 14266, pp. 152–175. Springer, Cham (2023). https://doi.org/10.1007/978-3-031-47243-5_9

26. Knublauch, H., Kontokostas, D.: SHACL-SHACL. http://www.w3.org/ns/shacl-shacl#. Accessed 01 Dec 2023

27. Knublauch, H., Kontokostas, D.: Shapes constraint language (SHACL). Recommendation, W3C (2017). https://www.w3.org/TR/shacl/

28. Mihindukulasooriya, N., Rashid, M.R.A., Rizzo, G., Garcia-Castro, R., Corcho, O., Torchiano, M.: RDF shape induction using knowledge base profiling. In: Proceedings of the 33rd ACM/SIGAPP Symposium on Applied Computing (2017)

29. Pandit, H.J., O'Sullivan, D., Lewis, D.: Using ontology design patterns to define SHACL shapes. In: Proceedings of the 9th Workshop on Ontology Design and Patterns (WOP 2018) Co-Located with 17th International Semantic Web Conference (ISWC 2018), vol. 2195, pp. 67–71. CEUR (2018)

30. Rabbani, K.: Quality shapes extraction (QSE). https://github.com/dkw-aau/qse. Accessed 20 Sept 2023

31. Rabbani, K., Lissandrini, M., Hose, K.: Extraction of validating shapes from very large knowledge graphs [extended version]

32. Rabbani, K., Lissandrini, M., Hose, K.: SHACL and ShEx in the wild: a community survey on validating shapes generation and adoption. In: Companion Proceedings of the Web Conference 2022, WWW 2022, pp. 260–263. Association for Computing Machinery (2022). https://doi.org/10.1145/3487553.3524253

33. Rabbani, K., Lissandrini, M., Hose, K.: Extraction of validating shapes from very large knowledge graphs. Proc. VLDB Endow. **16**(5), 1023–1032 (2023)

34. Rabbani, K., Lissandrini, M., Hose, K.: SHACTOR: improving the quality of large-scale knowledge graphs with validating shapes. In: Proceedings of the 2023 International Conference on Management of Data (SIGMOD-Companion 2023), pp. 151–154. Association for Computing Machinery (2023). https://doi.org/10.1145/3555041.3589723

35. The RINF: RINF: Railway infrastructure register. https://www.rinf-ch.ch/. Accessed 01 Dec 2023

36. The RINF: RINF XML Schema v1.5. https://www.era.europa.eu/domains/registers/rinf_en. Accessed 01 Dec 2023

37. Sommer, A., Car, N.: pySHACL (2022). https://doi.org/10.5281/zenodo.4750840. https://github.com/RDFLib/pySHACL

38. Spahiu, B., Maurino, A., Palmonari, M.: Towards improving the quality of knowledge graphs with data-driven ontology patterns and SHACL. In: Workshop on Ontology Design Patterns (WOP) at ISWC (Best Workshop Papers). CEUR Workshop Proceedings, vol. 2195, pp. 52–66. CEUR (2018)

39. Thapa, R.B., Giese, M.: A source-to-target constraint rewriting for direct mapping. In: Hotho, A., et al. (eds.) ISWC 2021. LNCS, vol. 12922, pp. 21–38. Springer, Cham (2021). https://doi.org/10.1007/978-3-030-88361-4_2

FidMark: A Fiducial Marker Ontology for Semantically Describing Visual Markers

Maxim Van de Wynckel$^{(\boxtimes)}$ ⓘ, Isaac Valadez ⓘ, and Beat Signer ⓘ

Web & Information Systems Engineering Lab, Vrije Universiteit Brussel,
Pleinlaan 2, 1050 Brussels, Belgium
{mvdewync,jvaladez,bsigner}@vub.be

Abstract. Fiducial markers are visual objects that can be placed in the
field of view of an imaging sensor to determine its position and orientation, and subsequently the scale and position of other objects within the
same field of view. They are used in a wide variety of applications ranging from medical applications to augmented reality (AR) solutions where
they are applied to determine the location of an AR headset. Despite the
wide range of different marker types with their advantages for specific
use cases, there exists no standard to decide which marker to best use
in which situation. This leads to proprietary AR solutions that rely on a
predefined set of marker and pose detection algorithms, preventing interoperability between AR applications. We propose the FidMark fiducial
marker ontology, classifying and describing the different markers available for computer vision and augmented reality along with their spatial
position and orientation. Our proposed ontology also describes the procedures required to perform pose estimation, and marker detection to
allow the description of algorithms used to perform these procedures.
With FidMark we aim to enable future AR solutions to semantically
describe markers within an environment so that third-party applications
can utilise this information.

Keywords: fiducial marker · ontology · augmented reality · pose
estimation

Resource type Ontology
License CC BY-SA 4.0
URL https://purl.org/fidmark/
Documentation https://fidmark.openhps.org/1.0/en/
Demonstrator https://fidmark.openhps.org/application/
Repository https://github.com/OpenHPS/FidMark/
DOI 10.5281/zenodo.10730905

1 Introduction

In computer vision applications, or more specifically augmented reality (AR)
solutions, superimposing virtual objects in real-world scenes poses a challenge

A. Meroño Peñuela et al. (Eds.): ESWC 2024, LNCS 14665, pp. 235–250, 2024.
https://doi.org/10.1007/978-3-031-60635-9_14

due to the lack of an accurate absolute position of the camera in the physical world. Various methods can be employed, such as creating virtual anchors based on visual features [7], anchoring these virtual objects to an absolute location based on GPS or indoor positioning systems [33] or using predefined visual landmarks that can be used as a spatial reference [26]. These landmarks, often referred to as fiducial markers, are used to determine the position and orientation (i.e. a *pose*) of an image sensor detecting these markers within its field of view [25]. While markers can be used to track the position of a camera or AR device, they can also help to position and scale virtual objects relative to these markers.

Applications using fiducial markers to determine a pose need to be able to detect and map the markers to their known position and orientation, which often requires a proprietary local or cloud-based database to retrieve this contextual information. In addition, the vast variety of available marker types [20,23], each with their own set of properties that are required to detect and identify these markers, make it difficult to generically define the contextual information of a marker.

Looking at existing ontologies and vocabularies, the Digital Imaging and Communications in Medicine (DICOM) ontology [19] describes fiducial markers and identifiers used within the medical field for use cases such as providing a visual landmark when performing radiology. Despite of being a domain-specific ontology, DICOM defines some generic concepts that are also found in fiducial markers for other applications. In the Machine-to-Machine Measurement (M3) Lite ontology, a description for the concept of a m3lite:TagDevice and tag device types such as a QR code or barcode are provided [12]. However, similar to the Schema.org vocabulary [11] also providing concepts for a generic barcode, it does not provide concepts for identifying different types of markers or individual markers for a specific type of marker.

When focusing on AR applications, fiducial markers are used for position and orientation tracking using both outside-in [35] and inside-out tracking [10]. With inside-out tracking, markers are placed within the physical environment and tracked by an AR device's image sensor. On the other hand, in outside-in tracking, markers are placed on a moving object such as a person, with fixed image sensors in the physical environment tracking these markers. Different marker types and variations exist that perform better depending on the environmental conditions such as scanning distance, scanning angle, light conditions or motion blur [5]. This makes it impossible to rely on a single type of fiducial marker when used for AR applications.

In order to support the interoperability of computer vision and augmented reality applications using fiducial markers, we propose the FidMark ontology that can semantically describe these individual markers as well as provide an annotated description on various marker types. Our ontology can describe the main properties of markers and their pose within a defined reference space. Being able to describe fiducial markers and their position within a physical space allows multiple actors to understand the semantics of a visible marker and even allows them to detect these markers. This enables future interoperability between augmented and mixed reality applications by describing a common reference frame relative to a marker.

We start by presenting our design approach and several design goals for our FidMark ontology in Sect. 2. The design of the FidMark ontology with some examples is introduced in Sect. 3. Finally, a validation of the FidMark ontology and discussion of a demonstrator application in Sect. 4 is followed by some conclusions and plans for future work.

2 Approach and Methodology

Our design approach for the requirements of our ontology is based on the Linked Open Terms (LOT) methodology [31]. Due to the already existing ontologies for describing fiducial markers in medical sciences [19], we decided to focus on fiducial markers used within the domain of computer vision (CV), primarily for markers which can be used for pose estimation [27] that obtains both a position and orientation. We started by analysing the different existing types of markers for applications within the domain of computer vision [20, 23]. Next, using this set of different markers with their use cases for different scenarios and environmental conditions, we have listed a set of use cases, design goals and required data for each type of marker.

Based on the marker analysis and their data properties, we determined the common attributes and properties of each marker. Two of the main common properties of each marker are the inclusion of an identifier and its ability to be used to determine a pose. Depending on the type of encoding and error correction, these markers use a dictionary that contains a set of possible identifiers that can be encoded within the marker. Computer vision applications that want to detect these markers should know which dictionary is used to perform the correct identification.

For the terminologies used for these data properties, we relied on common terms used within academic research as well as the standardisation of fiducials and their intrinsic properties for various domains [14–17]. We also investigated frameworks and libraries that scan for markers and the variable names that were used for expressing the data [1, 4].

2.1 Design Goals

In the following, we list the main design goals (DG1–DG7) we aim to achieve with our ontology. These goals will be used to scope our ontology to the required functionality and serve as a basis for the implementation and validation of the FidMark ontology.

DG1 *Enable the retrieval of a list of supported markers*: This design goal should enable applications to retrieve individual markers that are detectable by the hardware and software.

DG2 *Enable the retrieval of markers using the identifiable information*: This design goal should enable applications to retrieve marker information based on visually detectable and identifiable information such as the marker identifier or encoded data.

DG3 *Enable the description of a marker with a non-standard symbology*: In order to enable scalability for the ontology and marker types, variations on the symbology should be possible.

DG4 *Enable pose estimation of markers based on their description without ambiguity*: Two actors, each with their own marker detection implementation should be able to use all the available information to provide equal pose estimation for the same semantically described marker.

DG5 *Enable the positioning of virtual objects relative to a marker*: It should be possible to superimpose virtual objects around a marker, without having to to know where the marker is located in the physical space.

DG6 *A marker should be used as an engineering reference frame or image coordinate reference system* [15,16]: The marker should be used as a landmark when performing visual positioning. This entails that the marker should enable absolute pose estimation for an image sensor.

DG7 *Facilitate the integration of computer vision markers in frameworks*: Having a semantic description of a marker is required to decide what algorithms to use to detect and identify the marker. However, to further facilitate the detection, information should be available to decide what marker types to use and how to integrate them into a computer vision framework without having to perform a manual mapping. This in turn also relies on design goal DG4 that requires the detection of markers without ambiguity, as it also means that the description of a fiducial marker should not be framework dependent.

Each design goal poses its challenges. While we can determine multiple common properties for each marker type in our ontology design as shown later in Sect. 3.1, ensuring that markers can be described without ambiguity such as different marker origins (e.g. using the centre of the marker as the origin of its position) also requires a more detailed description of the necessary detection processes.

3   Ontology Design

As outlined in our approach, the proposed FidMark ontology is primarily designed to describe fiducial markers used in augmented reality (AR). However, one of our design goals is to ensure that our ontology can easily be extended and aligned to also describe fiducial markers for other domains.

In order that markers can be used for pose estimation, we have built our ontology on top of the generic Positioning System Ontology (POSO) [40] that can already describe visual landmarks with their spatial location and orientation. POSO allows us to add both *absolute* positions and *relative* positions to spatial objects, enabling the positioning of (virtual) objects relative to a marker. We expanded POSO to support different types and classifications of fiducial markers, their identifiers, image descriptors and calibration data. In addition, we also added two procedures to differentiate between markerless [28] and marker-based pose estimation via the `poso:PositioningTechnique` concept.

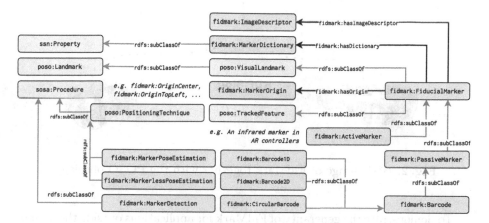

Fig. 1. FidMark main classes

The main classes of our FidMark ontology are illustrated in Fig. 1. We make a clear classification of active and passive markers [29] as this represents the major difference between different types of markers. We further subclassed passive markers into barcodes that can encode information such as an identifier. In addition to these main classes, we currently provide over 30 different types of markers as subclasses of the fiducial marker class[1], such as reacTIVision [21] or CCTag [5].

With our ontology we aim to describe different markers, their setup and their position relative to a certain reference space. The basic architecture and a use case for our ontology is demonstrated in Fig. 2. We describe markers, their identifier, position and orientation using the combination of FidMark and POSO. FidMark handles the description of the markers while POSO is used to describe the markers' absolute and relative position as visual landmarks. AR-capable devices with access to this description can synchronise their reference frame due to the common description. Any virtual object placed relative to these markers can again use the generality of POSO to indicate its relative position.

In our ontology, each type of fiducial marker is annotated with additional metadata describing the markers' visual and functional properties such as their shape, colour and encoding method. When available in OpenCV [4], we also provide the dictionary names of markers as they are available in OpenCV to facilitate the development as outlined in design goal DG7.

---

[1] For more information about the ontology profile and ontology statistics, please check the online documentation.

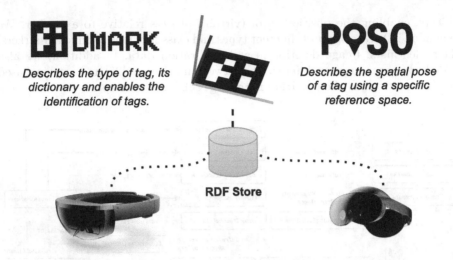

Fig. 2. Basic usage of FidMark together with the POSO ontology

To demonstrate the generality of FidMark for applications outside the domain of augmented reality, we provide the `fidmark-dicom` alignment ontology to align fiducial markers and POSO with the Digital Imaging and Communications in Medicine (DICOM) ontology [19] in our supplemental material.

3.1 Properties and Terminologies

Fiducial markers have a set of properties that are subproperties of properties on `sosa:FeatureOfInterest` from the Sensors, Observations, Systems and Actuators (SOSA) ontology [18]. They define how the marker should be detected, decoded and mapped to its location within the physical space. With fiducial markers being used to determine the relative translation, scale or orientation of visual objects within the field of view. The object and data properties we added to our ontology are also chosen to enable this description.

We provide the `:hasOrigin` predicate and `:MarkerOrigin` property to indicate the position origin on the marker itself. This origin determines the 2D or 3D location on the fiducial marker. An origin description is required to determine the accurate translation when performing relative positioning from virtual objects relative to the marker.

- **dictionary**: A set of marker identifiers that are available using a specified encoding scheme. A dictionary is also referred to as a *marker symbology* or *marker family* [17]. This encoding scheme can be generalised to both binary encoding in barcodes as well as the encoding with active markers such as infrared markers [37].

Fig. 3. Relative positioning of virtual objects and markers

- **origin**: The origin of the marker is an important design requirement in order to determine the relative orientation and translation to the marker. Our `:hasOrigin` predicate and `:MarkerOrigin` property are based on the OpenCV *pattern*. In Fig. 3, we illustrate how a virtual object is positioned relative to the `:MarkerOrigin`. The marker itself can be positioned relative to a known coordinate reference system or relative to other objects such as a room or building.
- **dimensions**: The known dimensions of a marker can be used to determine its scale. Our ontology supports the specification of both, a marker's width and height to support rectangular markers such as AprilTag [30].
- **hamming distance**: The minimum hamming distance between two codes, represented by the minimum number of bits that must be changed in one tag's code to reach another tag's code.
- **image descriptor**: The marker image descriptor links to an image URI or a Base64 representation of the image. Alternatively, the image descriptor can be described as a processed descriptor for natural feature tracking [3] as illustrated in Fig. 4.
- **identifier**: A numeric identifier that can uniquely identify a marker from a (pre-)defined *dictionary*. The identifier is (part of) the encoded data.
- **data**: Other than an identifier, some marker types allow the encoding of other types of binary data. An example of such a marker is a QR code, which can be used for both, pose estimation as well as the encoding of binary data.
- **codes & marker bits**: Frameworks with no prior knowledge of the concept of a dictionary or how it is computed require a list of all available codes that can be encoded with the available `:markerBits` and error correction.

Fig. 4. Image descriptor usage for markers

For a complete list of properties, please refer to the online documentation in our supplemental material also providing marker-specific object and data properties[2].

---

[2] https://openhps.github.io/FidMark/1.0/en/.

3.2 Procedures

The SOSA and POSO ontology both use *procedures* to indicate a process of computing data in a certain way. In Fig. 1, we already listed procedures for marker detection and pose estimation. However, in order to reduce the chance of ambiguity in pose estimation [36], we also extended POSO to add the most common Perspective-n-Point (PnP) pose computation algorithms used in existing AR and Computer Vision frameworks [6,8,22,24].

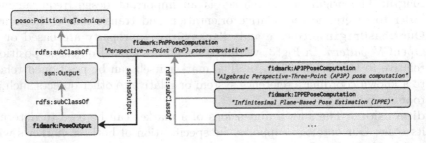

Fig. 5. Pose computation procedures in the FidMark ontology

The use of the PnP pose computation algorithms and the :`PoseOutput` associated with these procedures is illustrated in Fig. 5. Similar to the examples in the SOSA ontology, this output can be linked to a SHACL [13] shape to validate the output of an algorithmic procedure, which in this case would include a position and orientation.

3.3 Usage

In the following, we illustrate how FidMark can be used to describe markers in various scenarios. In Listing 1, we provide an example of an ArUco marker [9] described using our ontology. FidMark comes with a set of predefined dictionaries which in this example uses the original ArUco dictionary with a minimum hamming code distance of 0 and a maximum of 1024 identifiers. In addition to the marker information, the position and orientation are described. Computer vision applications can utilise this information to detect the marker and determine its position within 3D space. To avoid ambiguity, the origin of the origin of any object's position is positioned relative to the centre of the marker using the `fidmark:hasOrigin` predicate. The position of the marker is described using a well-known text (WKT) representation of a geo-referenced position [2].

Using the POSO ontology, we can utilise the `fidmark:FiducialMarker` visual landmark as a reference frame to position other objects. In Listing 2, we demonstrate how a simple virtual object is positioned relative on top of the AruCo marker from Listing 1 by indicating that it is positioned relative to

```
1    :marker-1 a fidmark:ArUco ;
2       fidmark:hasDictionary fidmark:DICT_ARUCO_ORIGINAL ;
3       fidmark:markerIdentifier 94 ;
4       fidmark:hasHeight [ a qudt:QuantityValue ;
5          qudt:unit unit:MilliM ; qudt:numericValue "100"^^xsd:float ] ;
6       fidmark:hasWidth [ a qudt:QuantityValue ;
7          qudt:unit unit:MilliM ; qudt:numericValue "100"^^xsd:float ] ;
8       fidmark:hasOrigin fidmark:OriginCenter ;
9       poso:hasPosition [ a geo:Point, poso:AbsolutePosition ;
10         ogc:asWKT "POINT Z(...)"^^ogc:wktLiteral ] ;
11      poso:hasOrientation [ a poso:QuaternionOrientation
12         poso:xAxisValue [ ... ] ; poso:yAxisValue [ ... ] ;
13         poso:zAxisValue [ ... ] ; poso:scalar [ ... ] ] .
```

[a]http://purl.org/fidmark/
[b]http://purl.org/poso/
[c]http://qudt.org/schema/qudt/
[d]http://qudt.org/vocab/unit/
[e]http://www.opengis.net/ont/geosparql#

Listing 1. Example ArUco marker using the fidmark[a], poso[b], qudt[c], unit[d] and ogc[e] prefixes

```
1    :object a sosa:FeatureOfInterest ;
2       rdfs:label "A virtual cube"@en ;
3       poso:hasPosition [ a poso:RelativePosition ;
4          poso:isRelativeTo :marker-1 ;
5          poso:xAxisValue [ ... ] ; poso:yAxisValue [ ... ] ;
6          poso:yAxisValue [ ... ] ] ;
7       poso:hasPosition [ a poso:EulerOrientation ;
8          poso:isRelativeTo :marker-1 ;
9          poso:pitch [ ... ] ; poso:roll [ ... ] ; poso:yaw [ ... ] ] ;
10      omg:hasGeometry [ a omg:Geometry ;
11         fog:asGltf "https://.../Cube.gltf"^^xsd::anyURI ] .
```

[a]http://www.w3.org/ns/sosa/
[b]https://w3id.org/omg#
[c]https://w3id.org/fog#

Listing 2. Example relative positioning using the sosa[a], omg[a] and fog[c] prefixes

this object. As a demonstrator, we utilise the Ontology for Managing Geometry (OMG) and File Ontology for Geometry formats (FOG) to describe the 3D geometry model that will be superimposed [38].

By enabling relative positioning with the marker, we satisfy design goal DG6 which requires the marker to be used as an engineering or image frame of reference. A marker can also be described without a position and orientation in the physical world, in which case it only acts as an engineering frame of reference for other objects positioned relative to the marker.

Some tags rely on the training of image data, preventing the possibility of only describing a marker using a dictionary and a simple identifier. To enable the description of fiducial markers that do not encode information or identifiers, we provide a `:hasImageDescriptor` predicate and `:ImageDescriptor` class. The image descriptor can be expressed as a raw image or pattern such as natural feature tracking (NFT) [3].

Tracked Markers. While previous examples used the description of markers relative to the markers with a fixed position, fiducial markers are also used for outside-in tracking [35] where stationary image sensors track the position of moving markers. The POSO ontology can be used to observe changes in the position of tracked markers and Listing 3 illustrates a marker with an observable absolute position.

```
1    :marker-1 a fidmark:ArUco ;
2        poso:hasPosition :marker-1-position ;
3        poso:hasOrientation :marker-1-orientation .
4
5    :marker-1-position a poso:AbsolutePosition ;
6        rdfs:label "Position of Marker 1"@en .
7    :marker-1-orientation a poso:Orientation ;
8        rdfs:label "Orientation of Marker 1"@en .
9
10   :position-1701946800 a sosa:Observation ;
11       sosa:hasFeatureOfInterest :marker-1 ;
12       sosa:observedProperty :marker-1-position ;
13       sosa:resultTime "2023-12-07T11:00:00+01:00"^^xsd:dateTimeStamp ;
14       sosa:hasResult [
15           ...
16       ] .
```

Listing 3. Marker with multiple tracked poses

4   Ontology Validation and Demonstrator

Our FidMark ontology has been validated using the OntOlogy Pitfall Scanner [32] and a set of SPARQL queries that answer the design goals DG1–DG7 listed earlier in our methodology. In addition, we created a demonstrator web application that can serialise and deserialise markers and virtual objects positioned relative to these markers. The web application will then use the deserialised information to superimpose virtual objects on top of markers detected with js-aruco2[3]. Our application[4] superimposing a 3D object ten centimetres above

---

[3] https://github.com/damianofalcioni/js-aruco2.
[4] https://openhps.github.io/FidMark/application/.

an ArUco marker with identifier 10 in a specific dictionary as shown in Fig. 6. This demonstrator was created using the OpenHPS framework [39] for aiding with the positioning and serialisation.

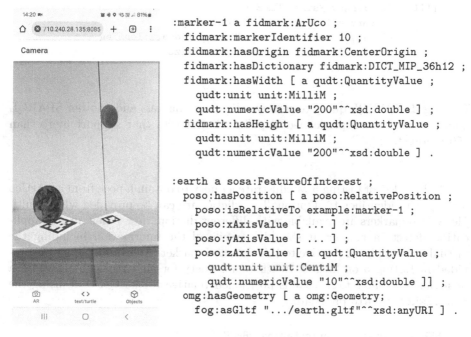

```
:marker-1 a fidmark:ArUco ;
    fidmark:markerIdentifier 10 ;
    fidmark:hasOrigin fidmark:CenterOrigin ;
    fidmark:hasDictionary fidmark:DICT_MIP_36h12 ;
    fidmark:hasWidth [ a qudt:QuantityValue ;
        qudt:unit unit:MilliM ;
        qudt:numericValue "200"^^xsd:double ] ;
    fidmark:hasHeight [ a qudt:QuantityValue ;
        qudt:unit unit:MilliM ;
        qudt:numericValue "200"^^xsd:double ] .

:earth a sosa:FeatureOfInterest ;
    poso:hasPosition [ a poso:RelativePosition ;
        poso:isRelativeTo example:marker-1 ;
        poso:xAxisValue [ ... ] ;
        poso:yAxisValue [ ... ] ;
        poso:zAxisValue [ a qudt:QuantityValue ;
            qudt:unit unit:CentiM ;
            qudt:numericValue "10"^^xsd:double ]] ;
    omg:hasGeometry [ a omg:Geometry;
        fog:asGltf ".../earth.gltf"^^xsd:anyURI ] .
```

Fig. 6. Demonstrator web application showing two markers with different dictionaries and two virtual objects positioned relative to these markers

Every SPARQL query is based on the design goals listed in Sect. 2.1. We have used the Pellet reasoner [34] on top of our ontology and an example dataset[5] which was created to test the queries. Fiducial markers have multiple subclasses that we query for all square fiducial markers in Listing 4 (lines 1–4) using the :shape annotation property on every subclass of :FiducialMarker. Similarly, other annotation properties such as the colours used within the marker can be used to determine the appropriate marker type for the available hardware.

Use cases where the ontology is applied to discover the appropriate marker type can also make use of the available dictionaries or marker families for markers that support identification. To demonstrate a scenario where we want to search for an ArUco dictionary that supports at least 150 markers, we can perform a similar query as shown in Listing 4 (lines 6–11). Each known dictionary will have listed its dictionary size, bit size and possible error correction methods.

---

[5] https://github.com/OpenHPS/FidMark/blob/main/examples/virtual_objects.ttl.

```
1   SELECT ?markerType WHERE {
2       ?markerType rdfs:subClassOf* fidmark:FiducialMarker .
3       ?markerType fidmark:shape "Square"@en .
4   }
5
6   SELECT ?dictionary ?size WHERE {
7       ?dictionary a fidmark:MarkerDictionary .
8       ?dictionary fidmark:supportedMarker fidmark:TopoTag .
9       ?dictionary fidmark:dictionarySize ?size .
10      FILTER(?size >= 150)
11  }
```

Listing 4. SPARQL query to retrieve all square markers and another SPARQL query to retrieve all predefined TopoTag dictionaries that support more than 150 unique tags

On lines 1–7 of Listing 5 we illustrate a query to obtain a pose from an ArUco marker with identifier 19. Optionally, a dictionary can be provided when multiple ArUco markers are available with different dictionaries. When an AR application detects a marker, it should retrieve all the information including the virtual objects placed relative to this detected marker. An example query is provided in Listing 5 on lines 9–16 where we query for all virtual objects with a poso:RelativePosition that is positioned relative to the QR code using the poso:isRelativeTo predicate.

```
1   SELECT ?position ?orientation WHERE {
2       ?markerType rdfs:subClassOf* fidmark:ArUco .
3       ?marker a ?markerType .
4       ?marker fidmark:identifier 19 .
5       ?marker poso:hasPosition ?position .
6       ?marker poso:hasOrientation ?orientation .
7   }
8
9   SELECT ?object WHERE {
10      ?object a sosa:FeatureOfInterest .
11      ?object omg:hasGeometry ?geometry .
12      ?object poso:hasPosition ?position .
13      ?position poso:isRelativeTo ?marker .
14      ?marker a fidmark:QRCode .
15      ?marker fidmark:markerData "001122334455"^^xsd:hexBinary .
16  }
```

Listing 5. SPARQL query to retrieve marker pose based on type and identifier and a SPARQL query used in the web application to retrieve all virtual objects placed relative to a detected marker

5 Conclusion and Future Work

In the presented work, we proposed the FidMark ontology for describing visual fiducial landmarks. FidMark can be used to semantically describe and publish the type and position of fiducial markers in the physical world. Augmented reality (AR) applications can use this description to detect, identify and position themselves or other virtual objects that are placed relative to the markers.

Our ontology is built upon the generic Positioning System Ontology (POSO) supporting the generic description of the absolute and relative position and orientation of markers and objects placed relative to these markers. Despite focusing on computer vision fiducial markers, we also provide an alignment with the DICOM ontology for fiducial markers in healthcare applications.

Based on seven design goals (DG1–DG7), we validated our ontology using a set of example SPARQL queries on top of our ontology and a generated test dataset. We also created an open-source demonstrator AR application that is available online and shows virtual objects relative to markers described with the FidMark ontology. This AR application demonstrates how the FidMark ontology can help to build interoperable AR applications that can use a commonly described reference frame.

Future work will primarily focus on expanding the annotation of marker types and dictionaries. While our ontology currently includes the most prominent AR fiducial markers according to recent surveys, we plan to expand FidMark with additional fiducial marker types based on other academic research that was not covered in the survey papers used for our initial release. Using these new marker types we will also expand the available procedures to detect and perform pose estimation for different types of markers, based on the different visual features offered by the markers. Finally, we will also develop additional FidMark use cases and examples to facilitate the synchronisation of reference spaces between multiple AR devices.

Acknowledgements. The research of Isaac Valadez has been funded by a Baekeland mandate of Flanders Innovation & Entrepreneurship (VLAIO, HBC.2020.2881).

References

1. Barone Rodrigues, A., Dias, D.R.C., Martins, V.F., Bressan, P.A., de Paiva Guimarães, M.: WebAR: a web-augmented reality-based authoring tool with experience API support for educational applications. In: Antona, M., Stephanidis, C. (eds.) UAHCI 2017. LNCS, vol. 10278, pp. 118–128. Springer, Cham (2017). https://doi.org/10.1007/978-3-319-58703-5_9
2. Battle, R., Kolas, D.: GeoSPARQL: enabling a geospatial semantic web. Semant. Web J. **3**(4) (2011)
3. Bermudez, F.F., Diaz, C.S., Ward, S., Radkowski, R., Garrett, T., Oliver, J.: Comparison of natural feature descriptors for rigid-object tracking for real-time augmented reality. In: Proceedings of the 34th Computers and Information in Engineering Conference, Buffalo, USA (2014). https://doi.org/10.1115/DETC2014-35319

4. Bradski, G.: The OpenCV library. Dr. Dobb's J. Softw. Tools Prof. Programmer **25**(11) (2000)

5. Calvet, L., Gurdjos, P., Griwodz, C., Gasparini, S.: Detection and accurate localization of circular fiducials under highly challenging conditions. In: Proceedings of the IEEE Conference on Computer Vision and Pattern Recognition (CVPR 2016) (2016). https://openaccess.thecvf.com/content_cvpr_2016/html/Calvet_Detection_and_Accurate_CVPR_2016_paper.html

6. Collins, T., Bartoli, A.: Infinitesimal plane-based pose estimation. Int. J. Comput. Vis. **109**(3) (2014). https://doi.org/10.1007/s11263-014-0725-5

7. Díaz, A., Caicedo, S., Caicedo, E.: Augmented reality without fiducial markers. In: Proceedings of the 20th Symposium on Signal Processing, Images and Computer Vision (STSIVA 2015) (2015). https://doi.org/10.1109/STSIVA.2015.7330431

8. Gao, X.S., Hou, X.R., Tang, J., Cheng, H.F.: Complete solution classification for the perspective-three-point problem. IEEE Trans. Pattern Anal. Mach. Intell. **25**(8) (2003). https://doi.org/10.1109/TPAMI.2003.1217599

9. Garrido-Jurado, S., Muñoz-Salinas, R., Madrid-Cuevas, F.J., Marín-Jiménez, M.J.: Automatic generation and detection of highly reliable fiducial markers under occlusion. Pattern Recogn. **47**(6) (2014). https://doi.org/10.1016/j.patcog.2014.01.005

10. Gsaxner, C., Li, J., Pepe, A., Schmalstieg, D., Egger, J.: Inside-out instrument tracking for surgical navigation in augmented reality. In: Proceedings of the 27th ACM Symposium on Virtual Reality Software and Technology (VRST 2021) (2021). https://doi.org/10.1145/3489849.3489863

11. Guha, R.V., Brickley, D., Macbeth, S.: Schema.org: evolution of structured data on the web. Commun. ACM **59**(2) (2016). https://doi.org/10.1145/2844544

12. Gyrard, A., Datta, S.K., Bonnet, C., Boudaoud, K.: Cross-domain internet of things application development: M3 framework and evaluation. In: Proceedings of the 3rd International Conference on Future Internet of Things and Cloud (FiCloud 2015) (2015). https://doi.org/10.1109/FiCloud.2015.10

13. Hogan, A.: Shape constraints and expressions. In: Hogan, A. (ed.) The Web of Data, pp. 449–513. Springer, Cham (2020). https://doi.org/10.1007/978-3-030-51580-5_7

14. ISO Central Secretary: Photography – Archiving Systems: Vocabulary. Standard ISO 19262:2015, International Organization for Standardization (2015). https://www.iso.org/standard/64219.html

15. ISO Central Secretary: Geographic information – Imagery Sensor Models for Geopositioning. Standard ISO 19130-1:2018, International Organization for Standardization (2018). https://www.iso.org/standard/66847.html

16. ISO Central Secretary: Geographic Information – Referencing by Coordinates. Standard ISO 19111:2019, International Organization for Standardization (2019). https://www.iso.org/standard/74039.html

17. ISO Central Secretary: Information technology – Automatic Identification and Data Capture Techniques. Standard ISO 18004:2015, International Organization for Standardization (2021). https://www.iso.org/standard/62021.html

18. Janowicz, K., Haller, A., Cox, S.J., Le Phuoc, D., Lefrançois, M.: SOSA: a lightweight ontology for sensors, observations, samples, and actuators. J. Web Semant. **56** (2019). https://doi.org/10.1016/j.websem.2018.06.003

19. Kahn, C.E., Jr., Langlotz, C.P., Channin, D.S., Rubin, D.L.: Informatics in radiology: an information model of the DICOM standard. Radiographics **31**(1) (2011). https://doi.org/10.1148/rg.311105085

20. Kalaitzakis, M., Cain, B., Carroll, S., Ambrosi, A., Whitehead, C., Vitzilaios, N.: Fiducial markers for pose estimation: overview, applications and experimental comparison of the ARTag, AprilTag, ArUco and STag Markers. J. Intell. Robot. Syst. **101** (2021). https://doi.org/10.1007/s10846-020-01307-9

21. Kaltenbrunner, M., Bencina, R.: reacTIVision: a computer-vision framework for table-based tangible interaction. In: Proceedings of the 1st International Conference on Tangible and Embedded interaction (TEI 2007), Baton Rouge, USA (2007). https://doi.org/10.1145/1226969.1226983

22. Ke, T., Roumeliotis, S.I.: An efficient algebraic solution to the perspective-three-point problem. In: Proceedings of the IEEE Conference on Computer Vision and Pattern Recognition (CVPR 2017) (2017)

23. Košt'ák, M., Slabý, A.: Designing a simple fiducial marker for localization in spatial scenes using neural networks. Sensors **21**(16) (2021). https://doi.org/10.3390/s21165407

24. Lepetit, V., Moreno-Noguer, F., Fua, P.: EPnP: an accurate O(n) solution to the PnP problem. Int. J. Comput. Vis. **81** (2009). https://doi.org/10.1007/s11263-008-0152-6

25. Marchand, E., Uchiyama, H., Spindler, F.: Pose estimation for augmented reality: a hands-on survey. IEEE Trans. Vis. Comput. Graph. **22**(12), 2633–2651 (2015). https://doi.org/10.1109/TVCG.2015.2513408

26. Mráz, E., Rodina, J., Babinec, A.: Using fiducial markers to improve localization of a drone. In: Proceedings of the 23rd International Symposium on Measurement and Control in Robotics (ISMCR 2020), Budapest, Hungary (2020). https://doi.org/10.1109/ISMCR51255.2020.9263754

27. Murphy-Chutorian, E., Trivedi, M.M.: Head pose estimation in computer vision: a survey. IEEE Trans. Pattern Anal. Mach. Intell. **31**(4) (2008). https://doi.org/10.1109/TPAMI.2008.106

28. Nöll, T., Pagani, A., Stricker, D.: Markerless camera pose estimation: an overview. In: Proceedings of the Workshop on Visualization of Large and Unstructured Data Sets (VLUDS 2010), Dagstuhl, Germany (2010). https://doi.org/10.4230/OASIcs.VLUDS.2010.45

29. Odmins, J., Slics, K., Fenuks, R., Linina, E., Osmanis, K., Osmanis, I.: Comparison of passive and active fiducials for optical tracking. Latvian J. Phys. Tech. Sci. **59**(5) (2022). https://doi.org/10.2478/lpts-2022-0040

30. Olson, E.: AprilTag: a robust and flexible visual fiducial system. In: Proceedings of the IEEE International Conference on Robotics and Automation (ICRA 2011), Shanghai, China (2011). https://doi.org/10.1109/ICRA.2011.5979561

31. Poveda-Villalón, M., Fernández-Izquierdo, A., Fernández-López, M., García-Castro, R.: LOT: an industrial oriented ontology engineering framework. Eng. Appl. Artif. Intell. **111** (2022). https://doi.org/10.1016/j.engappai.2022.104755

32. Poveda-Villalón, M., Gómez-Pérez, A., Suárez-Figueroa, M.C.: OOPS! (OntOlogy Pitfall Scanner!): an on-line tool for ontology evaluation. Int. J. Semant. Web Inf. Syst. (IJSWIS) **10**(2) (2014). https://doi.org/10.4018/ijswis.2014040102

33. Roberts, G.W., et al.: The use of augmented reality, GPS and INS for subsurface data visualization. In: Proceedings of the 22nd International FIG Congress (2002)

34. Sirin, E., Parsia, B., Grau, B.C., Kalyanpur, A., Katz, Y.: Pellet: a practical OWL-DL reasoner. J. Web Semant. **5**(2) (2007). https://doi.org/10.1016/j.websem.2007.03.004

35. Song, K.T., Chang, Y.C.: Design and implementation of a pose estimation system based on visual fiducial features and multiple cameras. In: Proceedings of

the International Automatic Control Conference (CACS 2018), Taoyuan, Taiwan (2018). https://doi.org/10.1109/CACS.2018.8606773

36. Ulrich, J., Alsayed, A., Arvin, F., Krajník, T.: Towards fast fiducial marker with full 6 DOF pose estimation. In: Proceedings of the 37th ACM/SIGAPP Symposium on Applied Computing (SAC 2022), Virtual Event (2022). https://doi.org/10.1145/3477314.3507043

37. Urtans, E., Nikitenko, A.: Active infrared markers for augmented and virtual reality. Eng. Rural Dev. **9**, 10 (2016). https://api.semanticscholar.org/CorpusID:29944026

38. Wagner, A., Bonduel, M., Pauwels, P., Uwe, R.: Relating geometry descriptions to its derivatives on the web. In: Proceedings of the European Conference on Computing in Construction, Chania, Greece (2019). https://doi.org/10.35490/ec3.2019.146

39. Van de Wynckel, M., Signer, B.: OpenHPS: an open source hybrid positioning system. Technical report. WISE-2020-01, Vrije Universiteit Brussel (2020). https://doi.org/10.48550/ARXIV.2101.05198

40. Van de Wynckel, M., Signer, B.: POSO: a generic positioning system ontology. In: Sattler, U., et al. (eds.) ISWC 2022. LNCS, vol. 13489, pp. 231–247. Springer, Cham (2022). https://doi.org/10.1007/978-3-031-19433-7_14

Author Index

Printed in the United States
by Baker & Taylor Publisher Services

Printed in the United States
by Baker & Taylor Publisher Services